Wyoming University

THE FIRST 100 YEARS
1886-1986

Deborah Hardy

Library of Congress Catalogue Card Number: 85-52346

ISBN 0-941570-01-0

 ii

edication

Without the previous labors of Professor Emeritus Wilson O. Clough, the publication date of this book would have been advanced well into the twenty-first century. He is a person of distinction, intelligence, imagination, scholarship, kindness, and warmth. To him, therefore, this volume is formally dedicated.

LARAMIE HILLS

I

The raw wind runs the hills like icy flame;
    Long slopes of sage lie low;
The lonely cedar hugs the granite rock
    And bows in scuds of snow.
Along the gray outcrop, against the wind
    Leaning, I move along,
And mark the briar's scant and withered tune
    Upon the faceless stone.
The frozen aspens group within the draw;
    Forlornly hangs the leaf;
Who pastures high will feed on slender fare,
    Austere and tough and brief.

II

Incredibly, the dun-limbed antlered buck,
    Unmoved in his retreat,
Merges within the mottled aspen boles,
    Snow dunes about his feet.
What catalyst compounds this crushed-sage scent,
    This dwarfed and fibered tree?
What rock-roomed distillation searches out
    The cedar's chemistry?
How came the buck, breathing the mantling snow,
    Wide pronged and proud to see;
Confronting thus this high, reluctant land,
    This chill frugality?

Contents

reface

This book is for the people of Wyoming. As an adopted citizen of thirty years' standing, I am not sure that I was most competent to write it, but I have given it all of my efforts over the past several years. Wyoming is my state as the University is my university, and if this volume brings to anyone a greater understanding of what the state University was, is, and hopes to become, that is all to the good. That would represent my special, personal reward.

When I agreed to write a centennial University history, I was far from recognizing the problems that would be involved. As a historian, I have researched and written monographs before, but I have never faced a surfeit of material — always I have had to scrounge and dig. In this instance, everything was opened to me, to the tune of literally hundreds of file drawers, boxes, cartons, notebooks, volumes, and ledgers. Many people in kindness volunteered personal help. Tours of warehouses unearthed dusty cases, and keys were proffered to locked storage vaults.

Looking back, I am keenly aware of the volume of sources that I have had to pass by as of the great quantity of documents I have consulted. Hundreds of materials remain untapped: These include such collections as the personal papers of many professors, the daily correspondence of many departments, the financial records of individual divisions, and even the memories of many people whose lives were interwoven with the University's history. To these individuals and institutions, I extend my apologies. A total history would represent more than a lifetime of work and would result in thousands of printed pages. In essence, this is a history of the University's core, and I hope that it will not diminish the sense of the institution's diversity, for not all trails could be followed around all windings to their ends. I believe that those neglected will understand.

I began this project with no special expertise regarding Wyoming and its university. I worked hard to make up the gaps. I ended with greater delight because we have experienced so much: Greater amusement because so many people were unique and exhilarating; greater respect because we have come so far in such a short century. This volume comes to fruition in the hopes that we will learn from our history and in the future reap harvests even greater than those of the past. For myself personally, it has represented a challenge and an agony, a frustration and a fulfillment, a lot of fun, a lot of work, and even a few tears.

Without the aid of friends, colleagues, and supporters, this manuscript would never have made it to the light. I am grateful to the committee which read it doggedly and critically: Professors Emeritus T. A. Larson and William R. Steckel, Professor Wilson A. Walthall, Vice President Peter K. Simpson, and Assistants to the President William G. Solomon and Vern E. Shelton. But it is impossible to list the many others who read and critiqued sections of the manuscript; who wrote summaries of their experiences or their departments' histories for my use; who tolerated my questions in long oral interviews; or who responded cordially to peculiar telephone calls late in the evening. To them I owe a great deal. Nobody has been less than kind.

Registrar Emeritus Ralph McWhinnie is a wonder, for he remembers everything and is always willing to share his vast knowledge and lore. Kevin M. McKinney, sports information director, has provided essential material, and G. W. "Hap" Arnold, former director of International Programs, assembled much important data. My graduate assistants William L. Hewitt, Deborah S. Welch, and Steven C. Schulte — all now holding UW Ph.D. degrees and beginning academic careers — aided me not only with routine chores but also with organization, analysis, and ideas. I especially thank my lovely, patient secretary Diane Alexander and the staff (including Norman E. "Skip" Roberts, Edward Rasmussen, D. Greg Thompson, Elizabeth Ono Rahel, and Carol Hale Stevens) of the University's Division of Communications Services, where publication was arranged.

Those readers with special interests and backgrounds in academic or historical studies may find themselves puzzled by the lack of reference footnotes. At this author's request, such notes have been deliberately omitted in order to protect — and even permit the use of quotations from — individuals. In most instances, the source of quotations is easily determined from the body of the text. However, should more exact citation be necessary to any reader, he or she may request access to the fully annotated text through the University president's office.

Deborah Hardy

Deborah Hardy
Laramie, June 28, 1985

Chapter One

Politics and Education
1887

he University of Wyoming, located in Laramie City, opened its doors in the autumn of 1887. The institution had been officially established by the territorial legislature in far from unanimous, and occasionally bitter, voting in the previous year. Certainly the new institution of higher learning did not grow out of a groundswell of popular demand, and its second president, A. A. Johnson, was probably right when he wrote seven years later that "This University is not the product of an educational desire on the part of the people of Wyoming."

It would nevertheless be simplistic to dismiss the founding of the University of Wyoming as the result of nothing but strategic political maneuvers. True, the territorial legislators of 1886 were eager to take advantage of U.S. laws that — through grants of public lands — guaranteed financial support to special, newly-established institutions of higher learning. True, the manipulations of legislators from various sections of the territory caused the proposed University to become a political football and its location to rate as a plum — although not by any means the juiciest — to be plucked and enjoyed. Still such single-minded analysis does little justice to a handful of territorial officials and legislators who from the start valued education as a matter both of practicality and principle. Territorial records cannot fail to evoke in the reader an impression of the pride, expansiveness, optimism, and exhilaration that genuinely motivated those early Wyomingites who entertained high hopes for their future state. And among these hopes, education played a primary role.

During Wyoming's early territorial years, several of her governors — political appointees all, and often men unfamiliar with Wyoming's vast and undeveloped expanses — took up the cause of education — and quality education — however it might be attained. The first territorial governor, John A. Campbell, appointed by President U.S. Grant and sworn into office in March 1869,

exalted education in his address to the first territorial legislators in the autumn of the same year. Recognizing the dearth of schools in the new territory, Governor Campbell urged the legislature to support education as a vital measure in Wyoming's move towards statehood: "In laying the foundation of a new state," he said, "[education] should be the cornerstone, for without it no durable political fabric can be erected." Two years later he reminded the legislators of the importance of education as a method of producing an orderly and enlightened citizenry.

Among the most potent auxiliaries in bringing about [such a citizenry] are the churches and school houses which have been erected in so many places throughout the territory. . . . I respectfully invite your attention to the report and recommendations of the superintendent of public instruction for information in reference to our educational interests. I do not doubt that the schools will receive from you that liberal support and encouragement which they deserve and which has always been accorded them by American legislators.

In 1873, the governor argued that it was necessary to establish a "uniform system of education throughout the territory" in order to attract that population deemed necessary to achieve statehood, for "no man with a family will make a permanent home where he cannot give his children all the advantages that can be assured to them in the most favored state." John W. Hoyt, territorial governor from 1879-1882 and later president of the University of Wyoming, was even more insistent on the need for promoting educational institutions. A gifted, articulate, and energetic man of considerable academic background, Hoyt produced a series of extraordinary reports on Wyoming. In an enthusiasm perhaps untempered by reality, Governor Hoyt reported that the educational institutions of Wyoming Territory

have been a surprise to me. The general school system is one of the best in the United States — resembling that of Michigan, under which all the grades are so related and correlated that each lower one becomes a proper stepping-stone to the one above it — and the public graded schools of Cheyenne and Laramie Cities are really among the best of their class in the country, being well directed and admirably taught. The school buildings are also excellent. . . . Attendance upon school is obligatory, teachers are liberally paid (male and female alike for the same service), and public provision is made for county superintendence and for regular teachers' institutes.

The enthusiasm of Governors Campbell and Hoyt for Wyoming education was echoed among early territorial legislators, who justified Hoyt's reference to their "fostering care" for the educational system. From its opening days, the territorial council (the upper legislative chamber) included a committee on education among its standing committees. In its first sessions of 1869, the legislature adopted a school act governing the system of educational administration, including the appointment and election of school officials; the right of county commissioners to levy school taxes; the definition of functions of county superintendents and school boards; and the establishment of the first territorial superintendent of public instruction — a job which fell ex-officio to the auditor, who was to collect information from county superintendents and draw up an annual report. Although the second territorial legislature in 1871 moved to abolish the state superintendency and caused local school superintendents to report directly to the governor, the third legislature (1873) revived the office and placed it temporarily and ex-officio within the competency of the territorial librarian, until such time (as Governor Hoyt stated) that "the field of labor has sufficiently enlarged to render it necessary [that] a superintendent . . . give his entire time to the work."

Although the legislature did not directly intervene in the founding of schools throughout the territory, it encouraged local citizens and educators to begin them. The first public school building had been opened in Cheyenne in January 1868, when Wyoming was still part of Dakota Territory, to great celebration and pride. Thereafter schools grew slowly in the sparsely settled communities in mining districts and along the Union Pacific line. Continued support was demonstrated by the legislature's appropriation of $3,000 to aid the Sisters of Charity in erecting a hospital and school in Laramie in 1875. This action was approved by Governor John M. Thayer with the disclaimer that in signing the bill he was not attempting to set a precedent of appropriating public moneys for sectarian purposes, but only recognizing that the institution was desperately needed.

The legitimate concern about education in Wyoming Territory included for some citizens a desire to extend the system beyond the grade school level. As a highly educated and academically oriented governor, Hoyt in particular stood firm in his conviction that higher education must be made available to Wyoming youth. In his report to the secretary of the interior in 1878, he deplored that there was yet no institution in Wyoming Territory beyond the high school level and stated firmly that "steps will soon need to be taken for the establishment of a college." He encouraged the foundation of libraries and in 1882 established Wyoming's first "Academy of Sciences, Arts, and Letters," which met in Cheyenne at the Baptist Church with the objects of

the encouragement of historical and scientific research; the promotion of the practical industries of Wyoming; the collection and preservation of authentic records of territorial history; the formation of historical, scientific and industrial museums; and the enlargement of the territorial library.

Still, the discussion of academies and institutions of higher learning must have verged on the esoteric for citizens of communities where primary and secondary schools were not yet in existence.

Had the establishment of a university not brought with it certain financial benefits, it is unlikely that the territorial legislature would have considered it at all. Luckily, the U.S. Congress had taken a positive stand on the development of colleges and universities well before Wyoming became a territory. For such men of vision as Governor

Hoyt, the dream of establishing a university became attainable because of federal funding policies. The Morrill Act of 1862 (first passed by Congress in 1857 but vetoed at that time by President Buchanan) represented a milestone in the history of public education with its promise of a grant to each state of 30,000 acres of land (over and above the acreage earmarked for the support of grammar schools), the income from the leasing and sale of which was to provide a permanent fund for

the endowment, support, and maintenance of at least one college where the leading object shall be, without excluding other scientific and classical studies, and including military tactics, to teach such branches of learning as are related to agriculture and mechanic arts, in such manner as the legislatures of the states may respectively prescribe, in order to promote the liberal and practical education of the industrial classes in several pursuits and professions in life.

In 1881, the Morrill Act was supplemented by "An Act to Grant Lands to Dakota, Montana, Arizona, Idaho, and Wyoming for University Purposes," by which statute 72 additional sections of land were granted to Wyoming. These sections might (within specific limitations and under careful supervision) be sold and leased to provide income for the upkeep of a university, without restriction as to subject matter such as set forth in the Morrill Act.

For Wyoming Territory, however, federal legislation contained a serious drawback, never really remedied by Congress. Although in its title the Morrill Act referred to "states and territories," the provisions of the law itself allowed grants only to regions that had attained statehood. Legislation proposing to extend the land grant clause to territories failed to pass Congress in 1866. The University Act of 1881 also restricted land income usage until such time as Wyoming became a state. No wonder that in his required reports to the secretary of the interior, Governor Hoyt frequently accused the federal government of dragging its feet as far as educational land grants were concerned. He deplored the fact, he wrote, that

provision has not been made by Congress for allowing to Territories while in their Territorial condition some of the advantages in aid of education with which they are favored when they have been admitted into the Union as States.

Old Main, under construction, 1886

His plea was to no avail. Hoyt won a minor victory in 1882 when, after several petitions, the secretary of the interior finally permitted the territory to make a preliminary selection of sections that might later be appropriated for university usage and approved the designation of the territorial superintendent of public instruction to supervise a land survey. But at that time, Hoyt had only a few months remaining in office and, busy with other projects (particularly a major Wyoming exhibition in Denver), he never seized the opportunity to act. Although some territories had appropriated lands and even begun the technically unauthorized construction of universities, Hoyt had not moved ahead. He ended his term as governor in 1882 still full of enthusiasm for a Wyoming university, but it was another four years before concrete plans were laid.

The former governor's dedication to higher education and the availability of federal land grants undoubtedly played their role in the territorial legislature's founding of Wyoming University. But when in 1886 the founding act was actually passed, it was local politics that fostered and hastened its adoption.

In his brief territorial administration (January 1885 to November 1886), Governor Francis E. Warren was faced with many problems of greater immediate importance to him than that of establishing a university. A lame duck appointee of Republican President Chester Arthur, and thus always insecure under the incoming Democratic administration, Warren found himself coping with

3

major troubles on the railroad and increasing difficulties with public and private lands. The Rock Springs massacre of Chinese workers in September 1885 put his administration to a test of statesmanship and decisiveness. The long run problems of the livestock industry, strongly emphasized by the new governor in his first annual report to the secretary of the interior, were part of ongoing conflicts concerning branding, rustling, fencing, and the fate of the public lands — problems of great concern to Warren, who was a Wyoming resident of eighteen years and had established a family livestock business of considerable importance.

Squabbling for spoils in the territorial legislature on the basis of south versus north, railroad versus cattle, was already a feature of political reality. If the power of early mining towns like South Pass City had already waned, that of the railroad cities along the Union Pacific had grown with their burgeoning populations. Their challenge from the north was based less on minerals than on cattle. The political clout of the livestock industry had soared with the formation of the Wyoming Stockgrowers Association, and the appointment of Warren as governor — he was the first Wyomingite to be so named — acted to increase the influence of ranching interests, as versus that of the brawling, squalling railroad towns, with their populations of immigrant laborers and transient toughs.

Warren had not himself received the benefits of a classical higher education — such as had so strongly influenced the priorities of Governor Hoyt — and there was little reason to anticipate emphasis on education from the gubernatorial appointee. Nevertheless, the new governor could hardly be accused of neglect. His lengthy first report on the state of the territory included careful statistics on public and private educational institutions in the then eight Wyoming counties. Upon achieving office, he had investigated the status of those lands that might legally be used to support a university once Wyoming achieved statehood. In spite of the secretary of the interior's earlier authorization of a survey and selection, Warren discovered that nothing had been done. The governor himself took no immediate action. But at the ninth session of the territorial legislature, political necessity brought the founding of a university to the forefront of Warren's plans.

The influential factors seem to have been Warren's desire that Cheyenne remain the permanent capital of the future state of Wyoming and that a building be constructed there so as to guarantee the city's preeminence and stand as a crown to his gubernatorial achievements. As a state capital, Cheyenne had advantages and disadvantages. It lay at an inappropriate site, for although its location in the southeast corner of the territory was understandable when the lands of Wyoming were governed from Dakota Territory, once Wyoming stood alone and its boundaries were extended to the west and north, Cheyenne lost its central location. Nevertheless, throughout Wyoming's territorial years the political center had continued to lie here, in a railroad town, in the territory's far southeast corner. Cheyenne's population grew: In 1885, the city boasted approximately 10,000 inhabitants, while Laramie City counted 5,000 and no other Wyoming community (even along the railroad) had reached a population of more than 4,000 souls. In 1885, according to Governor Warren's report, Laramie County (with Cheyenne its capital) contained greater assessed wealth than any other county in the state. In particular, Laramie County was home to more than 227,000 cattle, by Warren's estimate — a figure not touched by any other county, although the cattle business in the north was growing at a faster rate. Among the great ranches of Laramie County, the Warren Livestock Company was a large and prominent venture, and its presence here undoubtedly profited from the capital's location.

Cheyenne alone was not politically powerful enough to assign the state capital to itself, but it could clearly do so with the aid of its neighbor county. In 1885-86, the southeast axis of Wyoming Territory composed of Laramie (Cheyenne) and Albany (Laramie City) counties dominated the territorial legislature, where the two delegations combined controlled seven out of twelve votes in the council and thirteen out of 24 in the house (the lower chamber). Cognizant of the political potential of a southeast alliance, aware of the tenuous duration of his own appointment as governor, and driven by a desire to see the capital permanently located in Cheyenne, Warren seems to have proposed action to a handful of local delegates in the ninth territorial legislature, the only biennial legislature to meet during his first gubernatorial term. Indeed, as T. A. Larson, Wyoming's well-known historian, has pointed out, Warren

with his long experience in the territory, and acquaintance with most of the legislators, took charge more effectively than had been possible for past governors. His suggestions for legislation were generally carried out.

Threshing operations, Big Red Ranch, Ferris Cattle Company, 1898

In his message to the assembled legislators in January of 1886, the governor did not reveal his plans. Among suggestions included in this brief message was the location of an insane asylum at Evanston (Uinta County) and the establishment of a school for the deaf and dumb in Cheyenne. To the possibility of establishing a university, the governor referred only in passing. "The common school system," he said,

is more valuable to a growing community than the higher institutions of learning. The time, however, is rapidly approaching when both will be necessary to secure the best results of our educational system.

Nor did Warren announce his decision in regard to locating the capital permanently in Cheyenne.

It seems likely, however, that the governor conferred quietly with Albany County Legislator Stephen W. Downey. Like former Governor Hoyt, Downey had long hoped for a Wyoming university. As early as 1881, his daughter reported later, this prominent Laramie citizen had written F. L. Ames suggesting that the moneys proposed for an Ames monument along the Union Pacific might better be invested in a territorial university. Determined to "use all his influence" to steer an appropriate bill through the legislature, Downey later became known as the "father of the University."

It apparently came as a surprise to members of the territorial house when on February 24, 1886, Legislator N. J. O'Brien, a Warren Company agent from the governor's own county, announced that he would shortly introduce a bill for the construction of a capitol building "and for other purposes." Read before the house the next day, the bill provided not only for the sale of $150,000 in bonds to construct in Cheyenne such a capitol building as would seem to guarantee the permanent location of the state capital there, but also for the establishment of a state university at Laramie City, very probably Downey's price for his support. On Downey's motion, the controversial bill was referred to the committee of the whole. There it was read for the second time, slightly amended, and sent forward to the judiciary committee, of which Downey was chairman.

From the start, the governor's plan found the going tough and the opposition intense. In spite of the potential award of the state University to Laramie City, the Laramie *Boomerang* publicly smelled a rat in the building of the permanent capitol in Cheyenne.

This bill will be held over the heads of the members from Uinta and Albany counties as a rod of terror. In other words, if Evanston wants the insane asylum and Laramie the university, the members from those counties must vote to give the capitol buildings to Cheyenne, or the Laramie County delegation will vote down both the other propositions.

Delegations from other counties were equally angry and upset.

In the end, the Cheyenne and Laramie axis was too strong to counter. Colonel Downey, chairman of the judiciary committee, oversaw a number of minor amendments regarding the operation of the proposed University and steered the committee to a do-pass recommendation. On the floor of the house, he followed with an impassioned speech, described by the Cheyenne *Leader* as "eloquent, beautiful in diction, and inspired by noble motives." He was applauded by the southeast coalition but less well received by his colleagues from the north and the west. Debate was acrid. An angry delegate from Johnson County (north central Wyoming) proposed that no bonds be issued for funding either the capitol or the University until the measure was submitted to the voters at a special election, but his amendment was defeated by the coalition. The speaker of the house — J. S. Kerr from Carbon County — accused Albany and Laramie counties of "collusion to obtain public buildings at the expense of the territory." The southeastern delegates with equal violence denied a plot. The final ayes outnumbered the nays by the count of 15-8. At the last moment, two delegates from Uinta County (western Wyoming) suddenly changed their minds and voted in favor of the capitol and University bill. The reason became apparent when the proposal to locate an asylum for the insane at Evanston resurfaced for its final reading on the following day and was passed by the same voters and the same margin.

In the territorial council, to which the house bill was referred on March 2, opposition again was bitter. In anticipation, the house adjourned so members could hear the debates in the upper chamber. Angry delegates from Rawlins and the north and west voiced their objections to the crowded session. A delegate from Carbon County made an effort first to delete the location of Cheyenne as capital, then to reduce and restrict the bond issue for the University, both of which amendments went down to defeat. His colleague attempted in vain to require that the bill be submitted to voters at a special election. Over objection, the bill was immediately read for the second and third times. When put to the vote, it passed by 9-3, with the victorious ayes including the delegates

from Uinta County. A Carbon County council member issued formal protest against the passage of the bill and insisted that his statement be entered in the journal as a matter of record. By then it was too late. The bill became law when Warren affixed his signature on March 4, 1886. Just a week later, the governor signed the Evanston insane asylum into being.

In its final form, the act of 1886 contained not just provisions for financing but clear statements on the governance and operation of the new territorial University. The legislature provided for a university building commission, to be appointed by the governor and to oversee the issuance of the $50,000 in bonds and the construction of a university building. It also required that the governor appoint a board of seven trustees to be confirmed by the territorial council. The board received broad powers. In addition to many financial duties, it was authorized to select a university president, appoint professors, and prescribe courses of study and discipline. Presidential powers were primarily executive. The faculty was to "reward and censure students as they may deserve" and to confer honors and degrees. Carefully complying with federal strictures as provided in the Morrill Act, the legislature ordained that

> *No religious qualification or test shall be required of any student, trustee, president, professor, tutor or officer of such university, or as a condition for admission or for any privilege in the same; and no sectarian tenets or principles shall be taught, instructed, or inculcated at said university by any president, professor, or tutor therein.*

The University's goals were

> *to provide an efficient means of imparting to young men and young women, on equal terms, a liberal education and thorough knowledge of the different branches of literature, the arts and sciences, with their varied applications.*

In its last paragraph, the law authorized a one-fourth mill tax assessment on all taxable property in the territory, the funds from which should be reserved for use by the board of University trustees as operating expenses. Although clearly anticipating later federal aid, the legislature thus provided with some generosity for the territorial University, allotting tax funds to keep higher education solvent and bond issues to provide for building construction.

Jubilation from the victorious counties was accompanied by bitterness from the losers. Cheyenne was "wreathed in smiles," reported the Laramie *Boomerang*. "The passage of the bill," wrote the editor of the Cheyenne *Leader*, "will inaugurate a new era of prosperity in this territory," and the newspapers were filled with praise for the "selfless" action of the men from Uinta County. Even the Laramie papers came around to believing that a university was not all that bad.

Laramie has beyond question been awarded the first capital prize in being made the seat of learning for Wyoming for all time to come. . . . In making Laramie the educational center of the most promising territory in the union, there is attracted in this direction the attention of all citizens who are ambitious to see their children trained up to become educated and intelligent men and women. . . . Laramie will become known throughout the country beyond all its rival cities, as Athens is more famous than the country of which it is the capital, and as the names of Oxford and Cambridge, Yale and Harvard are more familiar in the household than those of older England.

But the "collusion" of the three counties — Albany, Laramie, and Uinta — rankled in other areas. The situation was not improved when a bill introduced by a Rawlins house delegate to provide for an institution for the deaf and dumb in his home town went down to defeat; Cheyenne received that plum, with Governor Warren's support. The Rawlins newspaper went so far as to question whether the actions of the ninth territorial legislature should be granted the force of law and threatened to take the matter to the Supreme Court because

the underhanded manner in which the capitol bill was railroaded through the Legislature has aroused a feeling of indignation among the people of all portions of the territory, Laramie County excepted.

A Sheridan writer likewise insisted that the southern counties had

for the time being gobbled up everything worth having. . . . It seems as though, after the Southern section has had all its own way so long, the people think they are all there is of Wyoming.

Such "collusion" was of course less negatively viewed in the counties that reaped the benefits, he continued.

The lion and the calf and the lamb will lie down together and divide the spoils. Cheyenne will get the biggest slice of the pie of course, if she didn't she would kick. Albany will get the university slice, and little Evanston be happy with a $10,000 crazy house. . . . For the first time in history Laramie and Albany had found a bone which they could gnaw together without growling.

Lighthearted words — but the northern counties were not assuaged. In the council of the tenth territorial legislature, meeting in 1888, the Johnson County representative introduced a bill providing for the erection of a normal school at Sundance and an agricultural college at Sheridan — the latter of which was intended to divert from the University the considerable federal grants under the Morrill Act. The bill failed to pass. In 1890, another northern councilman tried again, suggesting a teacher's school at Sundance and an agricultural college at Buffalo. Although his bill passed the council, it never became law, for the house adjourned without acting upon it. If these efforts were at first motivated by irritation, they were later sustained by arguments about Laramie's too distinctive location; not only was the University's home situated in the far corner of a state whose expansion was generally in an opposite direction, but neither altitude, climate, nor soils were conducive to agricultural experimentation nor typical of Wyoming resources. The location of the University and its agricultural station was contested through decades and remains a sore point to present times.

Riding high above the storm, Warren lost no time in meeting his obligations under the law and abiding by his promises to Albany County Legislator Downey. The governor's first appointments to the University board of trustees consisted of seven individuals, five of whom were respected residents of Laramie City (J. H. Finfrock, M. C. Brown, W. H. Holliday, J. H. Hayford, and Edward Ivinson); the statute provided that "at least three" members of the board were to reside in Laramie. In addition, Warren named to the board former territorial Governor John W. Hoyt, then living in California, and Samuel Aughey, the territorial geologist.

Old Main, c. 1900

Acting in conjunction with a joint resolution and memorial passed by the legislature on March 5, 1886, that requested congressional authority immediately to lease such lands as were set aside for the benefit of schools and the University, Warren also pursued the promised award of federal aid. Under date of April 13, 1886, the governor addressed the secretary of the interior regarding selection of the 72 sections of land promised under the special University Land Act of 1881 and suggested the appointment of F. W. Sawin, Laramie City, as commissioner to survey and select University lands from the public domain. Although territorial funds had been set aside for Sawin's operation, Warren asked for additional federal funding as well as approval of the commissioner's appointment. Approval received, Sawin immediately began his task. Although the process of leasing selected lands had begun, federal statute continued to prohibit any usage of the Morrill or University land-grant funds until Wyoming might achieve statehood.

The land-grant prohibition, however, did not discourage the building committee and the trustees from moving ahead under territorial statute and financing. By the act of 1886, the construction of a university building was to begin immediately and be completed within a period of eighteen months. In fulfillment of his legislative obligation, Warren immediately appointed a building commission composed of three Laramie City residents — Colonel J. W. Donnellan (chairman), LeRoy Grant, and Robert Marsh. The commission in turn moved to offer the authorized $50,000 in territorial bonds for sale and found a purchaser in the N. W. Harris Company of Chicago. Campus land — "the most desirable location that could be had" — was acquired by the commission through a gift of ten acres from Laramie City plus the purchase of ten additional adjoining acres from the Union Pacific Railroad. The plans of a Denver architect having been accepted by the commission and approved by the board of trustees, the first bids were all rejected on grounds of cost. Eventually the construction contract was let to a local Laramie firm — Cook and Callahan — for a total cost of $48,700. Local sandstone from quarries northeast of town was to provide the primary building material. By mid-July 1886, excavation for the University building had begun.

By September, construction was well along. On the 27th of that month, with great pomp and ceremony, the cornerstone of the University building now called Old Main was officially laid. On a bright and windy day, the dedicatory procession wound its way through the city, supported by bands, members of fraternal orders, and 500 school children, wearing bunches of fresh flowers and marching "like little veterans." Almost the entire city turned out to hear Reverend George H. Cornell, rector of St. Matthews Episcopal Church, who said:

And as we stand here in this unrivalled atmosphere, in view of some of the grandest works of God that either the old or the new world affords, and look down the vista of the coming ages, we see this edifice the center of a magnificent group of buildings, known as the University of Wyoming, with its rich endowments, its chairs of philosophy, of science and of literature occupied by wise men, and sending forth from its classic halls young men and women educated and well-equipped for the higher duties of life. This is no chimera. In this new west we are gathering all the energies of past civilizations. The glories of past ages are ours.

Reverend Cornell exhorted his audience not to confuse knowledge with wisdom and morality.

Have we not known individuals and nations who were distinguished for their intellectual acquirements and yet were morally corrupt? . . . Did the lustre of her genius, the liberality of her institutions, did the mighty roll of her eloquence or the sweetness of her song save Greece from the infamy of her obliteration when she perished by the canker of her favorite sins? Did the iron sceptre or the invincible sword, did the majesty of her government or the strength of her courage deliver Rome from the shame of her corruption and pitiable decay?

Even as he spoke, the chill wind rose, and the remainder of the ceremony had to be abandoned.

Among other effects placed in the cornerstone was a poem written by H. V. Groesbeck.

Ah, not for gain or garish show
Lay we this broad foundation stone,
Not for ourselves do we bestow
This largess of our desert zone;
But for the coming freemen great,
Who shaped the welfare of our state. . . .

We plant these academic trees
In sterner soil, yet nothing loth
For summer sky and sharper breeze
Shall stimulate a hardier growth
Beneath the eternal mountain snows
The fairest flower most surely grows . . .

Grand Master of the Universe
Who formed the mountains and the sea,
Move from this spot Thy primal curse,
Bequeath Thy light and liberty,
As hand-maids of our future state
To guard the portals of this gate.

A grand tribute indeed it was. For the cornerstone of the University was laid not just in recognition of the political clout of the southeast coalition and its Cheyenne governor; not just because funding was available; but actually in tribute, too, to the ambitions and foresight of a handful of territorial leaders, who saw education as a cornerstone for the future.

Chapter Two

John Hoyt, First President
1887-1890

The laying of the cornerstone for the first University of Wyoming building marked a ceremonial beginning, but also opened an era characterized by trials and tribulations. Once launched, the University's course led her through rough and turbulent waters. For her first few years, the University was commanded by a president of vision and ideals who nevertheless became involved in the politics of the new state's gubernatorial and senatorial campaigns. She suffered the indignities of low enrollments, lack of statewide support, and increasingly difficult economic times. The breadth — perhaps even the pretensions — of her curriculum contrasted sharply with the realities of Laramie dust and Wyoming population, although a handful of dedicated faculty struggled to make the courses work. In the end the president (whose head, the board thought, was sometimes in the clouds and sometimes preoccupied with political ambitions) lost his appointment through the irritation of a partisan political board.

Indeed, few could have anticipated an easy time for those citizens who set themselves the task of creating a state university on the Wyoming frontier. In 1887, Wyoming Territory was sparsely settled. Of the total population of about 60,000, only a few thousand adventurers had trekked northward to seek gold at South Pass or to establish livestock ranches in the Big Horn basin; most of the people settled the railroad towns in the south. Although the rate of population growth peaked in the decade of the 1870s at more than 200 percent, it thereafter fell well below that in neighboring states and territories. Distances across the state were huge, and for those who lived far from the railroad terminals, existence was rugged, lonely, and difficult. By the 1890s, Union Pacific's east-west route was supplemented by other railroads (the Burlington, Chicago Northwestern, and several less enduring lines) which constructed track north to Casper and Sheridan, south (from Montana) to Thermopolis and Cody. Even so, railroad travel was hardly luxurious. Wrecks were frequent, facilities were uncomfortable, and northern towns were often easier reached from Montana than from Cheyenne. Students at the University in the early twentieth century remember long, exhausting journeys from tiny end-of-the-line stations to Laramie, via many waits and changes.

The view from the train was hardly encouraging. Until the twentieth century oil boom, Wyoming was not a rich area. Sagebrush was the most common sight, for less than ten percent of the state's 98,000 square miles has ever been regarded as arable. Towns along the railroad showed few signs of permanent wealth. Cheyenne citizens had begun to build fine houses; permanent settlements erected churches (often empty, for the attendance was at best poor); and Laramie City boasted of several small industries (soon to collapse). But even in the largest of towns, winds circulated dust from unpaved streets and wafted trash and tumbleweed into every corner. Here and there along the railroad, a collection of abandoned shacks marked one-time construction camps; or a single log house, comforted by a few cottonwoods, indicated the home of an isolated sheep rancher. The cattle business that had seemed to promise prosperity was decimated by tough winters and hard times, until it represented less than a quarter of the territory's estimated wealth by 1889. If gold mining flourished at South Pass City, efforts to exploit other minerals or other areas proved futile or at most temporary. The coal mined primarily by Union Pacific brought the territory little wealth, for it was regularly shipped out of state to the company's profit. The miners were poorly paid, and mine labor was often imported.

Under the circumstances, few Wyomingites seemed inclined toward a university education. Most of them were struggling to survive. The demands of the frontier laid more stock on strong backs than on philosophical minds. For rugged men, taxed to endurance, rough responses came more easily than academic meditation. Violence was always close to the surface in the many bars and brothels. As late as 1883, a man accused of murder was seized from the Cheyenne jail; lynched by the crowd; and left hanging from a telephone pole at what is now the corner of Capitol Avenue and 19th Street. Cowhands carried guns in spite of town ordinances. In 1894, there were six high schools in all of Wyoming from which the University might hope to draw its freshman class; that year, these schools graduated a total of eight students.

In retrospect, it seems amazing that university education found such support and engendered such enthusiasm as it did. Support it found, particularly among the leading citizens of Cheyenne and Laramie City. In these older and larger towns gathered professional men who had received educations in the East. Here, too, were others who had journeyed to the frontier and worked their way to local respect through keen business sense, often coupled with pride and a feeling for community activity. Here lived established ranchers, who built town houses as residences for their families and rode out to the range as necessary. These few hundred determined citizens, the likes of whom were beginning to appear in other Wyoming towns, devoted energy and enthusiasm to the task of building education even on the frontier.

Such men were appointed by Warren as University trustees in 1886. The board of trustees worked hard and steadily during the University's first few years. Dr. J. H. Finfrock, chairman, and his Laramie colleagues W. H. Holliday, businessman, and Alfred S. Peabody (appointed 1888) stuck to their posts until the end of 1890 when Wyoming had become a state. Banker Edward Ivinson, also from Laramie, resigned from the board early that year but resumed service in 1891. These local trustees were deeply involved in University administration, for out-of-town members only sporadically attended board meetings. Their earliest problems, in the winter of 1886-87, involved coordinating with the building commission in regard to the construction of the first campus edifice. They met frequently throughout that winter and more so during the spring and summer of 1887.

Local politics and alignments haunted these Republican trustees through the administration of Thomas Moonlight, Democrat, appointed territorial governor in 1887. Moonlight disliked the attitude of the board, resented its independence from his own influence, and was convinced it was not properly performing its designated duties. The governor was bitter at his inability to push his own board candidates when vacancies occurred. In 1888, he was irrevocably at odds with the Republican territorial council, which was required by law to confirm gubernatorial appointments and frequently refused to do so. He complained that the law of 1886 by which the University was established failed to provide for necessary trustee responsibility and had not established any mechanism requiring the board to report on its fiscal and administrative actions. In his message to the tenth legislature in 1888, the governor suggested correction of the law "in the interest of good government." In this measure the legislature found no fault, and Moonlight had his way. Amending the act of 1886, the new law required the board to address to governor and legislators a biennial report,

giving a full and complete history of the work accomplished in the university; making an itemized statement of all receipts and disbursements; stating the number of pupils, together with their places of residence; and presenting a detailed estimate of the wants and necessities of the university for the two years next insuing.

In addition, the governor resented the rather cavalier attitude of several of Warren's appointees, who were not consistently and actively attending board meetings. He so addressed two "absentee" members — John W. Hoyt (former territorial governor) and Samuel Aughey (territorial geologist) — who were not even living in Wyoming in the spring of 1887. The governor wrote them that:

The members of the board of trustees of the University are very anxious for a series of meetings of the full board to make arrangements for a proper organization of the faculty. Much depends upon a good, fair, business like start or commencement. . . . Will you soon return to reside in the territory and will you be able to attend to your duties as Trustee of the University?

JOHN WESLEY HOYT

John Wesley Hoyt,
first president, 1887-1890

John Wesley Hoyt was a person of great distinction long before he became the first University of Wyoming president in 1887. Born in Ohio in 1831, Hoyt graduated from Ohio Wesleyan University in 1849, studied law, earned a degree in medicine, and became a professor of chemistry and medical jurisprudence simultaneously at three Ohio educational institutions, including Antioch College. In 1857, he and Mrs. Hoyt moved to Wisconsin, where Hoyt became publisher and editor of several agricultural journals, managing officer of the Wisconsin State Agricultural Society, and president and founder of the Wisconsin Academy of Sciences, Arts, and Letters.

Hoyt's political career began with his strong identification with the then-young Republican party and his support for the Union before and during the Civil War. He had campaigned vigorously for Fremont and Lincoln, and in 1859 he brought Lincoln to deliver a special address at the annual Wisconsin State Fair. In 1862, he championed the Morrill Act that established federal support for state agricultural colleges, and after its passage, he became deeply involved in that reorganization of the University of Wisconsin which the act occasioned. A personal acquaintance of such influential figures as Wendell Phillips, Henry Clay, Charles Sumner, and Horace Mann, Hoyt became a delegate to international exhibitions in London (1862), Paris (1867), and Vienna (1873), earning at the latter a special decoration from the Austrian government. Following the Paris exhibition, he remained in Europe at the request of Secretary of State W. H. Seward in order to report on European educational systems; Congress later published his conclusions in a mammoth document.

His reputation further enhanced by several state of Wisconsin appointments, various educational consultancies, and commercial negotiations with Latin American countries on behalf of the U.S. government, Hoyt was appointed governor of Wyoming Territory in 1878 by Republican President Rutherford B. Hayes. He served in the position for four years. Plagued by ill health, he retired in 1885 to California, where (after a period spent in a sanatorium) he became active in financing construction of a Santa Monica railroad. The call back to Wyoming to become first president of the University was irresistible to this idealist who regarded such a project as his dream come true. In 1891, at the age of sixty, an embittered man left Laramie for Washington, D.C., his health further diminished. Yet he remained active until the end of his life. His campaign for the foundation of a national university caused him to oppose the establishment of American and Georgetown universities under private funding. He lent his efforts to movements for peace and equal suffrage for women. Hoyt died of heart failure in Washington in 1912.

If the board of trustees dismissed Hoyt because he was too "visionary," some of the faculty who worked with him made a positive judgment from the opposite point of view. They saw him as "too big for the job."

CHAPTER TWO

The chastisement caused Aughey to resign, and he was replaced by the new territorial geologist. Hoyt's position was soon clarified.

Most of all, Moonlight resented the board's action in appointing a university president, an action taken in the spring of 1887. Several names had been mentioned in this connection, and the governor himself had taken an active hand in the search. Indeed, according to his correspondence, Moonlight had a favorite candidate — a professor from Kansas, which was his own home state — and a preferred second choice as well. He entered into personal correspondence with both of them and kept in constant touch with Finfrock about their potential appointment. He was therefore "incensed," in the word of a later scholar, when without further consultation, the board of trustees, meeting in Laramie on May 5, 1887, appointed as president one of its own members — former Governor Hoyt, who had just been reprimanded by Moonlight for irresponsibility. To Moonlight's great annoyance, Hoyt (who had never attended a trustees' meeting) wired his resignation from the board and accepted the appointment with pleasure.

A scholar, a philosopher, a man of imagination and ideals who had always propounded the importance of learning, Hoyt wrote later that the presidency of a university, especially in Wyoming, was the fulfillment of a dream.

The friends of learning and other citizens ambitious for the honor of Wyoming had been earnestly active in realizing my dream of an institution that should early become the State University of Wyoming; had secured legislative appropriations for a large and beautiful first building at Laramie City; had completed the same and were anxious that I should accept the presidency and commence the first year's operations in September (1887). This unexpected call . . . decided me to resign my presidency of the railway corporation, and to accept that of the new university — a position which, although equally or more important, belonged to a field with which I was especially familiar and could cultivate with but little strain upon my nervous energies.

Moonlight was less optimistic. In outrage, he predicted disaster. From the start, he thought Hoyt did not have the qualities necessary to be a successful university president.

It is not for me to misjudge the board, but I think the result will bear me out in surmising the complete failure of the institution under such management. The President of a University, College, or Normal School, or other public or private institution of learning must have a very strong business turn of mind, so as to be a practical worker, and not a mere theorist.

Dourly, Moonlight wrote Finfrock that he wished the University prosperity "in all departments of finance, members, and education: for without the first two, there will not be much of the latter."

The new president arrived in Laramie in time to attend the trustees' meeting of August 11, 1887. He found the University only partially ready for the opening date set in September. For one thing, the single campus building, the pride and joy of its designers, was far from finished; the vicious winter of 1886-87 had proved too much for the construction schedule. Required by territorial law to complete the building within eighteen months of the enabling legislation, the board had no option but to accept an unfinished job; moreover, the $50,000 building fund was close to exhaustion. Classroom equipment was sorely lacking. Only a few donated books stood on the shelves. Landscaping was nonexistent, and the tower of Old Main overlooked bleak prairies and dirt paths on all sides.

Hoyt was undaunted. Although his late arrival on the scene had caused the trustees to proceed with employment of faculty and three scholars had already been hired, Hoyt now sought out a teacher of mathematics, and the board approved the new president's recommendation for two other faculty positions. When W. I. Smith and Aven Nelson arrived from the East to assume the positions contracted for by the board, they found to their surprise that they were both expecting to teach English. As puzzled as they, Hoyt

asked the board and was told that it was his business to fit the two men into the teaching program — that they had been hired because of general preparation and not to teach a specific subject. After interviewing both men, Hoyt was convinced that Smith really desired to teach English, whereas Nelson said that he would teach Botany or Biology.

13

Board of trustees, 1896

So accidentally did the career of a great botanist begin. At once the president began a careful description of curriculum to be published as a supplement to the *Circular of General Information.* On September 3, Hoyt was officially inaugurated as president in ceremonies presided over by Finfrock as president of the board, and attended by Colorado University dignitaries as well as local population. The governor's hostility for Hoyt and for the board led him to refuse to attend Hoyt's inauguration. The half-finished building was dedicated. Three days later the University opened its doors to a student body of 36 young people, 33 of whom resided in Albany County, and 22 of whom were aged sixteen and under.

The president faced difficulties probably beyond the solution of any new administrator. New faculty, unfinished facilities, inadequate funding, a handful of students and an unusually authoritarian board — all these must have made the former governor's first year into less than the "dream" he anticipated. Moonlight's generally hostile attitude continued to cause troubles. In the winter of 1887, a few short months after the University opened its doors, Moonlight notified Hoyt to expect the "visiting committee" authorized by the University's founding legislation. This team of inspectors (I. C. Whipple, Rev. R. E. Field, and F. F. Shannon) returned to Cheyenne to report on the paucity of students; the inadequacy of equipment; and defects in University administration, which negative views of the situation Moonlight carefully included in his address to the territorial legislature of 1888. Hoyt was irritated and wrote the governor to protest, but he received only a chilly reply in which Moonlight hinted that conscience and decency required him to be honest, just, and firm. Hoyt responded by lobbying furiously for his University among the members of the tenth territorial legislature.

In spite of the governor or because of the president, that legislature was kind. It began by authorizing the sale of another $25,000 in territorial bonds to bring the first building to completion and to equip it more properly for use. In addition, it appropriated $9,000 from general funds to meet University operating expenses and increased the institution's tax levy from the previous one-fourth to one-half mill of assessed valuation. Angry as always, Governor Moonlight, whose consistent battles with the legislature were based on retrenchment and political hostility, vetoed the bill, but his veto was overridden and the legislation passed. The legislature's generosity stands as a monument to Hoyt's political influence and lobbying skill.

In another area, the governor's economic horse sense might have benefited the University, for he was eager to take advantage of the public lands set aside by the U.S. government for University use in 1881. These lands had already been selected by F. W. Sawin, surveyor and now mathematics professor at UW. Although he complained that he was unable to locate Sawin's records of the exact areas chosen, Moonlight wrote to the secretary of the interior to clarify the issue, called the attention of the board of trustees to the problem, and carried on considerable correspondence with individuals who were interested in leasing lands. In this unsuccessful effort, he was (for a change) supported by the territorial legislature, which again petitioned the U.S. Congress for an act enabling University trustees to rent the given lands and realize income from them. The memorial directed to Congress praised the new University.

A university building has been erected at [Laramie] city, at a cost of fifty thousand

dollars, and the university was formally opened last autumn with a full corps of competent instructors and with an attendance at this time of about seventy students. . . . [The selected lands] cannot be made available for the present pressing uses of the university under the terms of the present acts of congress in relation thereto although from their annual rental a handsome annual income might be obtained which would be of incalculable benefit to our university during its infancy, when it needs every fostering care. . . .

Since federal legislation anticipated the rental of these lands only after statehood was achieved, the legislators' efforts bore no immediate fruit.

Besides gaining essential funding from the territorial legislature, Hoyt was able, during his tenure in office, to set a tone for the University that it retains to this day. His greatest achievements lay, first, in designing a curriculum that admitted the necessity of career training, but that clearly centered around his beloved liberal arts; and, second, in selecting a faculty that remained for the most part extraordinarily devoted to this isolated frontier University — some of them for all of their lives. It is in these matters that John Hoyt left his irrevocable mark.

The earliest list of curricula, published in the summer of 1887 in what was termed a "second edition" of the University's *Circular of General Information,* represents a future plan as much as a reality. Hoyt envisioned a "University" that provided instruction on many levels. On the lowest level stood a "preparatory course," frequently referred to as the "Academic Department." This four-year curriculum, representing a concession to the nature of Wyoming's educational system, was provided on campus because the state's handful of high schools were not yet graduating many students of university calibre. As the *Circular* stated,

It is believed that, with a proper organization and management of the Public Schools, this [four year] time may be gradually shortened until ere long the preparatory work will be wholly done by them. Students who find themselves substantially ready to enter the High School may venture to apply for admission to the Preparatory Department of the University.

The first two years of preparatory work were strictly defined; for the last two, students could choose among classical, literary, or scientific options, the better to prepare them for full college work.

Preparatory or high school level students dominated the campus population. In 1894, 32 students enrolled for preparatory courses and 21 for collegiate in liberal arts; if the trend was temporarily reversed in 1897, in the following year the "preppies" again outnumbered their seniors. The presence on campus of so many students of high school age tended to be an embarrassment to an institution calling itself a university. "By force of circumstance and conditions," wrote Downey as president of the board of trustees in an 1896 report that was highly critical of Hoyt's planning and administration, "the institution began its work largely as a preparatory school." As early as 1890, the first year of the four-year "prep" course was abolished, but attempts to limit the curriculum to two years continued to be unsuccessful. Although a number of high schools were listed as "accredited" to prepare students for college entry, few students presented themselves, and the Preparatory School remained the University's main "feeder" well into the twentieth century.

The "collegiate" department, outlined under Hoyt's administration, was a liberal arts college as we know it today, and by the end of the century had indeed changed its title to College of Liberal Arts. It consisted of a four-year course with choices of "options" in classical, literary, philosophical, or scientific studies. Here freshmen, sophomores, juniors, and seniors (having duly completed preparatory work for entry) studied sciences, classics, languages, literature, philosophy, history, and mathematics. The curriculum changed and enlarged over the years as professorial instruction became available. Although the first two years of study were prescribed, considerable election of classes was permitted in the last two. Students graduated at first with bachelor's degrees in philosophy, arts, literature, or science, although later these all became traditional A.B. and B.S. degrees.

The most difficult measure of Hoyt's plan and the one that took longest to activate was the system of so-called "departments of practical arts." Hoyt envisioned such curricula in five fields: commerce, mining, agriculture, the Normal School, and (with the proviso that it would at first offer only occasional courses by outside lecturers) a school of law. By 1891, these were supplemented by a "School of Mechanics and Manual Training" and a program in military tactics and science in order that the curriculum meet the requirements of the Morrill Act. Hoyt's college of commerce boiled down to a course in bookkeeping offered to prep-aratory students and did not surface as a full University department until 1899; during that year its bookkeeping and stenographic courses attracted an astonishing total of 57 students aged sixteen and over, providing more than one-fourth of the University's enrollment. The School of Mines vanished temporarily but reappeared in 1893 when Wilbur Knight, a geologist by profession, was assigned to its teaching roster; in the 1890s, a school of irrigation engineering made occasional showing as well. Hoyt did not, however, anticipate a special "School of Music," established in 1895, in which the lone teacher gave lessons with no financial support from the University except for the use of space and piano. In view of the number of female students, it is perhaps strange that home economics did not become part of the curriculum until 1907, when it was requested especially by the State Federation of Women's Clubs.

Each of these "schools" set its own regulations for admission in terms of examinations; and their links with the Preparatory School and the College of Liberal Arts depended primarily on greatly overlapping faculty assignments. Still it is clear from some bulletins, and less clear from others, that not one of them at first operated on a strictly collegiate level. Not only did each department develop one or more years of "preparatory work" on its own, but even the designations "freshman" and "sophomore" — used in several instances to accord with federal regulations — were ill-defined as to age and level of schooling. Thus the Normal School, which offered one, two, or four-year courses of training, actually admitted students at the age of fifteen and provided, therefore, a high school level education, with one "professional" year open to high school graduates and those with teaching experience. The mechanical arts — later engineering — school awarded a bachelor of engineering degree after two years of "preparatory" or high school work plus two years of collegiate-level

training. Bulletins make it clear that the "practical" schools offered many programs for those who could not remain through a full college course. Not until 1905 was a determined effort made to begin upgrading these schools to a full collegiate-equivalent level. Then such a move was based on the desirability of providing a broad education (such as was provided by the general Preparatory School) at least through high school age before any special training was initiated.

Hoyt's influence remained; the *Bulletin* of 1905-06 listed the following academic units and degrees: The College of Liberal Arts with B.A. and B.S. degrees; The Graduate School, leading to masters' degrees; The Wyoming State Normal School, awarding a two-year bachelor of pedagogy degree (for grade school teachers) and a four-year B.A. in education (for high school qualification); The Wyoming State College of Agriculture (B.S. degree); The Wyoming State College of Engineer-ing (B.S. degree); The Wyoming State School of Mines (B.S. degree); and three non-degree colleges — The Wyoming State School of Commerce, The Wyoming State School of Music, and The Wyo-ming State Preparatory School. Most of these were of the first president's concoction.

With a huge breadth and variety of courses — functioning, offered, and proposed — a faculty of hundreds might not have been too many. Instead the original curricula were handled by a group of seven (including the president) plus Mrs. Hoyt, who, like her husband, was listed as teaching psychology and moral philosophy. On hand, sup-posedly, was a series of lawyers, state officials, judges, board members, and "practical" experts, all identified as "distinguished citizens of Wyo-ming and Colorado, who will lecture from time to time, and systematically, in connection with various courses of study."

Considering that a full program was offered in "preparatory" studies, that the collegiate depart-ment listed upwards of 100 required and elective classes, and that the "practical departments" each proposed between ten and thirty different offer-ings, the burden on each of seven faculty members sounds acute. The first *Circular* and succeeding bulletins throughout the decade contained multiple

First faculty, April 1891

listings of faculty members in different schools and departments. In 1887, Hoyt, who was also University president, was listed in addition as lecturer on didactics and the history of education for the Normal School; lecturer on the history of mining and metallurgy and on political economy for the School of Mines; lecturer on the theory and practice of agriculture and political economy in the agricultural college; and lecturer on the history of commerce, political economy, and international law for the School of Commerce. Concurrently, Aven Nelson was a lecturer on the methods of instruction in biology for the Normal School; a professor of physical geography in the School of Mines; a professor of "economic botany," zoology, and animal physiology and hygiene in the agricultural college; and a professor of "natural history as auxiliary to commerce" in the commercial school. He also gave instruction in calisthenics and supervised campus landscaping and grounds maintenance. For a time he served as librarian. Faculty members were all called upon to teach their fields in the Preparatory School, and the employment of a principal did little to ease the situation. In addition, of course, each taught his traditional field in the liberal arts college.

Although in later years, titles were not quite so rich and imaginative, University of Wyoming professors continued for decades to do double and triple duty in liberal arts, schools for career training, and high school level instruction. Writing to Professor Wilson O. Clough in 1935, C. B. Ridgaway reported that

in the spring of 1896, I was elected to the chairs of physics, mathematics, astronomy, civil engineering, electrical engineering, physical soil analysis, and weather forecasting. I was quite overcome with amazement at the presumption of my knowledge. However, I soon found that some of the other professors were likewise honored.

And indeed, in that same year, Justus F. Soule was listed as prepared to handle any of fifteen classes in Greek and an equal number in Latin. B. C. Buffum taught all six courses in agriculture, with the addition of four classes in horticulture, three in entomology, two in veterinary medicine, and one in irrigation engineering. No wonder faculty delighted when circumstances permitted a reduced load — glad, as Ridgaway put it, to be sitting finally on a chair instead of on a settee.

Luckily, the faculty and its sanity were preserved by the actual smallness of the student body. In 1887, the ratio of faculty to students was approximately one to seven, and most of the students were in the Preparatory School. The student statistic always included many "specials," young people and old who attended classes irregularly, part-time, and without a degree in mind. It was this ratio that saved the faculty. Seldom, if ever, was student demand so great as to cause any given teacher to take on a back-breaking load. Most classes listed as offered had no students at all.

But teaching on campus was only the beginning. Almost all of the faculty held administrative assignments. They were librarians, faculty officers, and directors for the soon-established geology museum and the Rocky Mountain Herbarium. Professors rotated assignments in standing committees dealing with admissions, promotions, degrees, athletics, entertainment, and other matters. Student discipline and its attendant problems — remember that most students were aged sixteen or under — occupied faculty meeting after meeting. Faculty put together exhibits for world's fairs and served as judges for county and state exhibits. Service to the state was a requirement for the job. Nelson was executive officer of the State Board of Horticulture for many years. E. E. Slosson served as state chemist. The University's president was the first chairman of the Wyoming Education Association, founded in Laramie in 1891; and the *Wyoming School Journal,* the association's publication, was managed and edited on campus by the leading professor of education. For some time, under the direction of Wilbur C. Knight, the University performed free assays of minerals on request; even after the amount of work became prohibitive and necessitated the assessment of fees, the geology department continued the service. Faculty were frequently called upon to teach "short" courses or institutes, or simply to lecture in towns across the state.

In addition to teaching and administrative assignments, faculty members, even in the 1890s, were constantly involved in scholarly research and practical Wyoming problems. The work of Nelson, Wilbur Knight, and Buffum, Nelson's assistant, took them on long field trips during the summer months; even in the 1890s, adventurous students were able to accompany them. Wonderful accounts of their travels through the "interior" of the state to collect fossils for the geology museum and botanical specimens for the herbarium occur from time to time in student and University publications. Nelson's extraordinary botanical survey of Yellowstone Park in 1899 was a feat of great scientific significance.

Meanwhile, all those associated with the College of Agriculture — and in the early years, that meant all professors teaching any kind of science — were pressed into service writing brochures to aid and advise Wyoming's ranch and farm population. In its first year of existence (1891) the Agricultural Experiment Station published four such bulletins, offering findings and advice on plant lice, sugar beets, and meteorology as well as a report from the "departments" in the College of Agriculture. Thereafter a similar series was initiated on mineralogy and geology. Knight's evaluation of oil resources, written with the collaboration of chemist E. E. Slosson, appeared in 1893.

Thus the position of professor at the University of Wyoming in the early years demanded breadth, specialization, administrative ability, classroom discipline, a willingness to travel, research interests, talent in public relations, and generally, great good humor. By the end of the century, the group selected by Hoyt was supplemented by such individuals as June Downey (who published extensively in her field of psychology) and shortly thereafter Grace Raymond Hebard, who served as secretary to the board of trustees, secretary for the Agricultural Experiment Station, president of the local camera club, business manager of the *Wyoming School Journal,* University librarian, member of the Wyoming State Board of Examiners, member of the committee on Rhodes scholarships, and (after 1906), associate professor of political economy. One wonders when she found time to write a textbook on Wyoming history and government or to become the state's champion woman golfer. The dedication of these individuals to the University assumed heroic proportions. Hoyt's legacy may be deemed to include a core of energetic, creative, and beloved teachers — among them Nelson, Soule, Wilbur Knight, and Henry Merz (French, German, education, and sometime orchestra conductor) — who gave a lifetime of service and set an example for many who followed.

The Hoyt plan for a classical and liberal education lent to the University a strongly academic atmosphere. In the bulletins following 1896, when Hoyt's value was coming to be recognized, the first president was recognized as a central figure.

As soon as possible after his election, he mapped out a broad and liberal policy for the institution. . . . During these years, a literary atmosphere pervaded the institution. Meetings, literary and historical, were of frequent occurrence, participated in by members of the faculty and by many citizens of Wyoming. The Wyoming Academy of Arts, Science, and Letters was instituted, and papers of more than passing interest were presented by persons from different parts of the state. The ideal held up before the students and community during these years was that learning and culture should be sought for their own sake and not from utilitarian motives alone.

Nevertheless, Hoyt's administration ran into considerable difficulties, almost from the start. Part of the problem lay in the president's relationship with the board. For one thing, the trustees retained absolute financial control of all University expenses, and one wonders how a former governor liked petitioning "very respectfully" for the return of such amounts as $12.50, expended out of his own pocket. On April 2, 1888, he wrote defensively to Finfrock to insist on his honesty and the necessity of certain payments called for audit by the trustees — payments for such items as stationery. "I have ordered some things we could not do without," Hoyt wrote, "but solely on my own account or that of the faculty," and "I have never, to this hour, ordered a penny's worth of either goods or services of any kind to be charged to the University." In the same month a controversy arose about Hoyt's salary, "pledged," in the president's word, in the amount of $2,000 temporarily but $2,500 as soon as legislative funds were available. Hoyt received the increase in June, but bad feelings were created all around.

Hoyt's involvement in politics — and he was a natural politician — made his university future even less secure. In April 1889, Moonlight had been removed by a new national Republican administration — undoubtedly a happy day for Hoyt and the board, for the Democratic "retrenchment" governor had never been a guaranteed friend to the University. Better still, his replacement was Francis E. Warren, the same governor who had originally appointed Hoyt and the others to the first board of trustees. Only a few months later, Hoyt was elected as an Albany County delegate to the convention that was to devise a constitution for a state of Wyoming. The University president may have made his first political misstep here, for he supported another Albany County delegate (M. C. Brown, once a University trustee) for convention president, and Brown was regarded by Warren as a maverick Republican. Still Hoyt was put in charge of drafting that part of the constitution that pertained to education and that included several paragraphs relating to the University, based on territorial legislation — regarding funding, lands, management, and anti-discrimination policies. His autobiography demonstrates that Hoyt was duly proud of this particular achievement.

As the last territorial governor, Warren was generally supportive of University programs. His report of 1889 to the secretary of the interior was positive. He continued to encourage the land program, and by 1890, he announced that the selection of University lands under the act of 1881 had been approved by the federal government, although such lands were technically not available for lease until later. The governor's committee to report on territorial institutions, while recognizing that some "needs and necessities" were beyond fulfillment under current financial conditions, told the legislature that the territory was not "justified in refusing" University requests in the amount of almost $9,000. It was hardly Warren's fault that the last territorial legislature adjourned (after many an argument) without agreeing upon an appropriation. Meanwhile the governor never threatened to upset the board, and the most influential members remained on that body from his earlier term.

During 1889 and 1890, however, cooperation between board and University president steadily disintegrated. The board's complaints — never recorded in the minutes, but stated with some acerbity in a later document addressed to the next board of trustees — included such matters as Hoyt's "lax and unsatisfactory" sense of discipline, whereby the president seldom backed the faculty in its censuring of pupils and instead permitted "the same mild rules . . . that usually govern in old established colleges," although most students were "in the preparatory department, too young to be trusted without constant supervision." Rowdiness in study hall was cited as a case in point. Complaint was raised against Mrs. Hoyt, who not only taught psychology but (when he was ill or absent) substituted for the president in his classes and assumed "other duties of a professor." In September 1889, Finfrock supposedly told Hoyt of the board's decision to end his wife's teaching on campus, and when she continued nonetheless, the board passed a special resolution (April 1890) insisting that only paid faculty be allowed to teach. Trustees said that Hoyt used "violent and intemperate" language in front of students on one occasion and complained of Hoyt's involvement in a quarrel between two campus literary societies. The president, they said later, developed an "unfortunate reputation . . . in matters of finance" (exactly the prediction of Governor Moonlight) that "weakened his influence and prestige."

At its July meeting in 1890, the board considered the status of the president, and the trustees later asserted that not only did they resolve that Hoyt should soon leave but that they notified him of this decision.

The Board was very loath to have him commence the new school year but, because of the

then approaching election and of his senatorial interests, yielded a point and upon recommendation of Doctor Cowhick consented to his holding through the fall term. Doctor Finfrock was deputed to notify him of this decision and, upon doing so, was informed by President Hoyt that, if allowed to remain until that date, he would then voluntarily resign his office. Upon this understanding the matter was allowed to rest. . . .

The board's statement does not coincide with Hoyt's later contention that he was removed from office "without warning," an action he referred to as a "sudden blow, wholly unsuspected on the part of the victim."

During the autumn months of 1890, the situation further disintegrated. For one thing, Hoyt was rather obviously a contender for the office of U.S. senator; two senators were to be elected by the first state legislature at its session beginning in November. Hoyt's campaign — if such it may be called — was hardly structured or ardently pursued, and there is evidence that even his friends believed he should have made his candidacy strong and clear. The president later contended that five other candidates had surfaced in Laramie, three of whom had close connections to the board of trustees, and that the board's attorney had told a friend that Hoyt had better "keep out of the senatorial contest [or] . . . lose [his] official head." In any event, the board's increasing irritation with the president may have been linked to his possible election as senator. In the long run, all were deceived, since Warren who had been elected first state governor in 1890, in spite of his pledge to remain at the post, resigned and became a U.S. senator himself.

Meanwhile, Hoyt had a political answer to the board's political outlook. In the first state legislature of 1890-91, he lobbied successfully for a law that replaced the rather vague territorial legislation on the University and its governance. The board was furious when it realized that Hoyt had managed to persuade the legislature to insist that future boards of trustees consist of nine rather than seven members and that no more than three be appointed from Albany County — a measure that, Hoyt contended, was essential to converting into a statewide institution the University that had practically been operated by a Laramie coterie. In addition, the new law in the trustees' view

"secured greatly increased powers" for the president by making him an ex-officio member of the board. One can imagine the board's anger, for in the past it had viewed the president strictly as hired help and invited him to confer with itself only twice in three years. Although the law of 1891 more carefully defined the functions of board and president, it can hardly be said that the president received any extraordinary authority. Nevertheless, it represented a victory for Hoyt over the trustees.

But the final victory was the board's. On December 13, 1890, five of the seven members meeting together dismissed Hoyt as of December 31. The trustees made no specific statement of causes except to express their conviction that they were acting "in the highest good of the University." To the press, the board members admitted that they had found Hoyt to be more visionary than practical. Immediately after dismissing the president, trustees announced that they planned a mass resignation, in order that acting Governor Amos Barber (Senator Warren's replacement) might select a new board under the new legislation.

In a confidential and undated statement to that new board, probably written in February or early March, the former trustees were more specific in their criticisms of the former president and referred to many of the circumstances noted above. "We have cumulative evidence," they told their successors,

that President Hoyt was very much out of place as an instructor of youth. We found him to be very impractical, visionary, extravagant in his views, autocratic, egotistic, artful, untruthful, greatly influenced by his family and persistently aiming to ignore the Trustees and override the Faculty. This may be strong language but our assertions can all be amply verified and we invite the most rigid scrutiny. We might add that we have wished and endeavored to avoid publicity and to spare his feelings, even making no record of the greater part of our proceedings in the matter. . . . There has been no fight, no harsh treatment, only necessity, with the honest regard for the best interests of the institution, on the part of this board.

CHAPTER TWO

Reference was made to Hoyt's poor health, and the board strongly suggested that the next president be a younger and sturdier man. Indeed, Hoyt himself wrote later that he was so ill that sometimes he "was obliged to hold on to the fence along the sidewalk to keep from falling."

Dismissal was a financial and psychological blow to the president, however, and no ill health could keep him from mounting a major statement of protest. The family felt friendless and isolated; in spite of student support in the form of a gift, no faculty members chose to take sides and no one came to offer sympathy. On January 12, Hoyt addressed a long letter to Grace Raymond Hebard, whom he probably knew; Hebard was one of the governor's new board appointees, recommended for the position by Joseph M. Carey, who had just (along with Warren) been elected to the U.S. Senate. Hoyt blamed his removal on the politics of the senatorial race, called attention to the broader composition of the board in accordance with the new University bill for which he had worked, and hinted that Hebard's appointment was in part the result of his own influence. But clearly, here was a man in unhappy straits; he speaks of "the injury to my reputation, dearer to me than life," and the "absolute integrity of purpose and utter faithfulness in meeting every obligation as University president," appealing to Hebard's "sense of justice" to help bring about his reinstatement.

Under date of January 13, Hoyt actually published a four-page statement of his position for circulation to friends and politicians. Herein he repeated his reasons for supporting the reorganization of the board of trustees; spoke to his achievements as president (especially in regard to application for federal agricultural support funds); and mentioned his "continued invalidism," with "consequent loss of nearly all the property I had and with great danger . . . of losing even my home, but partly paid for." In this document, Hoyt asked of his friends their support for a hearing before the new board. About the former board, he spared few words, calling the trustees:

a few ambitious men, most of them wanting, as came to be manifest, in nearly every requisite, [who] managed to get themselves placed in control and have since appeared to think they,

themselves, owned the institution. The men in control [in 1887] were, some of them, even narrower, more ignorant of educational matters, and, worse than all, more conceited than I knew — men who made no proper distinction between a university and a district school; who manifested none but the most general interest, never once in more than three years, as I remember, being present, either at the morning exercises or at any of the recitations; never once advising the faculty as to management, discipline, instruction, or anything else; yet sitting with closed doors, and there, without a word of inquiry, simply on rumor or sole testimony of offending students, berating the faculty for acts of discipline, and even reversing the unanimous judgment of its seven men. . . .

His dismissal he called a "vindictive act" and asked "the earnest help of my true friends in breaking the power of the corrupt combination here by means of . . . representations to members of the new board, in my behalf."

On January 28, Hoyt addressed the acting governor partly in regard to the necessity of immediately pursuing federal funding for agriculture and partly in the hopes of reinstatement. By now, the former board was furious, and in a last meeting on February 17, 1891, it angrily condemned Hoyt for having reproduced some steel engravings that the board had previously refused to purchase; such reproduction it called an "act of piracy" and ordered all the copies destroyed. The event had occurred in 1888.

The new board of trustees met for the first time on the University campus on February 24-25, 1891. Present were six of the nine appointed members: Reverend Albinus A. Johnson and Grace Raymond Hebard of Cheyenne; two of the three Laramie appointees (Stephen W. Downey and Frederick Scrymser, Bishop Ethelbert Talbot being absent); and one member (Charles Wagoner) from Carbon County. The new appointees from Evanston and Sheridan were not there. New trustees met in session with several former board members, and the written statement of the former board outlining the reasons for Hoyt's dismissal was adopted as part of the record.

On this date, the new board also received Hoyt's official eighteen-page application for reinstatement. Herein the former president reviewed his hopes for the University and the problems that had arisen, in particular because the trustees were unfamiliar with educational administration and had nevertheless been "accorded very large powers by the terms of the law," whereunder they had "little disposition to counsel with the president or, even in cases of first importance, to inquire into the facts absolutely necessary to just decisions." He commented on the notable *esprit de corps* among students and faculty, on the hopes he had for the University's curricular development, and on the necessity for immediate action in regard to federal agricultural funds. Clearly, Hoyt was bitter about the trustees' unwillingness to face him with the list of reasons for his dismissal. Reviewing his career and the success and approbation that had been his, he wrote that

> *It was reserved for a coterie of school trustees in this little mountain town to put me under the ban of their displeasure, and to mar, if possible, this record of a life devoted to the public good.*

Hoyt's message was received by the board, but it reacted negatively, resolving that since it did not "desire to pass judgment" on its predecessors nor to "assume the troubles of a past administration," it would decline to reinstate the former president. Bishop Ethelbert Talbot, who was absent from the meeting, wrote Downey to ask that his proxy vote be cast in favor of Hoyt. The support of this

Paleontology exhibit, College of Arts and Sciences, c. 1900

highly distinguished and widely respected trustee was indeed a strong recommendation for the president, but rather than taking into account the bishop's position, the board opted to disallow proxy votes altogether. Hoyt's statement to Johnson, whom the board chose as its president at this meeting, that if reappointed he would retire at the end of the academic year, had no particular effect.

Mechanical building workers, c. 1910

At the next regular board meeting, March 27, trustees moved to elect a new University president. In spite of the fact that at least six applications had been received for the position, only three candidates were considered: Hoyt, Professor John D. Conley (who had been appointed acting president after Hoyt's dismissal), and A. A. Johnson, then president of the board. Seven board members were present, and it took four ballots before any candidate received a clear majority of four. Hoyt received considerable support (on one ballot, he gained three votes), but eventually both he and Conley lost out to Johnson. Johnson accepted the new office, resigned as a University trustee, and was at once replaced as president of the board by his Laramie colleague Downey.

Hoyt had little recourse. His request for a hearing had not been heeded and the former board had never formally made clear its reasons for his dismissal. Hebard refused him access to the minutes of the meeting where his status was discussed. Under the circumstances, Hoyt could only write the board to request that his own statement be "filed in the same parcel with the said communication from the former trustees." As

early as March and persisting for some months thereafter, he filed his claim for salary through the end of the year. The board never agreed, accepting instead the statement of former Trustee A. S. Peabody that the board rehired Hoyt in September 1890 "with the expressed understanding that the engagement was for the first term only" and that under the statute then in existence the board's power of hiring and firing was without limitation.

In retrospect, the bitterness of Hoyt and his family was undoubtedly justified. The former governor had come to Wyoming to direct a university and had found what he himself called a "Laramie high school" instead. He had brought with him visions of a broad collegiate curriculum and had been faced instead with problems of disciplining sixteen-year-olds. The "magnificent" building to which all referred with pride turned out to be unfinished — only in Hoyt's last year were the final touches administered — and ill-equipped. As president, Hoyt's political ambitions were frustrated (in part by his own lack of firm intention), his wife was insulted, and his health further deteriorated. The board's dismissal was peremptory, and its refusal to permit him a hearing was arbitrary.

Still, perhaps the board had reason. Hoyt was indeed a sophisticated and well-educated individual with a "dream" that extended far beyond Laramie reality. He would undoubtedly have made an excellent university president elsewhere, and indeed he spent much of his remaining life in Washington, D.C. where he devoted himself to educational causes. He was the right man in the wrong place. Yet his ideas on curriculum in the liberal arts, his acuteness about federal funding, and his sound judgments in regard to faculty were to remain his legacy to Wyoming for years to come.

IN THE FIELD

ith the foundation of a state university, scientists of many genres gathered on campus, many of them eager to investigate the new and untried potential of their frontier locale. Minerals, plants, soils, and fauna of the frontier area were subjected to special scrutiny by young professors in frontierland. Early expeditions of research and discovery were frequently able to report new and dramatic finds. Shortly after their employment in 1891, B. C. Buffum and Dice McClaren, hired to direct the newly-established Agricultural Experiment Station, toured the field substations by wagon with new president, Albinus A. Johnson. As horticulturist, Buffum's assignment lay in potential arable and crop-growing lands, and he made special efforts to collect specimens of

Geology field camp, Green Top Mountain, 1898

native grasses occurring on the station lands. This collection Buffum sent to the Chicago World's Fair in 1893 under the custodianship of Aven Nelson and E. E. Slosson, chemistry professor; the exhibit won a medal in the category of grasses and twenty awards for grain. The beginning of Nelson's interest in a herbarium collection dates from Buffum's donation of these grasses to the young botanist for further classification.

IN THE FIELD

In 1894, Nelson and Wilbur C. Knight, geologist, undertook a summer trip by horse and wagon that led them from the Nebraska border to Jackson Hole, where they clambered up to a considerable height on the Teton Mountains. By 1895, Nelson's subsequent wanderings were adding an average of 5,000 botanical specimens to his collection every year.

Perhaps the most extraordinary summer investigations occurred in the year 1899. That summer, Knight invited geologists and paleontologists from throughout the country to join him in a search for remains of ancient animals on Wyoming's prairie. Spurred by the offer of free transportation from the Union Pacific Railroad, 100 geologists met in Laramie in June. It took them three days to organize their expedition, but eventually they set out for a summer of field exploration and rugged outdoor life on saddle horses; in covered wagons; and in lumber wagons, designed to carry heavy loads. Their success was measured in the collection of three wagonloads of prehistoric dinosaur bones, which were shipped to various schools and museums across the country. It was Knight's contention that Wyoming should sponsor a permanent geological field summer school, but the realization of his hopes — although on a far different basis — had to wait for the inspiration of his son, Sam Knight, a quarter of a century later. Meanwhile, Aven Nelson was also out collecting. Accompanied by his wife, their two small girls (aged ten and thirteen), and two student assistants, he set out for Yellowstone early in summer 1899. There he performed the first systematic botannical collecting ever to occur in the area. In his Nelson biography, Roger L. Williams has painted an extraordinary picture of the expedition: travel by horse and wagon, with horses often roaming astray; washing and cooking by campfire; tenting at night; wallowing in mud and suffering in rain. The entire party participated in the gathering and the careful drying of plants, always collected in several specimens to provide for later sale or exchange. One of the students had to be sent home after he stumbled into a hot pool and badly burned one leg. The munificent collection gathered by Nelson resulted in the official founding of the Rocky Mountain Herbarium, just as Knight's ancient animal bones formed the basis for what is now the geology museum.

To these pioneers and others, Wyoming science owes what it has become over the decades.

Chapter Three

Hard Times and Early Struggles
1891-1907

he responsibility you place upon me as President of the University is very great," wrote A. A. Johnson to the board of trustees at the end of his second year in office.

As busy men you depend upon me, as your executive servant, for plans and suggestions which when approved and executed will advance the interests of the University. To do this effectually I must sit in judgment on the work of my fellow teachers, must regard the interest of the State and her citizens as they center in this institution, and must ever bear in mind the highest and best interest of the students that gather in these walls. In this broad field conflicting interests must necessarily arise, and a harmonious and equitable solution must be found in order to avoid extremes, and maintain the unity of purpose and action so necessary to success. . . . I will give you my honest and conscientious judgment in all matters, as seen from my standpoint, being charitable in my views yet always seeking the best interest of the university. I assume that in the discharge of your exalted trust you do not know parties, creeds, or persons, but only desire to enhance the success and interest of the University committed to your hands. My report, therefore, shall be without fear or favor. A conscientious man can do no more.

The board responded favorably. Albinus Johnson was an individual of professional academic background, although at the time of his election he was serving as a Methodist pastor in Cheyenne. Before coming to Wyoming he had been founder and president of a college in Fort Worth, Texas. He was experienced in organizational and financial management. Johnson's honeymoon with the trustees may well have been predicated upon the fact that he was briefly a trustee and that it was thus not difficult for members of the board to consider him an ex-officio one of themselves.

But on the whole, harmony was by no means apparent in the years 1891-1907. Although board members worked well with each other, conflict with presidents was not unknown, and presidential authority remained limited. The constant struggle to expand the University's student body intensified with the depression years of the mid-1890s. Underfinanced by the state, the University came to rely on its federal funding, particularly that accorded for agricultural instruction and research. During these years its receipt of federal funds was continually challenged by groups in other areas of the state, where citizens contended — not without some justification — that federally financed agricultural research could best be carried on in lower elevations with less severe climates. In fighting for her federal funding, the University at Laramie was fighting for her existence. The issue was temporarily settled by a Supreme Court decision in 1907.

The years from 1891-1907 saw the trustees as strongly in command of University policy as they had sought to become under Hoyt's administration. Part of this control evolved from the nature of the board itself. The durable presence of a number of important figures among trustees during the years lent the board an aura of stability and authority. These might well be considered the Hebard years, for Grace Raymond Hebard received appointment in 1891; continued as a board member until 1903; and thereafter remained the board's paid secretary, an office she had held from the start. For seventeen years, Hebard's influence was all-pervasive, and in terms of the University's day-to-day operations, policy was often left in her hands.

 26

The board also boasted some important political personalities. Stephen W. Downey served as its president until 1897 when he was replaced by Otto Gramm, board member from 1895-1911. Gramm, a leading Republican political figure, joined Judge Timothy F. Burke (trustee from 1895-1918 and president after Gramm's resignation) and M. C. Brown (Republican from Albany County) as long-term board members whose presence lent a particular tone to the organization. Although Wyoming saw one Democratic governor (1893-95) during these years, the board was never threatened by more than token Democratic presence, and Republican politics dominated without challenge.

Under the new law of 1890, only three of the nine trustees could be citizens of Albany County — a measure designed by Hoyt to universalize the board in the eyes of the citizens of the state. Nevertheless, Albany County appointees, with the particular aid of Hebard, who resided at first in Cheyenne, continued their dominance of the board. For one thing, transportation was still such a problem as to make it greatly difficult for board members from remote areas of the state to attend meetings. But most importantly, the board's executive committee came to be authorized to perform many duties in the long interims between trustee meetings, and the executive committee was a strictly local group. Beginning in 1897, the membership of this committee always included Gramm and Hebard, and although the third — and often a fourth — member changed from time to time, he, she, or they always came from the southeast area. By June 1892, this committee was commanded (in consultation with a faculty group) to fill faculty appointments that became vacant between board meetings. After 1893, it was required to handle many financial matters. In some years the full board met two or three times and retained considerable control through its examinations of executive committee policy, but on occasion (for instance the academic year 1892-93) twelve months would pass between board meetings, and the executive committee became the trustees' powerful, policy-making arm.

Although she was technically only board secretary, Hebard had full charge of the day-to-day financial operation of the entire University. Unlike other trustees, she was paid a salary in addition to expenses. For much of this period of time she operated firmly and independently, her only restriction being that the books must be inspected and formally reported on annually by the board's treasurer. In June 1894, when the auditing committee reported that several accounts were overdrawn, the secretary was temporarily required to get authority for expenditures from the president of the board, but this regulation was rescinded a year later. After its formal organization in 1891, the important Agricultural Experiment Station was chaired by the president of the board (also president of the executive committee), and Hebard always served as its secretary too. From her appointment to the board in 1891, Hebard gathered a great deal of power and responsibility in her hands, although her decisions were always subject to confirmation by the executive committee, as the executive committee's rulings were to be confirmed periodically by the board itself.

Main entrance and barn, Saratoga experiment farm, May 1891

Under the circumstances, even Johnson — who had the respect of the board for financial acumen "seldom found in literary or University men" — was by no means a free agent in his operations. Trustee approval was still necessary for even the smallest expenses. Faculty appointments, student dismissals, curriculum, and legislative programs were all ultimately determined by the board or its executive committee, although often upon presidential recommendation. It became the practice for the president to present an annual report at the board's June meeting; such reports were accompanied by the reading of summaries from each University department. In these reports, the president outlined budgetary needs and problems for the coming year. Faculty appointments — always made on an annual contract basis — were determined at this time, but the board remained the ultimate authority.

In April 1896, Johnson resigned, the first of a series of presidents to leave the University voluntarily. In the case of Johnson, his resignation originated "for personal reasons" which the board, in its own words, "found it impossible to adjust to his satisfaction." The "reasons" had arisen suddenly, for Johnson had just returned from a trip to Washington, before which no problem seemed in evidence. It seems likely that one of the trustees had pressed him to recommend a faculty appointment that he found unworthy. In his last report to the board, dated June 10, 1896, Johnson said:

Were I to remain as President of the University, I am quite clear in my mind as to who should constitute the Faculty for the ensuing year, making my selection from the present Faculty and those who have applied for positions, and I am prepared to give clear and definite reasons for my judgment, based solely upon the efficiency of the applicant and the good of the University. . . . One thing is sure, and will be agreed to by all successful educators, and that is, that large freedom must be allowed the President of a University to select his Faculty, undisturbed by schemers, either among the public or in the Board of Trustees, to advance the personal interests of friends or those of partisans; and I would therefore recommend that you treat my successor better in that respect than you have the retiring President.

Rumors that Johnson's quarrel was with Hebard seem verified by the fact that when they made their decision, the trustees asked Hebard as well as Johnson to leave the room, although she was a full-fledged board member at the time.

That the board saw Johnson depart with reluctance is indicated by its resolution dated April 17, 1896:

We appreciate the fidelity with which he has discharged the difficult duties which have fallen to him, and we would specially commend his ability as an organizer, his superior power and mastery of difficult and diverse details, and the earnestness and untiring energy which characterize all his efforts.

Johnson was not so sanguine, and he wrote in some bitterness to the U.S. Bureau of Education; the letter has been destroyed.

Following Johnson, the succession of presidents continued. Those of short tenure left before problems developed, but those who remained in office longer frequently faced conflict with the board, which continued to perform as chief University administrator through the offices of Hebard and the executive committee. Frank P. Graves, elected by the board on the third ballot at its meeting of June 10, 1896, remained on the scene only two years. At 27, Graves was one of the youngest college presidents in the country. He came to Wyoming with a Ph.D. from Boston University, five years of experience in teaching classical languages at Tufts, and a reputation for scholarship based on his editing of several Greek texts. Graves was distinguished (the trustees wrote) as a polished gentleman, an able executive, and a person of strict integrity. In June 1897, the president was re-elected by the board, this time to an unusual three-year term, but less than a month later he informed Hebard that he wished to resign as soon as trustees could release him. They kept him for a year, until summer of 1898, when his resignation to accept the presidency of Washington State University was accepted.

Graves' successor, Elmer E. Smiley, remained at the helm for five full years. Chosen by the board in July 1898, Smiley held degrees in Semitic languages and theology from Yale. He was already known to the trustees as a Cheyenne minister; as a candidate for University president at the time of Graves' election; and as baccalaureate orator in June 1897, when his address was entitled "The Power Not Ourselves." With his dedication to the ministry, Smiley brought a different tone to the presidency, for although Johnson also had been a minister, the latter had an aptitude for everyday finance that characterized his administration.

As for Smiley, his special forte was the social gospel, and during his presidency he traveled the state preaching the social responsibility of religious

CADETS ON PARADE

or 78 years of Wyoming University's first century, every able-bodied male student was required to enroll in military drill, known by various names through its long history. After 1916, it was known as the Reserve Officers' Training Corps. By the provisions of the Morrill Act of 1862, under which Wyoming received those sections of land that were donated to a land-grant college, military science (along with agriculture, engineering, English, and other subjects) had to be made available to all students. As early as 1891, military drills began on campus, although (according to Wilson O. Clough) equipment and rifles did not arrive until the following year. The first uniforms consisted of gray West Point fatigues, and the first corps of 55 young men (most of them not yet 18) was directed by First Lieutenant D. I. Howell. A girls' cadet corps made periodic appearances on campus after the turn of the century, including an appearance during President Theodore Roosevelt's brief visit in May 1903.

Perhaps the best known of all of the officers who rotated in and out of campus service was Beverly C. Daly, who came to

Major Beverly C. Daly,
Reserve Officers' Training Corps,
later dean of men, 1899

ROTC machine gun class, c. 1917

Wyoming in 1911. Daly continued his army service until 1936, and upon retirement from that service he became the University's dean of men (until 1945).

In 1924, the military took over the University marching band, and thereafter marching band could be substituted by male students for ROTC membership. In 1929, Scabbard and Blade, the military honorary, established a branch on campus. The following year, the Wyoming unit received an "excellent" rating from the U.S. War Department for the first time.

The cadet corps survived a strong anti-military peace movement in the mid-1920s and 1930s, as well as a similar groundswell after World War II. Although court decisions in the mid-1920s found that the Morrill Act did not demand that military training be required of students but only that it be offered to them, it remained on the "must" list on the Wyoming campus until a faculty committee, with the approval of the president and trustees, abolished the requirement in 1965. Since then, the current voluntary ROTC system was in effect.

institutions, in particular as against gambling, a heated issue at the time. His reports to the board were less specifically financial than philosophical, to the point that on occasion they were distinguished by many quotations from the Bible. He sponsored the introduction on campus of the YMCA in 1900 and its sister organization two years later. In comparison with earlier presidents, Smiley's fear was that religion might be neglected on campus, and to that end he organized regular Sunday afternoon vesper services to supplement the several weekly assemblies that students were already required to attend.

In our anxiety that the University shall be above criticism in all matters touching religion, we must guard against giving the impression that religion is ignored altogether in our institution. During the past year the University Vesper services . . . have proven very popular and have been well attended by the students and townspeople . . . While everything looking toward sectarianism had been strictly barred out of these services, still they have been from the first more or less of a religious nature. And the feeling is unanimous that the results have been only beneficial to the University.

As it happened, the president coupled his religious beliefs with what some took to be an overemphasis on propriety, decent behavior, and seriousness. In 1901, he was attacked in the Douglas *Budget* for emphasizing religion and for the "coldness" of his strict behavioral codes. Even the generally supportive Laramie *Boomerang* admitted that "It may be that there are woven into the management of the institution a trifle too many theological ideas" and that Smiley might be somewhat too exacting in the rules of decorum. The president answered the complaint in his report to the board for the year 1901-02:

. . . The faculty claim to have gotten more good work out of the student body than they have been able to do heretofore. And the feeling is general on their part that it is better for all concerned to settle down to steady, plodding hard work even at the sacrifice of some of the dancing parties and student escapades. . . . One of the first problems in [my] administration was how to start a nucleus of influences that should make for seriousness and that should offset the influences that were making largely for frivolity in the institution. . . . I am glad for our young people to enjoy themselves. I am not opposed to their dancing nor to their good times generally.

But I do believe in moderation. And I believe it is a mistaken ideal for a university to turn itself into a merry mount where its students dance their time away and spend it in frivolity.

The board's answer was to renew Smiley's contract for another year.

Nevertheless, at the same time problems began to arise. Smiley was a gentle soul, and his complaint was always tempered, but clearly he was concerned about his duties, his relationship to the board, and particularly the role of its secretary. His 1902 annual report requested the board to clarify his role. "Am I expected simply to look after the faculty and students," he asked, "Or am I to take a general interest in and be ready to report on anything and everything connected with the university? . . . It is difficult for me sometimes to know just where the responsibilities of my office leave off and that of somebody else's begins." He made a rather charming analogy in asking whether he was a "kind of captain of the ship of this university . . . employed . . . to sail the ship for you," and if his position as captain put him in total command, so that "no one was allowed for a minute to divide his authority with him on board his ship."

If he was the captain, Smiley told the board, he was forced to report to the trustees that his office as "largely shorn of authority" in the eyes of faculty and students. There were on campus, he wrote, two rival officers, with divided authority, and when "authority is divided between the ship's captain and the purser, there will be mutiny amongst the crew." Mentioning her by name, Smiley made it clear that he had Hebard in mind. He had actually approached her on the problem more than once in the hopes that she might abandon her status on the board and take some other position at the University. Although she had occasionally agreed that administrative organization was far from perfect, she rebuffed his suggestions. Smiley now specifically asked the board to rectify the situation in his behalf.

I have felt obliged to force the issue. I ask now therefore that something be done in this matter. . . . Understand me, I have no grudge against Miss Hebard and am not trying to settle any old score. Personalities do not enter into the case in any way whatever. I am asking for a wrong situation to be righted.

The trustees did not directly address the situation in 1902, but a year later Hebard was not reappointed to the board. Instead, she became its hired and well-paid secretary. The truth is the change in status made little difference. Her continued authority in all facets of the University's administration played a major role in Smiley's decision to resign. The president's final report was presented to the board of trustees in June 1903, at which time — although he had no particular plans for the future — Smiley unexpectedly announced his resignation. He may be considered the second president alienated by Hebard's activities.

Smiley's replacement, Charles W. Lewis, selected by the board from a field of 24 applicants, assumed office in September 1903. Lewis, whose energetic tackling of problems at hand might have made him an ideal president, contracted pneumonia in Colorado and died during commencement week in spring 1904. He was followed in office by F. M. Tisdel, who was chosen by the board from among many applicants on July 21, 1904. Tisdel was perhaps the most highly qualified academic to achieve the University presidency in these early years. A one-time youthful resident of Rock Springs, he held the A.B. degree from Northwestern, M.A.s from Wisconsin and Harvard, and a Ph.D. from Harvard (1900). He had taught at Wisconsin, Oberlin, and the Armour Institute of Technology, and the year of his election to the presidency saw the publication of his book on English literature. Nevertheless, it took the trustees five separate ballots to come to a decision. They were undoubtedly influenced by the fact that Tisdel was the nephew of U.S. Senator C. D. Clark and a good friend of the influential Quealy family from Kemmerer. During the Tisdel administration the problems between board and president came to a drastic climax, but that is a later story.

Meanwhile, relations between board, secretary, and president did not impede the slow progress of the University as curricula were expanded, faculty developed in terms of numbers and interests, and the student body slowly increased in size and changed in nature.

During these first twenty years, University presidents were constantly struggling to attain stronger support for the institution, not just from Laramie but from citizens throughout the state. As early as 1893, President Johnson was not optimistic.

> *The people did not and do not feel the need of [a University], hence, its work of higher education is limited by our small population and must continue to be so for some years to come. I need not discuss how the University originated. It is here fully orbed and equipped. The pertinent question is how can it most benefit the state under these conditions. . . .*

Ten years later, Smiley, too, referred to "an old-standing criticism on the institution that it was launched too soon and before the state was ready for it."

In recognizing the problem, both presidents had suggestions. Smiley's attitude was that the citizens of the state had little cause to complain because, by the time of his administration, the federal government had contributed so much of the University's financial support. "The University had been a partnership affair," he wrote,

> *and the Federal Government has stood responsible for a large part of its bills . . . Up to date it has worked no hardship on the state to meet the conditions of the compact entered into with the general government.*

Johnson's solution was more positive. If the citizens of Wyoming were not yet ready to send their children to Laramie for college education, he said in 1893, then at least the University could help them in other ways. He thought particularly that University influence could be exerted in developing the resources of the state for its inhabitants, a task he clearly assigned to the Agricultural Experiment Station, a federally supported research project. Both presidents realized how dependent the school was upon federal aid.

What the administrators were most concerned about was the continuing small number of students who enrolled in campus classes. Only very slowly was the University managing to increase its student population. Statistics on enrollment are difficult to analyze, since each source presents different total figures, and some accounts actually seem to add first and second term enrollments together. But it seems likely that in 1887-88, 47 students signed up for courses on campus in fall semester; two years later, the total was probably 49. By the year 1896-97, the University boasted 160 students,

Sub-primary teacher training, Preparatory School, 1905-06

although at least sixty of these were listed as "irregular." In 1906, "irregular" students ceased to be tabulated as a separate category, and the total enrollment was 233. In this year, however, at least 115 students were not pursuing college degrees — namely, those studying music or commerce and those enrolled in the Preparatory School. Viewed from another perspective, the University boasted ten students in the liberal arts collegiate curriculum in 1890-91 and eighteen such in 1901-02. The presence of many students who were not seeking college degrees caused, as has been noted, considerable question about the University's real functions.

Two points of special criticism might be isolated. We have already mentioned the number of University students who were actually doing "preparatory" or high school level work. As high schools developed in the state, one might reason that this department would be phased out, and in 1896, it was reduced to two years with the statement that shortly it might be abolished. Instead, however, the three-year curriculum was restored. At that time seven high schools — including that of Laramie City itself — were listed as "accredited," in that their courses were accepted for admission purposes without special examinations. In 1906, the number of students of high school age still outnumbered those in collegiate classes. The Normal School, the music department, and the commercial department still regularly accepted students without high school training.

Secondly, in the early years, the University enrolled students mostly from Albany County. The first entering class showed only six from elsewhere. In 1891-92, the entire collegiate student body listed Laramie as a home town. Throughout the 1890s, only one-fifth and usually fewer of the students were from other communities. The University could hardly claim statewide significance when its students were gleaned from only the southeast corner of the state.

CHAPTER THREE

The hard times of the 1890s did little to help the University's growth. "The want of funds to pay expenses has kept quite a number of worthy students from attending the University," wrote Stephen W. Downey, president of the board, in his 1893 report to the governor. Two years later when enrollment (according to the board's statistics) had dropped by more than ten percent, he again reported that "the hard times and depressed financial conditions of the country have somewhat affected the attendence of students."

In these bleak years, recruiting students became part of the president's functions. Beginning with Hoyt, presidents spoke at innumerable ceremonies throughout the state — particularly high school graduations — attended meetings and preached from pulpits. Adventurous men like Graves (1896) "canvassed" Wyoming seeking students to enroll at the University. Hebard's early files are filled with letters to prospective students, but by the turn of the century this onerous duty had been turned over to the president, and Tisdel's correspondence shows literally thousands of letters that he wrote to high school graduates and their parents all over the Rocky Mountain area.

By 1907, it was regular procedure for the president to touch base with all Wyoming county superintendents of schools, with the aim of determining which graduates might make the best prospects. It hardly mattered, for all high school graduates were solicited. Bulletins mounted special pleas to parents:

> . . . it is assumed that our people will manifest their appreciation of the bounty of the Federal and State governments by according to their new University a most liberal support. The institution asks of them individually almost none of their money; simply that their sons and daughters, sufficiently advanced to avail themselves of its advantages, be sent to it for instruction, rather than to institutions abroad no better furnished; thus helping to build up at our own educational center a University that shall complete the school system, promote the highest culture, and add new lustre to the commonwealth.

In 1898, Smiley reported to the superintendent of public instruction:

> The next thing we need is for the people to know more about us. Really it is not generally known to the fathers and mothers as it ought to be, what are the advantages either for a practical or a higher education offered by our University; . . . We only wish that the teachers over the public schools of Wyoming were better posted in regard to our advanced state school, as to Where we are, What we are, and What we do.

In this campaign for students, all administrators recognized the strong rival call of other colleges. Eastern schools were particular rivals because of their prestige.

> Very often you will hear parents in the West with a sigh expressing their regret because out here their children will be deprived of the opportunities which, if born back East, they would have been afforded in the way of education. And it is true that we have not as richly endowed institutions as New England. . . . With the people of Wyoming all loyal to our University there is no reason why we cannot have here in this state . . . an institution of learning that will take rank with the best of these state schools.

Universities in Colorado and Utah were attractive to many Wyoming students. In addition, officials were concerned about the several denominational schools and their appeal to students, particularly young ladies. In Laramie, female out-of-town students were faced with the problem of finding places to live that would provide the proper oversight and atmosphere for young ladies. From Tisdel's correspondence, it was plain that the president involved himself in locating appropriate housing for such students. In 1900, Smiley announced with pleasure that "young ladies of all denominations" would be permitted to board at St. Matthew's Hall, run by the Episcopal Church. The president thought the solution excellent. But it was not until the actual construction of supervised campus dormitories for women that strict parents could feel more or less at ease.

As a result of these persistent efforts, enrollment began to increase by 1897 — not just from Albany

33

but from other counties as well. By 1900, Smiley could refer to

the return of more prosperous times. . . . Parents are in better condition financially and are feeling more able to spare their sons and daughters from home, and can better afford to send them away to college. In consequence, our attendance the past year has been the largest in the history of the institution.

In his report on the University's fifteenth anniversary in 1902, the president stated that average attendance for the first five years was 85; for the second, 120; and for the previous five years, 172, which figures do not entirely accord with other listings. Nevertheless, by this year, the University could boast at least one student from every Wyoming county.

Efforts to increase Wyoming's student body were counterbalanced by continuing drives to upgrade academic standards to the traditional level of other four-year educational institutions. It is difficult to assess the University's entrance standards with any accuracy, since examinations could be substituted in all cases for an accredited high school diploma. Still, the College of Liberal Arts in 1897 required such subjects as Greek for admission, and thus any student from any Wyoming high school (in none of which classic languages were offered) had to make up the hiatus after arrival on campus. It is noteworthy, however, that as late as 1905 the schools of mechanical engineering, mining, irrigation engineering, and agriculture required only one year of high school training for admission; in this year, the requirement was raised to two years. By then, admission to the Normal School was "almost" at the same level as for the College of Liberal Arts. By the turn of the century, the schools of mining, agriculture, mechanical engineering, and the Normal School were offering curricula of varying lengths, but all were granting bachelor's degrees to students who completed a four-year program — whatever the student's age or background. Non-traditional students enrolled in "short" courses, extension classes, and correspondence courses, and (after 1905) summer school accounted for a major percentage of reported enrollment.

Faculty did not have an easy time. Maintaining all of the research, teaching (on and off-campus), public relations, administrative, and disciplinary functions imposed upon them from the start, they suffered from occasional economic privation, as did the entire University system. On several occasions, during bad times, salaries were simply lowered. F. W. Sawin, professor of mathematics, suffered a loss of $200 in salary in 1892, and upon his complaint to the board was simply not reappointed. In 1894, the president reported to the board that it seemed necessary to eliminate several positions; one faculty member nobly resigned (and was especially commended by the board as a Christian gentleman held in great esteem) and the other was simply not reappointed (but also thanked). "Only the financial necessities of the University" in "times of depression" led to these dismissals, the board resolved. In 1895, all nine faculty members signed a petition addressed to the president and the board objecting to the decrease of salaries for all of them.

Tenure in office was a problem, and throughout the University's first few decades faculty members, granted only one-year appointments, frequently petitioned for longer contracts. In 1894, the board received a petition signed by all faculty asking five-year appointments for full professors. In support, two professors appeared before the board asking that appointments be made for definite, longer periods, but the board refused, because of (it said) problems with the legislature over budgeting. It may be accidental that two years later, both of these professors were requested to resign, although in both instances they were given high recommendations and expressions of appreciation from the board. The year was 1896, and these requested resignations may have featured in President Johnson's own withdrawal out of disapproval of Hebard's management of faculty appointments. In 1897, when the economy improved, the faculty tried again; its request for three-year appointments, following an original one year of trial service, was tabled at the June 24 board meeting. One small gesture was agreed upon; in connection with the non-reappointment of a faculty member in 1893, the board agreed that when its faculty committee presented an adverse report, the concerned faculty member should be notified at least three months before the end of the year.

Other personnel problems, of course, arose. A director of the Preparatory School was dismissed when pupils were judged not to have been properly disciplined. In a crisis in 1901, a professor of commerce was asked to resign because of the "indiscreet" behavior of his wife, who had given rise to such scandal that his own "influence and usefulness" as a professor were greatly curtailed. Occasional requests for leaves of absence were approved, but some (especially those of long duration) were refused. The overwhelming influence of Hebard as secretary of the board created problems for faculty as well as president, as Smiley clearly noted in 1902. On one occasion in 1896, Hebard's anger about faculty incursions into some unnamed quarter caused the board (at her request) to censure the entire faculty and change all the door locks. The iron hand with which she ruled campus and her general involvement in many policy decisions told on vice presidents, who were as a rule appointed from within the faculty. John D. Conley made it through his term as vice president (1891-96) although he was asked to resign (perhaps by Hebard) in the latter year, but Justus Soule, who followed him in the office, was at constant odds with the board's secretary.

Although administration, curriculum, faculty, and students would be problems enough, money was always at the heart of the University's difficulties. For its first twenty years, and particularly during the difficult depression of the 1890s, the University engaged in a constant struggle for what the trustees considered adequate funding. The board had several different sources of income it might tap, from in and outside of the state. A review of finances is appropriate here.

Some — but little — income was generated on campus. Since it was obligated by the state constitution to keep education as close to costless as possible for Wyoming citizens, the University never in these early years charged what might be called tuition. However, it did collect small fees from students; it accumulated petty cash in such matters as library fines; it came to assess a minimum charge for services like assaying; and it occasionally gained pocket money from the sale of student annuals or journals. Such income represented only a drop in the bucket as far as overall expenses were concerned.

From the state, as authorized by various legislatures, the University received a portion of its operating expenses in the form of an annual tax levy.

But in 1891, the first state legislature, undoubtedly anticipating the receipt of considerable federal funding, lowered the mill rate to one-eighth, and there it remained for six critical years. Thus during the depression of the 1890s, the institution found itself in particularly difficult straits. It was lucky in having Johnson as its president, for more than any of the other early administrators, he had an acute knowledge of finance and an almost intuitive sense about solving money problems.

Johnson termed the situation a crisis. In his report to the board in June 1894, not only did he present a clear picture of the funds on hand and expenditures (including certain overdrafts for which no state appropriations were available), but he predicted dourly that if the University were retained for a year on its current basis "one year hence you must face bankruptcy as far as the State fund is concerned." The decline in assessed valuation had caused income from the one-eighth mill levy to fall to only $3,000 per year. Proposing drastic measures (including the lowering of all faculty salaries to $1,600 per annum), Johnson correctly estimated that "we cannot expect one dollar from the next State Legislature" in terms of increased operating budget. The following March, he reported to the board that:

> During the recent session of our legislature, the University was subjected to considerable adverse criticism, much of which was unjust, and grew out of ignorance of the facts. . . . One of the objections urged was that the administration was and had been extravagant; that the Faculty was too large for the number of students, and that as the work of higher education was necessarily limited, because of our small population, the expenditures of the university should be considerably reduced.

That year several measures designed to take financing out of the board's control by fixing salaries and regulating expenditures failed to pass in the legislature or died in committee. Johnson reported that he had

> assured the Governor and other public men of the State that by the selection of an able and excellent board of trustees, economic management of all the departments of the institution could be secured, and that as far as my recommendations would go in the matter, I should surely plan and recommend the most economical management possible. . . .

The president kept his word; among other economy measures, he persuaded the board to disconnect all campus telephones as of August 8, 1895.

It was not until 1897, after repeated pleas from the board of trustees and when the economy seemed to be turning upward, that the legislature raised the tax levy for operating expenses to one-fourth mill. In 1905, the tax was further increased to three-eighths mill. In 1908-09, this fund netted the University more than $25,000, which total increased to nearly $34,000 the following year. But only in the prosperous days before World War I did this fund rise to substantial amounts.

Special appropriations from the state's general fund were made available for operating expenses only on a few occasions (in 1889, $9,000; in 1890, $1,200). In 1897, when the trustees expended certain federal funds in error and were refused further payments until restitution was made, the legislature came up with the requisite $3,800. After the turn of the century, occasional appropriations were allocated to special farmers' institutes. On the whole, however, the state's contribution to operating expenses came primarily from the standard mill levy.

Buildings, on the other hand, were financed in many ways. After 1899, once the depression had faded, special tax levies were occasionally instituted for construction purposes. That year the legislature authorized the construction of a hall of science and museum (the present geology building) to be funded by a special levy of three-sixteenths mill for a period of four years — an amount that had to be increased to five-sixteenths mill for the second two years, because of costs being higher than estimated. In 1903, in response to trustees' request, an armory and gymnasium was funded to the extent of $15,000, which trustees borrowed from a federally-financed fund and repaid through another special one-eighth mill tax. On occasion, the University was able to finance buildings out of other funds: The mechanical building, completed in

1893, was the result of a "windfall," when the federal government "repaid" the University $30,000 for previously completed work in agricultural experiments, and a wing for the same building resulted from an overdue rental payment from federally-granted University lands. Sometimes the legislature financed miscellaneous capital projects from the state's general funds: In 1901 it agreed to purchase another city block of land for the amount of $3,000, and two years later, when desperation had driven trustees to construct a more efficient heating plant without legal authorization, the legislature bailed them out to the tune of $16,000. Thus the sale of bonds (as for the original Old Main), special taxes, and appropriations all were used to finance campus construction.

In the first twenty-year period, by far the greatest portion of the University's income was received from the federal government. Some income derived from land grants. By the Morrill Act of 1862, the University received 90,000 acres of public land. The legislature, however, opted to accumulate rentals from this land in an agricultural land fund, and the University did not directly receive such rental income until legislative act of 1905. Receipts then amounted to an annual $3,800; as late as 1907, none of this land had been sold. The University Act of 1881 deeded to Wyoming 72 sections of land (more than 46,000 acres) for University purposes. By 1899, F. W. Sawin, as authorized by the secretary of the interior, had with difficulty chosen the requisite lands from throughout the state, more than 18,000 acres being located in Albany County; 11,000 in Carbon; 8,000 in Laramie; and the rest in other areas.

Once permission was received to lease these lands, the process began, but rentals were few and far between; for a five-year period, 1891-96, only a quarter of the lands were rented and a little more than $1,000 was realized. This amount was not actually turned over to the University until 1897, and thereafter rentals were duly paid each biennium. The amount so received in 1905 was nearly $3,000 and continued thereafter to rise. As late as 1910, fewer than 500 acres of University land had been sold. The capital received from sales served as an endowment, for it was placed in a special state fund and only its income was paid to the University for annual operating expenses. Thus the act of 1881, in spite of the hopes of the territorial legislators, did not provide a major source of income until the oil rush of the twentieth century.

Other federal acts were more generous in that they proffered cash. The Hatch Act of 1887 provided a straight $15,000 per year for support of agricultural experiment stations; in 1906 and thereafter, the Adams Act supplemented this fund with increasing amounts, beginning with $7,000 annually. The second Morrill Act of 1890 provided at first $15,000 per year for the support of a college of agricultural and mechanical arts, an amount increased at the rate of $1,000 every year until it reached $25,000 per annum.

These outright cash grants from the federal government antedated the establishment of the University, so it was up to University officials — with the aid of state governors and senators — to apply for them for the Laramie institution. After Wyoming became eligible through statehood, then-Governor Warren (at Hoyt's request) wrote the secretary of the interior (November 1, 1890) requesting $15,000 in Morrill Act funds. In this quest, the governor was successful. At the time, however, the board was not even aware of the possibilities of Hatch Act funding for agricultural experimentation. Only late in 1890, just when he was being dismissed, did Hoyt begin to consider applying for Hatch Act money. By January 1891, the former board picked up the ball. Acting President J. D. Conley was dispatched to Fort Collins to check out the agricultural experiment facilities there, and when he reported back and brought the board an actual copy of the Hatch Act, trustees at once wrote and telegraphed to the Wyoming delegations in Washington to ask assistance in applying for these funds. So deeply were they involved in negotiations that former board President Downey asked the new board to postpone meeting and organizing because the

old board is engaged in the important work of securing the appropriations from the government for the College of Agriculture of the University, and perhaps should be allowed to finish this work which they can perform with greater facility than their successors, as they are well-informed in this particular.

Inauguration dinner, Clyde A. Duniway, ninth president, January 24, 1913

The new board, however, opted to take over negotiations. On February 26, 1891, Johnson as president of the board again telegraphed Senator Joseph M. Carey for his support. In March, the board met with Warren (now U.S. senator). With his encouragement, it officially moved to establish a college of agriculture and mechanic arts, a course in military science and tactics, and professorships of agriculture in addition to botany and horticulture. Having done so, trustees promptly decreed an Agricultural Experiment Station, with an executive committee from the board of trustees, a director, and other research positions. A month later, they officially determined to set up experiment substations throughout Wyoming and began a search for donors of appropriate lands. Later that year, a council was established for the station, with Dice McLaren, director and agriculturalist, as its chairman; Buffum, Conley, and Nelson as members; and Hebard as secretary. Having established the administrative apparatus and leaning on Warren's aid, trustees had no difficulty in persuading federal officials to forward funds through Otto Gramm, then Wyoming state treasurer.

The board then pulled another major coup. Since the Hatch Act had actually been adopted in 1887 and since the agricultural school had officially been announced that year, it was able to argue that agricultural research had been in progress

37

from the start, as directed by Nelson, Conley, and others. In this regard, Warren's assistance was indispensable. He pushed through Congress a special act making back payments (covering 1887-89) available upon proof that the University had maintained the Agricultural Experimental Station during that period of time. In the matter of so proving, "Please exercise your ingenuity," Warren wrote to Downey in April 1891, and added (June 26, 1891) that it was his opinion that "it would take but a very little proof . . . to bring about what we desire." The senator even had some suggestions:

> I thought perhaps water had been used about the University grounds, that grass had been sown and raised, that trees had been put out in experimenting as to the growth of forest and shade trees, that some flowers or vegetables or other seeds had been put in to see what could be grown, on either the University grounds or some of the lands that it owned.

Proof of such efforts was indeed not difficult to find, and on August 18, 1891, Johnson was notified by Warren that $30,000 in back funding was available. With great delight, trustees moved to construct a second campus building, to be used for instruction in mechanic arts or engineering.

Thus from 1891 on, the University regularly received annual funding from the federal government that for many years eclipsed its small revenue from the state. In 1894-95, for example, the board reported that $18,492 for salaries had been paid from federal funds compared to $4,875 from state. In 1896, the figures were $15,065 compared to $3,559, and a year later, $17,326 compared to $2,925. In 1902, four professors were fully supported by the state, while twelve were funded by federal moneys. In 1904, the president reported that of total University income, the U.S. government provided four times that received from the state. Later in 1910, when a few unusually prosperous years had tipped the scales somewhat, President Charles O. Merica reported to trustees that since 1886, the state of Wyoming had contributed for all purposes (including construction, for which federal moneys were never available) an average of $24,000 per year, drawn from taxation, bond sales, and special appropriations. During the same period, federal allocations ranged between $50,000 and $75,000 annually. The strange situation caused President Johnson in June 1894 (a bad

year) to suggest perhaps ironically that the University abolish liberal arts, languages, literary and classical courses, and become an agricultural college altogether, until such time as the state might deem it appropriate to come properly to its aid.

Under the circumstances, one can understand the board's desire — if not absolute need — to use federal funds in every possible manner. Yet for many items these funds were not legally available. They could not be utilized for the purchase of land, the construction of major buildings, furniture, or maintenance. They could not be applied to the salaries of professors teaching philosophy, ethics, history, government, education, humanities, or ancient and modern languages, with the exception of English. Nor could general administrative salaries and expenses, except insofar as they pertained to the agricultural college or experiment station, be charged to their expense.

These restrictions and federal interpretations of the law caused frequent difficulties. In 1895, for example, Lorick Pierce, commissioner of education, refused payment for such items as wood, coal, light, postage, keys, and dues to the Association of American Agricultural Colleges under the Morrill Act, and since these funds had already been expended, they had to be replaced from the small state tax levy. In 1896, the federal government refused to pay for agricultural substations, and Johnson was informed that "The [main experiment] stations should at once abandon the policy of maintaining permanent substations unless the State will provide for their maintenance." Accordingly, over the next few years, the board divested the University of all recently-established agricultural substations, with the exception of that in Lander, which it leased out. For the year 1895-96, the commissioner of education refused payment of the salary of J. F. Soule (who taught Latin and Greek, but had also been reported as assisting in the library and in English); and, in part, wages of Irene Morse (German, French, and history); and Johnson himself, who was now listed as director of the experiment station and president of the agricultural and mechanical college. The amount of this deficiency totalled $3,825. The crisis was such that Johnson traveled to Washington in the spring of 1896, but in the long run, the state legislature had to be asked for an additional appropriation or federal funding thereafter might well have ceased. Incoming President Graves noted that several professors still being paid from federal funds should probably be transferred to the state payroll.

38

After the turn of the century, the federal government became stricter, and supervision over Morrill and Hatch Act operations became more efficient. By circular distributed in 1900, the Bureau of Education laid down the law on the Morrill Act, citing not only the original provisions but also specific decisions of the attorney general since 1890. In 1905, the commissioner asked Hebard for more careful definition of her term "supplies." The following year, the University's expenditures for instruction in English and education were challenged and partially disallowed, since the annual financial report hardly coincided with the *Bulletin* in its statement on professorial assignments. In addition, items for freight and books were queried, and Hebard was again requested to provide more specifics in future years.

Meanwhile, the U.S. Department of Agriculture was also tightening its requirements. Regular annual inspections of the experiment station took place. In 1903, on the department's request, Smiley ceased to be director of the experiment station and turned the title over to B. C. Buffum. Even so, when A. C. True, who was federal director of experiment stations, personally inspected the Laramie station, he had many complaints about its administration. The director, he insisted, should be "given general charge of the business and the funds of the station," and "control the planning and execution of all work." The secretary (Hebard) should not be the "final authority for the assignment of funds." True especially criticized financial procedures, and in view of the "indefinite" plans for certain projects in the coming year, he requested that the annual statements give more details on the work actually performed.

A year later in a special letter to Otto Gramm, True found so many items mischarged to Hatch Act funds that he found a need to threaten the status of the agricultural station.

We have repeatedly called attention to the irregularity of such items and have protested against the use of the Hatch fund except for purposes legitimately connected with the experiments and investigations of the station and the publishing of the results. . . . I am impelled to state that if clearly objectionable items, such as those indicated . . . , are found upon the station accounts

hereafter, I shall feel under the necessity of disallowing them rather than submitting to a transfer of them to another account after the year has been closed.

The threat hardly helped, for in November 1904, True again protested to Hebard about her charging the Hatch Act for expenses at meetings, the salary of the president's stenographer, laying a new floor in the physics department, advertising in a Cheyenne paper, all the equipment for the herbarium, and postage representing 10,000 stamps. Only later, when income from state sources substantially increased, did the constant pressure on federal agricultural funds relax accordingly.

It is in this context that the University's desperate efforts to retain federal funding and its campaign to keep the agricultural college as part of its own operations must be understood. Without such funding, the entire institution could have foundered. The political manipulating regarding the University's location, the bleakness and altitude of the Laramie plains for agricultural experimentation, and the richness of federal agricultural funding led to a constant series of challenges for relocation of the college and the experiment station in other areas of the state. Almost as soon as the nature of federal aid was revealed, neglected northern counties began their campaigns. For its first twenty years, the University was in constant jeopardy of dismemberment.

As early as 1890, shortly after the passage of the second Morrill Act, rumors circulated that Warren had promised the agricultural college, with its generous federal money, to a northern community in exchange for support of his senatorial candidacy. University officials were dismayed. But before the legislature met, the then-governor had nominated the University for Morrill Act funds. In his statement to the legislature that was about to elect him to the senatorial post, Warren called attention to the Morrill law

with the expectation that you will make such disposition in this matter as your judgment dictates. It may be advisable not to create a new institution which will draw appropriations direct from the State treasury for erection, establishment or maintenance until we shall have recovered from the extraordinary expenses made necessary at this time by causes mentioned elsewhere in this message.

In spite of Warren's support, however, the actions of the first state legislature were hardly favorable to the University. In December 1890, a bill was introduced into the house providing for the establishment of a Wyoming agricultural college, the question of the location of which should be placed before the voters of the state.

In vain University supporters sought to insert a clause into Hoyt's bill on University governance that would permanently entrust to the University at Laramie any federal grants for agricultural and mechanical purposes. Equally in vain, proponents of a separate agricultural college sought to cancel all such funding until a site for the new institution might be selected and appropriations for construction obtained. While northern legislators argued for lower altitudes with more typical climate and soil, the Laramie *Boomerang* continued to hint at Warren's "political connivance" and insisted that Laramie had the only operative institution available for federal support.

The idea now is to obtain a large tract of land from the land company on the west side of the [Laramie] river. The land at that point would be under water and a great agricultural experiment station will be established in Wyoming. This means a great deal, not only for Laramie but for the entire State. It will demonstrate the possibilities of the Laramie Plains and would be the means of clustering about this city a large number of ranchmen.

Cooks and mess wagons, Fossil Fields expedition, summer 1899

The eventual result was a compromise embodied in two pieces of legislation. The first was a law "providing for the establishment of 'The Wyoming Agricultural College,' " which act included intricate details for that college's purposes, activities, and governance, and designated November 1892 as the time for a public election to select its site. To the dismay of University administrators, the law limited such a site to a town containing at least 100 inhabitants and located at an elevation of no more than 5,500 feet — a provision which eliminated Laramie from consideration. The second "act as to government and maintenance of the university" provided little compensation, in that it gave the University permission to receive federal grants for agricultural and mechanic arts only until such time as a separate agricultural college might be established in the state.

Small wonder that the new board of 1891 went immediately to work, not only to acquire federal funds but so to arrange their management and status as to make it increasingly difficult and expensive for the college to be moved elsewhere. In 1891, the College of Agriculture, which listed Johnson as president, was "increased and strengthened" by the employment of Dice McLaren (agriculture), B. C. Buffum (botany), Edwin E. Slosson (chemistry), and F. J. Niswander (zoology), all promptly salaried out of federal money. A complete curriculum was set forth, laboratory equipment was purchased, and general facilities were improved.

The Morrill Act was followed to the letter. Rules for the offering of military tactics and science were established, although a military professor (supported by government funds) did not actually arrive on the scene until 1892. Foundations were laid for instruction in "mechanic" arts with the employment of L. C. Colburn, an engineer, and the board in its first annual report to the governor (1891-92) anticipated a full-fledged school of engineering. The construction of a new engineering building was gratifying since to reproduce such a structure elsewhere in Wyoming would have cost the state money.

In 1891, Dice McLaren was appointed director of the new Agricultural Experiment Station, and, with aid from local land donations, the short-lived substations previously noted were established at Lander, Saratoga, Sheridan, Sundance, and Wheatland. Faculty at the Agricultural Experiment Station immediately went to work publishing pamphlets of practical advice for Wyomingites.

Meanwhile, University bulletins regularly reprinted the texts of the Morrill and Hatch Acts, as if to lay exclusive claim to their benefits. Presidents and trustees in speeches, letters, and reports repeatedly pointed to the economies that resulted from the University's sharing of faculty funded by the U.S. government. If the agriculture college was actually operating with only a handful of students (its first graduate came in 1899; its second not until 1902), campus administrators looked the other way and emphasized the positive instead.

By November 1892, when the electorate went to the polls to choose an agricultural college location, the Laramie experiment station had published six brochures, the substations were operating, the mechanical arts building was under construction, the federally-authorized faculty members were in place and teaching, and the College of Agriculture was organized (at least on paper). Nevertheless, the voters of the state opted for regrouping and chose to locate the so-called Wyoming agricultural college, established by the first state legislature, at the town of Lander, Wyoming. All the board's aggressive efforts seemed in vain.

Salvation came from an unexpected source — namely, the general economic doldrums into which sank state and country in the early 1890s. The depression of these years lowered the state's income and decreased the legislature's willingness to appropriate funds for any new — and often for old — projects. Faced with the necessity of establishing a new campus at Lander — purchasing land, constructing buildings, providing for major furniture and equipment — the 1893 legislature demurred and passed no enabling financial legislation.

In 1895, the question arose again, but by now the depression was if anything worse. Legislators from Fremont County introduced bills to fund the Lander Agricultural College out of state tax funds and to cause it to be the future recipient of federal fundings; all these measures were either postponed or died in committee. In accordance with the law of 1891, the governor had appointed a Lander Agricultural College board of trustees, which lobbied vigorously and enthusiastically. Nevertheless, the University was again specifically awarded the Hatch Act funds, provided the board make an annual accounting of all of its expenses to the governor. The Laramie *Sentinel* rejoiced.

> *The great strain is removed. . . . The fact is that during the first half of the week a condition of uneasiness closely bordering upon a panic has prevailed among the faculty and students at the University, as well as among our citizens generally. It was freely asserted and generally believed that the proposed action of the legislature would cause the closing of the institution, even before the end of the present year. . . . A majority of one in the Senate saved the best thing in the State from annihilation.*

Jubilation was premature. In 1897, a bill was again introduced by Fremont County representatives to levy a tax for the purpose of building and equipping the Lander Agricultural College. Although this was a particularly difficult year for the University trustees — their keeping of the books and their financial policies in general were investigated by legislative committee following an episode of mis-accounting — the Lander college failed of support by one vote in the house. Two years later a similar measure was "indefinitely postponed" in the senate after having passed the house by a substantial margin (20-9). In 1901, the delegates from Fremont County pursued another tack, in that they proposed for Lander an "agricultural high school," with experiment stations potentially eligible for federal funds, but after considerable amendment and debate, this senate measure was defeated.

The situation of the non-existent Lander Agricultural College and with it the University's status became complicated in 1903, when a Lander resident died and bequeathed certain properties to the proposed college through its board of trustees. Phillip Wisser of Lander died in June 1903, and the final distribution of his estate was recorded in December 1904, at which time the appointed trustees of the Lander Agricultural College received better than $17,000 and a considerable grant of land. The trustees immediately purchased property on which the college might be located; devised a curriculum providing for instruction in history, civics, mathematics, agriculture, horticulture, and irrigation; and supposedly appointed a faculty, a president, and a staff for an agricultural experiment station in connection with the new college.

Faced with the actual establishment of a college, the authorization of which dated from a statute passed fourteen years before, the legislature of 1905 simply balked. After all, the University of Wyoming had had better than a decade to solidify its programs, both teaching and research, and to establish itself as the state's most viable institution of higher education. Both facilities and faculty had enlarged and improved (often at state as well as federal expense) in the years since the first state legislature's action. Accordingly, in 1905, legislators quickly repealed the 1891 act that set up a separate Wyoming agricultural college. When the Lander trustees appealed to the state treasurer for payment of Morrill and Hatch Act moneys into what they insisted were legitimate coffers, the treasurer simply refused.

In July 1908, the trustees of the Wyoming agricultural college at Lander filed a writ of mandamus, requesting the Wyoming Supreme Court to order the state treasurer to make payment to them of all federal agricultural funds under the state's jurisdiction; that included particularly the interest from the agricultural land fund, derived from the sale of Morrill Act lands, and rentals from such lands as were then leased.

In the legal actions that followed, the University was lucky to have the services of Timothy F. Burke, partner in the Cheyenne law firm of Burke and Clark, U.S. Attorney for the Wyoming district, and member of the University's board of trustees. The correspondence of Hebard, of Otto Gramm (then president of the board), and of University President F. M. Tisdel indicates that Burke was untiring in his efforts on the institution's behalf. It was he who suggested appropriate counsel (Nellis Corthell of Laramie, Judge John W. Lacey, and Charles W. Burdick of Cheyenne); he who contracted A. C. True of the Department of Agriculture, Office of Experiment Stations for advice; and he who shepherded University officials through briefs and arguments. Indeed, Burke knew as well as any of them the significance of federal funding. "It means life or death to the University," he wrote to Tisdel on August 19, 1905.

Before the Supreme Court of Wyoming in October 1905, the trustees of the Lander Agricultural College argued their case: that the establishment of the college and naming of its trustees constituted a contract binding upon the state; that the voters confirmed the location of the college at Lander by special election in 1892; that the University's primary thrust was not the teaching of agriculture and mechanic arts (as seemed provided under the Morrill and Hatch Acts); and that Lander, because of its central location, altitude, and climate, was a far more useful and reasonable site for the state's agricultural college. The University's attorneys, aided by the state attorney general, argued on the other hand that the legislature had every constitutional right to repeal the act creating the Lander college; that no contract existed to become impaired; and that the Lander trustees (having been deemed dismissed by the legislature) had no standing and no right under any circumstances to bring suit. On January 31, 1906, Justice Charles N. Potter found in favor of the University and refused to issue the requested writ. At once the Lander trustees filed an appeal with the U.S. Supreme Court. In this suit, the appropriate state and University officials were all named as defendants.

Virtually the same arguments were presented to the highest court in briefs filed in autumn 1906. In oral presentations before that body in April 1907, attorneys Corthell and Burke on behalf of defendants argued that the University was entitled by act of the Wyoming legislature to receive federal agricultural funding; that no act of the legislature granted such funding to any other agricultural college; that the allocation of funds by the legislature was completed legally and within the statutory requirements of United States law; and that the legislative repeal (1905) of the statute establishing a separate agricultural college was valid and did not involve the illegal breaking of any contractual relationship. In a decision written by Justice Moody, the Supreme Court sustained the Wyoming court, finding no error (as claimed by plaintiffs) in its decision.

The immediate crisis thus came to an end, but not without an aftermath of bitterness and anger. Few citizens of the mid and northern sections of the state took the view of A. C. True that a high-altitude, severe-climate experiment station must be considered for its unique contributions on a national basis; rather they sought an experiment station more attuned to the benefit of Wyoming agriculture and thus located in more typical terrain. In years to come, the irritation was somewhat mitigated as the state set up and the University eventually acquired direction of certain outlying

Aven Nelson and Edwin Slosson families picnic, Laramie Range, September 19, 1900

experimental farms and as further federal support set up a system of county agents throughout the state with the aim of addressing local problems. Even in recent times, voices have been raised in protest against the location of the University and particularly of the Agricultural Experiment Station at Laramie.

The University's first twenty years ended as they had begun — with a crisis centered around the receipt of federal agricultural funding. Throughout these years, the state had contributed comparatively little to its University's support — although that too would change. The role of the board and particularly its secretary in campus administration had caused three presidents to resign, and the problem of ultimate guidance and authority remained to be solved. Student population was sparse but was growing, particularly in respect to non-traditional enrollments. On hand, however, was a faculty to be admired, respected, and even celebrated as heroic; and a curriculum, first planned by Hoyt, that in spite of the few students in the classroom contained the germs of an institution determined to grow great.

WOMEN'S SPORTS

n recent decades federal legislation has mandated financial and administrative support for women's sports on campus, but feminine athletic prowess is nothing new to Wyoming. Lively young females of the turn of the century refused to be outdone by their male colleagues, and women's sports as curricular and extracurricular activities played a prominent role in the lives of early students.

Of course, physical education was required of women as well as of men. Before the appearance of the first woman teacher of physical education in 1915, faculty wives often directed and coached activities. Regular annual programs were presented by the women's gym class, included performances on dumbbells and waltz step exercises.

Women's gymnastics, April 14, 1909

The construction of the half-acre gym gave a great boost to women's athletics, as did the arrival in 1924 of Ruth Campbell, who was first hired to direct women's swimming.

Gertrude Gould Lindsay remembers Campbell's "Town and Gown Women's Polo Teams" which used horses donated by the U.S. Cavalry (Troop F of the 115th) and fought it out Friday afternoons. "My horse was named Jazz," writes Lindsay, "and he was trained in polo. He was a pro at following the ball. Jazz was responsible for any of my success." Lindsay, who taught health education in the women's physical education department, remembers, too, acting as ski coach during a variety of meets: One was held at Berthoud, to which the women traveled after dark since "there was less danger of avalanche on the road after sundown;" and another was held at the Libby Creek ski area above Centennial, at which everything that could go wrong did so, including the lift, which ran out of gas.

Professor Adolphe Dickman (French) offered an open fencing class, women invited. Early on, basketball ranked high in women's sports, and by the 1920s daring young ladies were even challenging men's predominance in the area of rifle shooting.

About all a male athlete could do without evoking female competition was to make for the football field.

Chapter Four

The Crisis of 1907

In 1907, the University celebrated its twentieth birthday with a zero hour that brought to countdown all those special problems that hung heaviest over the heads of its administrators since its founding day. All the pent-up angers seemed finally unleashed, as an original crisis that focused on the use and misuse of agricultural funds snowballed to involve the political commitments of the board; the relationship of board, president, and secretary; and even the role of the University as a "preparatory" school and the paucity of students in several academic departments. Before the crisis had subsided, it had attracted statewide attention and another president had lost his job. Still, in many ways the crisis cleared the fog. It hardly solved all problems, but it cured some, mitigated others, and opened the door to fresher air for the future. After 1908, the University came of age, and although many difficulties remained, the course of the future was on the whole steadier.

The crisis of 1907 began with the board of trustees, its practices, its principles, and its policies. The criticisms of petty graft that so easily arose resulted from the fact that board members represented but one of the two political parties and that, within the structure itself, authority continued to remain in a few powerful hands. In 1907, all nine members of the board — with the possible exception of one, whose affiliation seems not to have been clear — were Republicans. All had been named to their posts (and frequently reappointed) by a series of Republican governors and confirmed by a series of Republican state senates. All officers were from Laramie, and thus the executive committee was strictly a local body. Otto Gramm, member of the board since 1895 and president

since 1897, was a local Republican businessman of considerable wealth and great influence; his many interests included banking, a local coal company, ranching, and the drugstore business in which his career began. He had held a number of state offices (including treasurer), and in 1907 he was lessee and manager of the Wyoming State Penitentiary. He was thus a businessman of much prestige and a Republican of great influence.

Hebard remained the board's secretary. First appointed a trustee in 1891 by acting Governor Amos Barber, she had strong political connections in the Republican party through her father, a territorial legislator, and U.S. Senator C. D. Clark. Following the resignation of Smiley as president, Hebard was not reappointed to the board, but she remained its paid secretary. The change made little difference. She had served as campus librarian from the 1890s, and in 1906 the board found room for her on the faculty by naming her an associate professor of political economy. Unfortunately, the appointment only provoked more bitterness because an identical position had been granted to a man named Herbert W. Quaintance. Although Hebard was appointed "with the view of having her take the government classes of Professor Quaintance when he may be in the field on behalf of University interests," Quaintance's angry reaction was predictable, especially since (as board secretary, librarian, and professor) Hebard's salary stood at $1,800 compared to his own $1,600.

Of the other trustees, Arthur C. Jones of Laramie had been treasurer of the board since 1904; his name was never associated with any of the scandals that arose. The fourth Laramie member, Dr. Henry L. Stevens, had replaced political leader Stephen W. Downey in 1897 and was reappointed by Governor DeForest Richards in 1903.

Gramm, Hebard, and Stevens — in part, because of their location in Laramie — had come to assume special responsibilities for University operation. As Alfred J. Mokler — editor, writer, and board member from Casper — noted in the thick of the investigation, the great burden of work fell upon them. Mokler complained that annual meetings seldom attracted more than a bare quorum of board members, and that the state superintendent of public instruction, an ex-officio member, was almost never present. So much material was presented to the board by its executive committee about the year's operations that it was hardly possible to figure it all out, he said. Records were always made available, but time was too short. The result was an almost free hand for the Laramie board officers in the University's operation. The problem that Mokler isolated had, as has been noted, existed from the start.

Scientific party, Cycad Quarry, September 1899

The trustees who appointed F. M. Tisdel relinquished little power to the new president although for several years the new president — a Republican himself — enjoyed a honeymoon of cooperation. Tisdel worked hard. His correspondence shows hundreds of letters written to prospective students, numerous journeys and lectures around the state, and careful reports to the board on his problems and activities. He laid great stock on public relations and sent newsletters, the *Wyoming Student,* and the *Melange* (containing University publications) regularly to parents, students, and newspaper editors. He solicited money for scholarships from among well-to-do citizens of the state. He managed occasional disciplinary problems and located housing and jobs for incoming students. Considerable correspondence and much thought were devoted to the employment of new faculty members. Faced with declining enrollments in liberal arts and the Normal School, the president added (with the blessings of the state teachers association) a summer school in 1905 and encouraged Laramie residents to take campus classes, especially (when qualified) on a graduate level.

Unlike many presidents, he was greatly concerned with curricula. Tisdel was clearly a man of high standards. One student later called him "a Woodrow Wilson type." He had strong ideas of the University's mission. He found, he told the board, that the Normal School had been "a refuge for students who were unable to get on well in the harder courses;" he therefore raised its standards for admission and began the distinction between a "normal" course of two years for grammar school teachers and a four-year "school of education" for potential teachers at the high school level. Setting up grades one to three, he took the first steps towards establishing a full-fledged teachers' training school on campus. Likewise, he termed the commercial department "a refuge for students wishing a short and easy course." Although he did not abolish its high school level curriculum he added a standard four-year college course in business, on the grounds that classes in stenography and bookkeeping alone told adversely on the University's quality and purpose. Aware of the distinction between trade schools and professional colleges, he changed the curricula of the Schools of Agriculture and Engineering so as to include only two high school level years. In hopes of raising the usefulness of the School of Mines, he sent circular letters to mining firms throughout the state and received many — occasionally sharply phrased — suggestions about how the school's curriculum should develop — particularly through practical field experience for advanced students.

Tisdel's efforts to change curricula and improve standards undoubtedly made him some enemies, although it is impossible to isolate many of them. True, S. S. Stockwell, who had left his University position to become superintendent of schools in Laramie County, became irritated at the president's policies — or lack of them — in athletics; after a crisis over one football game, he wrote that it was doubtful that Cheyenne High School "will desire to renew athletic relations next year." Still, Superintendent of Public Instruction Thomas T. Tynan, an ex-officio board member, identified Tisdel with the positive when he wrote his formal report in 1906.

> . . . The growth, methods, power and number of [the institution's] faculty show an increase and material and substantial improvement. The University, through the efforts of its President and the faculty, has become closely allied to the graded and high schools of the State. . . .

As president, Tisdel could not control the rumors of graft and mismanagement that began to circulate, according to Mokler (Republican trustee and Casper editor), long before the scandal of 1907 came to light. Tynan did his share of complaining, for although he admired Tisdel, he found much to protest about in the rest of the University administration.

> Notwithstanding the increase of the number of graduates from our high schools, the student body of the University remains substantially the same, at least so far as the graduates of the high schools of the State at large are concerned. Why this seeming indifference to the chief institution of learning in this state? Is it due to the methods and personnel of the faculty of that institution, or to the administration?

In his biennial report, Tynan charged that the trustees were to blame, and he accused them in particular of trying to interfere with his own school policies.

> It is openly charged that politics is the chief concern of the majority of the present administration, and it is serving well the purpose of its head, the president of the board, in that particular, and a few of his immediate followers who are undoubtedly profiting at the expense of the institution. The endeavor to suppress the recent report of the State Examiner on two successive occasions and at meetings of the Board of Trustees is one incident toward which, if known publicly, sentiment would demand a change. Another feature which does not find favor with the people is the receipts and disbursements not passing through the usual channels, as those of other state institutions — through the State Auditor and Treasurer. For some time severe criticism has been rife as to the methods employed in its administration, and frequently over the State one will hear the charge that the institution, financially is not being conducted strictly in accordance with customs and policies usually governing state educational institutions.

In the quarrel between the superintendent of schools and the board of trustees, the president seems to have maintained his peace. But at the same time another issue arose in which Tisdel demonstrated considerably more interest on behalf of the University itself. This time state Republican officials came under the president's attack.

The question concerned the management of one-time federal lands set aside for University use. Although such public lands had been duly selected and confirmed, both under the Morrill Act (for an agricultural college) and the University Act (for a general university), the problems of their management had still not been solved. For one thing, the University had difficulty collecting the income from rental of these lands; it was the state's policy to manage rentals itself and to retain all income derived from rentals in a special fund. As early as 1891 the board of trustees set Hebard to check on rentals, but no change in policy occurred. Not until 1897 did state officials agree to turn over to the University such rents as were realized on University Act lands.

Annual board reports frequently complained that the University should have the use of agricultural land rental fees as well. Consulted by the board,

Faculty and staff, 1909-1910

the state attorney general informed Gramm that agricultural land (Morrill grant) rental funds could legally be used by the board only when the legislature authorized their disbursement from the state treasurer's office. Thus began a major campaign. One of Tisdel's first acts was to address a form letter to agricultural college presidents around the country regarding the use of rentals from Morrill Act lands. Although responses are not on file, they must have been helpful, for the legislature of 1903 finally agreed that rental fees from agricultural

lands should be made available to the board for immediate usage. Two years later, agricultural rents were finally being paid annually to the University — in 1905 in the amount of $4,400.

The sale of lands — both University and agricultural — was something of a different order. It seems clear that the state regarded the federal land grants as an endowment to be preserved forever and irrevocably. The legislature of 1899 awarded the University only the "profit and interest" that was paid on accumulated sales profits, as invested in federal, state, or municipal bonds. In 1902, the state attorney general upheld the decision, and informed Gramm that sales funds should be kept intact as a permanent endowment. Thus rentals and interest on sales profits were available for University use in terms of land granted both in 1862 and 1881, but in neither case could funds from the sale of lands be utilized for any immediate purpose.

The situation was complicated by a jurisdictional dispute regarding land management between the board of trustees and the State Board of Land Commissioners. Although all University property by constitutional definition was under the management of the board of trustees, the land board had been given broad authorization to handle all public lands granted to the state. Asked for his opinion, the attorney general informed Hebard in 1901 that rights of management seemed to belong to the trustees. Until after the turn of the century, however, the board seemed content to regard rentals and sales agreements as responsibilities of state officials.

The crisis of 1907 concerned both management and policy. In 1906 and 1907, the Wyoming congressional delegation at the apparent urging of state officials persuaded Congress to pass special acts (March 31, 1906 and March 1, 1907) granting the state the privilege of "relinquishing" certain lands (in Big Horn and Carbon counties) that had been selected for University use, thus returning them to the public domain. In their stead, the University would be granted an equal acreage of other government-owned lands. Much of the specifically designated relinquishable land was desired by an irrigation company that sought to build a canal from Shoshone River, near the site of a new federal reservoir then under construction. However, the company was unwilling or unable to purchase the lands directly from the University because of the $10 per acre that had been set as a minimum purchase price by Wyoming's Act of Admission. Such a dollar restriction would not pertain once the lands were returned to the public domain.

At first the trustees seemed unaware of any negotiations, but in his report to the board in June 1907, Tisdel brought the matter to their attention, basing his concern on a letter from R. P. Fuller, land commissioner, who was perhaps deliberately obscure. The president astutely put the problem in perspective.

Should plans like this for the development of Wyoming continue, the University would be put in an awkward position. Either the University must take the position of retarding the development of the state or it must submit to giving up its lands as soon as they become desirable for irrigation, taking other and probably less desirable lands which will not come into the market until later.

Even Tisdel's report came too late, for the state land board — "entirely on its own responsibility," as the trustees later wrote — had moved rapidly, and more than 5,000 acres of University agricultural college land in the Cody area had already been "relinquished." This raised, as Tisdel pointed out, the question of managerial authority.

If the custom goes on, who is to choose the new lands? And if the new lands are less valuable than the old, how are we to get a proper compensation for the transfer? The land may not be worth to an irrigation company $10 an acre, but if the University gives up its lands and takes others, the University ought in some way to get compensation for any loss in values resulting from the transfer.

On trustees' instructions, Hebard again wrote the state attorney general for an opinion regarding the functions of the State Board of Land Commissioners as versus the trustees; on June 15, the attorney general ruled that the lands "cannot be sold or relinquished without the consent and approval of the university, expressed through its corporate board of trustees." So notified, Fuller in turn cited legislation on the state land board and insisted that University trustees could not act without his permission. Carbon County land still remained to be "relinquished," and a challenge to the exchange of the Big Horn lands remained highly possible. Here the matter stood while another more acute crisis threatened.

THREE PIONEER PROFESSORS

 erhaps it was Wyoming's reputation as the "Equality State" that attracted three extraordinary women to the University before its twentieth birthday.

Of the early women professors, Grace Raymond Hebard stands out for the multiplicity of her interests and her accomplishments. Born in Iowa in 1861, Hebard defied custom by taking a degree in engineering. She moved to Cheyenne as a draftsperson in 1882. Her subsequent career as administrator, librarian, and professor has been described in these pages. Throughout her long lifetime — Hebard died at the age of 75 — she wrote many treatises on Wyoming, one of the most popular of which was a textbook on Wyoming government. Her work on Esther Morris and Sacajawea has been challenged as to accuracy; she was determined to advance the cause of women's equality. Indeed, Hebard had joined many early women's rights organizations, and it was she who brought about the award of Wyoming's first honorary degree to Carrie Chapman Catt in 1921. Among her many activities, Hebard was admitted to the Wyoming State Bar in 1898; she served as president of the State Board of Teachers' Examiners, working especially with education of aliens; she was also active in the Wyoming Historical Association. Hebard won state championships in both golf and tennis. To the time of her death, she was a dominant — and perhaps domineering — figure on campus.

Professor Grace Raymond Hebard, formal graduation portrait, c. 1880

Laramie born and product of a little-known Wyoming University, June Etta Downey was the greatest scholar of the lot. Daughter of an early Wyoming politician and member of the board of trustees, Downey was born in 1875, graduated with a B.A. at the age of twenty, a master's from the University of Chicago in 1898, and a Ph.D. from the same institution in 1907. She began her professional career as a UW instructor in English in 1898, by 1905 had become professor of English and philosophy, and after 1915 was a professor of philosophy and psychology and head of that department. Quiet and shy as a person, Downey's enthusiasm for psychology made her an exciting teacher. Her fertile mind led her first toward an interest in aesthetics and creative imagination that produced two books. Her Ph.D. dissertation and much subsequent research dealt with handwriting, including handedness and dextrality types. Her major and pioneering work lay in her studies of personality types and their testing. In the field of measuring personality, she attracted much attention among scholars and her contributions (although now superceded) may be regarded as opening new fields for scientific endeavor. During her lifetime, Downey published

Professor June Etta Downey, c. 1934

76 scientific works plus numerous other writings, including poetry, plays, short stories, and popular articles. She lived at home all her life, but died while attending a conference in New York in 1936.

Born in Oslo (then Kristiania) in 1857, Agnes Mathilda Wergeland was one of six children abandoned by their father and raised by a hard-working mother whose resources were modest at best. A lonely child, tall and sturdy, Wergeland was talented in music, art, and writing; Edvard Grieg accepted her as a piano student when she was nineteen. She was almost thirty when, with aid from friends, she went to study history in Munich. In 1890, she earned her Ph.D. at the University of Zurich — the first Norweigian woman to receive that degree. Always a feminist, Wergeland found no niche in her native land, a situation that caused her to speak out bitterly about Norway, which "had nothing to offer me but hunger and destitution." In 1890, she came to America, and following stints at Bryn Mawr, the University of Illinois, and the University of Chicago, she was appointed professor of history and French (later also Spanish) at Wyoming in 1902. Here she found friends, acceptance, respect, and happiness. Poet, musician, historian, Wergeland became an American citizen ("Norway has forgotten me," she wrote), but returned once to visit her native land. She died in Laramie in 1914.

Professor Agnes Mathilde Wergland, c. 1905

In the early days, women professors stuck together. For one thing, they were expected to abandon their careers should they ever decide to marry, and the necessity of such a sacrifice caused them to seek each others' society more eagerly than that of male companions. Wergeland and Hebard built the "Doctors' Inn" together, and each lived there until her death. More often than not, other women, too, shared homes. Moreover, they developed a closeness to each other that verged on exclusiveness. When they once founded a club, it delighted them to realize that any similar organization started by their male colleagues would have to be named the "Men Professors' Club." Although they never overwhelmed their male colleagues in numbers, Hebard, Wergeland, and Downey pioneered the way to a series of extraordinary women at Wyoming, all of whom achieved distinction in their own fields — such as Professors Laura A. White, history; Clara F. McIntyre, English; Lillian Portenier, psychology; Ruth Hudson, English; and Sara Jane Rhoads, chemistry.

The immediate eye around which the storm centered was the Agricultural Experiment Station, located in West Laramie and administered by the University under its considerable federal funding. Yet nothing might have come to a head were it not for a local school board election in May 1907. Otto Gramm and W. H. Holliday were both candidates for the board, and when returns were totalled and decisions announced, Gramm was said to have won a three-year and Holliday only a two-year term of office. The basis for the decision was obscure, and in a long blistering letter to the local Democratic paper, Holliday declined the position and called for the establishment of non-partisanship as a principle for school board service. His letter evoked a response from a young agronomist, recently resigned from the Agricultural Experiment Station, whose theme was that in the cause of administrative honesty the board of trustees should be non-partisan as well.

George E. Morton had come to Laramie in 1904 and had shortly been promoted to associate professor of animal husbandry. His public letter was actually a model of calm and gentility. Morton criticized the domination of the Republican board over the campus and contended that most faculty members were afraid to express "opinions at variance with the policy of the president or the secretary of the board of trustees." He himself was warned, he reported, that "criticisms of the policies of the president or secretary of the board would not be tolerated, even when made to a superior concerning matters directly affecting my own department." Faculty members, he reported,

do not even have full confidence in each other, and a certain uneasy, evasive attitude where dangerous topics are broached is frequently met with.

In particular, Morton decried the power of Hebard, who was still secretary to the board, secretary to the Agricultural Experiment Station, and University librarian in spite of her recent appointment (1906) as associate professor of political economy.

Last year at a station council meeting, Dr. Hebard, secretary of the board and of the council but not properly concerned in the investigatory or teaching work of any department save her own, very sharply advised us that if the law will not allow us to keep cattle for demonstration and teaching purposes by expenditure of the experimental funds, that we dispense with cattle

work entirely rather than demand state funds. . . . The discussion between Dr. Hebard and myself grew very warm. This indicates the influence that Dr. Hebard exerts. Her power is recognized by not only University people but by many townspeople, yet her clerical position enables her to throw the responsibility for any policy upon the executives.

Morton thereafter listed favors done for Otto Gramm and Trustee Stevens without charge at the stock farms; the fact that all University printing was done by the Republican newspaper; and that firms in which Gramm had an interest profited from the University's business. Gramm was unperturbed. "I see by the *Boomerang*," he wrote Tisdel laconically on official Wyoming State Penitentiary stationery in mid-May 1907,

that Prof. Morton has at last gotten rid of the bite that has been in his stomach. I did not know that the President and Deity had in any way intimidated him. The Board will meet in June. He should prefer his charges, bring them before the Board.

Morton's letter roused Democratic furor at the Republican regime far beyond what the minor charges and quiet tone might have logically provoked. The University, roared the Cheyenne *Leader,* was a "hotbed of graft and political jobbery" run by "a gang of cheap political shysters . . . in the interests of the Union Pacific party machine." The board was regularly referred to in the Democratic *Boomerang* as a "gang of ringleaders." Spurred by the chance for a challenge of the Republican machine, Democratic newspapers all over the state jumped on the bandwagon.

Papers generally picked up on the petty graft of which Gramm and Stevens were accused. Hebard and Gramm were accused of domination "so absolute that the faculty from president to janitor must sneeze when either of these two take snuff," that "the faculty . . . are afraid to say their souls are their own."

That this rascally management of the institution has destroyed its educational standards and general morale is shown conclusively by the list of high class men who have had positions in teaching corps or as officials who have had to "walk the plank." It's a standing remark in Laramie that no professor or employee of the institution

Early library scene, Old Main, c. 1906

*can hold his job without being branded "O.K."
by Miss Secretary Hebard, and whenever she
decrees it the president's head will fall in the
basket. This tyrannical and obnoxious supervision of affairs by a subordinate clerk is internally and externally resented by every person
connected with the teaching force and management of the university. Otto Gramm is equally
absolute and imperious in his control of the
financial and political business of the institution.*

Gramm was regarded, reported the local Democratic paper, "as one of the narrowest and most
unscrupulous partisan manipulators that has ever
inflicted an educational administration."

Other charges rapidly arose. The *Boomerang*
contended that Hebard had not given the courtesy
of a reply to its letter inquiring about possible
printing contracts. In addition to his contract for
coal and the University use of his bank, Gramm

was said to have benefited in his prison broom factory from "a large steam boiler, bought with university funds." Morton's brother-in-law, R. E.
Hyslop, who had also been employed at the experiment station, attempted to resign and was at first
persuaded not to, but in the midst of the barrage
was told by B. C. Buffum, head of the station,
that Gramm and Stevens (without, apparently,
consulting Tisdel, who was president) had decided
that he should go and were prepared to dismiss
him. Hyslop later contended that he was told that
Hebard was behind his dismissal. "In my opinion," he wrote in an open letter,

*the dominance of Miss Hebard is one of the
greatest drawbacks with which the university has
to contend. Her work is done in an underhanded
manner. . . . Shortly after I began my work
here, I was told by a superior officer that Miss*

Hebard had been criticizing me and that I could not stay here if I antagonized her. Under such conditions there are but two courses that a man can pursue. The one leads to a smooth, uninterrupted life and long position. The other leads to the outside, as Miss Hebard's power with the board is considered supreme. . . . Will the university with such a curse as this resting upon it ever be able to fully accomplish the higher, nobler, and purer purposes for which such an institution exists?

Quietly and with no publicity, Buffum resigned. Later Henry Knight, his co-worker, reported that he had run into some "social difficulties" and that his reputation on campus had caused considerable talk. Although his resignation may have been occasioned by personal considerations, it nevertheless added fuel to the fire.

Under such circumstances, the governor could hardly avoid intervention, especially since the demands from Democratic papers called for a new, non-partisan board to be appointed by himself. In early May, Governor B. B. Brooks called Morton to Cheyenne and conferred with him for several hours. Although Morton agreed to testify publicly to the points his letter had set forth, he refused to appear before a closed hearing of the board of trustees. On the first of June he left for his new job in Fort Collins, but as he travelled through Cheyenne he was subpoenaed to appear at a hearing before the state examiner.

This event took place on the University campus on June 4. During the questioning, it became clear that Morton had accurately portrayed the minor favors offered to board members at the experiment station and the travel of Otto Gramm to certain agricultural expositions. What also emerged was that Morton had resigned in some anger, which may have centered around his brother-in-law's situation. He and Buffum, at first good friends, had become estranged, and when Morton left the experiment station staff, he had told Buffum "what he thought of him" and his policies. Nevertheless, what the Cheyenne *Leader* called a "fearful indictment of the university management" actually boiled down to a few petty abuses of influence by the board of trustees. So far as can be judged by local papers, Hebard's position did not here enter into consideration. Minutes of the board of trustees indicated that she attempted to resign but that the board refused.

The situation was hardly enhanced by Class Night performance during commencement week of

1907. Traditionally, the skits composed by students for this occasion were carefully checked by faculty; this year, nobody remembered. A group of particularly lively students — knowing, as one of them said afterwards, about the "growing unrest among the faculty over the control of the President, faculty, and general University policy by the Secretary of the Board, who managed discreetly the President of the Board (a politician of politicians)" — decided to make their subject a Mother Goose play, in which Hebard became Old Mother Hubbard; Gramm, Prince Otto; and Tisdel ("who was in line for decapitation for alleged insubordination"), Little Dog Tray. The performance was apparently a roaring success. The faculty disciplinary committee, pressured by a horrified board, required that all participants personally apologize to Hebard before diplomas would be issued. The affair received considerable publicity. "We considered," wrote a ringleader,

that we brought about a change in administrative policy, from the complete control by the politically-appointed Board of Trustees to the President of the University as the responsible governing authority. Presidents since then have lasted longer.

Student pranks were exacerbated on June 7 when the *Boomerang* printed a letter from "a taxpayer" who brought up the land problem again, accusing the land commissioners, headed by the governor, of giving up lands in Carbon and Big Horn counties and substituting second rate selections elsewhere — not for money, but for "power." It was hardly fair, wrote the erudite taxpayer, to single out Gramm and Hebard when the state land commissioners were perpetrating such a scam.

Under the circumstances the board was compelled to act. It is impossible to know what negotiations took place between Gramm and Governor Brooks, but on July 4 (a month after the original hearing), the board formally and unanimously passed a resolution requesting the governor to

appoint such a commission as shall seem to him suitable, not only to investigate the truth of the charges preferred by Mr. Morton, but to hear any other complaints that may be made against the management of said institution, and likewise to hear any suggestions that may be offered or

*make any that may seem best to this commission
for the better operation of such institution to the
end that not only justice may be done in the
matter but that the largest possible good may be
secured to the people of the state through the
instrumentality of said institution.*

At the same time, the board made its own position
about Morton's charges eminently clear, by stating
that it

*deplores the attempt that is being made on the
part of some to drag this institution, which
sorely needs the support of all for its upbuilding,
into state politics and especially into the local
politics of the city of Laramie . . . that we
deplore and condemn the conduct of G. E. Morton in making his complaint preferred in his
charges through the press instead of to this
board while an employee thereof and a member
of the faculty of this institution, and we take
this occasion to denounce his conduct in so
doing as uncalled for, unprofessional, and dis-
honorable.*

Brooks did not hesitate to respond. Although he
had some difficulty finding commissioners that
would serve on such short notice, his appointees
soon included Martin R. Johnston, chairman,
Wheatland; Charles F. Maurer, Douglas; L. G.
Phelps, Meeteetse; L. C. Hills, Evanston; and
Charles A. Kutcher, Sheridan — legislators all.

In his letter of appointment, Brooks reported
that because of Wyoming's youth and limited population, the University's existence had been

*attended with manifold difficulties and
discouragements. A very substantial donation
comes from the general government annually
and with a reasonable tax levy, it is believed that
the school may be carried on and improved, but
in order to do this, the hearty cooperation of the
people of the state must be enlisted. I have concluded that a commission composed of responsible citizens of the state, to whom motives of
partisanship and sectional feeling could not be
attributed, and who, because of their undoubted
standing, judgment, business ability and patriotic
citizenship could make a thorough investigation
of the methods and management in each department of the University, followed by recommendations which could be carried out with mutual
benefit to the institution and our people*

should be appointed. In a further letter to one of
the appointees, Brooks asserted that he particularly

wished the commission to attempt a study "relative
to the wisdom of the use of certain funds for certain purposes." He appended a note on his disappointment at University enrollment, using as an
example his own daughter whose presence had
been much more seriously solicited by the University of Colorado.

The commission met in Laramie on July 17,
amid Democratic press accusations of "numerous
abuses of the privileges of offices of the trustees"
the "tyrannical rule of Miss Hebard," and the
"nefarious rule of grafters and boodlers." The
press sneered.

*The commission will go to Laramie, smoke a
few cigars with Editor Chaplin [The* Republican]
*and chew a few sticks of gum with Secretary
Grace Raymond Hebard and the exoneration is
complete. . . . Otto Gramm will continue to get
his and Grace will have her own sweet way
about it as she has in the past. . . .*

Arriving from Fort Collins to give testimony, Morton added fuel to the fire by reporting that Hebard
had repeatedly written the president of the Colorado agricultural college and sent "copies of resolutions which the board of trustees adopted
denouncing me for preferring charges of graft
against certain members of the board" in an effort
to threaten his position.

Tisdel himself was never accused of malfeasance.
His testimony before the commission refuted on
many scores the argument that politics played a
role in University policies on campus. He reported
that he had felt free to consult with the board,
that he "flattered himself" that Gramm had felt a
growing respect for his judgment, that faculty
appointments were generally in his hands, that he
had had a free hand in many items of University
management, and that political pressure upon him
and upon the faculty was generally nonexistent. In
all of his testimony (the only part of the record
now available), he remained strongly supportive of
the board of trustees, but he specifically included
Hebard's rival, Professor Quaintance, in his statement:

*Dr. Quaintance . . . came to me and said that
he had been approached by the Democrats of
Laramie to put his name on the Democratic
ticket for the Legislature, and asked me what I
thought of it. I told him — and the responsibility was entirely mine — I told him I felt any*

member of the faculty who went into a political campaign must be more or less active in the political campaign . . . that his attention would be taken from his University work during the campaign; that it would be necessary for him to be in Cheyenne six weeks of the winter term, and a substitute would have to be provided. . . . It seemed to me that the work of his department would seriously suffer, and I advised him not to be a candidate. He asked me if I felt that a member of the faculty in the Legislature could not be of great service to the University, and I told him I thought not. . . . I may have mentioned to Mr. Gramm what I was going to say to Dr. Quaintance, or what I had said, I am not sure but that I did. . . .

The investigating commission members took time to tour all campus facilities, most explicitly checking the agricultural experimental farms. They then sat for three days, encouraging the appearance of anyone who wished to testify. For Gramm and Stevens, instances of agricultural favors were quite specifically proven with impeccable documentation, in spite of Buffum's effort to defend the policies of the station. It became clear that not only were bids never let on University purchases, but Morton had been specifically told that no money was available even to advertise purchasing needs. At one point, a near fisticuffs occurred between Morton and a furious sheep rancher, whose prize-winning fleece had been only with difficulty identified at the station before it was sent to a fair.

For Hebard, the indictment was longer and more fundamental. For some time the hearing focused around her influence and activities, or according to the *Boomerang,* around

the real conditions under which the University is conducted. Is, or is not, President Tisdel president of the University, or does he allow himself to be governed in the management of the school by Miss Hebard's dictations?

In addition to Morton's testimony about the "petticoat tyranny," Justus Soule — one of the most respected campus professors — took the stand to describe his distaste for Hebard's "attempts to rule the faculty with an iron hand," attempts that he described as overbearing and galling to professors, including himself. In the face of these public accusations, Hebard in person made a strong and courageous impression. She had never, she testified, worked for anything but the best interests of

Faculty golf club, 1901

the institution, and if at times she had seemed overbearing, it was because of general professorial "laxity" about financial recordkeeping. "The board of trustees gave me a great deal of power," she admitted, "and I used it;" but not even the Democratic press challenged her affirmation of honesty and responsibility in keeping accounts and utilizing funds.

The commission proceeded directly from Laramie to Cheyenne to present its report to Governor Brooks. Although it refused to affirm accusations against any individuals — it found, for example, that the stock boarding and machinery rental by trustees had been properly paid for; that the prize wool belonged to its declared owner; and that although bids had not been let, prices paid had been reasonable — its recommendations in many ways were highly critical of the University, its policies, and its management. It found that the Agricultural Experiment Station — the original arena of Morton's complaint — was in deplorable condition — buildings in bad shape, weeds all over — and that "both farms are anything but a credit to the university." Services rendered should always be billed and paid for, whatever the previous policy. Worse yet, there was total misunderstanding as to the sense of the station's direction. Director, secretary (Hebard), president, and committee were confused. Buffum had regarded himself as master, but policies had been adopted without his concurrence. This lack of clear administrative function caused a "chaotic and distracted appearance." Although the commission found no undue political influence and no misappropriation of funds, it insisted that honesty was no excuse for mismanagement. It recommended that both station and University solicit competitive bids on all supplies more than $50 in value.

In terms of the University itself, the commission readily found "that there has been no interference by Miss Hebard." Nevertheless, here again administrative practice came in for shrewd criticism. The president, commissioners recommended, should be the administrative head of everything; he should be in command. His title should make him executive head of all departments and as such responsible to the board. As one of the commission members suggested to the *Boomerang,* the president should

be made the absolute power of the school and run it along his own lines. There have been too many bosses for the good of the institution.

From an administrative nonentity, he should grow into a chief.

In addition, in order that the University no longer compete for students with Laramie High School, the investigators insisted that the preparatory course be reduced to two years as soon as possible, strongly hinting that shortly the University should convert to a strictly college level institution. It suggested that professors should get out more, make more personal contacts throughout the state. It insisted — to the delight of the Democratic press — that the board should indeed be non-partisan, with only a bare majority from the dominant political party. And it ended with praise of faculty and institution and the recommendation that the state should love and support its university.

The board delighted in what it insisted on considering its total exoneration by the governor's commission. In the formal report to the governor for the fiscal year 1906-07, Gramm was able to write:

The facts in regard to the charges of graft at the University are, I believe, already in your possession in the report of the commission appointed by you to investigate the condition of affairs at the University. . . . It is gratifying to the authorities and to the friends of the institution that nothing in the administration of the institution could be found which could be called graft, that not a dollar of the University moneys had been misappropriated, and that the whole question

resolved itself into a mere difference of opinion as to the best method of administering the affairs of the University and in so conducting the Experiment Station that it might be of the highest possible use to the entire State of Wyoming.

He hoped, he concluded, that

the report of this commission will satisfy carping criticism, will clear up misunderstandings in regard to the University which have been widespread on account of the newspaper agitation of the subject, and that the University will henceforth receive a wider and more hearty support by the citizens of the State and grow more rapidly in numbers and influence.

The same euphoria apparently prevailed at the board meeting of August 30, 1907, called especially by the governor. Here Brooks discussed the committee report with the board, and all agreed on the value of certain of the commission's suggestions. There was, the governor pointed out, a "lack of harmony in the faculty," which he hoped the board would rectify. He thought perhaps the experiment station needed "overhauling." He would consider the recommendation that the board be made non-partisan; however, he insisted that no conclusions justified a request that the present board resign. He suggested that the University publicize itself more positively in order to gain confidence from citizens of the state. In particular, Brooks said he was glad that the charges against Hebard had not been confirmed and that she (secretary, and thus composer of these board minutes) emerged with flying colors and commendation for her devotion to the institution. Everyone may be said to have shaken hands all around.

It is not without significance that the governor brought land Commissioner Fuller with him to this meeting. A deal was about to be made. According to the board itself in a later publication, governor and commissioner explained the relinquishment of the Big Horn County agricultural lands

on the grounds that it would not only be the best thing for the University itself, by increasing its income but also a better thing for the State *of Wyoming. They set forth . . . that it was impossible for the promoters of the ditch to build the ditch and pay $10.00 per acre for the land, and that the building of the ditch would be a public benefit to the people of Cody and vicinity by placing arid lands under cultivation, and it appearing that other lands could be selected in place of the lands relinquished, the land board thought it would be best to order the exchange, as by the exchange the state would secure the construction of a fine canal which would bring fifty families to Wyoming and the University would secure lands for which $10.00 an acre would be paid in lieu of lands, part of which never could be sold at that price, and so they had ordered the exchange.*

When the *Boomerang* interviewed Brooks after the meeting, the governor only stated that he had made "some recommendations" in regard to the Carbon County lands still subject to relinquishment. Trustees did well by the governor's proposals. In what was obviously a fit of euphoric gratitude for the governor's support during and after the investigation, they resolved to turn all land management clearly and permanently over to the State Board of Land Commissioners. They asked only an annual report. Granting blanket approval in advance, trustees ruled that future land swaps would be out of their jurisdiction.

As to the University's operations on campus, the commission's recommendations brought about little immediate change. When Trustee W. G. Aber (Sheridan County), resigned in December, Brooks reported that he was seeking but having difficulty finding an appropriate Democratic replacement. Rumors of further resignations from the board proved inaccurate. Having been rebuffed in her effort to retire the previous spring, Hebard retained her position as secretary, her appointment as associate professor of political economy, and her functions as University librarian. Not until the board meeting in February 1908 was a committee set up to revise the bylaws and to work with the president in redefining his functions.

At the Agricultural Experiment Station, Buffum was replaced by J. D. Towar as director, and the two empty staff positions were shortly filled. "We believe," the board reported with some complacency,

that with the new staff the affairs of the Experiment Station will prosper and [it will] grow in

influence and helpfulness to the agricultural and stock raising interests of the state.

Repairs and clean-up were ordered, and Towar was soon able to display to visitors a construction site with sheds and barns being rapidly repaired and rebuilt. But basically so little seemed to have changed that the Democratic Cheyenne *Leader* cried whitewash again and portrayed a victorious board celebrating by deciding virtually to ignore the whole investigation. Wrote the *Leader:*

Resolving that Miss Hebard is an angel and Otto Gramm the highest Christian gentleman will not reform the university or satisfy anybody except the cheap G.O.P. politicians of the Albany County variety.

One individual seems not to have forgotten. Tisdel's testimony before the investigating commission had generally supported the board: He had spoken of considerate treatment; had insisted that politics did not enter into the administration of the University; and had claimed he had been unhampered in executive affairs. Nevertheless, he had spoken out against the land swap. By December, his attitude changed. Whether he suffered from the humiliation of being portrayed as a weakling or whether he regretted not having been firmer before the commission, Tisdel apparently became progressively unhappy with his situation. His irritation about the land exchange played a role. Later he said that he had hoped for changes that were not forthcoming.

It seemed at the time as if our problem might be solved by a gradual process. I knew the situation which had previously prevailed, but I fancied that I was to be an exception among our many presidents. The events of the last eight months have proved that this was a vain hope. Opposition was only being shifted from small to large things.

At the December board meeting, a number of Tisdel's requests were turned down and others were not considered. He was apparently told that the board felt that his administration had not been a success. According to one board member present, three trustees voted to dismiss him, three were "ready" to vote for him, and others declined an opinion. Rumors hit the local press that Tisdel had been asked to resign, and some speculated that he

58

had declined to support the exchange of University lands proposed by the governor on the grounds that those lands presently held were more valuable. The Democratic press proclaimed that the exchange was being arranged to the profit of the governor and Otto Gramm, Republicans both. Quietly, Tisdel began to solicit faculty support and circulated a petition endorsing his retention that a number of faculty members signed.

At a special meeting in February, the board considered a long letter from the president, who expressed his appreciation for not being fired and explained that his resignation could not improve the situation. His letter constituted an out-and-out attack on Otto Gramm.

> *No president of the University, in my judgment, could be thoroughly effective under our present methods of administration. One of the difficulties lies in the fact that it has not been made perfectly clear whether the President of the Board or the President of the University is the executive head of the institution. The respective duties of these two offices have not been clearly defined, and this has resulted in friction. No executive can succeed unless it is clear that he has the executive authority naturally belonging to his office.*

Tisdel insisted that he, and not Gramm, should be in control.

> *The president of our board is an active political leader and he has for many years been looked upon by the public as the executive head of the University. . . . [This] brings the University too close to politics in the public mind and makes it impossible to establish throughout the state a public confidence that the affairs of the University are administered independently of politics. . . . We are told [out in the state] that we cannot expect the hearty support of the state so long as the institution is run by a political boss.*

Like Johnson and Smiley before him, Tisdel deplored Hebard's assumption of special authority.

> *In an effective administration the President of the University must be closer to the Board than any other person in the organization. He should be their confidential adviser. During the present administration, and, so far as I can learn, during the three administrations preceding, there has been a prevalent belief that the confidential*

information concerning the University has gone to the president of the Board through the Secretary rather than through the President, and this has caused friction.

The board responded by reconsidering Tisdel's position; on this occasion, the vote was tied, 4-4.

Board minutes, of course, were not only kept confidential but were thoroughly laundered, so that only rumors could leak out. Tisdel himself chose to break silence — probably in anticipation of the board's next move — with a circular letter addressed to alumni and friends and dated March 21. The president's statement had been drafted by himself but (before circulation) read to an evening meeting of faculty and friends for their editing. They modified it before it was published. Henry Knight later reported that the meeting was supposed to be secret, but that the names of those present were slipped to Otto Gramm within 24 hours by an "informer." Thereafter, their own faculty positions were in jeopardy. Knight includes himself on the list of undesirables, but was certain he was saved by a local state senator and the intervention of several state officials.

In his public and well-circulated letter, Tisdel accused the board (and particularly Gramm and Hebard) of ignoring the commission's recommendations pertaining to his own role in University administration. It was well known, he wrote,

> *that President Smiley declared the University was injured by its close political affiliations and that the administration was hampered by [political matters]. The late President Lewis had served the institution only a year before he died, but he had already recognized the conditions and is known to have said that he would be compelled to resign unless a radical change could be made. The present president has been unable to centralize the executive authority in his office, on account of the determined opposition of the President and Secretary of the Board, and he has found it impossible to establish the educational institution because the President of the Board is an active political leader and is known to influence the smallest details of University administration through the Secretary's office which is*

not considered strictly subordinate to the office of President of the University.

Tisdel cited several national education experts on the problems and trends of college administration, especially in regard to the president, the board, and the traditional board secretary. He not only referred to the commission's report, but he published several personal letters from members of that group who urged that he be given the "widest possible authority," speaking of the handicaps the board had placed upon him, and offering him support. The crisis, he said, could not be solved by switching presidents, and he called the constant change in administrators — six in 21 years — "an educational absurdity." A few days later, however, he told a *Boomerang* reporter that he was planning to submit his resignation as of the end of the school year.

Tisdel's letter generated a new spate of publicity. The press across the state responded with accusations and counter-accusations. Editorials pointed out that the University had not flourished, that its enrollment had not kept pace with the growing wealth and population of Wyoming. Who was to blame? "Political graft and petticoat government in combination," wrote the Cheyenne *Leader.* Otto Gramm and Grace Raymond Hebard, said the Sheridan *Post,* who

have figured either directly or indirectly as the chief cause. These two officials of course have not done many of the things they have been charged with doing. But since the university is practically in their hands and its affairs largely administered by them, are they not responsible for the unenviable situation that exists today?

The *Boomerang* nastily hinted that "the scalps of Presidents Johnson, Smiley, and Tisdel [have] hung for many moons in the secretary's office as a practical demonstration of what a woman can do," and insinuated that Hebard had taken on those Indian characteristics she had long been studying. A local citizen (Republican) began circulating a petition calling on the governor to abide by the investigatory commission's recommendations. The Alumni Association in Laramie did the same, suggesting the appointment of more alumni to the board and the allocation of more power to the president.

On March 28, 1908, Tisdel formally submitted to the board his resignation, to become effective at the end of the school term. On the same day, after

carefully supplying the Laramie *Republican* with materials for its evening edition, a furious board of trustees dismissed Tisdel as president as of that exact date. The vote against him came from five members — Gramm, Jones, and Stevens from Laramie; Mokler of Casper; and J. F. Crawford, editor of the Saratoga *Sun* — while one member voted negatively, two were absent, and one vacancy on the board was yet unfilled.

In its long set of resolutions and justifications, carried within hours by the *Republican,* the board accused Tisdel of maladministration, insubordination, and untruthfulness. The latter accusation stemmed from Tisdel's cautious statements to the investigating commission, before which he actually aided the board; the "insubordination" applied to those faculty who had aided Tisdel in formulating his public statement. The trustees reviewed the investigating commission's report and claimed their full adherence thereto. Reprinting the entire appropriate sections from the law of 1891, they pointed out that the board had "almost unlimited" powers and that those of the president were legally restricted. Yet, they contended, the board of trustees

has always been generous in its administration of its affairs, delegating to the president much authority, being deferential to him on every action. To no president has more authority been given than to President Tisdel, which he verifies in his testimony given before the investigating commission. . . . In place of usurpation of authority and power, the board has repeatedly and continuously delegated to the president of the university, President Tisdel, more than to any one previously even to the initiative of measures and the execution of the smallest details. . . .

In further explanation, and probably to avoid making incautious statements of its own, the board sent to the *Republican* a Mokler editorial, scheduled to appear in the Casper paper. Therein Mokler stated that Tisdel had been chosen through "a political pull" (as nephew of Republican Senator Clark) and that

during the first year that he was at the head of the institution he showed an inclination to get into the political game, almost before he got his

seat warm. He went to the legislature as a lobbyist, and was severely criticized by the very newspapers that are now singing his praises, and it was a hard matter for his friends and the friends of the university to keep him at the institution where he belonged.

The Mokler article went on to assert that Tisdel's recommendations had been granted in full by the board until the December meeting and that "no man ever had more complete control of an institution than Mr. Tisdel had the first three years he was at the head of the university." The trustees, and particularly Otto Gramm, had insisted that he be given a free hand.

Mr. Tisdel was given a secretary at an expense of $1,000 per year, something which had never heretofore been done, and no more work was done after the secretary was secured than before. He was allowed to go wherever he chose in the state to interest prospective students, but the attendance did not materially increase; he attended state gatherings and tried to get the people interested, but no interest was taken; he made several trips east at the expense of the university and returned without showing any good results.

The board believed, Mokler reported, that

the university has not kept up with the progress of the state, and as the president has had full swing, as he has been given everything he asked, the failure to make good must not be attributed to the majority of the trustees. . . . Mr. Tisdel is an educated man, and he is a pleasant gentleman to meet, but he does not possess the tact, the simplicity and the commonness to be a success as president of a university in a western state. . . .

Roars of publicity again met the board's action, particularly from the Democratic press. Tisdel had many defenders: those who reported that he had been summoned to the legislature by Gramm to lobby against the Newcastle normal school project; those who said his whole problem was that he was "not a mixer;" those who blamed Hebard for dominating Gramm and for being personally responsible for Tisdel's fate and that of many University faculty. Cries of land graft arose again, although neither Tisdel nor the trustees accused anyone of petty malfeasance. The Laramie *Boomerang* predicted faculty resignations and reported

bitterness at Towar, the new manager of the Agricultural Extension Service, for agreeing to act as interim president.

On April 3, Tisdel sent an open letter to the local Democratic newspaper. In it he tried, not completely successfully, to explain his equivocation before the investigating commission. He spoke of the board's authority in financial matters, of its assumption of powers of faculty appointment, of the political influence of Gramm. He published his correspondence with the members of the investigating committee, the chairman of which wrote that the commission had found Tisdel "a mere figurehead." Again he asserted that much of his disagreement with the board stemmed from hiring policies, that in the previous eight months

Mr. Gramm and his executive committee have ignored the power of the president to recommend appointments and have assumed for themselves this privilege, even when the opposition of the president was known,

a repetition of the objections of A. A. Johnson more than ten years before.

Tisdel feared for the future, for he was sure that the committee appointed to devise new trustee bylaws would reduce rather than enhance the president's power. He called on the public not to be diverted but to recognize that the problem lay in the channels of administrative responsibility. Tisdel's letter fired a furious Gramm to respond through a "circular," most of which was later printed in the University *Melange*. This included the information released by the board and long quotations from Tisdel's testimony the previous summer, when he had remained loyal to the trustees and proclaimed that everything on campus was just fine.

In the wake of Tisdel's dismissal, the *Boomerang* dourly predicted that all who had professed loyalty to the president would be "axed." The rumor victims did not resign at once, but by the

Home economics department, 1901-1910

end of the semester Professors John Franklin Brown, Margaret Durward, Herbert Nowell, Frances Meader, and F. W. Gilkison had tendered their resignations to the new president. Henry Knight, who survived (he believed) because of his political influence, wrote later that the encouragement of these resignations was part of a deal made by Gramm with the incoming administration. Although it was rumored in the newspapers that Ridgaway, Nelson, and Minnie Stoner (home economics) would also lose their positions, they instead remained. H. W. Quaintance, however, was doomed; in spite of the witnesses he brought before the board to prove his own good character

and worthiness for rehiring, he had too powerful a rival, and Hebard moved permanently into the shoes she was supposed to wear only when Quaintance was out of town. When the names of these six faculty were added to those of the three from agriculture (Buffum, Morton, and Hyslop) who had left the previous year, the turnover reached the rate of almost thirty percent.

In addition, three trustees resigned from the board — Harriet Knight of Cheyenne, who had voted in favor of Tisdel; W. G. Aber of Sheridan; and Mrs. Charles Stone, Evanston, who seldom attended board meetings. After some difficulty (he reported), Governor Brooks replaced them with Democrats.

More to the point and highly publicized in the opposition press was Hebard's resignation as board secretary — a paid position, for she was no longer a trustee. In spite of her exoneration in the commission report, she was still under attack and widely criticized in the press. One of the most pointed editorials against her appeared in the Douglas *Budget,* where Bill Barlow blamed her for the entire mess in which the University found itself. Although she was a lady, Barlow wrote, a scholar, refined, cultured, and well-educated, she was too often wrong.

> *Of all the merry throng of talented gentlemen who have entered the portals of our state university to the tune of glad trusteeian huzzas only to be pushed or kicked out of the back door a few days thereafter, none of them bid goodbye to Miss Hebard as a friend from whom they parted with sincere regret. No man was ever handed his paycheck in the face of her protest. Always, singularly enough, there was first some slight disagreement with her — which grew and grew until the presuming upstart took the next elevator to make way for his successor.*

When Hebard had attempted to resign the previous year (although postponing the date of retirement until June 1908), the board had turned her down; now the resignation was promptly accepted. She undoubtedly meant it sincerely when she expressed to the board her

> *heartfelt appreciation for all of the confidences you have demonstrated that you held in me; for your consistent and loyal support (during the 18 years of annual elections I have never had a dissenting vote); for the splendid trust you have repeatedly imposed in me and for your faith in me. I have spent my best years in your service as your secretary, yet if I have in any material way by deed or influence added in the construction, growth, or upbuilding of this noble institution . . . then I am satisfied and compensated for the years. . . .*

In response, the board formally requested the new president to "consider her in the arrangement of his faculty for next year, with particular thought as to a professorship in political economy and librarian." The resolution tolled death knell for Quaintance, and Hebard again prevailed.

There is no doubt of Hebard's devotion to the University. Her gifts to the institution of her extensive library; her own records; the books that belonged to her dearest friend Professor Agnes Mathilde Wergeland, who died in 1914; scholarship funds and endowments; plus her lifetime of energetic involvement all attest to her dedication. But however noble her intentions, her position as faculty overseer and financial dragon had caused her to become heartily disliked. She lacked the sensitivity and tact to perform such chores with discretion and caution. Nor did she attack either scholarship or teaching with patience and humility. As one of her students later wrote, she was not

> *a first-rate scholar or a particularly good teacher. Her economics was primitive, her sociology subjective and emotional, her history romanticized. But she was a personality and a force. Nobody who passed through Old Main in that era will ever forget that Indian chieftain profile, that erect figure, that commanding manner.*

Hebard was promoted to full professor in 1908 and remained at her position (although finally in "partial retirement") until her death 28 years later. To the end she was influential and commanding, although shorn of her initial dominance.

In another way, the scandals of 1907-08 refused to be buried. For years thereafter, the board was touchy in regard to the problem of "relinquishing" lands. In spite of the governor's recommendation, it was reluctant to abandon title to the Carbon County lands, authorized for exchange by law of Congress in 1906. The board may have been scared off by Tisdel's opposition; there are indications that early in 1908, Tisdel had suggested to a friend that the "land steal" question actually be brought to the attention of the student body. Finally, in response to a letter from the land commissioner chiding him for not relinquishing the Carbon County lands while the market was good, Gramm brought the matter up again before the trustees, with whom Fuller met several times in 1908. Not until 1909 did the board finally set up a committee to check on legal procedures; request new secretary F. S. Burrage to locate all lands on a map and by

Music ensemble, c. 1915

description; and send a surveyor to check on potential use and values. After careful investigation, the board authorized the "relinquishment" of 3,860 acres, receiving, it stated, "in every instance another acre of land worth not less than $10 an acre."

Repeated "talk" and "criticism" continued to haunt the board, and trustees remained concerned about their "image" in regard to land sales and exchanges. In 1910, they considered requesting a public gubernatorial investigation. Instead, however, they decided finally to stand firm on the correctness and legality of their policies. Early in 1911, the board published a pamphlet edited by the new president and two board members, one a judge in Cheyenne. Herein the "land steal" rumors were explained; the "relinquishment" of the Carbon County lands justified (in terms of good financing); and the trading of the agricultural lands near Cody clearly assigned to the responsibility of the State Board of Land Commissioners. Seven pages of statistics detailed both University and Morrill Act lands sold, rented, or traded, and

R. P. Fuller attested to the truth and correctness of the statement. Although peace reigned for the moment, the question of long-term land management was still — considering several conflicting pieces of legislation — up in the air.

The scandals and problems of 1907-08 had evoked great bitterness and anger. They had cost the University a president, nine faculty members, three trustees, and a board secretary. Accusations, rumors, and criticism had been widely broadcast throughout the state press in such manner as to detract from the University's image and degrade whatever confidence it may have built throughout the state.

Under the circumstances, it is difficult to find anything positive to say about these trying years. Still, one might suggest that the board learned a lesson. With the public eye upon them, trustees were more cautious in their decisions and policies. Hebard's transfer removed a great cause for complaint. After 1908, the University enjoyed the services of three honest and energetic presidents, whose actions on the whole had board respect and support. The balance was shifting, and the revelations of 1908 slowly turned the institution onto a new course.

GO WYO!

ootball at Wyoming got off to a tremendous start. The UW team romped to victories in the first nine games it played, dating from 1893-97. With Coach Justus F. Soule (professor of Greek and Latin, later dean of liberal arts) cheering his men from the sideline, the UW eleven outclassed such teams as Cheyenne High School, the Laramie town team, a group called the "Wilson Beauties" (but not otherwise identified), the UW alumni team, and the No. 5 Hose Company. Following the defeat of the latter by a score of 16-6 in 1894, rumors spread that the University footballers had spent the morning turning in fire alarms to sap the energy of their opponents; the story is undoubtedly apochryphal. In

Coach Justus F. Soule's football team, 1896-97

1895 and 1896, the University team began to seek opponents out of state, and handily defeated Northern Colorado, Denver Manual High School, and Colorado State on their home fields. Thereafter, however, luck frowned, and the team posted a few losing seasons — although it still managed well against high schools, the Laramie Athletic Club, and (in 1904) the UW faculty. The season record by 1914 was twelve won, eight lost, and two tied. Some seasons saw only one or two games.

Coached by whoever would give it a try and captained by such student luminaries as Herbert and Fred Brees, M. E. Corthell, and Harry H. Hill, the UW footballers never had it easy. For one thing, the games were seen by University administrators as healthy extra-curricular fun, and rather than collecting perquisites, the team paid their own expenses and furnished their own uniforms. Home field was, in the words of Dean Soule, "almost granite," located in an undeveloped area near the present Prexy's Pasture. As a result, the rough and tumble games left participants loaded with scrapes and bruises, but never so many that "our arguing ability with the referees was impaired," according to Coach Soule. Opponents were sometimes awesome; in 1908, the Utah team outweighed the Wyoming players by 49 pounds per man and defeated them by a score of 75-0. In these early years, the team could claim little depth in the various positions, so whenever a player was injured, the game kept right on, sometimes with as few as eight men on the field. Players made up in spirit what they lacked in experience, for many of these freshman lads (and townspeople, who pitched in) had never seen a football game before they joined the team.

Not until 1915 did Wyoming have a professional coach. Thereafter the efforts of John Corbett, Lonestar Dietz, George McLaren, John Rhodes, and Dutch Witte garnered growing administrative support, but not until after World War II did Wyoming football begin to make its mark.

Football team formation, 1897

Chapter Five

Presidents' Progress
1907-1922

he crisis of 1907 and the governor's public investigation represented a milestone in University history. If not immediately, then within a few years, the report set the University administration on a better defined, more efficient, and more professional path. Although the trustees personally had reason to celebrate their public exoneration of charges of petty graft, mismanagement, and blatant political interference, the commission was not easy on many general board policies. Slowly and often quietly, governor, board, and University administrators recognized the validity of the commission's findings and moved to improve the University's situation and public image. In the years from 1907-1922, they were aided by a series of hard-working, fair, constructive-minded, and, on the whole, strong presidents. Only near the end of this period did hints of difficulties surface. Moreover, these were years of prosperity, and the University was able to claim its share of the state's newly-developing wealth.

Most important among the results of the investigation was a slow but steady movement towards non-partisanship in the composition of the board of trustees. At first Governor Brooks had seemed to demur, or at least he refused to seek the resignations of board members although he stated that he agreed in principle that the board should be less politically partisan. Press and private pressure continued. Among the governor's papers is a letter from the superintendent of the Cody public schools, who wrote Brooks that the University

does not have the standing up this way that it should have. As nearly as I can find out, people feel that the University has been a "political pie" too long. . . . In view of the sentiment that exists here, and as nearly as I can find out, the similar sentiment that exists in many other parts of the state . . . steps should be taken as soon as possible for securing in some way a non-partisan Board of Regents for the control of the University. To my mind, the University must be

lifted above the plane of politics and put upon a purely educational basis before it will command the confidence and support which it should have from the people of the state. If the present Board really have the best interests of the University at heart, seeing the muddle they have produced, they would resign at once and give you the opportunity to clear up the educational atmosphere of the state by the appointment of an entirely new and non-partisan board.

No wholesale resignation of board members was forthcoming, but a few did resign and Brooks appointed several Democrats to the board — the first time more than one at once had served on that body. Still, in 1909, the governor reappointed Otto Gramm, Republican, who (next to Hebard) had been most deeply implicated in the 1907 scandals. Gramm seemed surprised, but Brooks wrote him that

the course I have pursued has not only been to the best interests of the University, but has proven in a great measure a full and complete refutation of the numberless unjust charges and thoughtless criticism, which has been made against you in past years. I hope that some of these thoughtless critics will take a little tumble to themselves, and that affairs concerning the University may run smoothly in the future.

Two years later when the new Democratic governor requested Gramm's resignation, the latter at first refused, but he shortly agreed to withdraw, probably with the promise of a different political plum. With Democratic administrations in power from 1911-19, the less partisan nature of the board was assured. For more than thirty years, it remained well enough balanced between Democrat and Republican members so as to avert major criticism.

Lacking Hebard's strong presence and Gramm's political interests, the board became more disciplined, professional, and effective. Presidents served in rotation rather than in *perpetuum*. Judge Timothy F. Burke, president from 1911-18, performed his duties meticulously and devotedly until declining health forced his resignation. Mrs. Mary B. David from Douglas served as president for a year, followed by Alexander B. Hamilton, 1919-1922. David's term in office demonstrated that the board president need not necessarily reside in Laramie, and indeed as transportation improved, trustees from far corners of the state found it easier to attend regular quarterly meetings. Few sessions after 1908 had to be adjourned for lack of a quorum. The superintendent of public instruction began to appear fairly regularly, and (in part because of intricate financial problems), governors and other state officials frequently made it a point to be present. The governor became an ex-officio member of the board after 1922. The executive committee continued to meet monthly, but its business was generally routine and its policy-making powers declined as presidents became stronger and the board's operation more smooth.

During the years 1908-1922, the board chose to appoint increasing numbers of paid professionals to aid it and the University president — a move that greatly improved the efficiency and quality of general management. Hebard's replacement, Frank S. Burrage, operated with distinction in the role of secretary. A man of character, intelligence, and discretion, he was trusted if not beloved by one president after another. He handled their correspondence when they were away; provided small favors to all of them (such as supervising household arrangements); and remained on good terms throughout their administrations. He took classes, taught classes, served as registrar, reported regularly to the board, sang in the University chorus, found jobs for students, and eventually (supposedly when denied an adequate salary increase) resigned to become a Laramie newspaper editor. Fay E. Smith took office as secretary in 1922 after Elwood P. Johnson served for a short term.

When Burrage resigned, the board saw fit to divide his enormous responsibilities, of which he spoke with some pathos. It appointed a registrar (R. E. McWhinnie). In 1919, many financial matters that had been the province of the secretary were turned over instead to a professional fiscal agent. The appointment was devised as part of an effort to make clear "even to the lay mind" exactly how University finances were managed, and no doubt inspired by a bill nearly passed by the legislature, under which all University funds would have been handled by the Office of the State Treasurer. After the troubles of 1907, the board had adopted more stringent financial measures, and bids were carefully let for major purchases. Still, in 1919, further changes were inaugurated, in light of "the criticism that our accounts are indifferently kept and the records so incomplete as to make it difficult to secure a detailed account of the expenditures of the institution." At the same time, Nellis Corthell was officially placed on an annual retainer as board attorney. This multiplication of staff brought undesirable additional costs but it was clearly mandated by the complexity of University affairs. One secretary could no longer manage everything.

The most dramatic change in University administration occurred in the relationship between president and board of trustees. Even the 1908 board recognized the problem. Justifying Tisdel's dismissal, the board had cited the limitations of presidential functions according to the legislatively mandated bylaws of 1891, but at the president's request had agreed to review these rules with the aim of clarifying all responsibilities. Still, in its report of June 13, 1908, the appointed committee insisted that the bylaws "as fully and completely as the laws permit" defined the president's powers and the board's competency. However, the majority of the board (including Gramm, sitting as president) made a further effort at clairfying positions. Recognizing the value of

clear distinctions regarding the duties and jurisdiction among the various committees and appointments of the Board of Trustees in the management of the affairs of the University

the board resolved that

all questions of property and financial management pertaining strictly to business affairs that may arise in the interim between meetings of the Board of Trustees shall be in charge of the executive committee selected by the Board; and that all questions of educational management and discipline shall belong strictly and without interference during said interim . . . to the president with the assistance of the faculty of instructors that shall be chosen from time to time by the said Board of Trustees. . . .

Although trustees did not always abide by their own rules, relations between presidents and board ran a smoother course, at least until the early 1920s.

Thus over the years following Tisdel's dismissal, the board came to invest ever more authority in the University president and restrict more of its own actions to major financial and advisory and confirmatory functions. Much of this new attitude seems to have arisen from the trustees' confidence in three unusually competent University presidents to whom they permitted more flexibility than to their predecessors and whose guidance — even in financial problems — they came to respect and appreciate. These were in turn Charles O. Merica, Clyde A. Duniway, and Aven Nelson — all Ph.D.s, — a trio of men of extraordinary abilities.

From the start, Merica made a positive impression on the board and the University community. By one student he was described later as "ebullient, extrovert, and very popular." Henry Knight, who became Merica's good friend, said he was "very erratic, nervous, and high tempered," yet admitted that he was "a very lovable character" who won Knight's respect and that of his colleagues. A dynamic, articulate, and vigorous individual, Merica was elected president in May 1908 over several candidates of higher station, and no single trustee cast a vote for anyone else. Merica was a sociologist, a graduate of DePauw and Iowa Wesleyan, who had just received an honorary degree from Lawrence College, where he had taught as professor of economics and sociology. He entered upon his duties only a month after Tisdel's summary dismissal and probably after careful "agreement" about resignations to be elicited and accepted from among Tisdel's faculty supporters. Nevertheless, Merica won praise and support. Under the new president's management, wrote A. D. Cook, superintendent of public instruction,

there is an increased and an ever increasing interest in that institution. I am pleased with the force and energy displayed by President Merica in grappling with the problems pertaining to his office, and I predict a rapid growth of the institution under his charge.

The board was pleased too, and it so demonstrated. It began by granting him power to fill any faculty vacancy that might arise between its own meetings (subject to the approval of the executive committee). The board then applauded his immediately expressed interest in participating in financial planning; rearranged its meeting schedule so that he could make pertinent recommendations for the board's own annual report; obviously approved his plans for University expansion; and soon increased his salary by twenty percent — from $4,000-$5,000 in his second year of service. By December 1908, trustees added his name to their legislative — or lobbying — committee, a notable change of heart in that they had cited Tisdel's brief appearance among the legislators as cause for dismissal only a few months before. At Merica's suggestion, the president's annual report to the board — previously regarded as wholly confidential — came to be published and circulated, an action that brought University activities to the public eye and caused the president to become better known in the state. Merica's firm and certain presence can be sensed almost from the start in a reading of board minutes and of University and local periodicals.

Merica was a builder, both in terms of bricks and mortar and of academic expansion and program improvement. His optimism infected all around him. The legislature of 1909 might well have caused trouble after the investigations and scandals of the previous several years, but thanks to Merica's tact and Governor Brooks' silence, it in no way acted to the embarrassment of the University. Instead it was a good year. Collaborating closely with the board in its legislative request, Merica argued successfully for a $15,000 addition to the women's dormitory; for an increase in the University's tax levy from three-eighths to one-half mill, which amount was to enhance both building and operating funds; and — the victory that evoked the greatest irritation from northern county legislators — a special $50,000 tax levy to permit the construction of a normal school building, which solidified the University's claim to the state's teacher training program. In redefining qualifications for teachers and for nurses, the legislature in both instances recognized the University's interest and programs. Only F. S. King from Albany County — the integrity of whose prize-winning fleeces had been questioned by Morton — suggested that the University be duly inspected by a legislative committee. His resolution, passed in the house, was soon defeated in the senate.

In 1910, the president's recommendations to the board represented an even more strongly aggressive program. At the board meeting in December 1910, Merica presented an extensive report — later published and distributed to the press — that minced no words on what he considered the University's needs. He spoke in particular to construction and equipment necessities. Beginning with an analysis of the funding the University had received over the years from federal and state sources, the president demonstrated with little difficulty that the U.S. government had borne the lion's share of financing, a statement indeed not hard to prove. Merica's calculations, he wrote, were intended

as an answer to the opinion held in some circles that the university has been a great drain upon the taxable resources of the State. No other state west of the Alleghenies in its early years spent so little for the cause of higher education. . . . At no time during the entire history of the University has the State contributed for the maintenance of the University one half of the sum contributed by the Federal Government at the same time.

Moreover, by Merica's articulate definition, the purposes and nature of the modern university had changed. No longer could an institution of higher learning consist of a teacher on one end of a log and a young man on the other.

The university no longer confines itself to the old and inexplicable idea of culture. It has set for itself the business of being the very life of a people. It has become the business of the modern university to solve the great problems of industrial and social as well as so-called cultural life. It cost comparatively little money to build a building and hire a few men to teach Latin and Greek, mathematics and the humanities in the days when there were no libraries and laboratories and students bought their own text books, the only books used. Today the university undertakes to solve and demonstrate problems, for the solution of a simple part of which single appliances are often required costing thousands of dollars. The day of baby universities has gone by.

It was an almost revolutionary statement of the University's professionalism and its coming of age. Particular professions were in special demand in Wyoming, the president said, and the state ought to

maintain a university covering the usual work of a university in certain colleges which it believes are needed for the State or it should close its doors.

Merica's requests were so costly, his hopes so great, and his examples of classroom and laboratory conditions so shocking, that trustees endorsed his program with considerable uncertainty. The board of trustees, wrote Otto Gramm in his annual report to the governor,

recognize the fact that the state is new and that the assessed valuation of the property of the entire state is not large. It is the wish of the Board of Trustees that the state should not be unduly burdened in the care and support of this University. On the other hand, the Board of Trustees are most fully convinced that the work of the University will be much hindered, if not altogether defeated, unless most generous provisions are made for its upbuilding and maintenance.

After considerable discussion, trustees authorized the president to request from the legislature permission for a bond issue in the amount of $300,000 to be submitted to the people of the state at the requisite special election. Funds raised through the latter would be designated for a science building as well as an administration, library and auditorium facility, at a cost of $100,000 each, plus various lesser miscellaneous projects: shops, a veterinary building, the museum, and experiment station improvements. A special bond issue for University construction had not been authorized by the state since 1888.

The president was doomed to disappointment. In his message to the legislature in 1911, newly elected Governor Joseph M. Carey expressed faith in the institution; mentioned the amounts appropriated in the past biennium; and went on to announce that he did not believe in extravagance, as "it is not a waste of money that makes great institutions, but a proper expenditure of such reasonable amounts as may be available to cover the requirements." He referred to the University's "difficulties," and called for the removal of the management "from the suspicion of political influence.'' The governor's approach was adopted by the legislature too, and no request for a bond issue was ever debated on the floor of house or senate. Although the legislature again set the University tax levy at one-half mill (not to exceed in income the amount of $85,000 for each year, 1911 and 1912), Merica's plans for a university hospital were abandoned by the board (June 8, 1911). Student fees had to be raised (from $3-$5 per semester!), and hopes for a new science hall could be termed tentative at best.

The Wyoming School Journal, the editor of which was also head of the University's teacher training school, reflected general admiration.

He came to the University four years ago. In these four years the institution has made a progress of which the state of Wyoming may well be proud. First of all, it was evident upon his coming that he brought to the work an adequate vision of what the future of a great state university should be . . . The attention of the people of the

Botany class picnic, Saw Mill Creek, 1897

Merica's disappointment in legislative financial support probably formed the basis for his resignation in March of the following year. Trustees paid sincere tribute to their outgoing president both at their special meeting in May 1912 and in June at his actual departure. ''Again the University is called upon to bid farewell to her president,'' wrote the editor of the University journal, *Melange,* that spring.

Dr. Merica came during a time of confusion and so successfully brought order out of chaos, understood so well the needs of the University, was not only hopeful but really accomplished so much in meeting those needs, that it was hoped he had come to stay and would lead the University on to complete victory. That hope is not to be realized, and it is with great regret that the University gives up her leader.

state has been called to their institution with a directness and emphasis never before experienced . . . He has organized the University for future growth.

Merica's strength and professionalism left their marks, in spite of the legislature's failure to respond. It is because of his policies and visions that the University moved forward in the next decades. Leaving in disappointment and bitterness (according to Professor Wilson O. Clough, the University's historian, he destroyed all his papers and correspondence as president), he opted to return to his more successful work with recalcitrant boys and moved to a school in Minnesota. Later he returned to higher education once more.

In most respects, the new president carried on the tradition. Clyde A. Duniway, elected by the board in May 1912, with only one briefly dissenting vote, was in Clough's words ''scholarly, bearded, socially urbane, and affable.'' If Henry Knight commented on his ''lack of deep human emotions'' and ''cold . . . eyes, pointed beard, aristocratic face,'' it was probably because

Knight's own anticipations of being offered the presidency himself had been peremptorily dashed. Even in Knight's assessment, Duniway was "admired by some, respected by all," although the new president retained a characteristic remoteness, which he himself was always anxious to conquer. Once he asked Knight if taking up smoking might make him appear more congenial. He and Mrs. Duniway deliberately cultivated friendships with their Sunday afternoon open houses. Perhaps as a result, students found him attractive.

President Clyde Augustus Duniway was a peaceful, family sort of man. His grey Van Dyke beard conveyed the impression of fatherliness. His large soft brown eyes invited trust and confidence. While he was somewhat aloof from his faculty and the student body, he had the admiration and respect of all who knew him.

Duniway was a scholar of recognized magnitude. A native of Oregon, he earned his undergraduate degree from Cornell and his Ph.D. in history from Harvard University; for fourteen years, he served as professor of history at Stanford. The new president came to Wyoming from the University of Montana, where he had been president for four years. The experience undoubtedly prepared him for the particular problems he would face at another Western state institution. Unlike his predecessor he knew exactly what to expect.

Like Merica, the new president commanded respect from the board of trustees. On several occasions he was especially commended for the "fullness, interest, and comprehension" of his reports to the board, and after 1915, his annual summaries (with the exception of those parts regarded as confidential) were published. After his second year, Duniway's salary was raised to $4,700, in addition to which he received use of the presidential house, purchased by the board when Merica left.

Even more than his predecessor, Duniway played a major role in legislative efforts. His correspondence shows that he not only addressed the board regularly with recommendations for the program, but that he actively participated in pursuing University ends once the legislature was in session. On New Year's Day of 1913, he sent a long "personal letter just for your private use" to Governor Carey, explaining his view of the University's strengths and needs; he closed by asking the governor to honor him "not only with your friendship but with your confidence" in University affairs. He corresponded at length with Timothy F. Burke,

board president, about even the minutiae of the legislative action. Burke was located in Cheyenne (at the law firm of Burke and Riner) and served as go-between for the University and legislature, but Duniway had a hand in all decisions: He drafted proposed legislation, worked with Burke on deciding which legislator should be requested to introduce bills, conferred with the Albany County delegation, wrote to the governor, sounded out the superintendent of public instruction, conferred with the chairpersons of committees, lobbied (at Burke's request), and personally petitioned all members of the house ways and means committee. In 1913, he invited the entire legislature to come by special train to Laramie for his inauguration; and, in 1915, he repeated the invitation for the formal dedication of the new agriculture building, which events he carefully coordinated with the legislative schedule. He virtually moved to Cheyenne for the last days of the legislative sessions. His personal relationship with Judge Burke seemed consistently close, and in this regard the heads of board and University were again as closely linked as in the Gramm and Hebard days.

Duniway's requests of the legislature were less demanding than Merica's, and his experience had conditioned him to settle for compromises when necessary. In 1912, operating under the half-mill tax levy, one-eighth mill of which was earmarked specifically for construction, the board began construction of the agriculture hall. But in spite of Duniway's intensive efforts, the economy-minded legislature of 1913 decreased the mill levy to three-eighths. The president was undaunted. His report to the board in June 1914, commented on "substantial" progress, a splendid spirit of cooperation, and what one newspaper editorial had called the "Era of Good Feeling for the University of Wyoming." It was axiomatic, he wrote, that any healthy, growing institution of higher education would need and seek more funding than was available to it. He predicted a fine future.

Is it too much to hope under these circumstances that the people of the state through their representatives in the Legislature will put into the hands of the Board of Trustees of the University of Wyoming sufficient resources to enable this institution to fulfill its high destiny? Is it too much to expect further that men and women of independent means seeking to share their fortunes with the people of the state in beneficent

ways will make their State University the trustee of funds for the training of youth and for the development of art, industry, and science?

The legislature of 1915 was more generous. In addition to restoring the mill levy to one-half (of which one-eighth mill was to be expended for building construction), it finally allocated the University one-fourth of the income from "omnibus" land rentals and one-fourth the interest earned on capital from the sale of such lands. These lands represented a federal grant for education, charity, and other support as authorized when Wyoming became a state in 1890. Although Democratic Governor John B. Kendrick was reluctant to put his signature to the University bill, a last-minute lobbying effort by University and board officials (reportedly leaning over his shoulder) caused him to change his mind and sign. On the basis of the allocation, the board contracted for a new women's dormitory.

Fiscal year 1914-15 saw income from the state tax rise to $101,000, thanks to the increased mill levy. In 1916-17 the University received $108,000; in 1917-18 (when the legislature renewed the half-mill tax), $118,000. The flexibility accorded to the board in determining construction priorities within the eighth-mill allocation signified a great step forward. Duniway might regard this mill levy increase as a triumph of his legislative chores.

In the spring 1917, the president signed a regular contract with the board, but in June he came before it to request a release. He had been offered a firm $7,000 plus housing and other perquisites to become president of Colorado College. Duniway told the trustees he would abide by his contract if the board so desired. When it agreed to release him for the position that must be "considered an advancement," there was no rancor on either side. He left with good feelings, commenting on the cordial relationships and good working conditions he had enjoyed.

Pressed with a last-minute resignation, the board asked Aven Nelson, official vice president since l9l4, to accept the acting presidency. Nelson agreed. For several months, the board undertook a search for a new president; in the files is a letter addressed to former Governor J. M. Carey from one university president who declined the offer because the University of North Dakota

pays a salary of $6,000 and in addition furnishes horses, carriage, coachman, and heats and lights the President's house . . . In addition to this I

find that the University of North Dakota has a very much larger income and a wider recognition than that possessed by the University of Wyoming.

Two months later, in spite of a search for a permanent replacement and the candidacy of a number of off-campus figures, the board requested Nelson to continue throughout the academic year in an "acting" capacity.

One of the so-called "Old Guard," Aven Nelson was well known to board, faculty, and citizens of Wyoming for his work with the Agricultural Experiment Station, in the field, and as teacher of botany and many related subjects. The Rocky Mountain Herbarium, founded by Nelson and enriched by his collecting and his loving care, remains one of the jewels of the University even today. A quiet, self-effacing, nineteenth-century Christian gentleman, Nelson was, commented the *Wyoming Student* upon his election,

very reserved but unable to avoid the popularity which his winning personality and lovable nature have brought him.

The faculty held him in "affectionate regard," and students found him unique, versatile, and a great teacher. His botanical expeditions to the mountains and the countryside had become legendary. As an administrator, however, Nelson gives somewhat the impression of a fish out of water. Henry Knight, who again hoped for the presidential job, thought Nelson lacked strength and decisiveness. Several students later remarked that Nelson was a better professor than president.

The board's action in hiring Nelson on a temporary basis in 1917 may have reflected a wait-and-see attitude, but then the country was at war, and a change in administration was probably deemed unwise. Through the 1917-18 year, the trustees' confidence in their botanist-president grew, and as early as December they talked of asking him to stay. In June 1918, at a meeting filled with praise that Nelson himself did not hear (having been asked to leave the room), the board unanimously and "with enthusiasm" appointed him permanent president. The decision was abetted by a petition signed by more than fifty members of the Alumni Association, which had not particularly supported Duniway. Nelson could not help but be pleased and gratified.

The University of Wyoming campus, c. 1920

hen Aven Nelson arrived at the University of Wyoming in 1887, he was a young man of 28, anticipating making his name as a teacher of English and literature. Fate in the form of the trustees' blunder shifted his responsibilities into the field of biology. When he died in 1952, Nelson had gained fame as one of the country's leading botanists, and its uncontested authority in the field of Rocky Mountain flora.

Born of Norwegian immigrant farmers in a log cabin in Iowa, Nelson had from the start been set close to nature and had come to understand her beauties. If in his academic work he had chosen to work in English language and literature, the decision may have represented his parents' hopes — they did not easily read and converse in English — that he would become a man of the new country. According to his biographer, Roger L. Williams, Nelson never did credit his academic interest in botany to his early life on the Iowa farm — perhaps the association was too deep for him to recognize.

Once engaged, he became totally committed. In 1893, Nelson traveled to the Chicago World's Fair, to exhibit some Wyoming grasses collected by a colleague and horticulturist, B. C. Buffum. The exhibit won a prize and Buffum donated the specimens to Nelson, stimulating him to begin his career of categorizing and cataloguing flora of the Rocky Mountains. In 1896, he published his first report on the flora of Wyoming. By then, he had begun to establish his reputation, in particular through correspondence and exchange of views with leading botanists in California and the East.

Each summer Nelson took to the wild trails of Wyoming, gathering and drying plants; the story of these field expeditions — often with his wife and their small daughters — is told elsewhere in these pages. In 1899, the young botanist approached the trustees with a report on the magnitude of his collections. That year the board officially established the Rocky Mountain Herbarium, the result of Nelson's many investigations. By 1902, the herbarium contained 40,000 specimens; by 1913, 75,000. All were gathered by hand in duplicate, so that extras could be sold or exchanged. The herbarium continues to be a unique and wonderful collection even today — a tribute to its founder's foresight and hard work.

In the course of his collecting, Nelson identified many new species, some of which were named for their discoverer. He found himself caught up in the grand debates on taxonomy that absorbed the nation's botanists in the pre-war years. Before his career was over, he had served as president of the Botanical Society of America and of the American Society of Plant Taxonomists. To his Ph.D. from Denver University, the University of Colorado added the honorary D.Sc. degree and the University of Wyoming the LL.D

Aven Nelson, tenth president, 1917-1922

As a scholar, collector, and teacher beloved by his students, Nelson found time to act as landscape architect for the bleak Wyoming campus. Many of the trees we see today, he planted with his own hands. "Nelson Day" in the spring marked a time when students pitched in to plant, prune, or pick up after the long Wyoming winter. In the files is a letter, written by the eminent botanist only a few years before he became University president (1917) begging relief from some of his heavier gardening chores.

At the time of his resignation from the presidency in 1922, Nelson was 63. For twenty years he continued to work and to encourage young scholars in the field. When he finally retired, on the pittance that was allowed, Nelson had supervised his own replacements: as botanist, W. C. Solheim, and as herbarium curator, C. L. Porter. He had also felt the beginnings of ill health and suffered the loss of his first wife. This astonishing man found happiness in a second marriage to a sympathetic and loving woman, also a botanist. He died in Colorado Springs at the age of 93.

Nelson's administration was prosperous for the University as none before. In spite or perhaps because of wartime inflation, funding had never been more generous or secure. Throughout the Nelson years, the legislature continued its policy of granting to the University three-eighths mill from the general tax assesment for operating expenses, plus another one-eighth mill for purposes of construction. By the fiscal year 1920-21, these tax appropriations amounted to almost $200,000 annually; as property evaluations in the state continued to rise, the University's income kept pace. In addition, the budget was boosted by increasing incomes from federal lands granted to the University, including those from the original Morrill Act (1862), from the University Land Act (1881), and the UW percentage of the "omnibus" land grant (1890).

In 1921, the University made a special campaign of its legislative requests, with the board even addressing a special plea to University alumni with a cry for help.

Without that help, your Alma Mater can never hope to fill her days with usefulness and honor. . . . She is not a beggar with cap in hand. Only a part of her income is the gift of the taxpayers of this state. . . . Her graduates are her assets. She looks to them to see to it that public sentiment continues to advance to the end that higher education in this state will take its fitting place above local jealousies and national politics and policies. This year an election will be held. Will you help so that every candidate for the Legislature will, if elected, take office with a mind free from prejudice and with some sympathy for the leading educational institution in the state?

Aven Nelson, Rocky Mountain Herbarium (science hall), 1912

Whether the alumni influence dominated or not, the University received from the 1921 legislature a special $100,000 earmarked for buildings: namely, a library, a new gymnasium and armory, a new power plant, an engineering building, and expansion of Hoyt hall dormitory. As Nelson wrote in his quarterly report to the board in March 1922, "It is generally recognized that, never in its history, has the University of Wyoming received such generous legislative support as was accorded it in the 1921 session." Prosperous times, of course, played a major role, but Nelson's own performance as chief administrator must be given due credit.

One special measure of financial prosperity must be noted: During Nelson's tenure as president, the University benefited from extraordinary discoveries of oil on University-held lands (all of which derived from federal land grants).

As early as 1893, Wilbur C. Knight and E. E. Slosson had published a geographical report on Wyoming's high potential for oil development in the Salt Creek area; but because of remoteness, poor transportation, and lack of contemporary demand, the state's oil production as late as 1897 was valued at only $54,000 for the year. Salt Creek oil was not truly explored until 1908, and other fields lay in abeyance until the motor car's popularity inflated demand for black gold. Between 1916 and 1918, Wyoming's oil production doubled, and thereafter into the 1920s it continued to increase. University lands on which oil was discovered were located primarily in the Big Muddy area east of Casper. The resultant extraordinary increase in funds included income from oil royalties and rentals. Royalties alone brought as much as $29,000 per month (September 1920), although the amount varied enormously ($5,000 for July 1921). In addition, the moneys from land rents (including also interest on sales profits) increased to more than $55,000 annually in fiscal year 1921-22, in large part because of the value of mineral resources.

Oil was gold, and gold delighted the board of trustees, but the procedures of collecting and utilizing oil royalties and the problems of determining fair value of lands for lease and sale purposes dominated board concerns after 1916. In that year, with considerable foresight, Duniway anticipated the extent of new oil discoveries. In his annual report to the board, he recommended a conservative policy, suggesting that oil royalties either be reserved as a permanent endowment, on which

only interest would be available for use, or utilized specifically for permanent (construction) improvements. The board agreed, and in December 1916, in spite of the protest of board member and former Governor Joseph M. Carey (who clearly understood the implications of the move for continuing state appropriations), trustees voted to place all oil royalty money into a special permanent building fund.

The problems of administration of oil lands were nastier and led the board into considerable conflict with other state authorities. Who should negotiate and determine the assignment of oil leases and how should the value of such leases and properties be determined? Legislation was contradictory, seemingly granting authority to the trustees and to the State Board of Land Commissioners. In the midst of the 1907 land scandals the board had authorized the land board to act in its stead, particularly in regard to the Morrill Act (or agricultural) lands.

Oil made the problem acute. The land commissioners had issued a number of extended leases (for five years or more) on University lands that seemed at the time to be worthy only of grazing stock; when oil was discovered, the board was stuck with those leases in effect at the original low rental scale. The issue came to a head in early 1917, when Governor Kendrick and the state board were attacked for what was deemed mismanagement. In February 1917, Secretary of State Frank L. Houx appeared before the trustees and insisted that

While the Constitution of the State vested the University lands and the right to lease them in the trustees of the University, the same constitution was also just as emphatic in saying that all leases should be approved by the State Board of Land Commissioners and that these facts, taken in connection with the resolution of the Board of Trustees of the University of August 30, 1907, in his mind established without doubt the right of the State Board of Land Commissioners to make the leases that they had made. He said he wished to emphasize what Governor Kendrick had said that they had made these leases in perfect good faith and also that in light of the facts that they had at the time the leases were made, their terms were just as good as possibly could have been obtained.

Faced with a number of lessees who stalked the corridors for fear that original contracts might be canceled and an equal number of potential lessees who hoped for the same, the board stood by its decision of 1907 and voted that all current leases be deemed legal and binding. Having confirmed existing leases, however, the board declared that in the future it would manage its lands by itself, and that

from this date on all leases to all oil lands belonging to the University shall be granted by the Board of Trustees, the terms of such leases to be approved by the State Board of Land Commissioners, but applications for leases to be made as heretofore to the Secretary of the State Board of Land Commissioners; and further be it resolved that the resolution of August 30, 1907, as found in the minutes of the Board of Trustees on p. 233 of Book II, be repealed and is hereby repealed insofar as it is in conflict with the motion above passed.

In taking over its own business, the board had no idea of the magnitude of the Pandora's box it had opted to open. Meeting after meeting was devoted to the assignment, renewal, and investigation of oil leases. Company representatives regularly appeared before the board, some of them angrily. Policies were slowly set: Oil leases were to be granted at auction to the highest bidder; public notices were to be posted; forms were established; a percentage royalty scale was adopted; and lands for grazing were to be leased only with mineral rights reserved. Board members personally went to check land on which oil had been discovered. Subleases were considered, and lessees of large tracts were required to offer bond. In June 1918, the presentation of the president's report was interrupted by the appearance of oil company executives, and in July of the same year the board began a series of meetings held near oil-rich properties: Glenrock, Casper, and Midwest. By this year the board was attempting to offer royalty oil (paid in kind) for sale.

Trustees hired several experts to aid them in checking lands, including agricultural holdings; E. O. Fuller and his assistant inspected 29,922 acres of University land and 14,820 acres of agricultural college land by November 1920. They did not hesitate to call on faculty members to help: S. H. Knight made a special report on Big Muddy lands in 1917, and board Chairman A. B. Hamilton made a trip to Rock River to check on some land that the State Board of Land Commissioners

had already appraised — only to announce that in his opinion the land was worth more than the commissioners believed.

Throughout all of its involvement, the trustees consistently spoke of the value of a "friendly suit" to solve

the various questions which the experience of the past indicates will rise between the University and the State Land Board and other State Officials from time to time. A settled policy will avoid controversy and stabilize the State's growing land business.

But by 1921, the board was clearly exhausted and in over its head. In March of that year, the trustees turned management of the public lands back to the office of the commissioner of public lands, since, as they pointed out, that office was far better organized and equipped to perform such routine and "ministerial" duties. They retained the right to "supervise" the commissioner's decisions. Plans for a "friendly suit" to determine actual legal responsibility were retained but placed on the back burner.

Meanwhile, the question of the usage of these extensive revenues rose again. The board's ruling that oil royalties should be utilized only for construction purposes was supplemented in 1917 by a resolution that money received from mineral leases should also be treated "as permanent funds," although rental fees had long been used for current operating expenses.

Two years later, in June 1919, board member and former Governor Carey made an impassioned plea to his colleagues for saving *all* royalty fees and not spending them at all. He was sure that

the move to utilize money derived from oil royalties in buildings at the University or in current expenses would be the worst thing the institution had ever done. He cited instances of other States disposing of such funds and thereby depriving coming generations of the endowment which should be theirs. He said that if the University should succeed in getting from the State Treasury oil royalty money to be used for current expenses, every county in the state would get after the board. Judge Carey stated that public opinion was against any such use of royalty moneys.

Robert D. Carey, son of Joseph M. and currently Wyoming governor, echoed his father.

It would be better for the University to be content with the present mill tax levee which would soon become a fixed policy and enable the University to be entirely free from politics. He said that it would be foolish to use royalty money in this way and thereby throw the University into politics. The question would go much further, he said, embarrassing the State officials in their endeavor to build up an endowment for educational purposes.

Still, Nelson spoke strongly of the great needs of the University in terms of buildings: a new heating plant, dormitories, library space, and others. In the end, the board rescinded its former decision and instead asked that one-third of the money from oil royalties that was not actually invested in "permanent securities" be made available at once for "urgent purposes;" the rest could be credited to the University Permanent Land Fund, on which only interest could be expended.

The question thus basically remained unanswered, and problems were shortly enhanced, for after 1920, in addition to the income from its own federal land grants, the University came to receive nine percent of Wyoming's share of oil royalties from all public lands within state borders leased out by the federal government. In the long run, the problem was handled by legislative action. Prosperity was not always easy to manage.

But prosperity warmed the campus, and students and faculty seem to have shared a sense of well-being. In the years after 1900, American higher education was expanding as never before, and Wyoming students participated in the nation's optimism about the values of education and the lifetime opportunities for young college men and women. Strong and respected leadership enhanced faculty morale too. Expansion continued apace. A campus population of 245 students in 1911 more than doubled by 1920, not counting students in the preparatory high school. Faculty increases almost kept pace, for a 1909 faculty of thirty (a figure that does not include classroom and research assistants) had grown to 52 by 1920.

Physical facilities also vastly improved. A campus that had once contained no more than a towered building on the prairie by 1920 boasted nine major edifices, including Old Main (by 1920 considered the home of liberal arts); separate structures for science, engineering, agriculture, music,

and education; a gym that served as campus social center; and two women's dormitories, named for Presidents Hoyt and Merica. Nelson's years of toil were bearing fruit, for pictures of campus before World War I show rows of deciduous trees, small but healthy evergreens, shrubs, and even grassy lawns to replace the old sagebrush. At the famous botanist's plea, upkeep of the roadways, walks, lawns, tennis courts, and playing fields was finally turned over to a professional campus gardener in 1917; but for years students celebrated Nelson Day in spring, an occasion on which everyone pitched in to pick up, prune, and plant.

By 1910, too, student activities were assuming dimensions similar to what we know today. Music had become an increasingly important part of campus life. By 1909, it had formally joined the University curriculum, with student fees paid through standard financial procedures and regular credit granted. Enrollment in music classes continually increased. Credit was given for orchestra performance, and the orchestra actively participated in Laramie's first music festival with a performance of *Cavalleria Rusticana* in 1917. A University band, led by Wilbur Hitchcock, grew from eleven men (mostly faculty) in 1913 to 29 a mere two years later. In 1913, music students and budding actors cooperated in the performance of a Gilbert and Sullivan operetta. Theater was always a major source of extracurricular pleasure, although most plays (many directed by the talented Mabelle Land DeKay) were sponsored by student social organizations for financial benefits. By World War I, literally dozens of plays had been performed, from Shaw to Shakespeare, particularly by local sororities. Both sororities and fraternities were springing up on campus, most of them soon achieving national chapter status.

The campus was elated with the victories of its debate teams, particularly in the years following 1918 when Wyoming debators posted extraordinary winning seasons in regional competition. If athletic teams were not quite so successful, still the program burgeoned with the introduction of minor sports, women's activities, and teams in football and basketball organized for collegiate and pre-collegiate competitive levels. After 1908, agricultural students took scores of stock show prizes, until the money won at national exhibits was often sufficient to cover costs of travel and transportation. Local prizes and scholarships engendered competition too.

In these years, student publications flourished. *The Wyoming Student,* which had appeared regularly since 1899, became the *Branding Iron* in 1923, and was supplemented after 1909 by an annual *Wyo,* and from time to time by the publications of an enterprising language club or a writers' association like Quill. The Associated Students of the University of Wyoming was officially founded in 1913.

Through all the academically-oriented activities, students found time to attend an annual series of glittering — or sometimes just light-hearted — balls, dances, and banquets. The traditional Cadet Ball was enhanced by a junior prom after 1911 and the Engineers' Ball after 1916, as well as by numerous imaginative less formal events. Roman banquets and Washington's birthday celebrations called forth imaginative menus and dress. In 1914, Old Main was lit up from outside by student electrical engineers, just two years before its landmark tower was demolished for reasons of safety. By the end of her first quarter century, the University boasted more than 200 alumni, many of whom enthusiastically involved themselves, through Alumni Association and its activities, in campus affairs.

Through the years from 1907-1922, curricular expansion proceeded slowly but steadily. Presidents, working smoothly with the board, seemed keenly aware that small enrollments precluded vast curricular empire-building, and the result was frequently a tightening of the belt in an effort to bring programs up to higher standards and integrity. In 1914, for example, the department of commerce was reorganized to admit no students below the eleventh grade; as a four-year program, then, it provided two years of high school training plus two years of college-level instruction. The decision was in line with criticism of the University as being a mere extended high school. The law school rather tentatively opened its doors in 1920. Still Duniway had recognized that the University was not truly prepared for graduate instruction, and so

the former graduate school, which existed in skeleton form, has not been continued. As students may ask for post-graduate courses, the several departments of the University will endeavor to meet their needs. Usually, however, graduates holding Bachelor's degrees from this University are encouraged to go to larger institutions where graduate schools are fully developed.

More important to the future than the curricular changes for regular students were the enormous efforts concentrated on non-traditional student programs after 1905. Among them, summer school was the most startling success. Directed primarily at teachers and first established (1905) at their behest, summer school enrolled an increasing number of students from throughout the state as the standards for grammar and high school teachers came to demand more and more formal training. The original enrollment of 25 students rose to 307 by 1916, and although the war years somewhat decreased overall attendance, by 1920 there were 353 students enrolled. A similar enormous increase occurred in correspondence study; by 1920, the number of students enrolled in such courses (724) exceeded the number of those working regularly on campus.

A more difficult area and yet one of great promise lay in extension courses. The first formal extension courses were the "short courses" in agriculture, conducted by individuals like Buffum and Wilbur Knight as early as the mid-1890s in various communities around the state. In 1905, the legislature appropriated $2,000 especially for a series of farmers' institutes, some of which were conducted on campus. Demand for extension credit soon embraced many other subjects as well; in 1913-14 Duniway, who took over direction of the extension program himself (relieving a perhaps unenthusiastic June Downey), taught seven different extension courses, presumably in his field of history and political science, in towns as far away as Casper, Douglas, and Sheridan. The war increased enrollment in many off-campus programs; in 1917-18 (Nelson's administration), campus enrollment decreased while correspondence and non-traditional courses leaped forward. Following the Smith-Hughes Act of 1917, the University stepped up its program in teacher training for home economics, agriculture, and mechanical arts. Wyoming's College of Education was designated as the state school in charge, but the paucity of students made teacher training in home economics and industrial arts borderline for federal funds, and no courses in teaching agriculture were ever established because of the "very meager registration."

Men's gym class, c. 1920

From the nature of presidential reports and correspondence, it seems clear that curricular problems were centered in two areas, both of which were concerned with statewide career training and federal funds. Teacher training in Wyoming was a problem from the start. The shortage of teachers throughout the state in the 1890s caused standards for entering the profession to be lax if not non-existent. High school graduates, by passing the simplest of examinations, could proceed straight to the front of the classroom. Only after the turn of the century did the State Department of Education move to place teacher training on a professional level; by 1905, the department began requiring education for teachers beyond the twelfth grade.

The decision to do so greatly enhanced the University's operations. As has been mentioned, summer school was almost exclusively geared to teachers who were required to undergo further training. By 1904, the University responded by revising courses to provide for a "continuous,

well-articulated, and well-graduated line of study." The result was what was then regarded as a combination teachers' college and normal school. Requirements for entry were raised to a standard "practically" the same as that of the liberal arts college; that is, "practically" high school graduation. A two-year "normal school" course prepared some students to teach at the grammar school level; students graduating after two years were granted the bachelor of pedagogy degree, replaced in 1917 by a diploma in elementary education. A four-year course (the equivalent of the teachers' college) granted the degree of B.A. in education, with its graduates trained to teach in high schools throughout the state. The combination of elementary and high school training, reported Otto Gramm to the legislature,

is almost unique and solves a good many of the problems which are pressing upon the normal schools and the colleges of the country. It is a

combination that we have been able to make with very great economy from the fact that the state normal school is part of the state university.

Nevertheless, as late as 1912, only one "professor of education" was listed in the *Bulletin,* with one director of "normal" training.

The increased requirements for professional courses for school teachers issued a challenge to the University in terms of its monopoly on teacher training. For teachers already employed and for prospective teachers unable to move to Laramie during the winter months, correspondence courses, extension training, and summer school helped to meet that challenge. Still, enrollment remained low and the teacher shortage was intense. In 1904, the B.Ped. degree was earned by eleven students — that was more than all other degrees together. In 1921, six diplomas (similar to the old B.Ped. degrees) were granted in elementary and rural education, but no one in that year opted to earn a regular four-year bachelor of arts degree in education.

The acuteness of the teacher shortage led the State Board of Education to attempt to supplement the University's teacher training efforts. By 1917, laws had established "normal" courses in state high schools and commanded the University to give credit for such courses to students entering its own programs. In 1918 came the "threat" of the establishment of a fifth year in all state high schools, to consist strictly of teacher training. In 1919, Nelson feared that separate normal schools would be established elsewhere in the state; indeed, bills were introduced to do so at this and many legislative sessions, but all failed to pass. A jurisdictional struggle in establishing standards emerged between the University on the one hand and the Department of Education on the other. In l921, Nelson reported to the board:

We have upon this campus every facility for teacher training. What we do not have is a sufficient number of students definitely committed to training for teaching . . . I feel that the advocates of an additional Normal School will realize their wish within a very short period of time if we do not at once institute a campaign state-wide for the finding of those who can be

induced to come into residence for teacher training. While perhaps we have in no way been to blame, the truth stares us in the face that the number in training remains unjustifiably small.

During these years, the school of education enhanced its program in teacher training with the addition of a special school for practice teaching. The first three grades were established in the year 1905-06, and others followed, so that grades one through eight were operational by 1914.

This "training school" solved a great University problem, for the former Preparatory School originally attached to the College of Liberal Arts, was eventually transferred to its jurisdiction. For years — and especially by the commission of 1907 — the University had come under criticism for maintaining pre-collegiate courses on campus. High schools so resented the competition that eventually Nelson insisted that the University school accept students only from those communities lacking secondary schools, in order to "remove the criticism that we have continually and more or less justly faced." The legislature resented supporting a University high school, when secondary education was supposedly the fiscal responsibility of the local districts. The transforming of the "Prep" school into a teacher training high school seems to have been Nelson's idea. Even by 1921, the idea was not entirely accepted by the legislature, and Nelson reported that

. . . no one thing connected with the College of Education has developed so much criticism and misunderstanding as our University High School. During the recent session of the Legislature, the mention of a High School upon the University campus drew sharp inquiry or even retort. . . . The existence upon this campus of a grade training school can be justified but only in so far as it serves teacher training. The state naturally assumes no responsibility for the education of Laramie's children as such. The state will support a grade training school to the extent of furnishing the practice teaching, under trained direction.

Still, in the long run the plan proved viable.

Problems in teacher education were infinitely more easily solved than those of the College of Agriculture. During the years after 1907, the enrollment in agriculture remained small while federal funding still provided a great portion of the

University's resources. Personnel conflicts added to the agricultural college's difficulties, as did the complex administration of extension and experimental work. The University's monopoly position in regard to overseeing (and receiving funding for) the statewide Agricultural Extension Service was complicated by a new series of extension plans, both state and federally sanctioned.

In 1912, with the resignation of Merica, the *Farm Journal* especially praised the former president's policies in regard to agriculture. Optimistically, the *Journal* professed that Merica had "found an agricultural college only on paper. He leaves it one in fact." The assertion was bold and not necessarily accurate. Although enrollment in agriculture had increased somewhat over the previous ten-year period, the college still boasted only a handful of students, few of whom actually finished their degrees. In 1908-09, only seven individuals were majoring in agriculture; in 1909, the college awarded no degrees. Two students received the bachelor of science degree in agriculture in 1910, but none did so in the following year. In 1912, three students graduated. To the board, Nelson reported in 1921:

> . . . *Among the criticism made upon us is that, in its present location, very few register or work in Agriculture. While I am absolutely certain that the cause is not due to [the location of the Agriculture College] yet it is a criticism that would be largely shorn of its force if, through the various available channels, primarily personal contact on the part of our Agricultural College and Extension Faculty, a marked increase in registration could be secured. The reckless statement made by some uninformed people to the effect that more students from Albany County were registered at Fort Collins than the entire number enrolled in Agriculture in Laramie of course is not true.*

Still, Nelson was highly optimistic about the future of Wyoming agriculture and the college. "Agriculture in its large aspect — production in all lines (crops and stock) —" he predicted, "will increasingly represent the source of the state's prosperity." He urged the College of Agriculture forward in that "we have not yet measured up to all that may be reasonably expected from us."

Whether or not his prediction proved accurate, the truth was that many farmers' sons in these early years seem to have believed that an ounce of experience in the field was worth a pound of education. To experience in the field — that is, through extension work, farmers' institutes, experimental farms, and the system of county agents — the University came increasingly to devote its efforts. The College of Agriculture on campus remained a comparatively small operation in terms of students enrolled.

At the same time, federal funding for agricultural projects and instruction remained high. The government's money provided direct income for instruction in agriculture, engineering, and certain other fields; for the experiment station; for agricultural extension, including the system of county and home demonstration agents; and for the training of teachers in agricultural, engineering, and home economics.

To its credit, the board exercised more restraint after 1908 in the matter of charging items against federal funds. In 1914, to be sure, the U.S. Bureau of Education disallowed a number of expenses applied against Morrill Act funds — "a crushing blow," Secretary Burrage reported to the newly-elected and yet not installed Duniway — but Duniway was able successfully to defend the expenditures. As state funding and oil revenues increased after 1917, federal funds became a somewhat less dominant feature in University budgeting.

In spite of the Supreme Court decision against the erstwhile Lander Agricultural College in 1907, state legislators often called for relocation of the agricultural college. As Nelson reported to the board in June 1922,

> *The introduction of a bill for the separation of the Agricultural College from the University is a biennial event. I had the opportunity to talk with some of the promoters of the proposition at the time the question was before the Legislature. . . . It seems to me that they fail to recognize that the location of the Agricultural College is in no wise dependent upon the agricultural possibilities inherent in said locality. An Agricultural College is an educational institution, necessitating an administrative force, a faculty, buildings, and equipment. . . . A Government Experiment Station, on the other hand, . . . is not necessarily located in immediate proximity to the College.*

Building construction, College of Agriculture, 1913

The construction of a new College of Agriculture building in 1914 not only raised morale of the faculty but materially decreased the possibility that the college might be relocated elsewhere.

The Agricultural Experiment Station provided a separate but even more complex issue. For decades, citizens in other parts of the state had protested that Laramie's climate, soil, and topography were not typical of Wyoming and that agricultural and stock experiments had best be conducted in other locales. In 1911, legislators who objected to the federal policy of non-support took the bull by the horns and began setting up a series of experimental farms in different regions of the state, all to be governed by the State Board of Farm Commissioners. Within the next few years, state experimental farms were established in Sweetwater, Goshen, Uinta, Laramie, and Sheridan counties, in addition to the horticultural commission station in Lander on acreage rented from the University. The University's experimental farm — located west of Laramie — continued to be supported by federal funds.

The creation of a statewide network of farms administered by a separate authority disturbed University officials. When the first such farms were proposed, Duniway wrote freely to Timothy F. Burke, chairman of the board and by nature the University's foremost lobbyist, of his concerns.

I am fearful lest the raising of the question may produce jealousies, especially among the official circles in Cheyenne. At the same time, I am not satisfied to let the subject alone when they are going ahead to develop competing agencies with special appropriations for the work which the faculty and staff of the agricultural departments of the University ought to be doing. The subject comes up pointedly . . . [in regard to the bill] providing for a state experiment farm to be conducted in Sweetwater County and to be supervised and controlled by the Board of Farm Commissioners. The presentation of this bill, and there will doubtless be others of similar nature, makes me wonder whether the University Board ought to take up the subject actively with the proper committees and with the Governor and the Boards concerned.

"It is the same spirit," Burke responded, "that has suggested the lopping off of the agricultural college and the normal college, etc."

Duniway's concern was shared by Henry G. Knight, dean of the agricultural college and director of the experiment station at Laramie, who (in an undated report to the president) recommended immediate extension of the station's research interests and the cancelling of the Lander lease so the University could begin experiments on that property. "All of the scientific and demonstration work for the state should be centralized in the University," Knight wrote. Duniway went so far as to write the U.S. secretary of agriculture, urging that his department declare its lack of support for the state farm board,

an organization which has a separate state appropriation and is not, in fact, connected with the Agricultural College. Probably at the time cooperative work of this kind was inaugurated, the Agricultural College of the University of Wyoming may not have been in a position to do its part. Circumstances have changed, however, and I believe the time has come when all these agricultural activities in Wyoming should be administered through the Agricultural College no matter in what section of the state the work is to be done.

Secretary of Agriculture D. F. Houston responded cordially but made no commitment.

Duniway was unsuccesful in his campaign, and the Wyoming legislature of 1915 continued to expand the state network of experimental farms. Four years later, however, Nelson was able to persuade the legislature and Governor Robert D. Carey (whose father was a University trustee) to support a consolidation of agricultural work under the supervision of the director of the Agricultural Experiment Station. By legislative enactment in that year, the law of 1911 was repealed and all state experiment farms were transferred to University management. An advisory agricultural board of five members was appointed to assist in administration and policy. The state granted $40,000 for the running of all such enterprises for the next biennial period.

The passage by the U.S. Congress of the Smith-Lever Act (1914) for the establishment of extension service and the system of county agents also enhanced the University's responsibilities and federal financial allocations. Of course by 1914, the University had entered into sundry extension services, not just in agriculture but in all areas. Institutes throughout the state were common, particularly in education and in agriculture. In accordance with a program advanced by H. G. Knight, boys' and girls' agricultural clubs were sponsored; judges were provided at county fairs; prizes were offered for young peoples' achievements in agriculture and home economics; and secondary education in agriculture was encouraged, particularly in rural schools.

The Smith-Lever Act, however, proposed the permanent establishment of county agents to serve as advisers and demonstrators in agriculture and home economics throughout the state and to be supported by a combination of federal, state, and local funds. Knight was delighted, and so of course was Duniway. Clearly, the new program would involve adjustments and problems, but clearly too it would add to the University's prestige. In the legislative session of 1915, Duniway lobbied hard for approval and funding of the Smith-Lever plan. One legislator feared that such county agents might be used as a "political machine." Duniway answered that the danger seemed to him unreal because of "the nature of the University organization and the quality of the educational men who are or will be on our staff." The president wrote,

I start with the assumption that there should be a system of county agents under competent state supervision. That being true, what state agency would be less likely than the University to be influenced by political considerations or to be subjected to political dominations? The University Board is non-partisan. Its members are appointed for six years by successive governors. They are not subjected to political pressure by the immediate presence and participation in their business of any politically elected officers. The State Superintendent of Public Instruction is an ex-officio member but without the right to vote. . . . is there any form of state wide organization than the University with its constitutional status and with the absence of politically elected officers in its membership?

That the president was politically effective is demonstrated by the legislature's approval of the Smith-Lever system and its authorization of the University trustees to administer it. An annual $8,000 plus increments was appropriated by the state to match county money (within certain limits) at the rate of $2 for every one. Federal funding was assured. Although only two county agents were operative in the first year, by 1917 Duniway was able to report that all but five counties were by then involved in the enterprise.

The counterposition of agricultural college, agricultural experiment stations, and agricultural extension service necessarily caused considerable administrative turmoil and uncertainty. J. D. Towar had been appointed director of the station by the Gramm and Hebard board in the midst of the formal investigation of 1907. Only a year later, however, Merica as new president recommended that Towar not be reappointed, "giving his reasons for his decision and these were approved by the board." To replace Towar as head of the college and the experiment station, Merica promoted Henry G. Knight, a chemist, whose keen thinking and hard-working service did the agricultural college proud. Knight became Wyoming's first academic dean. He and Merica worked together well as good friends and colleagues.

With the introduction of agricultural extension under the Smith-Lever Act, administration became more complex. From the first, Knight indicated uncertainty about the extension service administration and wrote to Duniway that this was "a serious matter and should be given first consideration." Duniway recommended that for the first year A. E. Bowman, who had joined the faculty in 1913, become director of extension under Knight's supervision. Bowman proved himself and became permanent director of extension work. In 1917, Knight resigned and A. D. Faville, who had been second in command of both the College of Agriculture and the experiment station, took his place.

Becoming president with an intimate knowledge of both agriculture and the extension service, Nelson was more aware than his predecessors of internal problems that existed. As a botanist, his ideas by no means always coincided with those of the College of Agriculture faculty and deans, for Nelson frequently lauded the benefits of raising crops as opposed to grazing cattle. Perhaps he remembered his Iowa upbringing; in any case, he regarded farming as supplying a type of life and social milieu far superior to that of bronc-busting and stock herding.

Nelson's personal convictions may have influenced his relations with the College of Agriculture and engendered hostility and misunderstandings. In December 1921, he recommended that the College of Agriculture and the experiment station become administratively separate entities. The board took his recommendation under advisement, but in executive session (that is, without the attendance of the president, hired officials, and other ex-officio members) voted to consult with Washington as to what changes "would be desirable" in the agricultural college and the extension service as well. By March 1922, the chief of the Office of Experiment Stations in Washington reported that he preferred to see the deanship of agriculture and directorship of the experiment station remain in the hands of one individual. In executive session, the board debated many hours and finally decided by a vote of 4-2 to follow Washington's advice. At the same time the trustees appointed two of their number as a committee "to suggest ways and means of improving the College of Agriculture." The committee recommended some reorganization of assignments. In 1921, because of a reduced appropriation, Bowman was asked to simplify and reorder the extension service as well.

In 1922, then, the previous organization of agricultural sciences at the University still maintained. Faville was dean of the College of Agriculture although he was to resign at the end of the academic year. The college listed a "resident division," consisting of instruction in agriculture and home economics; the experiment station, directed also by Faville; and an extension division, headed by Bowman.

Meanwhile, Nelson's administration was marked by an extraordinary situation: the country's involvement in World War I. Thanks to inflation, oil, and an enhanced financial position, the University was able to survive the nineteen months of U.S. participation in the war with a minimum of difficulty.

Of course, a certain amount of temporary disruption was inevitable. In the president's report for 1916-17 (presumably prepared by both outgoing and incoming chief executives), the reaction to the declaration of war was said

> *to produce a feeling of unsettlement and disorganization among faculty and students. All wished to be of help in the national emergency. A certain number of the young men proceeded immediately to go into military and naval service. Others took examinations for commissions in the Reserve Corps. Women became active in relief work including Red Cross activities, and engaged seriously in first aid work. When Officers' Training Camps were announced, a generous number of young men in proportion to our numbers promptly applied for admission and mostly were accepted. . . . Student organizations in various ways promptly demonstrated their appreciation of the situation. They abandoned announced plans for formal social functions and greatly curtailed informal affairs of this kind. The young men discontinued spring athletics in order to devote more time to military training, cadet officers volunteering to give special aid to the commandant.*

The faculty voted to grant credits to students of satisfactory scholarship if they withdrew to enter military service or to take up work in agriculture in response to the government's fears of a food crisis. During the course of the war, eight faculty members entered government or military service. Faculty and students alike volunteered for Red Cross work, for YMCA activities, and donated heavily to the campaigns for liberty bonds. As representative of the Woman's Liberty Loan Committee, Hebard stumped the state to raise bond money. Thurman Arnold, S. H. Knight, H. C. Dale, and Ralph McWhinnie toured with an army tank in the same cause.

Various courses and curricula were changed to accord with the war effort. In early 1918, in accordance with a recommendation from the National Security League, the political science department began offering a new course in international politics since 1900. A war emergency course in foods was made compulsory for all women students. A school for nurses at Ivinson hospital, for a time affiliated with the University, began but did not endure. A class was offered in "Trench French." Various curricular changes were announced by the military department. A "radio-buzzer" school functioned for a few months. Military classes were particularly well attended, and extra drill hours were carried by all men students without complaint.

In June 1918, Nelson reported to the board that

A degree of seriousness and earnestness has been imparted to the scholastic atmosphere by the patriotic desire to prepare for whatever service the nation may require. From among the college prepared folks have been drawn in very large measure those who give directions to the affairs of the nation in this crisis and those who hold the commissions in our armies. The University of Wyoming has been doing its best.

Indeed, a spirit of sacrifice, unity, and hard work seemed to prevail.

In the summer of 1918, Nelson contracted for a unit of the Students' Army Training Corps, in the number of 250 men, to enroll on campus. Perhaps the most difficult immediate problem caused by the war was the need to feed and house these young men. Drawing on the example of Fort Collins facilities, which several representatives had inspected, the board authorized the construction of a mess hall and decided to use the gymnasium, the basement of the agriculture building, and several available fraternity houses for sleeping quarters.

Scarcely had these arrangements been completed when armistice was signed. It was a matter of considerable disappointment to the University administration that almost all of the SATC students opted to drop out of school without finishing their courses when the corps was demobilized in December 1918. In hopes of persuading them to stay, the administration called a special meeting — at which, commented the student newspaper sarcastically, Justus Soule's was the only speech to emphasize "other advantages than the pure material" — but to no avail. The inevitable decline in enrollment was only a temporary manifestation, and numbers shortly built up again.

Still, the war may be debited with a number of undesirable consequences. For one thing, the University's courses in the German language were dropped for the year 1919. Nelson conveyed to the board with a no recommendation a petition he had received from "citizens of this state" recommending that instruction in German be eliminated, and the board opted to do so, primarily for political reasons.

While some members of the board were of the opinion that it should be possible for students to study German in the University, yet it was the sense of the Board that owing to the status of public opinion it might do the University more arm than good to make it possible for the few who wished to study German to have classes in the same in the University of Wyoming.

Consequently, German classes were cut from the curriculum "until a Treaty of Peace shall have been signed between the United States, the Allies, and Germany," with unfortunate effect on Mabelle R. McVeigh, teacher of German in the Preparatory School, who had quickly to brush up on French. Teaching of German resumed in 1921.

In the autumn of 1918, the widespread influenza epidemic closed the University's classrooms for several weeks. The basement of the agriculture building was set up as "detention quarters" to which all students feeling symptoms were urged to report, pending improvement or hospitalization. Instruction was resumed, at Nelson's recommendation, by November 7.

Finally, the University was ill-equipped and poorly organized to meet the post-war influx of students seeking strictly vocational training. As late as 1922, Nelson reported to the board that the program for former service men, in a stage of "development" for two years, was still barely off the ground. "The work can scarcely be said to have flourished," he told the board, and

> *much unfavorable comment has come to us because of this fact. The Federal representatives in the state as well as our own local business men felt for a time that we were not using due diligence in providing the type of instruction which should prevail in what must be essentially a trades school. It is to be remembered that the purpose of this rehabilitation training is not to provide a college education for these men but rather to prepare them, in as short a time as possible, to become self-supporting citizens by fitting them for some one occupation.*

For incoming veterans, interested in career education, one counselor had been appointed after another. But registration continued (in Nelson's word) "unstable," and many students complained of unsympathetic treatment and lack of courses adapted to their career-oriented needs. By the end of 1921, it seemed necessary to rejuvenate the program or to cancel it. It is perhaps typical of Nelson that he viewed its continuation as a "duty" and part of the University's service to government and state. He summoned a special committee to reorganize courses and establish new ones along vocational lines. When even this did not bring much progress, he isolated the problem as one of administration; he thought that the several faculty administrators were clearly unenthusiastic if not obstructionist in regard to the program. Nelson's answer was to centralize responsibility in the hands of Professor Philo Hammond as "Acting Director of Vocational Work." At the time, the president anticipated further reorganization — perhaps establishment of an actual state trades school. Such an institution never developed as veterans' demands soon leveled off.

In spite of the inevitable ups and downs, the University operated remarkably well under the administrations of Merica, Duniway, and Nelson. All these presidents, in particular, seem to have worked well with faculty and earned the respect of their colleagues on campus. Of course personnel problems occasionally arose, and these were generally handled by presidents with the backing of the board. Sometimes a faculty member was not recommended for reappointment, but these occasions were by no means frequent, and in all cases

seemed to have centered around special conduct of the individual concerned. On several occasions, heads of departments who were functioning poorly in respect to their peers were requested to step down, and usually they did. Trustees seem to have leaned over backwards to accommodate faculty members, as for example in granting of a leave of absence with fractional pay to a professor of whom it was understood "that at the end of this year his connection with the university will be severed."

The greatest difficulties within the faculty occurred in a quarrel between several members of the College of Engineering, or as Nelson put it to the board, the "lack of harmony between the different divisions . . . [which] resulted in an unfortunate incident on registration day which had caused him to write a letter to the various professors in this college." The board solved the problem, at Nelson's recommendation, by dissolving the separate College of Engineering and placing its faculty under the dean of the College of Agriculture (then the "College of Agriculture and Mechanic Arts"), although "it feels impelled to say that it is not pleased with the evidence of personal antagonism which is inconsistent with the spirit of true scholarship." The independence of the college was restored two years later when one of the professors involved duly resigned. Similarly, in 1917, Nelson reported on the "inability or the unwillingness" of the home economics department to cooperate with the extension program, but the problem was solved when the head of home economics resigned her position.

Meanwhile, Duniway and Nelson in particular lent their support to plans for salary adjustments, fringe benefits, and eventually faculty participation in University governance. In 1913, 1914, and 1915, Duniway lobbied with the board for faculty salary increases. With a slight surplus in the faculty salary funds as of June 1913, he recommended that full professors be moved to $2,200. A year later he reported that the salary of professors (especially those on the payroll for a number of years) was $400-$900 lower than in other Western states.

> *If we seek to do justice to the older members of the faculty who have given consecrated service to the University; if we heed the dictates of good policy in establishing the standard of remuneration sufficient to attract and retain talent of a*

88

high order; if we seek merely to meet the competitive conditions prevailing in our neighboring sister states, we must endeavor to raise the maximum of a professor to at least $2,500 just as rapidly as financial resources will permit.

The president did not immediately achieve his aim, for when in December 1914 the board instructed him to increase salaries as funds permitted, the building program was devouring most of the University's income. In 1915, salaries for full professors were raised only to $2,300 and $2,400, with "moderate" increases established at other levels. Although the president managed to gain board acceptance for the principle of sabbatical leaves, such leaves were to carry only such pay as was available after a substitute had been hired.

It was Nelson who faced the most difficult task yet he who accomplished most for the faculty. Following the wartime mustering of enthusiasm, unity, and self-sacrifice, the postwar years brought about a disintegration in spirit and intensity. Nelson called the year 1919

the most unusual in the history of the institution. In common with every other college and university, we have had the problems of the reconstruction period. The spirit of unrest has dominated the entire social fabric of the nation . . . The high cost of living has had as its twin problem the general discontent arising out of a mental attitude most difficult to explain. There had developed during the war period a high sense of duty and responsibility which apparently was replaced after the armistice by a relapse into irresponsibility and indifference as marked as had been the higher attributes during the period that "world ideals" dominated. . . . It has required no end of patience and forbearance to keep faculties and employees in such a frame of mind as to secure a reasonable measure of cooperation and a fair and continuing attention to the daily tasks and to the problems that are dependent upon well co-ordinated team work.

As a longtime faculty member himself, Nelson was particularly well equipped to cope with his colleagues' discontent. In 1919, he made an effort to increase salaries, adjusting them twice during the year in "relationship to services rendered and responsibility assumed." The following year, Nelson raised the issue with trustees again, and having no response after his efforts in June, he spoke even more firmly in July.

The president is charged with the responsibility for a satisfactory faculty. . . . The minds distracted by the cares incident to less than a living wage or even by the thought that they are earning far less than they might elsewhere are not the minds of those who will render notable service. We cry contentment, but there is no contentment. We say "forget it," but they are not allowed to forget their bills. I do not willingly harrass you with this question again, but if no action is taken now, we shall go into the new academic year in September with the very framework of our faculty organization broken down.

The president won his point, and although certain "inequalities" remained, he was able to report later that year that salary increases had "improved the morale and . . . tended to minimize the dissatisfaction that was so strikingly evident in the earlier part of the year."

In 1921, Nelson began his mid-year report to the board with a long discussion of faculty and its importance as "the heart of the university." He lectured trustees on faculty ranks, on men and women faculty, on relative responsibility, and on deanships. He called the board's attention to the functions of deans in agriculture, education, and (projected) engineering, as compared to those of executive dean of the College of Liberal Arts and the deans of men and women. Having explained the faculty and administrative structure, Nelson moved in his next report (of June 1922) to recommend a scale of minimum and maximum salaries for faculty ranks and increased salaries for deans. Again he spoke strongly of the plight of professors, who did not receive substantial raises at a time when "it seemed necessary to think first of instructors and others who were receiving the minimum wage." Inflation caused the lowest paid group to need help "in order that they might even exist." Although inflation was hard on the faculty, Nelson was able to adjust only a few salaries upward.

In his efforts to aid professors, the president was firmly backed by a special and startling report devised by the Rotary and Lions clubs of Cheyenne, published in 1921:

In the matter of salaries paid professors and instructors we [the investigating committees of the above organizations] found the average scale

to be from twenty-five to thirty-three and one-third per cent below salaries paid in educational institutions in the immediately surrounding states. We found that the salaries had been raised only to the extent of about thirty percent since 1913 and an average of about ten percent since the commencement of the war. . . . The salary scale has naturally lost to the University many of its best men and women instructors within the last three or four years. . . . and in this connection your Committee wants to call attention to the spirit of self-sacrifice and self-denial shown by some of the present members of the faculty, who have placed patriotic duty above self-service, who have stood by the University through stress and storm, and who have disregarded every temptation to seek more lucrative fields of effort.

The report especially named Nelson, Soule, Hebard, and Downey. It proposed that oil royalties be released from restrictions and admitted for use as operating expenses.

Even more than Duniway, Nelson was aware of possibilities of faculty self-governance. In 1917, while he was still acting president, he petitioned the board to give the faculty "a voice in appointments and dismissals of its members." With this end, he recommended establishment of a faculty advisory committee to work with the president on personnel and related matters. Trustees considered and then approved the election of such a committee of five individuals from the faculty.

In 1920, Nelson called the attention of the board to possibilities of a pension system and a workmen's compensation scheme. In 1921, he reported on the need to pay railroad fares (which he estimated generally as about half the out-of-pocket expense) of faculty members attending national professional meetings. Nelson also got the board's approval for faculty members to receive compensation for consultative and other outside employment, so long as this may not "curtail in some degree the efficiency" of their employment or in any way threaten the institution's reputation.

Nelson might well have been proud of his accomplishments, but by 1922, he was more than ready to retire from the presidency and return to his positions in the botany department and as curator for his beloved herbarium. As early as December 1919 (only eighteen months after he had become permanent president), and again each subsequent year, he had in his self-deprecating manner

suggested that trustees consider returning him to his teaching and research. It is likely that he had assumed the presidency more from a sense of duty than from great enthusiasm. As administrator, he was less popular than as teacher and botanist; he was "part poet," one student reported, a "great teacher" but an "indifferent administrator." His stern Methodism may have told against him with a student body more prone to festivity than to decorum. There are indications that some faculty were restive too, and in the spring of 1921, a group seems to have protested some of Nelson's policies to the board.

Although Nelson retained strong support from Trustee (and former governor) Joseph M. Carey and from Carey's son Robert, then governor — the Careys were old family friends — his relationship with certain other board members became less happy as the years went by. In 1920, Nelson took it upon himself (in his annual report that July) to write a long analysis of ideal relations between trustees, president, and faculty, as quoted primarily from the American Association of University Professors. Faculty, he said, provides curriculum content and offers instruction; the president selects faculty and develops general academic policy; and the board selects the president and occupies itself with financial affairs. Some question may have arisen in regard to Nelson's consultation with his faculty advisory committee, for the president defended the committee and its role throughout this report. The old presidential-board disputes about administrative jurisdiction seemed to be recurring.

As before, Nelson proposed that the board reassign him to botany.

That you have deemed me worthy to serve in an executive capacity fills my cup of happiness to the brim, but I want to be sane enough to know and big enough to feel and to say that my personal ambitions and desire must be wholly forgotten in the large problems we are collectively called upon to solve. . . . When the time comes, whether it be sooner or later, that some one with larger vision, with greater ability to bring things to pass becomes available, I want you to feel absolutely free to restore me to my department position. . . .

Picnic trip, 1919

In executive session, trustees considered his suggestion and rejected it, agreeing that

> *the best interests of the University would not be served by any consideration or discussion of Dr. Nelson's successor at this time. We believe Dr. Nelson should have a free hand in organizing and carrying out his plans for 1920-1921, . . . We found Dr. Nelson's position eminently fair and that his first interest is the welfare of the University.*

That year or the next, according to Roger L. Williams, UW history professor, in the biography *Aven Nelson of Wyoming,* a volume that liberally utilizes Nelson's private papers, the president was disturbed by the "falsification of the Minutes," apparently those of a board meeting, although the episode remains obscure and the date unstated. Nelson was clearly upset, for he reported later to the full board that he had tried hard

> *to prevent becoming embittered or suspicious . . . since that time I have tried to "carry on"*

and to treat the two men involved as friends just as if nothing had ever happened.

Again in March 1921, the president submitted his annual request for reassignment or a vote of confidence.

> *If . . . you believe that the University's welfare will best be promoted by continuing me in my present position, I shall appreciate more than I can tell you the vote of confidence that would be implied in my reelection today [March 22, 1921] for the year 1921-22. Such action would give me renewed courage and inspiration. . . . I have strength for anything that may lie just ahead, if your strength becomes mine through my being permitted to feel that you are unitedly with me. I covet services in harmony with your kindly counsel. May I know today your plans for me?*

Painting and drawing class, fine arts department, c. 1920

The elaborate resolution of the trustees is in itself an indication that troubles were looming. They resolved that the president continue in office and that

> *Dr. Nelson as president be directed to exercise all that authority given him under the law as chief executive officers, and all powers, responsibilities and duties usually pertaining to the position; [and] . . . that the Board of Trustees, recognizing his high integrity and deep interest in the University, pledge to Dr. Nelson as President their cooperation and support both in letter and spirit.*

Such cooperation was surely lacking, however; Nelson discovered in December 1921 that the trustees' president and acting secretary (since Burrage's resignation) were for unknown reasons making copies of his confidential reports on personnel matters. It seems likely that former board President Hamilton stood at the center of trustee opposition to the president.

In early 1922, Nelson made several controversial decisions that apparently split board and faculty alike. He proposed to separate the Agricultural Experiment Station from the deanship of agriculture; the board debated hotly and turned the suggestion down, but A. D. Faville was permitted (probably under pressure) to resign from the joint position. Williams has found indications that Nelson also sought to reassess the position of football coach John Corbett, who had become a powerful and independent campus figure.

Thereafter the president submitted his resignation once more, clearly with the knowledge that it would be accepted, the understanding that "it is now the wish of this Board to take up my standing suggestion that I be relieved from the responsibilities of the presidency and that I resume my former place in the Department of Botany." A gentleman to the core, he chose not to mention differences.

Instead he wrote:

In the two and a half years since [1920] not only my willingness but my desire to be returned to the Department of Botany has been kept before you. In the nature of things a long administration is impossible in my case. . . . Many pieces of research and publication were first interrupted by the war and then by the duties to which you called me. My ambitions are not diminished. I am keenly eager to round out my botanical career by some teaching in these riper years, and by the publication of papers now on file and nearly complete. . . .

And further:

The past five years have been years of unremitting responsibility but the cares and anxieties have been shared by so 'many — by members of the Board, by faculty members and by students as well as by hundreds of friends in this city and in the state — that the load has been halved and the joy doubled. This being so, I rejoice in the experience that has been mine. . . . I shall continue to pray that an overruling Providence may minimize the effects of my failures and may somehow bring this institution, into which most of my life has gone, into an ever enlarging service for the state and for humanity.

The board's response was to grant Nelson a leave of absence, which he was finally able to take only when the new president was in place. Traveling around the West with his wife, he was notified to his delight and satisfaction that he had been officially appointed ''president emeritus.'' In its citation, trustees wrote that he had

served this University in various capacities from the infancy of the institution, in all of which he has succeeded to a high degree . . . his industry, his patience and his scholarship were controlling factors in carrying the University of Wyoming through the World War and the reconstruction period thereafter to its present success . . . The Board . . . appreciate more fully than we can express his splendid loyalty and labors; that we extend to him our sincere wishes for a continued pleasant relationship upon his return to his former position as Professor of Botany; that we bespeak for him and Mrs. Nelson a long and happy life and all the joy and satisfaction which come from real service and the knowledge of a duty well done.

Privately, Robert Carey wrote Nelson less happily.

It has taken me four years to find out what was wrong with the University, and I wish that I could be in the office for another four years if for no other reason than an opportunity to straighten out matters in connection with that Institution. The trouble with the University has been that there has always been interference by certain members of the Board of Trustees, and no institution can be run under dual management.

The last years of Nelson's presidency, then, harked back to the difficulties that had arisen between presidents and boards previous to the Merica and Duniway administrations. Nevertheless, the years had brought progress. The University had made it through the war with few scars. Prosperity had brought some flexibility in solving its financial problems, and campus had seen three administrators who were keen, sensitive, and at least ready to define the problems. New programs had been instituted, primarily out in the state. Income increased, and enrollment, recovering from the war years, moved slowly upward. The University of 1922 was looking to the future.

Vedauwoo pageant, experimental dance theatre, 1924

THEATER

ll the world's a stage, and all the men and women of the University of Wyoming's early years enjoyed theatricals as much as any other extracurricular fun. The two literary societies (the Lowell and the Olympic), founded almost as early as the University, served partly as reading and discussion groups, partly as debate clubs, but partly, too, as a source of amateur theatricals. Before the turn of the century, the Olympic had produced *She Stoops to Conquer* and *The Rivals,* ambitious undertakings indeed. Alpha Omega sorority (later to become affiliated with national Pi Beta Phi) did the latter again in 1908, with Mabelle Land DeKay directing. Thereafter campus saw *Midsummer Night's Dream* and *Arms and the Man* as well as *Merchant of Venice* (F. S. Burrage acted Shylock) and the Gilbert and Sullivan operetta *The Mikado.* In 1914, a pageant of Greek life and legend was presented by the Pi Phis, who persuaded Justus Soule to deliver an appropriate lecture beforehand. Most of these dramatic efforts were designed by organizations for their financial benefit through ticket sales.

The most ambitious early dramatic undertaking — rated a financial success, thanks to a contribution from trustees — was the pageant of *Veedauwoo,* written, directed and supervised by Mrs. DeKay in 1924. A kind of allegory, the four-part pageant traced the development of Wyoming from the origins of time to the founding of the University, through days of Indians, pioneers, and cowboys. The epic-style plot dealt with the wooing of Miss Wyoming, daughter of Teton, the god of the mountains, by the earthbound Veedauwoo, who finds her soul rich and beautiful. A cast of more than 65 sang, danced, and recited against the background of the dramatic rock formations east of town. Mrs. DeKay sent out calls for scarves and formal gowns, but it is uncertain whether she found the live meadowlark and bluebird that she hoped to include in the pageantry. The music department prepared genuine native American music to accompany the first acts; and Leona Gage, dancing the character of Fire Flame atop a rock, 200 feet above the audience, was provided with a rope safety strapped around her waist. The rope was held by her husband Jack (later Wyoming governor) from an invisible spot behind her.

In spite of the fact that weather caused the postponement of the pageant by a week and that during the performance it was ''more like November than June,'' the pageant was viewed by 1,500 people, who agreed with the *Boomerang* that it was ''a wonderful conception'' and an ''extraordinary event.'' Viewers commented on the startling effects of a beautiful Wyoming sunset, against which the last act was performed. Reviewers later lauded the ''presiding genius of the author, her tireless industry, her inexhaustible

Vedauwoo pageant, experimental dance theatre, 1924

patience, her intense faith in what she was trying to accomplish, and her abundance of resourcefulness and courage seldom matched.''

Courage may have been less essential, but resourcefulness was always necessary in the many future productions — too many to list here — that came to be part of campus life. Memorable performances were recorded by students, faculty members, and townspeople. After 1947, dramatic endeavors were directed by Richard Dunham and enhanced by the costumes designed by Charles M. Parker. Not until 1951 did Dunham organize a special department of speech and theater, which formalized the long-successful dramatic endeavors on the University of Wyoming campus. Later, these two divided and theater joined dance as a department.

Chapter Six

Crane, Building, and the Depression, 1922-1941

inancing the University was a major concern during the 1920s and 1930s, especially during the depression years, a period in which progress was temporarily halted and cutbacks in University operations were inevitable. During the years of A. G. Crane's tenure as president, a building program that would have delighted the heart of former President Merica took shape and rock was quarried for the construction of seven major campus projects. Such construction seemed the core of the new president's program. His policies in financial regards stood well with board and legislature, at least until the last few years of his tenure in office. Crane was less successful in his relations with faculty and students, and several times he plunged into controversy.

Arthur Griswold Crane was elected president of the University on the first ballot taken by the board in August 1922, after one of the most thorough searches the trustees had yet conducted. They had heard reports of a sub-committee, met with the governor, and interviewed a number of candidates. Major Crane — for he had held that military rank in a Washington, D.C. job during World War I — held a Ph.D. in education and came to Wyoming after having served as president of two state teachers' colleges (North Dakota and Pennsylvania). He worked well enough with the board to be granted a three-year contract the following spring at $8,000 a year, with prescribed $1,000 annual increments. In 1926, the board proffered another three-year contract, this time at $10,000 per year with $500 increments annually, but (perhaps with thoughts that he might move) Crane would only sign for twelve months. A few years later when the president received an offer of $12,000 from the University of Nebraska, the board countered with a year's contract at the offered salary and gave him a $2,500 bonus in addition.

Crane himself took an ever-active part in financial planning, budgeting, and campaigning for the University, primarily in constant efforts to enhance funding, in particular for the building program. Although it is difficult to assess his relationships with the governors who marched in and out of the state house in these years, it is clear that politics in the legislature was Crane's personal bag. More than most presidents before him — with the possible exception of Merica — he took the legislative program into his own hands. Not only did he (as in the past) forbid any University employee from approaching the legislature without special permission, but he clearly thought of himself as director of the campaigns.

Judging by the material left in the University archives, legislative matters took up a vast amount of Crane's time and attention. Once the budget was formulated as indicated above, Crane set up a series of conferences throughout the state with businessmen, legislators, political leaders, and the press. Material was mailed to University alumni. He made it a point to accumulate a careful directory of legislators, involving not just a card file of names but an analysis of background, position, party, and any ties with the University, whether son, daughter, or wife might be a graduate of the institution. He went to great lengths to provide interesting entertainment and programs for visiting legislators or committees on campus. Reams of supportive documents — literally hundreds of pages — were gathered in reports from deans and departments, sometimes 25 or more pages on each division. Special problems were tackled with pages of tables and statistics — for example, the use of space in buildings (thirteen pages, 1929), or surveys on such matters as telephone use or per student costs. Sometimes materials were organized by topics of importance; sometimes "briefs" were composed justifying the University's position on particular bills — all carefully bound like legal documents in light blue paper. In 1933, the president sent his published ten-year report to all 89 members of the legislature; such massive mailings were the rule rather than the exception.

Documents indicate that Crane kept careful track of the progress of all legislation that might affect the University even indirectly. Laden with statistics compiled by E. O. Fuller and Fay Smith, he appeared regularly before such important committees as appropriations. His activities at one point reached such a peak that rumors flew as to the University's undue influence in lobbying. In 1929, both he and W. C. Bond, then president of the board, were called in by the president of the senate and accused of so influencing Senator H. H. Horton (Albany County) as to cause an impasse in the organization of senate committees. Crane and Bond insisted that

it was the set policy of the University officials not to concern themselves with any legislative matters of organization or in the passage or repeal of any bills not directly affecting the University or education. This policy of refraining from the use of University influence in any legislative matters not directly affecting the University has been followed steadfastly for the past ten years. At times it has been embarrassing to refuse help and assistance to friends of education who asked help on their own bills or in their own controversies.

Crane benefited from the assistance of the accomplished staff that Nelson and his predecessors had set into action. Throughout his years, E. O. Fuller operated as fiscal agent; a hardworking, meticulous man, Fuller was responsible for much of the smooth running of the financial edifice. In 1926, when the board set up a committee to evaluate the University's administrative efficiency, it was Fuller who did the lion's share of the careful and thorough report. The resultant board resolution proposed only minor changes and had nothing but praise for Fuller himself.

In its transition from the status of a small University to a larger one, the present set-up of administrative organization is operating admirably and without confusion. . . . The committee . . . recommends that the Board allow no proposal of economy to induce them to dispense

with those services of the Fiscal Agent that have come to do with the safeguarding of the University's use of its lands and incomes. The Committee desires to commend Dr. Crane for the splendid prestige of the University he has established throughout the state and for the effective way in which he had assumed the duties of business administrator, publicity agent, educational director, and legislative pleader for the University. We commend his efforts and achievements to the Board. . . .

These were the long years of the tenure of Fay Smith as board secretary, and one senses the power he drew around him and the confidence the board apparently placed in his judgments. Ralph E. McWhinnie supervised operations as registrar; Nellis Corthell was attorney; W. A. Hitchcock and William Dubois were University architects. In 1938, the board appointed a superintendent of buildings and grounds in order to relieve Fuller of these chores.

Meantime, the handling of many issues became routine. The board met quarterly except for special problem sessions. Monthly, the executive committee approved interim expenses, appointments, and other matters, postponing major decisions until board meetings. President, fiscal agent, and secretary presented formal, written reports on the occasion of all meetings. In calculating budgets, the financial office devised forms to be sent to each dean and department head asking estimates of "essential" and "desirable" items for the next fiscal year and calling for a tabulation of actual expenses during the past several budget periods. President and deans conferred in an effort to fit requirements into available moneys, as estimated primarily by Fuller's office. Every March, the trustees debated a tentative budget, detailed enough so the president could notify faculty of reappointments and salary scales. In June, the final budget was acted upon.

Over the course of these years, efforts were made to streamline financial processes. In 1925, when the assistant state budget officer "made several constructive suggestions and criticisms for the betterment of both academic and business operations," the University administration could accommodate the suggestions and pride itself on general high marks in financial administration.

The early 1920s for the University were years of relative prosperity. Oil royalties on University lands varied greatly from month to month but continued to pour in. According to Fuller — whose office handled all business concerning lands and their income — oil royalties on the Big Muddy and Rock Creek tracts amounted to nearly a quarter of a million dollars in fiscal year 1921, although they decreased to $116,000 the following year; between 1924 and 1928, they varied from $97,000-$128,000 annually. By board ruling, these royalties were preserved in the University Permanent Land Fund, of which only the income was used for operating expenses. By the end of June 1922, this fund totalled more than $1 million, and of course it continued to increase. Annual income from the investment of this fund stood at $56,000 in fiscal year 1924-25 and $82,000 in 1928-29. In 1925, Fuller estimated that these University lands were worth $1.3 million. The University continued to benefit from its share of the "omnibus" and agricultural land income funds, but since no oil discoveries were involved, these funds only yielded $23,000-$30,000 in interest per year. Such amounts were applied to operating expenses throughout the 1920s, as was the standard three-eighths mill tax levy authorized by the legislature ($166,000 in 1924-25; $147,000 in 1928-29; but varying highly in accordance with property evaluations).

Meanwhile, the University's share of public-land oil royalties that the federal government returned to the state of Wyoming continued to provide a financial boon. In 1921, the legislature had authorized ten percent of the state's federal royalties for University use with an upper limit of $375,000 per annum. Moreover, it had agreed to preserve such funds for use in capital construction and building only. Federal oil royalties were simply combined with the state-authorized one-eighth mill tax levy that was set aside for building purposes; this fund came to be known as the University Building Improvement Fund. Its continued replenishment was challenged in 1923, when what Crane called a "highly organized powerful highway lobby" proposed to divert the University's share of federal oil royalties to the construction of roads. Crane lobbied vigorously.

Time and again the issue hung in the balance, the bill endorsed twice by the Senate Committee gave all the University's share to the highways. Friends of the University owe a debt of gratitude to its stalwart friends in the legislature of 1923 and outside in the third house. . . .

Eventually he was successful, but the board had to agree to some compromises. Only nine percent of the federal oil royalties were to be assigned to University permanent construction, and never more than $360,000 per fiscal year. Amounts in excess had to be placed in the University Permanent Land Fund, where only interest could be used — a transfer occurred in fiscal year 1924-25, when oil royalties attained a peak. As part of the deal, the legislature revised the one-eighth mill building levy to permit its use for current operating expenses.

Two years later, the decision to apply federal oil royalties to permanent construction only — a decision dear to the heart of Crane, whose ambitions centered around campus building — was challenged in a legislature which found itself shouldered with payment of considerable University operating expense. In 1925, senators from Sheridan and Thermopolis, with the strong support of their Casper colleagues, introduced several bills which would cause the University to apply its share of federal royalties to regular operating costs. Crane was once more at work and on the defensive. These bills, he reported to the board,

are a threat at the very life of the institution. If carried as they now stand, the institution will have to close many of its departments. Besides this it will mean a complete cessation of its building program. . . . We have very sound but unattractive arguments that this is an unsound policy to use in expending these royalties. We have the further argument that if Wyoming ever expects to get a standard University now is her opportunity and probably the only opportunity she will have in a century. . . . I wish to urge, with all the force at my command, that the conversion of this oil royalty fund to current expenses is bad financing, breaks faith with the Federal Government, and absolutely dooms Wyoming's hope of securing a standard University within the period of our lifetimes.

Crane won his way and the bills were defeated, but by 1924-25 the boom had faded, and the president was speaking in terms of the need for "all possible economy" and extreme budgetary caution.

Strict economy was easier said than accomplished, and many problems plagued Crane, Fuller, and Smith. For one thing, income for operating expenses varied enormously from year to year,

Board of Trustees, 1927

depending on the assessed property valuation throughout the state; the generosity of a fiscally conservative legislature; and to a lesser extent on the volume of the University Permanent Land Fund (composed of oil revenues from University lands), interest from which was applied to operating expenses. Drops in income were difficult to anticipate: In 1925-26, for example, the three-eighth mill tax provided $30,000 less than originally estimated, but the interest from the University Permanent Land Fund brought in $4,000 more than anticipated. A 1931 statement (probably devised by Fuller) indicates that receipts were more often over than under estimated, while expenditures often exceeded the annual budget.

Having deliberately placed the major part of its revenues beyond reach for operating purposes, the administration often found itself in a tight bind when it came to meeting everyday bills. In an effort to increase mill-levy revenue for annual expenses, the board in 1926 mounted a campaign for the collection of delinquent taxes. Three years later, it criticized the state's investment policies for the low rate of return on permanent funds. Still, it could hardly avoid borrowing money to cover vouchers on a short-term basis, a policy that Crane defended.

Running on close margins with revenue dependent upon irregular tax collections has at times required loans from the banks to maintain cash payments on monthly vouchers, but never at any time in the decade [1922-1932] have there been actual operating deficits when bills have been met and income due been collected. The legislature has never been called upon to appropriate for a deficit. When the small size of Wyoming's population and assessed valuation is considered, it is remarkable that a respectable University has been possible with such low per capita tax for higher education.

ALUMNI

n 1922, an energetic Samuel H. Knight gathered a handful of husky students and willing alumni together and all labored mightily to finish constructing the bleachers on old Corbett field in time for a special football game. Knight had sold seats at $10 each to all comers, but the amount earned failed to meet the costs of the project, so "Doc" and his crew chipped in. The completion of the bleachers occurred only hours before the football team raced out onto the field. The occasion was important: "Doc" Knight had organized the first football homecoming for University alumni.

For many years, a June banquet climaxed annual alumni efforts. The meeting of graduates took place regularly in the spring. Alumni activities — including a play, a banquet, an official meeting, and small-group gatherings — occurred during commencement week. At that time, returning graduates mingled with new ones and shared the festivities such as baccalaureate, commencement

Alumni Association board of directors, September 1984

100

itself, and the gala Cadet Ball. Other alumni projects came about sporadically. In 1911, two graduates edited a volume called *Chronicles of the Alumni,* which remains a major source for early University history. Generally the association, dependent almost entirely on the imagination and labor of its president, saw years of ups and downs.

President from 1921-24, Knight was one of the most dedicated and energetic of the early officers. During his tenure, the first issue of the *Wyoming Alumni Magazine* — later the *Alumnews* — was distributed (February 1921). But the major change that "Doc" achieved was the transfer of the annual alumni weekend to a "homecoming" during the autumn months. Beginning in 1922, homecoming came to involve activities designed especially for the enjoyment of alumni: class reunions, open houses, the homecoming dance, and the big football game. Among them, the homecoming parade stands as most memorable, with its ever more intricate floats provided by campus organizations and its themes that range from dinosaurs to spaceships. The first full-time secretary for the Alumni Association was appointed in 1937. By 1941, the title changed to director. In 1946, one such director — General C. L. Irwin, a 1916 graduate — set up a formal constitution for the association, with a board of directors as governing body. Now the directors of the association are chosen by Alumni Association members who submit nominations. These nominations are then reviewed and placed before the paid membership in May.

In the 1950s the association began to name the special "Distinguished Alumnus Award" winners. Samuel H. Knight was the second to be so honored; the first was Admiral Emory S. Land, University graduate of 1898.

Today Wyoming alumni clubs exist in major cities throughout the country. Through the years, the University has called on her graduates to support her legislative requests, to finance special buildings, or to donate to special projects. Alumni have provided some of the institution's most enduring gifts.

If her graduates think of the University with warmth and delight in the benefits she extended to them, the coin also has another side, for without alumni who remember, a University would not be worthy of the name.

Homecoming parade, 1934

Constant petty overdrafts were covered by local banks, which accepted University vouchers as security and charged interest on money advanced. To save the operating budget, the University also came to charge many items against the more prosperous oil-royalty building fund: furniture and equipment; salaries for janitors; repairs; and even library books, on the grounds that the latter were "permanent in character."

State examiners were frequently angry about the constant operating overdrafts, especially since payment of interest was involved. Smith found himself often in conflict with state auditing officials, whom he regarded as unfair in their interference and use of their power. In 1923 he complained to Crane that

the State Auditor frequently put arbitrary interpretations on laws governing expenditures, and in this manner causes a great deal of inconvenience and difficulty. The law reads that if he is satisfied it is a true and correct bill, he will pay it. This places a great deal of authority and power in that office, and they are not afraid to use it.

In most years, however, the University managed to squeak by with the aid of local banks in day-to-day deficit budgeting.

Far more difficult was the situation in regard to campus construction, Crane's most extensive and expensive program. In 1923, the new president presented to the legislature an ambitious program of building, the cost of which he estimated at $2.25 million. Legislation in 1923 and 1925 made it possible to plan a building program based primarily on the University's share of the oil royalties that were returned to the state of Wyoming by the federal government. Anticipating a continuing fall of manna, Crane and the board constructed a gymnasium (1925, cost of $430,000), shops (1926-27, $135,500), a stadium (1926, $12,000), an engineering building (1927, $181,000), and a men's dormitory (1928, $195,000) before the depression put an end to immediate construction. All of these buildings were constructed not on the basis of cash on hand, but on anticipation of future revenues which would supposedly be sufficient to cover contractor payments.

But indeed, such optimism turned out to be unjustified. Oil revenues reached a peak of $430,000 in 1925 and plummeted to $89,000 by 1929 in a fluctuation due to the price of crude oil and to production variables. As a result, the University's building fund operated almost constantly in the red. As early as 1922-23, it was apparent that *annual* payments from the federal government would not cover anticipated *quarterly* payments to contractors. Crane professed to the board that he was not overly concerned. In spite of the fact that the gymnasium was running over cost estimates, he said he believed that Laramie banks would be willing to cover vouchers with cash loans. The federal government eventually came to the University's aid by paying royalties more regularly and in more frequent installments.

Construction budgeting was always so tight, however, that Smith was on the telephone monthly to Washington in an effort to estimate exact payments forthcoming so that arrangements might be made to hold contractors at bay. By 1924, the board had borrowed around $25,000 to carry on the building program; in 1927 it was unable to meet its payment to the gymnasium contractor and had to pay both penalties and interest. By 1929, the construction funding was in the red by approximately $200,000, and Smith was estimating that it would take two to three years of the decreased oil royalties to pay off the debt. Having set aside federal funds for construction purposes, state legislators volunteered no assistance to the building program after the $100,000 appropriation for an addition to Hoyt hall in 1921. Legislatures of 1923, 1925, 1927, and 1929 confined their aid to operating expenses and the appropriations necessary for matching funds in agricultural extension.

Nobody anticipated the crash of 1929, and unfortunately the policy of spending future income sent the University into the depression already deeply in debt.

The depression took enormous toll from the University. Revenues on all levels shrank to ten-year lows. Although tax revenues somewhat increased in the uncertain year 1930-31, mill levies for 1931-32 were the equivalent of those for 1922-23. Federal oil royalty revenues dropped to $73,000 in fiscal year 1931-32. A nervous legislature — pressed since 1925 into supplying "contingent" operating funds through appropriations — budgeted a record $131,250 for biennial expenses in 1931, but by 1933, began a series of drastic cuts. Federal funding for agricultural programs was constantly threatened by adverse Congressional proposals.

The first program to hit the dust was the president's favorite. Building expansion had come to a standstill after 1928 until such time as the $200,000 debt (June 1931) could be repaid out of federal oil royalties; however, such royalties were dropping well below the anticipated $100,000 per annum. Crane was unwilling to give up. In the winter of 1930-31, anticipating the legislative session, he approached Dean Charles H. Kinnane of the law school for an opinion in regard to a bond issue for construction of new buildings, the bonds to be retired out of future federal oil royalties and the anticipated income from the University Permanent Land Fund. Kinnane believed that precedent would support use of future income to cover such indebtedness, but Nellis Corthell, University attorney, pointed out that by the constitution no public debt could be incurred without approval of the voters of the state — a procedure which the board was understandably reluctant to undertake.

Nevertheless, in January 1931, Crane brought to the board a "brief" on financing new buildings. The president therein proposed to construct certain additions to the experimental farms (estimated at $50,000), a liberal arts building with auditorium ($200,000), a home economics building ($100,000), and a College of Education building ($150,000), with the possibility of an agriculture building strong on the horizon. Allowing that construction this time must be accomplished on a cash rather than an anticipated-income basis, Crane remained unwilling to wait until the accumulated debt might slowly be retired and cash would be available once more. Instead, he proposed that the legislature either provide tax funds so that new buildings could be contracted for at once, or that some system be devised to pay off indebtedness and free current oil royalties for immediate construction needs. Ultimately, the board chose to sponsor a refinancing plan that called for the issuance of $200,000 in bonds to pay off the building debt, thus freeing current funds for immediate construction. Such a plan was presented to the 1931 legislature.

The bill for a bond issue did not pass, although the board threw all its support behind the proposed legislation, to the extent that it even gave up protest against a mammoth University audit proposed in the senate. The ways and means committee reported the bill favorably to the house, and here it passed by a vote of 40-13, but in the senate it was "indefinitely postponed" — because of, Crane thought, a "natural distrust of debts and refinancing plans" among budget-conscious legislators. Meanwhile a second plan that would make University vouchers acceptable as an investment for state funds also failed to gain legislative support.

Still, 1931 was not a disastrous year for all University projects. Although income from mill levies decreased by 23 percent, the legislature was relatively generous in its "contingent" operational funding. The legislature was presented with a budget request for the biennium July 1, 1931 to June 30, 1933, that called for an increase of $60,000 for expansion and an additional $20,000 to offset income shrinkages for the previous years. It came through with a two-year appropriation of $200,000 (an increase of $30,000) plus the necessary funding to match federal contributions in agricultural extension. There was also a special award of $15,000, lobbied for by the State Federation of Labor, for "home education classes." In his "brief" on the operating budget as presented to the legislature, Crane reported that a trustees' committee recommended that if more major economies be demanded by the legislature, the University might save $20,000 by abolishing correspondence study (an area where growth had leveled off); the department of mining engineering; and the department of music. Protests poured in, including one from the entire committee on ways and means. The threat worked, and the legislature "generously" (in Crane's words) appropriated an extra $25,000 for the continued maintenance of these departments. The biennial state funding for operating expenses thus stood at $225,000, while $145,000 was appropriated for Agricultural Extension Service matching funds. Ominously, by September 1931, the overdraft on UW funds totalled $284,729.

Still, the depression did not seem so bad. The student newspaper in September 1931 thought hard times might be performing a service.

The remark was once passed that a period of depression had no effect on college students, for

they never had any money, anyway. At least it is quite evident that Wyoming University has not suffered for want of students due to the industrial depression. . . . In times of depression such as these, a person finds the very best opportunity of getting an education. Where many jobs are to be had at a high salary a person is likely to feel that he cannot afford to go to school. Yet if the opposite conditions prevail to such a degree as to force former students to return to school they may, in a sense, be termed worthwhile.

The *Branding Iron* spoke too soon. By 1932, the real wrath of the depression exploded in Wyoming and the University. Local and national signals pointed to a distress that could no longer be written off or ignored.

To its credit, the board made a manly effort to reduce expenses in anticipation of declining state and federal University income. The year 1932 — and particularly the spring, when the budget for the following fiscal year was traditionally fixed — was filled with such efforts. Early that year, partly because of economic conditions but also arguments over policy, the state high school tournament was suspended; this event usually represented a major part of the University's student recruitment efforts. At their March meeting, facing the fact that estimated income for the next fiscal year would clearly drop both in terms of mill levy and oil revenue receipts, trustees instructed Crane to cut $50,000 or more from the budget he proposed, suggesting optimistically that funds should be found where decreases would cause least permanent damage and could most easily be restored. In spite of Justus Soule's appearance to beg for salary retention and Crane's frequent statements about retaining good scholars, the reduction of faculty pay levels was discussed as was elimination of the high-cost, low-enrollment law school. The dean, Kinnane, had just resigned.

Science camp tents, Snowy Range, c. 1930

Meanwhile, budget overdrafts continued to mount in spring 1932. The state budget official assigned to investigate University accounts agreed with Crane that "it would be folly to eliminate necessary departments or parts of such departments," but deplored what he obviously regarded as signs of fiscal irresponsibility in current accounts.

It would appear that either insufficient funds were appropriated or expenditures have been made without due regard for the Budget provisions. It should be required of administrative officials that, so far as possible, they live within the specific amounts set out for certain activity, as well as to have regard for the sum total appropriations for all purposes.

At the April board meeting, Crane suggested reductions in supplies and travel funds; replacements of retiring personnel at lower salary levels and leaving vacancies unfilled; reduction of the athletic coaching staff; and suspension of certain curricula, which would result in the dismissal of faculty members whose salaries might then be reassigned. In a long and tough session, the board took these and other possibilities for budget reductions under consideration. It ended by reducing travel allowances, refusing all costly sabbatical leaves, and agreeing to leave certain open positions temporarily vacant.

Further economies were also anticipated. Certain agricultural and entomological positions might be consolidated with state-financed offices. Dean R. L. Rhoads of the College of Engineering was offered an ominously "conditional" appointment, no doubt because of his clash with Crane over student behavior at the Engineers' Ball. In a measure that was to become the focal point of much discussion, the board ruled that "due to the present stress of economic conditions" it would not renew any contracts with married women nor employ married women in the future. At the end of a long meeting, Crane dramatically volunteered a ten percent reduction in his own salary to protect faculty from any across-the-board decrease. The board accepted his gesture with gratitude, but it had the foresight nevertheless to

reserve the right to reduce the salary carried by [all faculty contracts] at any time after January 1, 1933, if in the opinion of the Trustees, financial emergency demands it for the welfare of the University.

Budget savings may have temporarily engendered optimism among University officials, but the general outlook was gloomy. In April, the First State Bank of Laramie closed its doors — one of seven Wyoming banking institutions to do so in 1932. The University had quietly withdrawn some funds during the previous year when the bank's position seemed in jeopardy, and the result was that it stood to lose little, if anything, in the closure. During the summer, the Commons, an eating facility which had been the source of a small supplementary income, was closed for lack of demand, and in autumn it was able to reopen only with reduced services. Enrollment in fall of 1932 was down by eight percent compared to the previous autumn, with freshmen enrollment experiencing an even greater decline. In the spring, a Wyoming Tax League (later the Taxpayers Association), founded in Casper, began its campaign to avert tax increases and to reduce spending. Throughout the year, it subjected the Agricultural Extension Service to attacks of increasing intensity.

Again officials reacted as firmly as possible. Retrenchment was in the air. In September 1932, the board announced that the 1932-33 budget would provide for

the utmost economy consistent with the maintenance of the present program and without lowering present quality of service, but without any expansion of program. In general an effort shall be made to retain all present savings anticipated in this year's budget.

To the special meeting at which it formulated a legislative request standing at $90,000 per year lower than that of 1931, the board of trustees carefully invited not only the assistant state budget officer but the president of the Wyoming Tax League. The 1932 November election placed in office a Democratic governor, who talked economy and retrenchment, together with (for the first time in history) a strongly controlled Democratic house. Meanwhile, the president as usual approached the legislative session with vigor and hard work, as is attested by his enormous compilations of statistics, reports, press releases, and speeches.

There is little reason to believe that Crane and his colleagues anticipated legislative disaster before it was hard upon them. As it turned out, 1933 was the worst year in the history of the University as far as funding was concerned. The University's original request basically proposed continuance of the tax levy at a total of one-half mill plus the standard one-tenth mill for operation of those state farms turned over to UW for management in 1917. In addition, the president asked an operating fund of $271,350 for the biennium, a reduction of approximately twenty percent from the appropriation for the previous two years. For agricultural extension (to provide matching funds for federal grants), the board pared its request to $98,000 in the face of gubernatorial intransigence and the attacks of the Wyoming Tax League. However, it was apparent that the mill levy would produce so little (assessed property valuation in Wyoming dropped from $338 million in 1929 to $300 million in 1935) that the budget would require replacement of the amount lost. Crane also sought special funds to cover existing deficits.

The first blow was delivered by Governor Leslie A. Miller, who recommended in his legislative address that the University's operating appropriation be reduced by more than $50,000 and that the funding for the Agricultural Extension Service be set at $61,000, better than one-third below the request. Crane was devastated. Acting rapidly, University alumni established a "State Committee for the Protection of Education in Wyoming," the leaders of which included Milward Simpson, Jack Corbett, Velma Linford, Mrs. H. T. Person, and others. In a series of bulletins this committee rallied to the defense of the University, asking its supporters to contact legislators, the governor, and any other influential citizens and groups. In a matter of a few weeks, nine bulletins were published and circulated, to "arouse interest in protecting the future of the University and help avert disaster for [our] Alma Mater." Still the courteous day-long hearing granted University officials by the house ways and means committee — a presentation by three trustees, the president, and several financial experts on January 25 — apparently accomplished little. From every angle the University was under attack.

Among bills introduced in the legislature of 1933 were measures to eliminate completely the Agricultural Extension Service; to provide high school certification for teaching; to end the University's extension course division; to establish two-year or junior colleges; and (a bill sponsored partly by Scotty Jack) to return the University to the status of an isolated local institution by refusing funds to cover membership in such organizations as the North Central Association of Colleges and Secondary Schools. In the long run, the legislature refused to pass any of those above except for the teacher certification changes.

Financial deprivations were of far greater importance. Most drastic — "disastrous," Crane said — was the repeal of legislation supporting the University through mill tax levies. Since 1887, some sort of tax levy had provided the bulk of state-supplied operating expenses. Throughout the 1920s, three-eighths mill had been set aside for operating expenses; another one-eighth mill for construction and maintenance; and a supplementary one-tenth mill for the running of the state farms. In the wording of the bills abolishing these tax levies,

introduced by the house ways and means committee, the legislators made it clear that they sought to make University funding "subject to direct legislative appropriation each biennium" as a matter of principle. Crane deplored the change.

This will be a disastrous measure to the University because there is no possible assurance that an appropriation would be made equal in amount to replace the millages. Further, it would make it impossible for the Board of Trustees to lay long time plans for the development of the institution. The millages are always under control of the legislature but they carry an assurance of continuance which enables the Trustees, by business planning, to make a little money do more than a larger amount would do if received in uncertain biennial appropriations.

Although Governor Miller had obviously not anticipated the legislature's action, he signed the bills into law.

The ways and means committee also wrote sudden death to hopes for a major appropriation bill. Following the governor's cut of the University's request to $210,000, the committee reported favorably on only $120,000, a figure which was approved by legislature and governor alike. The Agricultural Extension Service, threatened with extinction, was rescued to the tune of $61,000, as compared to $145,000 in the previous biennium. Thus, appropriations which had stood at $375,000 for the two years past were reduced to $181,000. It was small consolation that the legislature postponed extinction of the three mill-levy taxes until the end of calendar year 1934.

Before the ways and means committee, Crane had volunteered a salary cut for faculty members on the same basis as any cut demanded of state employees. His statement probably represented an effort to curry favor, for the president's papers are filled with arguments against cutting faculty salaries: He spoke of the miseries of underpaid teachers who had to take jobs on the side; the loss of good faculty to institutions elsewhere; the continuing need for research to benefit the state and its citizens; and the positive effects of merit increases on faculty achievement. The senate resolution demanding specific salary cuts according to an ascending income-related scale failed to pass, but budget cuts made salary reductions almost inevitable and the governor spoke of a figure of around twenty percent. Moreover, the economy-minded legislature proceeded to reduce the president's salary permanently to the sum of $8,000 per year — $1,500 above that which the governor was drawing. Crane (who had voluntarily in 1932 taken a cut of ten percent from the $12,500 he was earning) protested vigorously against this encroachment on the board's autonomy and impediment to future presidential quality.

On February 16, the appropriations bill was passed, and the student newspaper cried "ruin of the institution." The following day the campus went into mourning: The flag was flown at half mast, the ROTC band played Chopin's "Funeral March," and the bugler sounded taps. Crane appeared with a black band around his arm. A few days later to the board's executive committee, he reported that budget constrictions would probably mean program retraction and even the end of some departments.

The next several months saw frantic attempts to construct a budget that would fall within income restrictions and still keep the basic campus program of courses and curricula functioning. To a board meeting on March 22, 1933, Crane made an "elaborate" report on finances. What became immediately apparent from Fay Smith's statistics was that even current year expenses would have to be cut; there was, Smith reported, an "acute shortage of cash" in the treasury account, coupled with large overdrafts being temporarily carried by local banks. Bills from several months back were being held for lack of money, and banks had refused to extend already-overdrawn accounts. To the board, Crane brought news that $65,000 was needed before June in order to balance the current budget and pay current debts. He had already ordered that no supplies be purchased except in emergencies; approved the disconnection of nine telephones; and proposed the immediate closing of Merica hall, for women's dorms were occupied only by 55 and the men's by 38 percent, and at least three-quarters occupancy was needed to break even. Still there seemed no way to avoid carrying debts into the new already-deficient year and trying to pay them out of the new reduced appropriations.

Under these circumstances, Crane reluctantly proposed an immediate salary cut to balance the budget for the current fiscal year. After due consideration by a special committee, the board unhappily ordered its executive committee to

levy a cut on a general basis of twenty percent on the salaries for March, April, May and June, sufficient to pay the deficit in this year's operations of the present budget to June 30th . . . and authorized [the Committee] to draw upon the University contingent in the State Treasury in case such salary cut, in the opinion of the Committee, appears unduly harsh. . . . Reductions shall be spread upon all employees, but lighter on those in the lower brackets. The draft upon the University contingent [for the future biennium] for use in this current year, however, shall not exceed $30,000 before June 30, 1933.

Accordingly, the executive committee opted to take ten percent of the first $1,000 annual salary; twenty percent of the second; and increasing amounts thereafter. Crane told the board that these moneys would balance the 1932-33 budget by June 30.

Current year expenses, however, were only a fraction of the board's headache. Crane went to the March "budget" board meeting with the knowledge that expenses for the coming biennium would have to be slashed. At a conservative estimate, income for operating expenses would total less than $550,000, and maintaining the budget at current levels would involve expenses of $654,000. Even with the continuance of the proposed payroll cut, $60,000 had to be found somewhere. Crane was adamant about cuts.

Prudence demands precaution against disaster, but drastic cuts should not be made so heavy as to preclude taking advantage of financial improvement. Cuts at this time might be made so low as to destroy the institution's chance of rising when conditions improve. We must not cut so deep as to kill the patient.

Indeed, the president's fundamental optimism led him to believe that the worst was over. President Franklin D. Roosevelt had avoided the bank crisis and announced his New Deal, in which Crane had considerable confidence. "Give the institution," he told the board, "a chance to cash in on the prosperity of the 'new deal.' "

Still tough decisions had to be made. Crane recognized that activities and departments would have to be curtailed. Clearly, the president favored first and foremost a suspension of the expensive football program. The University could save $8,000 a year and the Associated Students would save $3,000, much of which could be invested in other student activities. The suspension of football, Crane thought, would provide funds that

> *would add greatly to the educational and cultural advantages of the institution. Through a period of years, the money devoted to football would provide a very strong and varied program of local sports and entertainments for the students. Laramie possesses some very fine natural advantages, both in Winter and in Summer, which could be developed and capitalized so as to benefit all classes of students.*

Crane also suggested the ending of branch summer schools, canceling the already contracting correspondence department, ending the physical education requirement for juniors and seniors, restricting the music department to lessons only, and closing the department of mining engineering. The law school, with Carl Arnold now dean, was no longer threatened.

Meeting again ten days later in emergency session, the board responded to Crane's recommendations. It declined his suggestion that football be eliminated — partly on the basis of adverse publicity that had somehow leaked out across the state. Crane was instructed instead to reduce the athletic budget without reducing competitive sports. Programmatically, trustees cut $4,000 out of the physical education budget; suggested an end to the second summer session; recommended that the law school be continued on its restricted basis (the addition of a faculty member to be indefinitely postponed); and agreed to Crane's plan for a savings of $12,000 in engineering — a solution probably quietly pushed by the president in that it permitted the dismissal of Dean Rhoads in the name of economy as a cover for Crane's lingering hostility. Besides miscellaneous reductions in budget, it was clear that salary cuts in the aggregate of fifteen percent or more would have to be adopted.

By mid-April, Crane was able to present the board with a balanced budget for the next biennium on the basis of criteria trustees had set. By grading the salary cuts between twelve and 37 percent, he actually managed to include $15,000 for a "safety margin" and set aside $5,000 to apply to the deferred overdraft. Because of previous publicity and pressure from a group of legislators, the music department was not cut back, but mining engineering was eliminated (with the dismissal of Professors Joseph R. Guiteras and A. C. Dart) and Rhoads was fired. Other cuts, as anticipated, were made in the athletic budget, in physical education, in summer school, and in miscellaneous areas.

What clearly upset the president the most were the salary cuts. He wished audibly to the board that there was some way to avert them. In addition, he feared federal cuts that would reduce salaries and staff in the Agricultural Extension Service, the Agricultural Experiment Station, the vocational education program, and those many departments supported under the Morrill Act. Indeed, the U.S. Congress in August proposed to take 25 percent from each of these programs, but postponed the effective date. Thus Crane's contract statements to faculty included a statement reserving the right for further salary reduction, but also stated that the cancellation of federal funding might be "sufficient grounds" for dismissal. The first federal project actually to close was the U.S. Petroleum Research Laboratory, connected with the department of engineering.

Readjustments of the board's budget continued through the rest of 1933. With the retirement of Justus Soule as acting dean of men, the board simply raised the salary of Major Beverly C. Daly, longtime head of the ROTC program, and added the deanship to his duties. In September, the board's committee on administrative reorganization recommended combining the positions of registrar, fiscal agent, and secretary of the board of trustees, but the recommendation was tabled. All three faculty members on emeritus service — Soule, Aven Nelson, and Grace Raymond Hebard — were continued at their current $3,000 "salary" level (for no provisions existed for actual retirement pay), since their incomes had already been reduced by board action. J. R. Rhodes, who resigned as athletic director and head football coach in 1932, was not replaced; instead, his functions were turned over to Willard Witte, who was basketball coach as well. The College of Engineering, under the temporary administration of an "acting" dean, suffered the most. In June 1933, the board received a petition from engineering students, begging for the retention of the dean, professors, and mining program. The trustees "regretted," they replied.

Merica hall, women's dormitory, 1935-36

Rumors of courses dropped and programs ended may have had a positive influence on legislators, but they had a negative effect on prospective students. As enrollment declined (1931-32, 1,402; 1932-33, 1,238; 1933-34, 1,191), the student newspaper told prospective students that "few" courses had been dropped. The cut in the College of Engineering, the editors wrote, amounted to ending a mining department which attracted very few students and the curriculum of which consisted "largely of combinations of abilities trained in the other divisions of the Engineering College." Changes in physical education involved only the discontinuance of teacher training, and since there was little demand for such teachers in Wyoming, the measure might even be seen to protect students from entering into an undesirable career. The University had lost nothing in standing among other schools, and most routine changes in courses emphasized the "progressiveness of the institution."

Through it all, Crane maintained a dogged optimism, based in part on national policies. In a talk to the student body in February 1934, he refused to commit himself to a positive view of the New Deal, but he recognized with some enthusiasm the historic role of the National Recovery Act. The country would never go back, he thought, and a new era of stronger "social control" was in the offing. America was setting out on a new trail, he told students, like a pioneer crossing an unknown continent. He saw social security and welfare programs as an enormous field for future young people, particularly researchers, for "If we had had the same amount of research in human problems that we have had in the fields of science, we would not have been in our present trouble, probably." Schools and government should cooperate in interpreting and disseminating information.

The New Deal and the new territory through which we will pass during the next decade will require new schools, new emphasis, and more schools adapted to the needs of a new order,

Crane concluded. All in all, budget cuts and even faculty salary decreases seem to have been accepted as miseries of the time.

As far as the University was concerned, the president's optimism turned out to be justified, as state and University slowly pulled themselves out of the depression and its mentality. At the special legislative session of December 1933, called by Governor Miller with the aim of reorganizing government and retrenching finances, the legislature and governor alike avoided the panic mentality that had swept both in the previous spring. Now the legislature responded with conservative caution to the sweeping governmental reforms proposed by its committee on organization and revenue; almost all of them met defeat. Among the measures introduced was a major change in the educational system, by which University and school system would be centralized under one statewide board, but it was "indefinitely postponed" by the committee of the whole in the senate.

Budget strictures for fiscal year 1934-35 (under the previous biennial appropriations) were still tight; and although Crane and Smith foresaw a slightly improved income, it was impossible to replace equipment or repair diminished salaries. We are "inviting disaster," Crane told the board in March 1934, reporting that 23 people had left the University for better jobs since 1929. Included in the budget request to the 1935 legislature was a program for the restoration of faculty salaries — at the rate of half in 1934-35, and half the following year. The item was rated top priority. The legislative appropriation of $550,000 together with rising interest from the land funds permitted restoration at the rate the president requested. When the board in March 1935 voted to restore half of the salary cut, "a feeling of optimism pervaded the campus," according to the *Branding Iron,* student newspaper. A year later, when salaries of 1931 were totally restored, the Wyoming branch of the American Association of University Professors formally extended its thanks to the board of trustees.

With economic indicators slowly turning upward, legislators proved fairly generous in appropriations for operating expenses to replace the property tax on which the University had leaned so long. In 1935, of the requested appropriation of $600,000, the legislature produced $530,000, adding $75,000 for the biennium for agricultural extension (mostly to match federal funds) and $45,000 for the operation of state farms. The appropriation may not have achieved all the president wanted, but it made the University richer by $50,000 per year than in the previous biennium. Crane's optimism spread to Fay Smith, who wrote the newly-elected U.S. Representative Paul R. Greever (Democratic Cody lawyer) that

> *We came through the Legislature in excellent shape. Never has the Legislature been so friendly toward us. This may or may not have been due to the fact that we did absolutely no lobbying. . . . Governor Miller has certainly done a lot for this institution and this fact is known and appreciated. . . . The University is in better shape today than it has been for ten years. The price of cattle has doubled, wool is up, oil is up, drouth is over, the depression has ended, and everything is all right!*

By the end of fiscal year 1934-35, Smith was able to report to the board that the deficit in the operating budget had been wiped out, and nearly $10,000 surplus was on hand.

From 1937 to the end of Crane's administration, the legislative appropriation for operating expenses was gradually increased in all areas: the main University funds, those for agricultural extension, and those for state farms. At the same time, the board was gratified by the gradual increase in interest paid from the omnibus, agricultural, and University land funds and by an increase in oil royalties. The federal government played its role in that the proposed cuts in federal aid to education and agriculture were rescinded by Roosevelt in 1934. The following year Senator Joseph O'Mahoney succeeded in winning an appropriation to reinstitute the Petroleum Research Laboratory. A threatened withdrawal by the State Board of Education from the Smith-Hughes Act vocational program in agriculture was averted in 1934. Crane's request for legislative appropriations in 1939 included several programs in vocational education, agricultural experimentation, archeology, and industrial research that involved matching federal funds. By fiscal year 1940-41, University operating income totaled $835,000 per annum, of which $349,000 came directly from state appropriations.

Federal support also figured prominently in the revival of Crane's favorite project — that of adding buildings to the University campus. Here the president again took strong initiative. In December 1933, he reported to the board on various possibilities for federal loans and grants such as had already been achieved in Montana, Utah, and Minnesota for building purposes. His thorough investigation included an estimate of the relief that construction projects might bring to the locally unemployed. First on the president's list was a liberal arts building with an auditorium, at an estimated cost of $300,000. In spite of three negative votes from trustees, the board agreed to Crane's borrowing plan, which instructed trustees to borrow up to $300,000 from the Public Works Administration, moneys to be gradually repaid by the income from the University Permanent Land Fund. A proposed bill was drawn up by the administration and checked by the attorney general. A special "brief" was prepared, and the governor's approval was solicited and received. House Bill 92 was introduced into the special legislative session by the committee on buildings and institutes, the backing of which the president had specifically sought. The bill passed the house by a vote of 43-15, the Senate by 14-12, and was signed into law by Governor Miller on December 20, 1933.

Lengthy and detailed negotiations followed. The PWA eventually agreed to provide an outright grant of more than $80,000, but asked of the board that it provide security for a loan of $228,000 through the sale of University bonds. Such a bond issue had never been attempted by the University itself, and indeed a similar plan had been turned down by the legislature in 1931. Many questions arose. Would bonds sold by the University constitute a general state debt and thus have to be approved (according to the constitution) by the state's voters? How would University bonds be rated and sold? Would such bonds be a legal investment — like those of Wyoming cities, counties, and school districts — for state-held funds, such as the University Permanent Land Fund? If so, bonds could be purchased by the state treasurer and interest thereon paid by the University into its own fund for its own use.

Suit was brought to ascertain the constitutionality of the plan. In June 1934, the Wyoming Supreme Court ruled in favor of the University on all counts. Justice Fred H. Blume ("speaking individually") took the opportunity to ask

Is there no end? Many of us were not brought up in the bosom of luxury, nor did we sleep in marble halls. The village schools and their humble surroundings and the university campus graced with edifices hoary with age seemed to us to satisfy the longings for learning. We heard at that time of the wrecks and ruins of the past brought about by mortgaging the future. . . . We heard of the existence in the past of cities, once humming with the glad refrain of thousands of happy human beings, lying now desolate with their stately baths, their roomy porticoes, their sacred shrines in ruins, because no space, no corner, no nook had become exempt from the invasion of public burdens. Do ruins tell tales merely to be scorned? Times change. . . . The tide of the day sweeps us along into whirlpools which seem giddy. We can but hope that they may not be what they seem.

Nonetheless, the plan was put into effect. Bonds were issued, without an election, and all were purchased by the state treasurer with money accumulated in the University Permanent Land Fund.

With the funds from the PWA, the liberal arts building (in spite of some problems with cost overruns) was completed in 1936. Similar imaginative financing led to the construction of the Wyoming Union, authorized by the legislature in 1937. In this instance, the board operated through a Wyoming Union Corporation, which received a $75,000 grant from PWA. The board also issued an extra $150,000 in University bonds, half of which were to act as security for a PWA loan. The debt would be retired and the loan repaid through a special levy of $1 per student per term; matching money from the Associated Students (which actually also derived from student fees); an annual faculty levy (termed "dues"); and income from the Union itself. The governor, not the legislature, balked at Crane's plans to construct two new dormitories through similar loans plus appropriations. Vetoing the plan, Governor Miller pointed out that dormitory income in the past was erratic and not to be relied on to support carrying charges. Students petitioned and protested to no avail.

Crane's building program received a blow when even after his assembling of "voluminous data," the PWA refused to lend more money to the University for construction, since its "limited allotment [for Wyoming] . . . crowded out" the University application. In 1939, the president had to turn to the legislature for help. His proposal, about which the board contacted newly-elected Governor Nels H. Smith, was huge. It suggested twelve projects for building construction and remodeling, some of which were self-liquidating and some not. Crane got a little but not all that he wanted. Construction of a women's dormitory, the

Snowshoeing, science camp, Snowy Range, c. 1926

bond issue for which was to be liquidated out of dorm revenue, was now approved, with a $60,000 appropriation to begin with; an electric power plant, necessitated by the extra dormitory, was authorized; and greenhouse construction was financed to the amount of $4,600. Two years later, Crane was less lucky, for no major projects were authorized and Governor Smith (no friend to Crane nor to the University) vetoed the legislature's appropriation of $205,000 for construction of an education building.

In review, President Crane must be credited with many financial accomplishments. True, national economic trends cannot be discounted, and such funding as derived from the mill levy or oil royalties was basically beyond the president's control. Still, he put extraordinary efforts into legislative proposals, devising numerous statistical charts and tables, providing hours of arguments, and lobbying with intensity and conviction. In the last four years of his administration, when legislative funding replaced the traditional mill levy, Crane saw the University's biennial appropriation rise from

$622,000 in 1937 to $760,000 in 1941. Funding for the Agricultural Extension Service — always subject to legislative debate — increased as well. During Crane's administration, eight major and numerous minor buildings arose on campus. Many remodeling projects bought older facilities up to date.

Crane steered the University through the depression as best he was able. The abolition of the property tax income was a major defeat. In retrospect, the temporary reduction of faculty salaries and the cut-back of some programs seem virtually unavoidable.

In spite of the depression, then, the University president had reason to pride himself on his financial successes. Crane was an imaginative financier. His policies regarding buildings — the use of oil royalties for construction, the gaining of federal support, the management of bond issues and bond redemptions — set patterns for future University presidents. One must believe that in any business enterprise, Crane could have made his way. That he was not so adept at managing people is the other half of the story.

SCIENCE CAMP

n New Year's Day 1923 in New York, Samuel H. Knight — no stranger to Wyoming's prairies and mountains — proposed to a friend from the Columbia University geology department that they cooperate in setting up a Wyoming field summer camp. It did not take J. F. Kemp long to agree. Thus the S. H. Knight Science Camp was conceived.

Conceived — but only slowly born. That summer, Knight and Kemp set up a temporary camp in the Laramie Range, some thirty miles northeast of Laramie. There they taught the two students who formally enrolled in the course, and entertained a number of faculty and friends who found their way to the camp to visit. The next year, with growing support, the two geologists set up camp near Camel Rock and persuaded Aven Nelson to add botany to the courses offered. Thereafter it was time, Knight felt, to find permanent shelter. The road from Centennial to Brooklyn Lake had recently been opened to automobile travel. Knight selected a small meadow where cabins could be tucked into a clump of trees a few hundred yards from the road.

Construction began on June 1, 1925, when Knight and five geology students began clearing the area to build tent houses. Kemp, colleagues, and students from Columbia came to cooperate. By 1926, 24 students enrolled in the course, hauling themselves and their gear in a caravan of bright yellow, air-cooled Franklin touring cars (purchased secondhand) across the prairie and up into the mountains. Every year the department awarded as many as 12 working scholarships to students, who then spent two weeks preparing the site and cabins before classes began, assisted with camp chores, and stayed long enough after classes were over to chop wood for the following year. Courses offered came to include botany, zoology, and, on occasion, art.

The most ambitious building was the main lodge, for which construction began in 1929. Let "Doc" Knight tell it in his own words:

In order to support the heavy winter snow load, this building was constructed of spruce logs a foot or more through and up to 50 feet long. These logs were cut in the area, trimmed and snaked to the site with a team of horses and built into the walls and roof. The north wing (lecture room) was built in 1929, the central assembly room and kitchen in 1930, and the dining room in 1935. Just how this was accomplished by inexperienced student crews with a minimum of skilled supervision is difficult to explain. . . . The construction of the electric plant which still supplies most of the power for lighting the camp was one of the most interesting enterprises undertaken by the student-staff crews. To describe the construction of this power plant would be a subject in itself . . . The ingenuity that went into the plant can be appreciated by the fact that for several years the power was transmitted from the turbine to the generator by the rear axle assembly of a junked automobile. Full credit for the idea

Summer class, main lodge, science camp, c. 1940

and installation of this novelty belongs to students. It suffices to say that once their interest is aroused, American youth is hard to stop. Luckily, New Deal labor crews were there to take over major building from 1935-1937.

Thousands of students — at the rate of sixty to seventy a year from more than 100 different schools in geology alone — have come to love their science camp experiences. Many still remember ''Doc'' Knight — his black mustache and eyebrows later turned grey, his high laced boots and cowboy hat that were part of his inevitable costume — as he charged up slopes with panting students attempting to follow along. Once he almost dismissed a class when a woman showed up in trousers, but that was in the early days. Once he made a wild dash into Laramie — then one had to open and close nearly twelve gates — to deliver a student wife to the hospital only half an hour before the birth of her child. Other summers were less eventful but always memorable.

In 1973, because of a change of schedule in summer courses, the geology department dropped out of the science camp consortium. Zoology and botany classes continued at the camp until 1976, when the facility was found to be in need of repairs so drastic as to be financially inexpedient. After that summer, the University's summer field offerings were transferred to another area. With the passing of the Knight Science Camp, an era came to an end.

Chapter Seven

A President Loses Touch
1922-1941

In the American Heritage Center's biographical file on Arthur Griswold Crane is a striking photograph (reproduced later as a mural in the Wyoming Union) of the new president's entry into Laramie in 1922. Staring from the window of a stagecoach, into which he had been "kidnapped" by the welcoming committee, Crane shows little emotion and less enjoyment. Out from the window he peers like a prisoner; he is neither smiling nor waving nor eagerly surveying the sagebrush around him. If anything, the camera catches a tone of disapproval for this youthful, high-spirited prank.

The picture gives a quick glimpse into the character of a man who was always somewhat remote, seldom a social mixer, and frequently given to sternness and stiffness. To the board of trustees, Crane was known for his excellent head for figures and talent for financial management. To a student working regularly in an office down the hall from his own, he never paused to say good morning. To his colleagues, even in friendly correspondence, he was always "Dr. Crane." Although in their early years the Cranes occasionally invited students or faculty into their home, Fay Smith reported to Crane's successor in 1941 that Crane seldom entertained. Faculty and students seem to have regarded Crane with considerable respect but less real affection. It is difficult to tell whether he and his wife established any warm social contacts or found any deep and enduring friendships among the faculty. Perhaps Major Beverly J. Daly, professor of military science and dean of men after 1932, became a friend; of all his colleagues, Crane admired Daly the most and the two of them shared an interest in military matters. The new president may have made friends among local businessmen. Still, no real evidence remains.

Crane's remoteness from faculty, colleagues, and students plus his seeming coolness in public did not keep him from supporting a good many projects and causes with considerable intensity. His intricate written reports to the trustees and their executive committee reveal a man of strong objectives, an eye for the future, and occasional violent distastes that sometimes drew him into petty tactics. Some of Crane's policies were popular and others were out of step with the times, but there is no doubt that all represented a deep attachment to the University as he saw it. Thus his term of office saw extraordinary advancements in many fields, over and beyond the building construction to which he was so strongly committed.

Crane's vision of the University — of its objectives, curricula, and functions — was more practical than classical in orientation. His background lay in educational administration and not in the area of liberal arts or scientific theory. In his speeches to students and to the public, he consistently emphasized the services that the University provided to Wyoming and its citizens. He urged students to consider careers when they selected courses; and he suggested, in particular, that they study fields linked with the wealth of resources that Wyoming offered. With the coming of the depression, when a need for survival pressed upon everyone, his practical orientation made its strongest showing. Yet he was wise enough to recognize that the world was changing, and he wanted students to study human relations, to "set the best scientific minds at work" to solve social problems, which he regarded as far more difficult of resolution than problems of a purely scientific nature. Crane's dedication to professional training for the real world never kept him from recognizing humanistic achievements or scholastic endeavors. As he told graduate students in 1930, he held a "dream of this institution," for he believed it could have a "greater future than any other institution of its kind in America."

Like all Wyoming University presidents before him, Crane was perennially concerned with enrollment and devoted enormous efforts to increasing the campus and off-campus University population. Although Wyoming's population had achieved a level that prohibited personal contact with all potential students, such as Tisdel had once attempted, recruiting efforts continued to divert a great part of the president's energies. "Traveling Crane," the student newspaper called him, in connection with his many trips and speeches around the state. Catalogues, brochures and pamphlets on the University were sent to all Wyoming high school graduates. Spring "High School Week" became an annual event which included visits to campus by potential students who competed in sports, oratorical, and other events. Alumni were urged to contact potential students. Crane's administration saw the first efforts at coordinated public relations, with volumes of news releases dealing with all aspects of campus life and activities prepared for statewide distribution. By 1928, the Episcopal Cathedral's radio station was devoting air time to "Wyoming Day" programs throughout the state.

Recruiting efforts paid off, for enrollment steadily increased during the 1920s (from 388 in fall quarter 1918 to 1,054 in 1929). Although the depression saw considerable setback, it rose to the new record of 2,110 in the year before World War II, Crane's last year in office. A similar pattern saw summer school students increase from 276 in 1918 to 894 first term, and 469 second term, in 1940.

One might expect a consequent dramatic increase in courses and curricula, but here Crane's stern sense of efficiency and economy caused him to move with great caution. His first announcements to the faculty in 1922 called for an end to small classes, and in 1923 the president's advisory committee, composed of professors from each college plus the college deans, voted to cancel courses that enrolled fewer than five students. The president was convinced that the resultant "efficiency" would mean better teaching, for he always believed that small classes lacked the dynamics for good communications. Annually he reported to the board on "progress" in elimination of courses, and by 1932, he estimated that fewer than ten percent of all classes — and those primarily on a graduate level — stood below the minimal enrollment.

Introduction of new courses was infrequent, and all proposals for innovation had to be justified before the advisory committee. Often approved courses followed Crane's preference for the practical and vocational — new classes in journalism, a course on choosing a career, farm shop work, and (1933) a course in how to discover gold. Crane's own personal interests (he was chairman of the National Association of State Universities' Committee on Education by Radio) were reflected in the addition — after much difficulty — of a curriculum in radio broadcasting, through which the president envisioned spreading educational programs across the state. At his instigation also, a "flying school" financed by state and federal governments was established at the Laramie airport in 1939, although its quality did not meet with the president's approval for several years. Meanwhile all was not vocationally oriented; for example, the English department developed remedial courses in writing and even a writing laboratory in the early 1920s. In 1935, at the instigation of the Mormon Church, a faculty committee, the president, and the board approved a plan allowing credit for off-campus religious courses; soon other local church groups — of which the Methodist was particularly active — joined the system.

A few departments continued an unusual expansion. The graduate program, for example, substantially increased. As early as 1922, the board complied with a faculty recommendation to establish graduate assistantships. In 1937, the graduate committee, faculty, president, and trustees in turn approved Ph.D. programs in the Colleges of Agriculture and Education as well as in the liberal arts departments of chemistry and geology. Off-campus and adult education courses did well too. An annual branch summer school for teachers, co-sponsored by the State Department of Education, rotated from one community to another from 1923 until the depression ended the plan. An ambitious program for extension courses around the state also fell victim to the depression and was only slowly reestablished. The very special field program established by Professor S. H. Knight at the science camp in the Snowy Range was soon strongly supported by the president; here several departments — geology (the strongest), botany, zoology, art, and others — offered special summer mountain fare.

Others managed not so well. In 1933, with the legislature's cry for retrenchment echoing in every hall, Crane brought to campus a team of investigators from the Carnegie Foundation for the Advancement of Teaching with the request that it analyze the University's strengths and weaknesses and recommend areas where cutbacks might be made. Besides recommending certain consolidations and more efficient practices in the business office, the Carnegie team suggested cutting far back on the College of Engineering (where it felt that equipment was too minimal to maintain reasonable standards of instruction), ending the law school entirely, reorganizing the department of physical education and the College of Liberal Arts, dropping courses in journalism, and greatly consolidating classes in such departments as history and languages. Observer suggestions to reduce the "overemphasized" football program caused great grief, for in some mysterious way (apparently never even discovered by Crane, in spite of his meticulous search and inquiry) the report was leaked to the press in Casper and caused considerable comment. Many of the recommendations were slowly carried into effect — a number of engineering courses disappeared along with the college dean, who was in Crane's bad graces, and physical education was somewhat consolidated under Major Daly's athletic direction. Crane held firm on the law school, however, and the football program (in spite of Crane's personal hopes to terminate it to save considerable money) remained virtually intact.

Major curricular innovations, affecting all University students, can be counted on a few fingers. In the early 1920s, the faculty voted to combine certain groups of requirements, with the result that fewer classes were actually required and more electives permitted. In 1927, the faculty debated reducing requirements once more, but (according to the student newspaper) the plan presented by Dean P. T. Miller of the liberal arts college was so violently contested that it was tabled indefinitely. With the depression, Crane began talking of curricular "experimentation;" and an extended advisory committee, chaired by the president himself, dedicated years of debate to a plan that lowered the number of required classes again. The purpose, as the *Bulletin* explained, was to accommodate "individual student needs."

Many students are seeking training to meet changed economic and social conditions. Many old types of training have become obsolete. Great opportunities exist in new fields of activity.

Consequently, the 1936 *Bulletin* listed 38 "options," combinations of majors and two-year study-plans from which a student might choose, thereafter working with an adviser to design a program to suit his or her special purposes. Traditional curricula were still available, but the new choices especially emphasized career training and shorter periods of time.

The truth is that Crane's interests in curricula were slight. Within certain broad guidelines, he generally left initiation and development up to the faculty. Indeed, this president leaned on the assistance of deans and faculty committees more than any administrator before him.

During Crane's years, faculty governance began to be the practice, if at first on an informal level. Higher education was becoming professionalized. Crane needed the aid of faculty, department heads, and deans alike in collecting the volumes of statistics necessary for legislative programs, for the National Association of Land-Grant Colleges and Universities' survey in 1927, and for the Carnegie Foundation committee in 1933. Accrediting associations and national honorary organizations called for constant assessments. Twelve cartons in archives contain surveys conducted by faculty committees and deans.

The network of committees formed a system respected by Crane, although the president carefully reserved for himself a place on each of them. Faculty members (as opposed to deans, who were there by dint of their titles) on the president's advisory committee were elected by their peers. A branch of the American Association of University Professors had been active on campus since before Crane arrived. During this administration, the faculty institutionalized its role and performed its functions with considerable independence.

here has been a great movement of people to the cities and this movement is still going on," reported the UW agricultural college bulletin of 1912, "but it is nevertheless true that most of our people who honestly get a living get it from the soil, and it is true that this must in the nature of things continue to be so. . . . There is no occupation which has more downright creating in it than farming. There is no line of production where as many marvelous laws are in operation."

As one of the foundations for the University's existence, through the grants of the Morrill Acts, instruction in agriculture began on campus, spread throughout the state via the Agricultural Extension Service, and expanded its scope through information brought to light by the experimental stations.

In the early years, ties between the Agricultural Experiment Station and the College of Agriculture left no doubt about their closeness. In experiment station bulletins, Aven Nelson published his first botanical surveys and Wilbur Knight not only wrote about Wyoming geology but also about Wyoming birds. By 1904, when B. C. Buffum became director of the station, such a teacher as Nelson had found himself swamped with his heavy class load, his summer investigations, and his curatorship of the herbarium. His reports as "station botanist" frequently deplored the lack of time in his schedule to complete station bulletins. At the same time, Buffum

Stock farm showmen, c. 1955

began to seek an emphasis on experimental agricultural research to supplement the many surveys of flora, fauna, and terrain that were still "of much interest" to people in the state. In 1902, the station began to work on range management (particularly on poison grasses and their elimination) and on wool.

It was in the latter connection that the station (in 1907) acquired a "specialist" and the University, shortly thereafter, an associate professor of animal husbandry. John A. Hill was to rise to positions of national esteem and receive a University honorary LL.D. degree to celebrate his accomplishments.

Born on a farm in Ohio in 1880, Hill never had it easy. He was the eldest in a family of eight children, and the list of jobs he undertook in his youth and young manhood ranges from hired hand to waiter. In 1901, he moved to Cody, where his uncle owned a ranch, working as a hand and (later) in a mapping project before he enrolled in the University as a "Prep" student in 1902. He found his vocation in animal science. In 1906, the winter before he graduated, he transferred to Philadelphia for advanced training in wool and wool scouring. Meanwhile, in spite of his smallish stature, he played tackle on Wyoming's varsity football team.

Immediately after his graduation, he was tagged by Buffum to become a wool specialist at the experiment station. His pioneer work on the strength, measurement, and scouring of wool brought him national attention. Publications appeared at first locally, but later in widely-read journals. Sheep ranchers in Wyoming — at first uninterested in Hill's experiments — were soon sending him samples by the hundreds for testing and analysis.

Married in 1911 to Evelyn Corthell and father of five children, Hill served in the army as a battalion commander in World War I.

In 1923, this ebullient man was appointed dean of the College of Agriculture. As such, he became head of the experiment station as well. Hill encouraged students to compete for prizes in judging, where they were unusually successful and saw the winning of many firsts in livestock at national and international exhibits. In the 1930s, he brought to his staff Robert Burns, who was to publish more than 100 articles, to travel as a wool consultant through Iran and China, and to serve as chief of the University party in Kabul in 1956-58. Alexander Johnston came to UW in 1937. He was a native of Scotland and later author of a volume on wool preparation and marketing.

A favorite dean on campus and off, Hill earned further respect from his colleagues when he served as chairman of the council of deans that administered the University in 1941. He was one of the first alumni elected to the new chapter of Phi Beta Kappa. In 1932, he had been president of the American Society of Animal Production. That group honored him as "Outstanding Livestock Man in the United States" in 1949. By then Hill was retired on limited service as vice president of the University.

John A. Hill died at the age of seventy in March 1951. "A little man with twinkling eyes and a perpetual smile," wrote the Laramie *Boomerang,* "Above all else, he was a man who enjoyed life to the fullest." The obituary credited him with a great contribution to "the expansion and development of the West." He was also one of the pioneers in his field, and he created of that field a specialty for which Wyoming is still recognized.

Seed planting experiment, 1930

Crane's support of the faculty appears clear in every presidential report to the board of trustees. Faculty accomplishments in research and other areas were regularly called to the board's attention and played a prominent role in reports to academic associations. Beginning with his first years in office, Crane made annual pitches for increased faculty salaries. He gathered statistics on pay scales throughout the nation to prove that the University's faculty were less well paid than schools of surrounding areas.

If Wyoming ever hopes to have a superior faculty which shall be worthy of the dignity of our service, Wyoming must pay above the market. Our handicaps of distance, isolation, and high living expenses are distinct handicaps which desirable faculty members consider when balancing our offers with those from other institutions. For years, the attitude of our progressive, younger members has been that Wyoming is a springboard to better fields and larger rewards elsewhere. These considerations should be taken into account when discussing and acting upon the . . . budget. . . .

Of all Crane's biennial budgets, only that of 1926 — a "retrenchment" year — did not see him request salary increases for faculty — until, of course, the depression hit. If, in 1931 and 1933, the president was forced to abide by gubernatorial and legislative edicts on reduced salaries, no one was more saddened than he, nor was any University official more ardent than he in the pursuit of salary reinstatement.

In 1929, acting upon a suggestion from Fay Smith of several years before, Crane asked the board to investigate a program for faculty retirement funding. Since 1917, an informal plan had been in effect whereby the salaries of senior faculty members had been decreased and these individuals had been placed on a reduced teaching load — one that supposedly would maintain until their deaths. By 1933, those involved were Nelson, Soule, and Hebard, although the latter persisted in teaching a full load in spite of the president's consistent admonitions. During the depression, Crane urged "generosity" on the trustees and managed to avoid eliminating these "pensions." After 1935, no single project of faculty and president absorbed so much

time as the working out of a formal retirement plan. O. C. Schwiering, dean of education, coordinated efforts with the Wyoming Education Association: Legal opinions were solicited; insurance companies were consulted; and suits to establish legal validity were prepared. All was in vain, for both state insurance commissioner and attorney general insisted that the University could offer no payments of any sort to any non-working employee, so that retirement plans seemed *ipso facto* out of consideration. No breakthrough was made until 1944, when the Wyoming Education Association managed to get legislative approval for a teachers' pension system.

Crane did insist on a sick leave policy for faculty and employees as recommended by E. O. Fuller, the fiscal agent; this policy paid to family the maximum sick leave sum in case of the employee's death. Regular medical payments, similar to workman's compensation, were paid to employees injured at work. In some unusual cases — such as nervous or mental breakdowns — the board adopted fairly generous provisions for support, always at Crane's recommendation. Sabbatical leaves, however, continued on the basis of forty percent salary, whether for one semester or one year; this policy was criticized without result by the Carnegie Foundation. During the depression, all such leaves were simply tabled.

More successful were efforts to develop policies on hiring, "permanent tenure," dismissal, and promotion during the years of Crane's administration. In his intricate report to the Carnegie Foundation team, the president pointed out that although tenure was not written into faculty contracts, the "established policy" of the institution decreed permanent tenure in the fourth year of service, following a series of one-year contracts. The president's advisory committee ruled on dismissals, promotions, and tenure, and anyone threatened with discharge at any stage might file an appeal with the board of trustees. In practice, the president had always approved the committee's decisions, and so had the board. In 1939, a special faculty committee approached Crane with a report on tenure, based upon some studies prepared by the local chapter of AAUP. Although the committee recommended no basic changes in University policy, it requested a much more concrete system for investigating faculty candidates during their probationary period. The committee also questioned the role of the president's advisory committee in faculty dismissals. Crane seems, in general, to have

Board of trustees, 1946

accepted the faculty recommendations, although their integration into official trustee rules remained for a future date. Meanwhile, the faculty also began to set requirements for associate and full professorships (1932) and recommended, as early as 1928, that non-teaching staff be afforded ranks, although not tenure, on a basis comparable to that of faculty.

Two particular employer practices endorsed by the board might be mentioned here. One was a policy decrying nepotism, the strict enforcement of which Crane endorsed in 1936.

. . . often times employees are of excellent quality. It is, however, a very dangerous policy as the engaging of relatives grows on itself. It

creates serious embarrassment to the heads of departments, deans, and other administrative officers. In general, it results in lowered efficiency as, too frequently, it places employment not strictly upon the basis of efficiency but upon family and group relationships.

Although the policy was applauded by the board, from time to time exceptions were allowed because of the competence, long tenure, or special circumstances of a given case.

During the depression, the board also chose to adopt a firm ruling excluding all married women from employment, except in cases where the husband was "incapacitated and unable to support the family." Here, too, married women "of long service" on campus were sometimes exempted. The ruling resulted in considerable grief and many investigations, such as that of a home demonstration agent in Laramie County who was "reported to have a husband" or a secretary in engineering who married a law student and failed to inform her employer. The most highly-publicized case caused the University more than local criticism.

It occurred when Caroline F. Ware, employed as a summer school teacher by the history department, was discovered by Professor Frederick L. Nussbaum to be the wife of Gardiner Means of the National Consumers' Advisory Board. Petitions from Nussbaum, Professor Laura White (head of the history department), and the summer school director made no impression on the board, and the contract was duly withdrawn. Ware protested with some justification that the withdrawal constituted legal breach. In spite of a few articles in the press and the protests of several women's organizations, the board held firm. Trustees were supported by many Wyoming citizens who favored denying women's right to enter the marketplace in times when men were going unemployed.

During the 1920s, student activities burgeoned and branched, and although Crane was not always immediately involved in their planning, he kept an overseer's eye on what went on and often provided the students with support. The Associated Students of the University of Wyoming, founded in 1912-13 and headed by an executive board that included a number of faculty members, was technically in charge of "all general student activities," including a range of functions from publications to debate to competitive athletics, although actually president and board managed the latter firmly from above. In 1922, women students founded an organization of their own. At first, the group was sponsored by the dean of women, whose efforts to stand *in loco parentis* had resulted in a series of strict dormitory regulations and whose hopes were to lure women students to agreement by arranging a committee under her control. Shortly, however, the Associated Women Students gained at least a modicum of independence by electing their own officers and affiliating with a national women students' organization.

Meanwhile, clubs associated with academic majors multiplied, and the campus was soon alive with Ag Club, Home Ec Club, Potter Law Club, foreign language and drama clubs, clubs affiliated with religious organizations, and W Club for men who had won letters in intercollegiate athletics. All of these organizations had faculty sponsors, but all involved students in planning meetings and activities. Nationally-affiliated honorary societies in various academic fields authorized chapters on campus (sixteen such were listed by the dean of men in the early 1930s), and local honorary groups supplemented the roster. As early as 1929, the University set up an office to handle funds for all student organizations that so desired — a measure of the number and complexity of those that were developing.

Theater and music organizations were particularly popular. In the 1920s and 1930s, they provided a whole series of campus programs and occasionally even took productions on tour across the state. In 1924, Mabel Land DeKay, longtime teacher of drama, proposed a vast historical-dramatic pageant to be staged at Vedauwoo, the rock-pinnacled mountain site east of Laramie, and the board underwrote its costs to the tune of $1,000. Two thousand people came to watch, and the pageant became a spirited (and financial) success. Two or three plays a year were produced under the auspices of Theta Alpha Phi, dramatic honorary society established in 1921, and usually supervised by members of the English department faculty. Likewise, the University Glee Club, orchestra, and band (after 1924 part of the ROTC program) regularly provided music for campus events. Local programs were supplemented by a "public exercises" series, through which lecturers, musicians, and other artists were imported for special appearances.

Living accommodations for students were always of concern to parents and administrators alike — witness Crane's constant lobbying for new dormitory construction. Women's dormitories appeared early on campus — Merica hall in 1907, Hoyt hall in 1920 — and Crane supplemented them with the new Knight hall (1941), which also housed a cafeteria to replace the old commons.

CHAPTER SEVEN

Here all women dormitory students were required to eat, and if proper fees were not paid for board (as well as room) coeds might actually face suspension (1928). The first men's residence hall was built in 1928 under Crane's administration; a dormitory for forty male athletes was constructed in 1940; and 24 male students were regularly housed in the Wyoming Union, built in 1939. Still, a great many students — and particularly men — lived in rooming houses or with families in Laramie proper. Here the University occasionally attempted forms of inspection, and gloomy pictures were reported (especially during the depression) about the nature of housing available.

Crane's plan for a fraternity-sorority "park," an area in which University land would be sold for construction purposes to social fraternity and sorority chapters, represented an effort to provide campus housing for students otherwise living in town and an attempt to bolster the whole fraternity-sorority system. By 1936, there were twelve such organizations registered at the University, and the next five years saw two additions to the list. Interfraternity Council, dating from 1923, managed male rushing and other activities, while Panhellenic Council oversaw women's organizations. Through the years between the wars, occasional attacks of social exclusiveness surfaced in the college newspaper, which once called fraternities a "decidedly undesirable influence." The view was not shared by the president. At the start of Crane's administration, most of the fraternities and sororities sponsored houses near campus for social meetings and a handful of roomers and boarders. Crane's fraternity park plan took some time to catch on, although the University stood ready to extend credit terms for land purchase and construction. The first building erected was the Pi Beta Phi house, which was ready for occupancy in 1931. The president would have liked to continue fraternity park and dormitory expansion, but the termination of his tenure in office kept him from pressing more plans.

By nature, Crane had a great mistrust of youthful enthusiasm, excitement, fun, pranks, and games, but he nevertheless remained a strong supporter of the students at the University. The president delighted in student academic achievement. He frequently reported to the board his pride in the victories of debaters or the careful revision of the ASUW constitution or the addition of new honorary societies. On his recommendation, the board occasionally bailed out senior classes that

had not made it through without sinking into debt, just as it once bailed out a men's faculty club which could not keep its head above water. Crane's concern for students caused him to inaugurate a major campaign to raise money for the loan fund (established in 1921 and maintained at first by student contributions), resulting in a considerable increase in its resources in 1935. In 1929, he inaugurated a full student health insurance plan, providing for hospitalization when necessary. At his suggestion, the board conducted a survey of other universities' student health services, and the result was the addition of a University physician (1938) to come to the aid of a longtime, hard-working nurse.

Both Crane and the board were reluctant to raise fees or tuition, fearing a drop in enrollment and respecting the Wyoming constitutional provision that education should remain as "nearly free" as possible. In 1941, tuition remained at $75 a year for Wyoming students; and fees for student health, the Union, activities, and other special items were generally less than $5 a quarter. On many occasions, Crane backed legislation to reduce or refund rail fares to Laramie from remote corners of the state, but such legislation always failed to pass.

The greatest crisis for University of Wyoming students came in the depression years, when financial pressures caused many to drop out of school and those remaining to seek whatever employment they might find. Enrollment dropped from 1,247 in fall semester 1931 to 1,027 two years later, and administrators counted themselves lucky that the decline was not even greater. Desperate students shoveled coal and loaded railroad cars. Delinquent student fees multiplied in number and amount, and many who had lived in dormitories cut expenses by moving into dark basement quarters or by reneging on their agreements to take meals in the Commons. In 1931, Crane set up a special student employment committee, which made a vast effort to utilize student labor on campus wherever possible, whether in cutting stone for construction or maintaining the skating rink. As a result, almost a third of the students were provided with 292 campus jobs in the 1932-33 academic year; besides outdoor labor, they worked part-time in the library, the bookstore, the gymnasium, and other campus buildings.

123

Campus aerial view, 1930

In 1933-34, the federal government stepped in to help, and Crane's Washington lobbying brought federal aid through financing of campus jobs for an additional ten percent to twelve percent of the total enrollment. Faculty members contributed; they instituted a plan for student relief through a donation of five percent from one month's salary for each professor — even at a time when salaries had been reduced. A special student welfare office handled the loan funds. The president's report to the board in December 1935 indicates how untiringly he had worked for all kinds of funding — and particularly federal aid — on the students' behalf. Without his efforts, the student body would have suffered far greater misery and trauma during depression years.

Still, Crane had difficulties, and they arose not from his support of student body or faculty *in toto* but from his inability, personally, to change with new social mores and his rigidity, if not pettiness, in dealing with individuals in crisis. The period between the wars in this country was characterized by swiftly changing social and intellectual currents. Peaceniks and flappers mingled in the twenties, while prohibition competed with the "jazz age." A strict and unyielding moralist like Crane was necessarily out of step with the times. The depression brought America up short, replacing the nation's optimism and playfulness with fear, hunger, and threats of social upheaval, with which a solemn and humorless president could better cope and against the background of which he rose to fuller heights. Throughout his administration, Crane had trouble dealing with individuals who in some way crossed or opposed him. At such times, he could become petty and even vindictive. Not all of the faculty and students saw his irritation, and many perhaps did not even dream it existed. Nevertheless, as president, Crane showed little tolerance for radical innovations or for variety in human individuality.

Take, for example, the pacifist and anti-militarist movement that swept across many college campuses in the mid-1920s. True, Wyoming students and the Western states in general were affected less than those of the East, where religious leaders (especially Quakers, but also groups like the YMCA) joined educators in a peace movement. Organizations such as the Committee on Militarism in Education boasted a national council that included individuals like David Starr Jordan, Alexander Meiklejohn, Reinhold Niebuhr, Carlton J. H. Hayes, Zona Gale, and many others. Speakers toured college campuses — and a number of them, including Sherwood Eddy, came as far as the University of Wyoming. Citizens like John Dewey, Robert Morss Lovett, and Paul H. Douglas lent their names to groups that were (according to a memorandum in the files of Major B. C. Daly, professor of military science and tactics) "busily subverting our educational system and transforming it into a number of socialistic centers."

With his background as a military man and his concept of military virtues, Crane (a lieutenant-colonel in the Officer Reserve Corps) had little sympathy and less respect for the pacifist cause. He gloried instead in such ceremonies as National Defense Day (so established by President Calvin Coolidge in 1924), at which he spoke with fervor. After 1929, he persuaded the board (and indeed he may have provided some funding) to offer a special scholarship to that Wyoming student who made the best record at summer ROTC camp. He was pleased to see organized the first campus military band, which students might join as a substitute for required drill. No one enjoyed military ceremonies more than the University president (as witness the student newspaper's report on the 1930 flagpole dedication). One of Crane's pet Washington projects after 1934 was finding federal funds for armories and other military buildings. If Crane had a friend on campus it was Major Daly, whom he consistently applauded and of whom he stated "There is not a member of the entire instructional staff of the University whom we would rank higher in general value to the institution and in instructional ability." Consequently,

when Daly was occasionally threatened with replacement and finally retired as a military science professor in 1932, Crane protested to the secretary of war, transferred Daly to the position of dean of men, and later saw to his assignment as athletic coordinator. In 1936, Daly compiled a history of the military department and its honors, a meticulous source of information for the historian.

It was fitting that in the late 1920s, Crane became chair of the Committee on Military Organization and Policy for the National Association of Land-Grant Colleges and Universities. Crane's committee acted as liaison between the academic world and the U.S. War Department, working closely with the government in matters affecting college ROTC units. In 1928, when a group of pacifists appeared before the committee to argue against a military presence on campus, Crane wrote to the head of the land-grant college association that he had 'little sympathy with this propaganda because of the character of the men who are most active in it," by which he seems to have meant Quakers and other religious conscientious objectors.

The particular cause espoused by the pacifist organizations was that of abolishing or restricting campus military activities and organizations. It had long been assumed by land-grant colleges that the wording of the Morrill Act demanded that military training be required of all campus men, but in June 1930, the U.S. attorney general confirmed a judicial decision regarding a University of Wisconsin case asserting that this was not so; the Morrill Act required that military training be offered, but not that it be made compulsory. Some years later, in 1934, a legal suit brought by the University of California (and supported by many land-grant institutions, including Wyoming) determined, however, that any given college had the right to require ROTC of its students.

Crane's position was clear: Never did Wyoming vary its requirement that all men join either the ROTC or the military marching band. The military science department had been founded on the premise that the Morrill Act set an absolute requirement, and the *Bulletin* was merely reworded after the Wisconsin decision.

Recognizing that preparation for the national defense is one of the important obligations of

citizenship and that the qualities of patriotism, loyalty, discipline, leadership, and respect for constituted authority inculcated by proper military training are valuable in the formation of character, it has been the consistent policy of the University to co-operate with the Federal Government in making the Department of Military Science and Tactics as effective as practicable. To this end, military training has been made compulsory for male students qualified and eligible therefor.

The *Bulletin* always insisted that ROTC enrollment was not "in any sense conscription." Furthermore, a land-grant college survey, run by Crane's military committee, demonstrated that most administrations favored the granting of official credit for both basic and upper division campus military courses.

Crane's stance on military duty and the ROTC brought him hostility not just from national, but from local organizations. As early as 1926, many Wyoming citizens — particularly those belonging to labor unions — wrote the president requesting that compulsory military training be abolished. For the 1927 legislature, Crane compiled a large file for use in case the University's policy was attacked. Although the campaign quieted for a time, it revived again in 1935 and 1936, at which point Crane not only heard from Wyoming church officials but from the students themselves. An "anti-war strike" and demonstration, sponsored by several student peace committees, was held in the Old Main auditorium in April 1936 as supported by local church groups and the poetry society. Even the student newspaper called for the abolition of the ROTC.

Once again the local ROTC unit is parading daily, accompanied vigorously by the well-meant, if somewhat irregular, playing of the band. During morning drill periods, the unit appears in unpleasant-looking "monkey suits," which keep their wearers very warm, but which do not fit any too well . . . Look closely at this group of young men when they are in uniform. Does their appearance and the "highest honor rating" which the unit will get after inspection seem worth the $50,000 invested annually in the corps?. . . . Even if this "training" may not be actually harmful, its abolition is certainly justified because of the extravagant waste of time and money it represents. . . .

Although Crane stood firm against all critics in his policy on the ROTC, militarism was at the heart of the first scandal that shook his administration in the years 1924-26. During this period, the president clashed almost openly with a young radical professor who came to Wyoming from the University of Oklahoma and who rose to the headship of the mathematics department in 1923.

H. C. Gossard was a competent academician and administrator, a pillar of the Methodist Church, an acquaintance of former President Aven Nelson (who was chairman of the board of the local Wesley Foundation), a member of the Lions' Club, and active in the YMCA. Gossard's repeated criticism of Crane probably had its origins in the military issue. In 1924, the mathematics professor brought Sherwood Eddy of the Committee on Militarism in Education to campus as a speaker, and even persuaded the president to suspend classes for this "all-University" assembly. Instead of speaking on Russia, from which he had just returned, Eddy preached a veritable sermon against militarism and the campus ROTC. In future years, similar appearances on or around campus were sponsored by the YMCA, with Gossard's assistance. In 1925, John Nevin Sayre (Episcopal minister, executive secretary of the Committee on Militarism in Education, and official in the YMCA) spoke in Laramie where he very likely made Gossard's acquaintance. It was probably Gossard who supplied Sayre with charges published later in a pacifist journal, wherein Sayre claimed that Daly, the

commandant of the ROTC at the University of Wyoming, is a fine Christian man, sincere and courteous, but very conservative and hopelessly set in his views. Because of his ability he has gained a dominant place in the faculty and is now chairman of the Speakers' Committee. No one can get on the campus to speak without his O.K. The President supports the captain [actually major since 1922] very strongly, for he is a keen preparedness man.

Crane and Daly furiously denied the accusation, which had been picked up by the Associated Press.

Gossard was almost certainly also involved in the scandal sheet called the *White Mule Boomerang,* a mimeographed and anonymous publication that appeared mysteriously around the campus in mailboxes and under doors on the morning of Easter Sunday 1926. The term "Boomerang" was drawn from the local newspaper, originally named by humorist Bill Nye, while "White Mule"

President Arthur Griswold Crane, 1922-1941

referred to a drink outlawed by prohibition: "Only a fool fools with White Mule." The *White Mule Boomerang,* which became a *cause célèbre* as soon as it appeared, dealt with another searing issue of the day in accusing President Crane of ignoring student drinking, partly in a local cafe, partly at four different fraternities, and partly in general.

Crane's reaction was characterisically intense. True, these were days of prohibition. But in spite of the fact that Wyoming seems to have been among the wettest states of the very wet West, Crane was a letter-of-the-law man, and of course he had parents to deal with too. No measures were spared in tracking down the *White Mule Boomerang's* perpetrators, and shortly the print type was traced to the Methodist Church mimeograph machine; a hired, imported handwriting expert identified the title as written by Raymond H. Laury (part-time student and Methodist student minister); and even the paper was traced to its purchase in a local shop. Under some pressure, Laury and three young students (all originally from Sheridan) confessed. One of the students was the son of a University trustee.

A shocked faculty by unanimous vote dismissed Laury as campus minister. As it happened, Laury was a boarder in the Gossard household, and the president was sure that Gossard and the second Methodist minister, W. L. French, were involved behind the scenes. Although Gossard asserted his innocence, Crane wrote to the trustee father:

The boys were influenced by Reverend Laury and he in turn is controlled and guided by a group consisting of Reverend French, Dr. [Aven] Nelson, and Dr. Gossard. Though the young men have sought in their testimony to fully exonerate any of these faculty members, nevertheless it is plain that had the faculty members manifested in the past disapproval of such tactics and such broadside accusations, the White Mule would never have appeared.

Laury left town; the other students were suspended; and Nelson, a strict teetotaler, resigned from the board of the Wesleyan Foundation. Called to task, Gossard agreed to take a year's leave of absence at partial pay in order to work for the YMCA as a traveling representative. It was agreed that his contract would be terminated after a year. His friend Bernice Sanford, dean of women, lost her job in 1926.

Nevertheless, the *White Mule Boomerang* scandal died hard, and Crane long remembered. To the board, he preached patience.

From all evidence that we can secure, including information from the Federal Enforcement Officer, intercollegiate visitors to our campus and general observation, the conditions at the University of Wyoming [in regard to prohibition violations] are much better than those prevailing in similar institutions in other sections of the country. There are, of course, and always will be infractions of the rules and social conventions. The question at issue is one of procedure. The administration believes that quiet, steady, unobtrusive, and persistent action will bring more lasting and better results than megaphone methods, particularly if these are supported by careful analysis of the facts.

Keenly aware of prohibition's problems and perhaps inspired by the methods of Laury and his friends, who had literally become informers for the federal enforcers, or T-men, Crane used liquor violation to cause the dismissal of the head of the foreign languge department. Professor O. C. Gebert was no great friend of the president's, and the files contain transcripts of testimony privately solicited by Crane from the professor, students, and the household's young boarders. In December

1926, in part on the information of an illiterate letter received from a temperance advocate in Cheyenne, Gebert's house was invaded and the T-men discovered a small quantity of homemade wine. A gentleman to the core, Gebert offered to resign. In accepting his suggestion, trustees were kind enough to continue him in his position through the academic year in regard for his generally good conduct. The victory was Crane's, and it was not out of character. Transcriptions of Crane's command performance interviews with friends, family, and faculty were frequently introduced as evidence before the board in dismissal cases. Occasionally the president's own notes were utilized, as were his reports of rumors and secondhand gossip he had heard.

Gossard's name appeared once more in the University's most sensational scandal of the twenties — the accusation, published widely in the press, that the University of Wyoming directly paid its football players or arranged illicitly for their support. In the 1920s, such financial support was deemed scandalous, for college football was still a strictly extracurricular activity. Football conferences maintained stern rules about recruiting and eligibility, and Wyoming had apparently already briefly (1912) run afoul of one of the regulations. That colorful head football coach, W. H. "Lonestar" Dietz, had brought several key players with him from Louisiana in the autumn of 1924 could scarcely be debated. That he continued to "invite" other players from his home state to join the Wyoming football team, and that he offered various rewards for their doing so was the question in point, as raised in the first instance by an Associated Press release in Louisiana. Dietz vigorously denied that he had "directly or indirectly" invited the players. Affidavits were collected from players involved, and evidence began to be accumulated. In the fall of 1925, Dietz's victories on the field caused a flurry of publicity and the revival of the "professionalism" complaint. Not until 1926 did Crane discover that Gossard was involved. Apparently the young mathematics professor, a crusader of high principles, had approached representatives of conference schools on several occasions to complain that Wyoming athletes were accepting money, loans, and scholarships. As a Lions' Club member, Gossard's firsthand knowledge of a fellowship presented to a star basketball player and a plan for offering loans to indigent athletes impressed conference members.

Coach W. H. "Lonestar" Dietz, c. 1920

Crane investigated with all his usual diligence. Testimony was solicited from faculty members in person and in writing. All presidents of conference schools were asked whether Gossard had contacted them on any occasions. Athletes gave testimony, and members of the Lions' Club swore depositions. Professor S. H. Knight, representative to the athletic conference, wrote a 26-page report touching on all episodes and all possible complaints. Crane himself took pains to explain the situation to faculty and to local businessmen.

Gossard's intervention eventually turned against him, for he was condemned by a faculty committee that reviewed all of his activities, expelled from the Lions' Club, censured by the president, and deplored by the board of trustees. His subsequent appeal to the American Association of University Professors for payment of his full salary during his year's leave of absence resulted in a two-year investigation and several on-the-spot hearings by a committee of that body. The AAUP found essentially in favor of the University, and Gossard dropped his appeal. Still, rumors of unfair athletic practices continued to haunt Crane and the administration. In 1927, Dietz resigned, supposedly as the result of a losing season.

No sooner had the athletic scandal died down than the engineering college provided Crane with another cause for investigation. Here, students were involved, for here (as the Carnegie Foundation team later reported) facilities were inadequate and equipment was short. Several professors were scarcely abiding by their contracts, and students complained that profs skipped classes, borrowed tools for their own use, and paid little attention to laboratory conditions. As a consequence of their complaints, a group of students in 1927 conducted what was later termed a "popularity" contest for engineering professors. Earl D. Hay, dean of the college, won low place on the totem pole by an overwhelming vote, and indeed his professional conduct had been the brunt of most criticism. The most popular professor was J. C. Fitterer. Irritated at the students for violating discipline, Crane conducted the usual full-fledged investigation, with depositions, sworn statements, letters, and transcripts of interviews with faculty and students alike. In spite of much testimony to the contrary, Crane may have accepted Hay's word that Fitterer was so close to the students as to be involved in contest planning from the start. But the most unpopular and the most popular engineering professors were dismissed in 1928: The one for general lack of competence, the other for what can only be termed disloyalty to the boss.

Crane's rules and expectations were just as strict for students as for faculty. Here, too, his lack of humor and want of good-natured tolerance stood at variance with the financial and other support he was eager to offer. He was sure that the University must act *in loco parentis* during times of changing social behavior and growing social distress. Student activities were always closely monitored. Having dismissed one dean of women for her apparent friendship with Gossard, he watched the new dean — "by the smoothest and most courteous bit of railroading ever done at an assembly of any description" — push through a rule that freshman girls be in their rooms by 8 p.m. in spite of angry protests. Although attendance was voluntary, he deplored absences from the weekly assembly as a sign of "poor citizenship." He spoke of the need to educate "ladies and gentlemen" as well as well-informed scholars. He did not care much for student social activities, and when he refused to permit the hiring of the usual out-of-town music group for the Cadet Ball, he explained that

there is an ever increasing tendency for increased expense in these student social functions due to the natural rivalry and the effort to "keep up with Lizzie." Effort should be made to promote a counter tendency of simplicity and reasonableness.

Firm rules required students who "contemplate" being married to report their intention to the proper officials; clandestine marriage could be cause for suspension. Crane was particularly upset by Sneak Day, that traditional junior-senior celebration when upperclassmen slipped out of town for a picnic and some spring cavorting. The president was concerned, he said, because the "advent of the automobile" added a note of "danger" to the undertaking.

Automobiles were indeed the president's *bête noire* and the cause of another great crisis, although certain observers felt that he deliberately chose time and place because of his old antipathy towards the engineering school. On December 4, 1931, on a chilly winter evening, Crane made an unusual appearance at a campus social function and took note of a "wholesale exodus" of about fifty young people of both sexes from the Engineers' Ball. Following, he discovered the erstwhile dancers had taken refuge in parked automobiles near the gymnasium, where the event was being held. Angrily he whipped open the car doors, "visited," "interviewed," or "accosted" (all his own words) a number of couples he found there, and expressed "amazement and chagrin." To one or more of the couples, he shouted, in his own words, "Such actions belong on First Street [the Laramie red-light district]" or, according to the students,

You come out here for all your drinking and petting. You ought to go to First Street where you belong.

This above all precipitated the ensuing troubles, and eventually Crane, who pointed out that the remark "has been given the worst possible interpretation," explained to the board that he *should* have said

Your actions are such that you are throwing yourself open to grave suspicion, to adverse comment, and to the charge that these actions are such as to justify comparison with the actions which one sees in the Bowery sections of our cities,

hardly a shouting phrase. Following his inspection of the parked cars, Crane found new (1928) Dean R. L. Rhoads of the College of Engineering, and together they counted (noting the identities of) all 43 students who returned to the ballroom following intermission.

The "First Street" remark and the president's entire attitude aroused the ire of many students.

Although the ASUW refused to take formal action, on the following Monday a committee of 24 young people from various student organizations sent four of their number to demand an apology from Crane. The president told them "not to hold their breath." By evening, he had somewhat calmed himself, though the students had not. At a "mass" gathering, Crane suggested the students present their case to the board of trustees, but instead they declared a "strike," scheduled to continue until an apology was presented. When "strikers" congregated the next day, Crane made an effort to continue classes as usual, but his anger showed in his decree that those who were not in class had "voluntarily ceased to be students of the University," were barred from campus and their residences, and forfeited any University jobs. That afternoon, Crane called in the police to break up "large groups" of picketers.

Deans, businessmen, faculty, the press, and the chairman of the board eventually got into the act. The result was that a chastened student committee persuaded colleagues to accept the president's terms: reinstatement, a hearing before the board, committee action regarding jobs, and a high-level student-faculty committee to investigate. Just 24 hours after it started, the "strike" had ended.

To the board on December 14, Crane presented a 25-page document detailing the events. Although he was close to apologetic for his "First Street" analogy, he did not spare words. Since the war (1918), he told trustees,

there has been a general tendency toward license and laxity of conduct in many things where stricter standards of conduct formerly prevailed. This tendency has been marked in the habits of our people. The youth movement, the doctrine of natural development, the relinquishment of parental control, the misuse of automobiles, Bolshevism, student strikes, and bizarre modernism have all contributed their share to the frenzied abandon of youth. . . . It is high time that an institution of learning like this one set an example which shall aid conscientious parents and shall not tear down the careful instruction and nurture of years when their young people leave home to attend college.

After the student committee reported to the board, trustees issued a conciliatory statement, condemning strikes, violence, agitation, disloyalty, and disturbances, but averring that the whole incident had been greatly exaggerated and had arisen from certain misunderstandings. At least one trustee said later that the students had presented their case "effectively and with commendable decorum, but the board obviously had to back the President." As the president had promised, the students had been officially reinstated, and shortly they got their jobs back. The student-faculty committee proposed more careful chaperoning of dances (including the hiring of a doorman); designation of special areas for smoking; and the "loyal cooperation" of the students in a "code of honor." The moratorium imposed on social events was lifted in early February. Less happy was the fate of Dean Rhoads. The angry president who reported on the dean's "lack of support for the administration . . . in the entire recent crisis," an attitude "of long standing," and recommended that Rhoads be "immediately removed from official duties" was persuaded by the board to withdraw his request. Still, it was no accident that Rhoads was the first to go when the depression in 1933 required programmatic and faculty cut-backs.

The "First Street" episode and the student strike were not happy affairs. Considerable publicity was given both to Crane's actions and those of the students, not only in the regional press but in a Sunday supplement of national circulation, where a cartoon showed Crane wresting open the door of a parked automobile. Most response locally (and Crane presented pages of material to the board of trustees) favored the president's disciplinary approach. Years later students (both those pro and those con) remembered the event with various reactions from amusement to regret.

Discipline on campus undoubtedly increased. Crane began presenting long reports to the board about minor episodes of cheating, thievery, and disorderliness. Student activities of all sorts were more carefully supervised. In 1934, Crane showed the board a careful organizational chart to demonstrate the duties of various student committees. The immediate cause of alarm was a "yellow sheet" edition of the *Branding Iron,* whose young editor, an erstwhile campus radical, was suspended for his reference to president, dean of men (Daly), and president's secretary (Ida Moen) as the "holy trinity." A few years later, a tauter and more explicit new constitution was adopted by the ASUW. In March 1936, somebody (almost certainly on Crane's orders) removed three nude paintings from a traveling art exhibit, thus evoking protest from the American Artists' Congress and amusement from the *Nation*. Two years later there was a brief scandal involving student experimentation with marijuana, but the center of operations was found to be located far from Laramie and no disciplinary action was taken.

On balance, by 1940, Crane had a great deal of which to be proud. In spite of his strict and disciplinary stance, he was not unpopular with students — after all, students came and left, and he was far from the most important individual in their campus lives. The students could hardly be said to be suffering from lack of social activities. The student handbook for 1941 lists fourteen annual special balls and dances, sponsored by their own clubs and organizations, and unnumbered less formal "mixers" besides. Crane had seen student enrollment more than triple during his administration; he had provided students with dormitories, health service, loans, jobs, and general support. If some faculty had suffered almost arbitrary punishments, most were extremely grateful for the president's support during the depression — his restoration of salary cuts (especially commended by the AAUP); his fight for fringe benefits; and the beginnings of the retirement system for teachers passed by the legislature in 1941. Crane was in turn proud of the faculty: the increasing number of Ph.D.s among it, the honors accorded by the Colorado-Wyoming Academy of Science, the continuing recognition of research. He delighted in the accreditation of the tiny law school and the admission of the University to the Association of American Universities. Perhaps one of his happiest moments before the board came when he reported not an athletic victory but the authorization of a Wyoming Alpha chapter of Phi Beta Kappa in 1940. Crane had hoped to gain a PBK chapter ten years before, but the application was refused. Its installation remained a credit to the efforts of a dedicated faculty committee. Sigma Xi had come to the campus in 1929. No one was prouder of these achievements than Crane himself. They probably meant more to him than his personal triumph in being elected president of the National Association of State Universities in 1939. A man of 63, the president undoubtedly looked forward to a dignified retirement in two years.

The blow that was delivered to Crane in 1941 was probably the more devastating because it was unexpected. In all the years of his administration, the president had seemed to be managing well with the board of trustees. On several occasions during the twenties, Crane was considered for other university appointments, and in 1927, he was offered the job of chancellor at the University of Nebraska at a salary of $12,500. The board unanimously voted to meet the offer, although with somewhat muted enthusiasm. However, on several other occasions, trustees specifically commended Crane for a job well done.

Politics had seemed remote from University administration. A Republican, Crane meticulously kept out of politics and insisted that University employees follow his line. A brief flurry on a "political stand" he was rumored to have taken in Casper in 1924 seems never to have made the headlines. If any University official assumed a political role, it was Fay Smith, secretary to the board, whose Republican preference was well known and whose correspondence leaves little doubt that he aided Republican candidates in electoral campaigns. Moreover, during Crane's administration — up until 1939 — Democratic and Republican governors alike maintained a near political balance in their appointments to the board of trustees. Of the nine members, five were always of one party and four always of the other. Indeed, trustees prided themselves on their own fine spirit.

The members of this Board work together harmoniously, with a wonderful spirit of cooperation and fairness to the State, to the University and to each other. At no time in the history of the State have the various sections and industries of the State been as equally well represented on this Board as now. [The president feels] that this condition is one which will result in much good to the University and to the State.

Crane never expressed disapproval or mistrust of any single gubernatorial appointment decision, and although his rather formal social attitudes kept him at some distance, as late as 1939, he seems to have regarded several board members as his "close personal friends."

The long honeymoon came to an end with the election of Nels Smith as Wyoming governor in the autumn of 1938. A Republican cattle and wheat rancher, Smith had little experience in politics. Rumors were that he was a puppet of James B. Griffith, the Republican party chairman, who was also state land commissioner. No friend to education (he vetoed the teachers' retirement program passed by the Republican legislature in 1939), Smith became the brunt of jokes about his use of the English language as well as his political pork-barreling. It seems clear that he was impressed more by Crane's enemies than by the president's accomplishments. According to Professor T. A. Larson, Wyoming historian, "Nothing caused Governor Smith more grief or gave him worse publicity than his inept handling of university affairs." Nevertheless, ultimate victory was the governor's and the loss was Crane's.

Smith's first three appointments to the board of trustees were Republicans all. Milward Simpson was well known in the state and was to become the Republican candidate for U.S. Senate in 1940. Frank Barrett was a Lusk Republican and future U.S. senator. The third appointee, the relatively unknown Peter Sill, was a Laramie businessman and baker. Although no single Democrat voted against the appointment, Crane reported later that the governor's move

was protested vigorously . . . by Republican officials who maintained that Sill was not fitted for such a position. He had the support of a small faction in Laramie, which, for years, had been notoriously antagonistic to the University administration.

It seems likely that Sill was indeed chosen to facilitate the president's dismissal. More important was the Republicanizing of the board.

Quarreling began almost at once. In the spring of 1939, trustees questioned the reappointments of eight members of the University faculty. Crane conducted his usual investigation, primarily through secretive personal interviews with faculty colleagues, and the board eventually chose to renew contracts and take no particular action. In July, Simpson (one of the new board members) not only challenged several appointments (manager of the bookstore and head of the physical education department) but also debated the executive committee's right to make them between board meetings. Along with the governor, Simpson (who said he spoke for "scores of alumni and businessmen throughout Wyoming") thereupon called for a legal opinion from the attorney general in regard to the duty of trustees and executive committee in appointments and dismissals. Attorney General Ewing T. Kerr found the executive committee competent to make professorial appointments as long as the board subsequently approved.

A worse crisis occurred in September 1939 when at Simpson's urging the board refused to approve Crane's recommendation for dean of the College of Education and appointed O. C. Schwiering instead. Trustees subsequently claimed that the president "made an attack on Schwiering's character" and "became angry" when the new dean's name was mentioned. Schwiering was, Crane reported later, a candidate of whom he "vigorously disapproved." At the same board meeting, trustees requested Crane to report on the competence and number of his own administrative staff. A month later trustees set up a committee of six to make a "complete study" of all University departments, a resolution moved by Evelyn Plummer of Cheyenne and seconded by Simpson, who was promptly appointed to the committee.

In January 1940, on the eve of a scheduled board meeting, the governor invited a group of five trustees to dinner in Cheyenne and included with them Griffith, the state Republican chairman, to whom Governor Smith felt strongly attached and whom he invited to many subsequent board meetings. Although trustees later denied it, Crane was convinced that the social occasion was actually a coverup for a planning session on his discharge. The next day, following the business meeting of the board, another "informal caucus" took place at a Laramie hotel. Crane was not present, but late in the afternoon he was called before a committee of three — Trustees Milward Simpson, Wallace Bond, and D. Marshall — and informed that the board was not "entirely happy" with his policies. The president later claimed that he was explicitly told that the governor wanted him out, although trustees denied saying so. The board later considered this episode as full notice of the president's pending dismissal, but contended that

notice was given quietly, courteously and by a group of his friends. He was informed that he could "write his own ticket." This meant a generous pension and possible election to emeritus standing. He could have gone out in a blaze of glory by means of the publicity he knows so well how to handle.

Formal declarations and decisions were postponed, but rumors began to circulate. On January 25, the student newspaper published reports of the possible dropping of the pilot and, registering indignation, summarized Crane's multitude of accomplishments over the years.

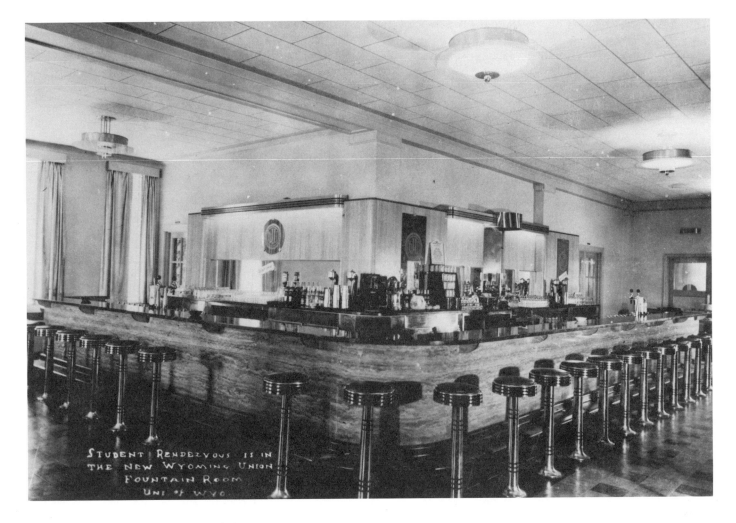

Wyoming Union fountain room, c. 1940

The night before the next meeting of March 25, the "anti-Crane trustees" caucused to the wee hours in a Laramie hotel with frequent telephone calls to the governor in Cheyenne. Governor, Republican party chairman, and rebellious trustees were two hours late to the formal meeting. Here Simpson read his notes on the earlier "executive session," apparently to explain away the fact that Crane was not present. In executive session and with some apparent opposition, the board resolved to create the position of a comptroller — a move actually suggested by the Carnegie Foundation team in 1933. By the board's reasoning

> *. . . due to the great growth and consequent increased volume of business some of the financial and business affairs of the University have been handled in a decidedly loose and unsatisfactory manner and the Trustees have determined that drastic, effective, and immediate steps must be taken to correct that situation.*

> *. . . To that end the business administration, purchasing activities, financial affairs, public relations in business matters with other departments of the State . . . [shall] be consolidated and centered in the hands of a Comptroller appointed by and under the supervision of and answerable only to this Board.*

Official amendments to the bylaws were hastily composed by Simpson during the noon hour and adopted by trustees. Thereupon the board offered Crane a one-year contract at $6,000, a salary reduction of $2,000, justified on the grounds that the comptroller would relieve him of many heretofore pressing duties. Crane requested two weeks to consider the offer.

133

Governor Nels Smith nearly blew the whole ball game. On April 1, in a one-sentence letter with no explanation, the governor ordered Fay Smith to instruct Crane to "hold in abeyance" the contracts of eleven University employees until the board's next meeting. Among the names listed were those of Carl Arnold, dean of the law school; Ralph D. Goodrich, dean of the College of Engineering; and H. T. Person, professor of engineering and future University president. All of those named in what became called the "purge" had received routine contract renewals at the previous board meeting. How the governor derived his list remains uncertain, but he explained that

a number of instructors at the university, drawing in the neighborhood of $4,000 a year, actually spend but one hour a week in classroom instruction, and in many instances some teach as little as two or three hours a week.

If Nels Smith expected to undermine either Crane or faculty with his tactic, he must have been surprised at the result. Crane immediately accepted the offer of a contract with reduced salary. Schedules and salaries of the "purged" were compiled and publicized. Students, faculty, and, in general, the press deplored the governor's high-handedness and cried politics. Meeting on April 8, the board found itself united with the president. If nothing else, its own independence was at stake. Rapidly, trustees adopted a resolution reaffirming the contracts they had authorized and ordered the governor so advised. On second thought, trustees managed to get in touch with the governor, who was fishing at Saratoga, and requested him to join the meeting on his return trip.

What occurred has not been fully recorded, but the governor shortly backtracked. The board's resolution announced that "all misunderstandings have been settled satisfactorily" and that "Governor Smith is entirely satisfied with the manner in which the Board is managing the affairs of the University of Wyoming." Perhaps as a compromise, trustees authorized a complete "audit and report of University fiscal and academic affairs." But at least temporarily, Crane and the board had joined forces. It is significant that four days later in Greybull, Simpson introduced Crane to the local alumni club as "a great president of a great university."

The show of unity could not last, and Crane's uncertain tenure kept him at his job for only another year. The 1940-41 academic year was filled with rumors, publicity, speculation, and uncertainties. In August 1940, Crane published a report emphasizing his accomplishments and circulated it widely through the state. Trustees complained later that he made much of whatever publicity he was able to rouse. By now, Crane had lost the powerful support of Fay Smith; and when Smith was nominated for comptroller (and actually received the office in 1941), Crane apparently attempted to enlist the support of law school Dean Carl Arnold in his effort to get Simpson to cast a negative vote.

With the legislature of 1941, Crane conducted his usual campaign. Although Nels Smith opted to veto the portion of the appropriations bill that would have financed a new building for the College of Education, the governor did sign into law the largest appropriation the University had ever received — more than $750,000 for the main University alone. To the legislature Crane carried a large "brief" on the possible election of members of the board, but no bills resulted. More to the point, the governor again filled three vacancies on the board of trustees, this time with two Republicans and an alumnus Democrat, Bard Ferrall, who had expressed opposition to Crane's administration.

The vote on Crane's contract occurred on St. Patrick's Day 1941, with the long expected results. In spite of petitions and committee requests from students, alumni, and townspeople, the board in executive session voted not to renew the president.

Serious difficulties on policy having arisen between the President, Dr. Crane, and this Board, and it appearing to be to the best interests of the University to terminate his tenure of office with the University, the Board hereby terminates his services as of this date and agrees to pay the balance due on his contract and to pay him an additional three thousand dollars and to permit him and his family to occupy the University house to the end of his contract, June 30, 1941.

The vote against Crane was 7-2, with Milward Simpson and V. J. Facinelli favoring renewal. The board published no explanation other than the above.

Nevertheless, an explanation may be advanced. Crane and his policies had alienated many individuals, and often those who had powerful political forces behind them. Among his personal enemies, the president could count state politician Scotty Jack, with whom Crane had gotten into "a scrap." The dismissal of Dean Rhoads of engineering, following the student strike, called forth the irritation of powerful state Senator Harry Horton, a good friend to Rhoads. The board's contention that Crane had "political ambitions" was enough to evoke irritation, if not rivalry. Even greater opposition to the president had developed among many alumni who favored a strong and competitive intercollegiate athletic program. In 1933, Crane had urged the board to drop football to save money. Thereafter, the team could not manage a strong winning season. Several trustees were lifelong sports fans. Indeed, at the same time that it fired the president, the board reorganized the administrative structure of the athletic program and hired a new football coach.

Nor did faculty leap to the president's defense. In spite of his many efforts on their behalf, professors had undoubtedly become aware of the stubborn streak in Crane's nature, his prying into personal affairs, and his tendency to isolate himself and operate alone. His general animus towards the engineering college was common knowledge on campus, and rumors circulated that he was about to attack again to get rid of a "young Turk" named Person who later, incidentally, became the University president. Historian Wilson O. Clough, who was there, asserts that "even close friends found it increasingly difficult to advise him." When he was dismissed, few faculty seem to have protested, although the student newspaper cried politics and demanded explanations.

Under the circumstances, the election of Governor Nels Smith had provided an opportunity for packing the board and permitting the president's dismissal. In actual manipulations and planning, the new trustees found an ally in powerful Fay Smith, long-term secretary and newly-appointed comptroller. Smith, in turn, was a good friend to Frank Barrett, who (according to a trustee colleague) "engendered and nurtured and continued" the fight against Crane. Like several new board members, Barrett enjoyed athletic events, both on the football field and the basketball court. It is notable that he and the new football coach became good friends. In one of his appointments, however, Governor Smith misjudged. Two years of working with Crane changed Milward Simpson's mind, and in the crunch Simpson voted to retain the president.

An angry president contested his dismissal. Within a few weeks, Crane circulated to colleagues and acquaintances a letter crying political pressure.

Like little Orphan Annie's goblins, the politicians will get you if you don't watch out. In fact, they may get you even if you do watch out. For nineteen years I have fought a small band of hungry politicians. My nine predecessors' average tenure was less than four years. Combination of political mishaps has given the gang trump cards in a Governor whom they can manipulate.

Without informing trustees of his plans, the former president filed a long protest with the National Association of State Universities in which he summarized his administration's accomplishments and the series of events through which he was dismissed. Quoting a statement he had first devised in March, Crane repeated his accusation that his firing was an act of politicians and urged that Wyoming citizens keep close watch on appointments and policies at the University. He appended 129 pages of news releases and editorial comments on his dismissal and the events that preceded it.

Fine arts building, c. 1930

Caught by surprise, the board responded in an angry brief of its own, in which it described Crane's inability to provide necessary educational leadership, his supposedly inadequate performance with the legislature, the various depression-age overdrafts, Crane's frequent absences from campus, and what it termed his "political ambitions." Three members of the board carried the brief to a meeting of the committee appointed by the NASU to investigate Crane's case. No formal hearing occurred. But on December 10, 1941, the committee simply resolved not to carry Crane's case for further investigation. Ironically, even the $3,000 voted by the board as a terminal bonus seems to have been denied to Crane, for the attorney general (at the state auditor's behest) ruled that such a "gift" was not proper use of state moneys.

Crane was not finished. Failing in his bid for the Republican nomination for U.S. Senate in 1942, he was elected secretary of state in 1946 and automatically became governor in 1949 when Lester C. Hunt moved to the U.S. Senate. He served in that capacity until 1951.

Crane's myriad accomplishments should not be overlooked in consideration of his last difficult years. He loved the University; his intentions were beyond debate; and he served for nearly twenty years, working with eight governors, ten legislatures, numerous board members, and even more faculty and colleagues. Crane was not far from wrong when he wrote in his own campaign literature in 1942 that

> *the University stands today, lasting evidence of his ability as a business executive and practical administrator. He guided the institution through nineteen critical years, including the disastrous decade of depression, and brought it through — larger — stronger — better built — and with all this — financially sound. Under his leadership it became an institution of recognized merit, a University worthy of Wyoming.*

Even the trustees came to agree. In 1946, the University granted its former president an honorary degree and in 1950, the title "emeritus." When his term as governor was over, the board occasionally petitioned him to represent it at national educational meetings. When he died in 1955 — after years of failing health — trustees resolved that they had "lost a beloved former member and intimate friend" who

> *during his twenty years as President of the University, a period beset with economic depression and the beginnings of the Second World War, not only led the way to academic survival in trying times but also stimulated and directed its growth from a small, inadequately housed University to an excellently appointed one, a University grateful for his contribution to its past and confident of its future.*

Glee and mandolin club, c. 1907

rom the moment in 1895 when trustees gave Mrs. LeRoy Grant permission to use campus facilities to teach piano, music has been part of the curriculum and extra curriculum at the University of Wyoming. For many years, staff provided instruction upon payment of fees, but after 1909 music pupils were expected to register as University students too. In 1929, the music department granted its first bachelor's degree to Cecil R. Nussbaum. In 1940, the master's degree was offered for the first time.

In October 1899, Professor Henry Merz first lifted his baton to direct the University orchestra. "He was a scholar of the passing type," writes Wilson O. Clough of this talented gentleman, "a man of rounded preparation rather than the more narrowly specialized." Indeed, Merz fit orchestra practice into a schedule already crowded, for he taught social science, political science, philosophy, and education as well. He directed the cadet band too. After 1914, students could earn credit for playing in the orchestra, and three years later it performed *Cavallaria Rusticana* for a Laramie music festival. The first symphony to be played by the orchestra was Beethoven's *Symphony No. 1* in 1932.

Meanwhile, in the spring of 1913, Wilbur Hitchcock organized a band, consisting of seven faculty members and four students; a few years later, enthusiasm brought the number to 29. At first it held practice sessions in the Old Main physics lab on Sundays. The first actual band concert apparently occurred in 1916, although well before then the band had paraded in athletic and other outdoor events. In 1917, the organization toured the state from Cheyenne to Cody.

After 1899, faculty and music students held regular recitals and concerts. After 1919, Handel's *Messiah* became an annual event. In 1925, Sigma Alpha Iota, the music fraternity, established a local chapter, and by then the Laramie Musical Arts Club was sponsoring concerts and music events. Allan Willman came to campus in 1936, fresh from his Paderewski award for creative composition; barring time served during the war, he remained at Wyoming until his retirement, for 33 years as department head. Professors Robert Becker and George Gunn joined the department just before World War II.

The summer music camp for high school students began in 1946. A few years later, the creative arts workshop (including literary, artistic, and theatrical personalities) brought to campus such luminaries as Darius Milhaud and the Pro Arte string quartet. By the mid-1960s, the music department could count more than 150 majors. Every year following 1951, the department was accredited by the National Association of Schools of Music.

Music in the classroom was only part of the joy — other pleasures lay in extracurricular musical activities. Thus by the turn of the century, there was a University Chorale Society. Like the girls' glee club, the mandolin club was directed by Mrs. Justus Soule. Often they performed in concerts with the mens' glee club and the orchestra.

What the "Comedy Four" had to do with great music is still debated. Barbershop, hymns, harmony, improvizations — they did it all, touring the state as well as delighting the campus. Their "warbling," "jazzy accompaniments" and "sweet tenor voices" made them, said the *Wyo,* a most popular organization — one that was "always sure of a welcome," wherever it went.

Chapter Eight

The War and its Aftermath
1941-1950

The war years (1941-45) at the University of Wyoming were characterized not just by the necessity for flexibility, but by such sweeping changes in enrollment and assignments that adjustments, readjustments, and counterreadjustments became virtually the order of the day. War was declared following the Japanese attack on Pearl Harbor in December 1941. Thereafter, enlistments and conscriptions into the armed forces were only part of the picture. Government policies in regard to campus-based operations changed dramatically from up to down. University officials struggled to maintain a semblance of normal scholastic programs against all odds. Then after the war came the great upsurge in enrollment caused by returning veterans using their "G.I. Bills" — no one could guess how many nor exactly what courses they might choose. Post-war years brought special crises in financing, building, and athletics. A new two-year college system upset University administrators, and an investigation into textbooks angered faculty. Altogether, the return to "normalcy" took five years after the war's end.

Following Crane's dismissal in the spring of 1941, the board chose not to appoint an interim president but opted instead to request a committee of deans to take over administrative leadership. John A. Hill of the College of Agriculture was chairman. The deans were assisted by Fay Smith, now comptroller as well as secretary to the trustees. At first the deans expressed some uncertainty as to their policy-making role. In the long run, however, this interim government managed well. The deans began reporting to executive committee and board just as Crane had reported over the years, and their concerns were remarkably similar. During the months of interregnum, sundry personnel and curricular projects were dealt with routinely. The only crisis that arose concerned the

Branding Iron and its editorial policies during the period of Crane's dismissal, when the student newspaper had made it clear that it stood on the president's side. The deans investigated, reported, and recommended to the board that no censorship policy be instituted, but rather that the publications committee (on which two faculty members sat together with students) be charged with evoking a more responsible policy in the future. As late as autumn 1941, Fay Smith reported that, with the deans in charge, things were running "quietly and smoothly."

Meanwhile, the selection of a new president got under way almost at once. The files show applications from 53 individuals. From among them the board eventually selected five who were summoned to Jackson for interviews in August. Among finalists was Chancellor Chauncey S. Boucher of the University of Nebraska, who was making a positive impression as chairman of the committee considering Crane's protest, and Robert W. Miller from the law school at Syracuse University. One other candidate withdrew when it became apparent that guaranteed tenure was not to be part of the package. Miller seemed the favorite at first, and he had the powerful support of Fay Smith and the backing of law school Dean Hamilton. But he was a young man with little administrative experience, and in spite of Smith's late-night defense, his name was placed low on the list because, as one board member wearily reported, "there is a universal prejudice against youth." Miller's defeat saddened at least one trustee, who wrote Smith that

I can say without equivocation that he is twice as big in every respect as any man I have ever met in school business. I am naturally sorry that he was not selected because I am convinced that the time is not far off when he will have attained an even higher position than what the University of Wyoming could have offered him.

Instead of making a firm decision at Jackson, as was expected, the board asked Smith to inquire of Boucher and of another finalist, J. Lewis Morrill, vice president at Ohio State University, whether either would accept the position if offered. Boucher was a man in his fifties, due to retire in about ten years. He considered and then declined, primarily on the grounds that he was still in charge of the Crane investigation; he might have reconsidered had the board been willing to wait several months until the investigation was concluded. Instead, trustees offered the position to Morrill — even though at Jackson he had impressed Fay Smith as "almost too smooth . . . but on the other hand if he went to the State Legislature, he might be able to bring home the State Treasury." By the end of September, trustees tendered an offer of $8,000 (the legislatively imposed salary limit), the president's house, maid service, and an allowance for entertainment. Morrill accepted. On October 2, he was officially introduced to faculty and students in a special assembly.

That the University got lucky is attested by all who remember Morrill and worked with him. A graduate of Ohio State, Morrill had made a career as editor of the Cleveland *Press* and had returned to his alma mater to teach journalism and to serve in several administrative capacities. His doctor's degree was the honorary LL.D. from Miami University in Ohio. The new president came at a time of crisis, for he took office on January 1, 1942, just a few weeks after Pearl Harbor. In 1917, he had served with the Ohio branch of the Council on National Defense, and his experience stood him in good stead. He steered Wyoming University firmly and effectively through the storm of World War II.

On campus the immediate reaction to the declaration of war was no different from that throughout the country — a shock of horror and uncertainty. "Officials Guarding against Hysteria," proclaimed a *Branding Iron* headline.

The flash of war bulletins, the rumble of recruiting officers has the male students, on campus, in a state of minor turmoil. The local draft board and the University military department has [sic] been swamped with students wanting to enlist and others asking questions concerning their immediate action in the present national crisis. At the present time all branches of the service and all offices connected with the government civilian defense program are in a terrible muddle since the outbreak of the war.

Telegraph wires are jammed with reports and orders for men already in the service of the country; hence no definite measures have been taken concerning the present selective service program. It is believed that the men who have received their numbers will be called as prearranged except for the speeding-up factor proceeding [sic] the first flare of excitement.

And elsewhere:

While men students bone away at their military courses or prepare to be drafted, there is a real service that Wyoming girls may perform — knitting. Prosaic as it sounds, it is the only Red Cross activity that will be carried on the campus for the time being . . . As soon as the Christmas holidays are over regular hours for the knitting group will be established. . . .

Yet the immediate effect of the war on the University campus was slight. Enrollment for the new quarter (beginning January 8) dropped less than expected; winter quarter enrollment was traditionally lower than that in fall. The *Branding Iron* speculated that the small decline resulted from the board's new cash-in-hand policy on registration.

The planned emphasis on vocational courses and curricula continued as before. The previous summers a "defense school," sponsored by the State Department of Education, had operated on campus, although a number of courses, including blacksmithing and auto mechanics, were dropped in 1941 because of underenrollment. A similar trade school had been closed because of the "default" of the state director of vocational training. For some months, the University had been negotiating with the U.S. Office of Education for "defense training courses," and the first such — a twelve-week night class in radio communication sponsored by the College of Engineering — held its initial meeting in January 1942. A pilot training program, partially funded by the Civil Aeronautics Authority and dating from 1937, continued.

Trustees set policies on faculty and staff leaves for military and civilian war service and (with faculty approval) notified all seniors that those who were within one quarter's work of graduation would be granted their degrees if conscripted into the armed services. Morrill announced formation of a War Activities Council (formerly called the Defense Council) to be headed by Professor O. H.

Rechard. The board increased its executive committee's authority to act between meetings on emergency problems. Generally, however, the University managed its business as usual.

In the next quarter, effects of the war began to show. Spring term enrollment in 1942 was 22 percent below that of the previous spring term. Morrill responded with a special "recruiting" effort, through which current students were instructed on how to persuade younger colleagues to attend school. War-oriented courses began to appear: Evening and weekend vocational programs (engine mechanics, telegraphy, home nursing, first aid) were supplemented by new offerings in fields like languages and history. Assemblies concentrated on armed forces training programs, and war bond drives began.

More importantly, in April 1942, the University acquired its first armed forces training contract with official U.S. Navy Department approval for a program comprising two years of study (with possible further training) leading to naval reserve officerships. Announced in June was an aviation cadet plan, whereby an enlisted air force private might receive deferment to study until graduation and become commissioned as a second lieutenant — all subject to air force needs and regulations. By August 1942, the Marine Corps and the so-called Army Enlisted Reserve Corps added similar programs for preliminary officer training during University years. The ROTC, a campus institution since World War I, continued to function.

At the end of summer, the student newspaper conducted a campaign to persuade young people to enroll at the University in spite of dislocations.

More than ever before the movement over the nation is "back to school," or in the sense of the college freshman "on to school." This attitude has been emphasized by army and navy cooperation with reserve programs in the colleges over the country. Wyoming is a university especially prolific in these "help stay in school" programs. . . . The student who stays at home and waits for the draft is in reality holding up his country in the war effort. . . .

The *Branding Iron* further remonstrated against those who objected to student draft deferments.

There has been heard the usual grumbling from some people like "My son was on the Lexington, or my boy is in the army, and why should these guys be allowed to stay here at home where they are safe?" That is a very poor attitude. There isn't a one of those in college under one of the military programs who wouldn't be glad to get his chance to fight in this war. And what's more, they're going to get it. The value of the college-trained soldier has definitely been shown. . . . Don't criticize the man in the University. He is as much a soldier as the man at Fort Warren.

Nonetheless, fall quarter enrollment in 1942 stood at its lowest point since 1934 and had declined around 22 percent from the previous autumn. Winter quarter saw an even greater decrease. In his message to the legislature, a sympathetic Governor Lester C. Hunt reported early in 1943 that

Your State University faces perplexing problems. A great many of the teaching personnel have been called into the armed forces. Student enrollment and student fees are down approximately thirty percent. With the drafting of the eighteen-year-olds very few male students will remain unless they are assigned there under courses prescribed and initiated by the War or Navy Departments. . . . While the University cannot expect to operate as usual, nevertheless we must maintain the institution on a high standard, maintain the physical plant, and be prepared to take care of any type of training the War Department may assign to the University, and to return to normal functions following the war.

Of the 195 degrees awarded to graduating students in spring of that year, 99 were granted in absentia.

Early in 1943, the U.S. War Department announced a change in its policies towards college-aged students training for the service. Beginning as soon as reorganization could be accomplished, men from current university service training programs would actually be inducted into the army. Instead of enrolling directly in school, new recruits would be put through basic training, tested, and only thereafter (as full-fledged military personnel) sent to acquire whatever schooling might be deemed advisable on contracting college campuses. On completion of the assigned collegiate program, they would take up active military assignment. Thanks in part to Morrill's involvement in the national educational war effort, Wyoming was selected as a testing university as well as a participant in the new Army Special Training Program. By May, the army had contracted for use of University facilities and faculties for both.

In 1897, Harold D. Coburn (captain in the army and University commandant), Charles D. Abrams (later of Grant's Pass, Oregon), and J. W. Taylor (to become a clergyman in South Dakota) walked to the podium in the Old Main auditorium and received the University's first master of arts degrees.

Business department, College of Commerce and Industry, 1901

It can hardly be said that a formal graduate school was in existence at such an early date. Nevertheless, the *Bulletin* had ambitiously promised to students what graduate work might be offered by existing faculty. Abrams and Taylor had worked in geology with Professor Wilbur C. Knight. Coburn received his degree in political economy. In the next four years, five more degrees were granted, one or two at a time. But enrollment was slim. By 1922, only 23 students had received masters' degrees. Four of them were women.

After the turn of the century, a "graduate school" made a brief appearance in the University bulletins, always on a modest scale. The *Bulletin* of 1911 guaranteed graduate instruction only in "some" departments. Nevertheless, it listed procedures for admission, residency requirements, and courses. Work towards graduate degrees was to be directed by professors, but each plan was to be approved by a committee, then consisting of Agnes M. Wergeland (history), June Downey (psychology), and Aven Nelson (botany). The president, too, had to grant his permission. Any college could award the M.A., but only engineering, agriculture, and the department of commerce and the division of home economics were allowed to give the M.S. degree. A scattering of courses were acknowledged as "graduate." The *Bulletin* stated firmly that the Ph.D. degree would not be awarded and that the University "does not feel disposed to encourage graduate work except on the part of its own graduates."

In 1914, "inasmuch as the University is not prepared to carry any large amount of graduate instruction," President Duniway officially abolished the Graduate School. Students might still request particular graduate courses, but those seeking degrees were "encouraged to go to larger institutions where graduate schools are fully developed." Between then and 1923, only four masters' degrees were awarded. In the years just before the war, between eight and fourteen undaunted students were nevertheless listed "in graduate standing."

Not until after the depression did the demand for graduate study soar upwards. In 1936, 28 masters' degrees were officially awarded. Encouraged, the committee on graduate study persuaded trustees to authorize the granting of the doctoral degree in agriculture, education, geology, and chemistry. No individual earned such a degree until after World War II. In 1940, the Plan A and Plan B programs were adopted for the master's degree, the former continuing to emphasize thesis and the latter providing for additional course work instead.

In 1946, on the recommendation of the curriculum committee chaired by W. G. Solheim, President Humphrey reestablished the formal Graduate School. Back from the naval training school at Chapel Hill, Professor Robert H. Bruce (psychology) was appointed the school's dean. Bruce at once began to coordinate the allotment of a number of paid assistantships for graduate students. The dean also set up special courses on teaching skills for such students. According to his later report (1959) he was keenly aware of the faculty-student relationship that lay at the heart of graduate work and of the need for superior and dedicated faculty to keep the program at the requisite level of academic excellence. Accordingly, Bruce sponsored research grants to faculty in graduate departments as part and parcel of his commitment.

Thereafter programs grew apace. In 1949, the University awarded six doctoral degrees, all in education. Chemistry soon followed. In the 1950s and 1960s, doctoral programs were established in many fields, including eventually all of the sciences in the arts and sciences college and (in spite of the objections of its faculty) history as well. In 1984, 49 doctoral degrees were awarded, thirteen of them to women; other years had seen an even greater number.

Robert Bruce was recipient of many honors in a long lifetime of service: He worked for a year as chief of the country's major graduate fellowship program and received a special award from Ohio State University in 1970. Bruce retired from his post in 1972. He had been dean of the Graduate School for a quarter of a century. His efforts had institutionalized policies that still endure.

Major Beverly C. Daly,
dean of men, 1936-1945

Wilson O. Clough's published history, *The University of Wyoming: A Land-Grant College in War* (1946), gives some impression of the hectic efforts of faculty and administration to meet the challenge of these wildly changing assignments. In mid-March 1943, a special assembly bade farewell to past University ROTC and Army Enlisted Reserve students being called to full-time duty. Within a few weeks, contingents of 200 or more army men at a time were arriving on campus for testing. Having passed a preliminary test, they were directed through intensive ten-day refresher courses; given a barrage of special examinations; and thereafter either failed (to return to active duty) or passed (and assigned for further training at one of the designated technical schools or universities). On June 1, there were 700 such men on campus; the average for the six-month transitional testing program was 600 men at one time. Faculty members to teach the required refresher courses were in high demand, especially since by mid-year around fifty teachers were on leave in service or essential war jobs. Those who were left found themselves pressured into areas barely related to their own, for the army particularly required help in chemistry, engineering, mathematics, medicine, languages, physics, and psychology. A series of short refresher courses was inaugurated for faculty members willing to change their teaching fields. Residence halls were commandeered for troops, and a new health service was set up. Military commanders arrived to supervise special units. In six months, Wyoming processed more than 5,000 men through the testing program.

By mid-summer, as the transitional testing program waned, the University's contract for an Army Special Training Program took effect. In ASTP, men were presumed to be assigned for regular academic terms in accordance with the testing that had been administered and that the War Department now opted to manage itself. Under regular military discipline, 1,000 men (September 1943) attended courses for up to forty hours a week, specializing in engineering, military and physical training, and foreign area studies. Refresher courses were provided in special fields when necessary. Again, dozens of UW faculty taught outside their own specialties, and many instructors were temporarily hired. Syllabi, textbooks, and course content all had to be approved by the War Department. Classes were held in military drill fashion. Acceleration left faculty exhausted and complaining of the mechanical and rote learning necessitated by rapidity and prescription. But before Wyoming's program was six months old, rumors flew that the ASTP would soon be liquidated. Indeed, the War Department reduced student quotas in January. At the same time, a similar (but smaller) navy program came to an end. By the end of March 1944, almost all of the men had left.

An exhausted faculty and administration took stock. The men had vanished overnight. With enrollment standing at only 497 for spring quarter — the lowest since 1921 — teaching faculty found little to do. Some left for other positions; others were reassigned by the board to assess University policies or proceed with their own research. The addition of 100-200 seventeen-year-olds, supported by the government in their studies before being conscripted through a program called Army Specialized Training, added little to enrollment. The G.I. Bill, passed by Congress in June 1943, brought a few demobilized veterans to campus, but the major swell in enrollment was to wait until after the war's end. In vain, Morrill vigorously renewed the student recruitment campaigns. By 1944, 74 percent of the University's regular staff were on leave for one purpose or another. The underpopulated law school had been closed since 1943. Campus seemed close to deserted, with most of its dormitories locked for the duration. The 730 students who enrolled in autumn quarter — all but 204 of them women — determinedly carried on.

Nevertheless, the academic year 1944-45 was one of optimism for administrators and faculty alike. The favorable military situation in Europe did not necessarily signify the end of the war against Japan, but events following D-Day in June 1944 led to hopes that at least partial victory lay in sight. With this in mind, in spite of the difficult immediate situation on campus, Morrill and the board began a series of post-war plans in reference to programs postponed throughout the war period and in anticipation of the tide of veterans who would return on G. I. Bill benefits at the end of the war.

Foremost among board concerns was that of building. Before the 1945 legislature, the board issued a brochure containing a ten-year post-war building plan. First among its requests was expansion of the power plant, already operating at capacity and not yet serving several small buildings on the fringe of campus, acquired by the University during the war. Beyond power necessities, trustees set as their primary need a new building for the College of Education (with its elementary training and "Prep" high school); Crane's hopes for such a structure had been dashed by the legislature in 1941 and further retarded by the war. In 1943, the Wyoming Education Association had strenuously urged improvement of teacher training and educational demonstration facilities, and the subsequent unusually detailed evaluation by a North Central Association accreditation team was highly critical of understaffing, physical plant, equipment, and the small number of pupils enrolled in the school.

Other major projects were a new building for the College of Agriculture (still occupying and even sharing with liberal arts the structure completed during World War I) and, after many years, an infirmary building. The present student infirmary was located on the top floor of the Union, reached by no elevator and far from the basement kitchen, while clinic offices were housed in the gymnasium next door. Finally the report projected a fieldhouse and stadium to bring Wyoming up to par in the Mountain States Intercollegiate Athletic Conference — with the strong suggestion that such a structure might result in winning track, football, and baseball teams. Other proposed improvements included a classroom building, a number of wings and

ROTC pistol exercise, 1923

remodelings of older structures, and some basic improvements such as curbs, gutters, and paving.

The total price tag on the board's request stood at $3.9 million. Trustees were quick to point out that during Crane's presidency, the legislature had provided only $60,000 for construction purposes, and other sources (bond issues, oil royalties, Public Works Administration funds, and local income) had provided more than three times that amount. From the buildings completed during Crane's presidency at a cost of nearly $2 million, outstanding bonded indebtedness still remained at $509,000.

No one seriously proposed immediate building to the legislature of 1945 because the war remained — and indeed, the optimistic outlooks of the previous autumn "when the prospect of European victory seemed fairly immediate" had faded into what Morrill called uncertainty. In his message to the legislature, Governor Hunt urged post-war planning and general support for the state's four-year institution.

It is my considered conviction, based on my own observation and interest as a statutory ex-officio member of the Board of Trustees, that our University of Wyoming deserves, by virtue of its war-training activities for the Army and Navy, the pride and commendation of the citizens of the State. It therefore merits the generous support of our taxpayers and challenges us to give attention to its major needs during the years just ahead.

Nevertheless, uncertainty dominated legislative thinking. The main University operating budget, which had stood stock still at $924,000 for two biennial sessions, was raised only by $130,000; as was becoming usual, legislators carefully earmarked special funds for student labor, equipment and library books, industrial research, and other categories.

Even the president did not dare plan far ahead. In his memorandum to deans and department heads on budgeting for the year 1945-46, Morrill requested conservatism: Enrollments had not substantially increased; a fund was necessary if the University was to set up a retirement system (the legislature had cut the $121,000 requested for this purpose); and it seemed wise to set aside the greater portion of appropriations for a second biennial year in which expenses (and student population) might indeed increase. About the only

budget decision in which the president might have rejoiced was the increasing appropriation for "industrial research," an institute (the Natural Resources Research Institute) which Morrill had persuaded the legislature to establish in 1943. Other matters fell into the category of future decisions.

Meanwhile, faculty, too, were planning for what lay ahead. In May 1944, at the recommendation of its curriculum committee, the faculty suggested the appointment of a director for veterans' relations and an advisory committee to aid him. Morrill promptly named O. H. Rechard to the post and as chairman of the advisory group. Recognizing the need for specific skills as of prime importance to many returning servicemen, the deans and the veterans' director agreed that such career training should be available in the College of Education, primarily because engineering and agriculture deans demurred at taking over. A department of vocational education was established in the education college, and a one-time dormitory was remodeled as labs and classrooms for teaching vocational skills. At the same time, the faculty reorganized the "individualized" curricula established at Crane's behest in 1935; abolishing thirteen of them; transferring others to the pertinent department; and retaining only twelve as interdisciplinary or non-departmental courses.

During this last academic year of World War II, special data were gathered by the curriculum committee from each college in regard to desirable modifications and expansions. From the committee's progress report to the faculty, dated June 1945, it is apparent that most faculty found it imperative to return to solid, traditional education. Accelerated programs, such as had disrupted campuses during the war, were deemed educationally unsound, although veterans were to be encouraged to finish school as soon as they possibly might. Admission policies, "general education," a sound background in reading and writing skills, innovative teaching based on discussion and "student participation" (as well as lectures) were all regarded as important. As an aid to veterans, a number of "certificate" programs (one year of "vocational agriculture," for example; or a "surveying and mapping" two-year sequence in engineering) were proposed by different colleges. The curriculum committee recommended the separation of the adult education program into a special division and the establishment of a graduate school. Needs for more staff and more space were considered to be likely but unpredictable.

At a special faculty meeting in November 1944, President Morrill announced his intention to resign as of June of the following year. As universally respected as any other previous president, Morrill had accepted the position of chancellor of the University of Minnesota, at a salary increased by fifty percent. Among the many tributes to him during the following months, one senses the great personal regret of Morrill's colleagues at his decision to leave. The board had already once persuaded him to remain — in the summer of 1944, when he was asked to become an air force educational administrator — and it had demonstrated its confidence by raising his salary to $10,500 in 1943, when it persuaded the legislature to revoke the $8,000 salary limit set against Crane in the depression years. "In the all too short three years since Morrill's coming to Wyoming," said Milward L. Simpson, president of the board,

> great forward strides have been made here. By his tact and diplomacy, by his indomitable courage and zeal, he has guided our University through turbulent and discouraging times. . . . President Morrill is an excellent gentleman. . . .

The student newspaper echoed the trustees' sentiments under the headline, "Good Luck, Prexy."

> Now that we must look forward to a parting, it is almost impossible to summarize the good works Dr. Morrill has accomplished for the University. . . . It was through the efforts of Dr. Morrill that the University of Wyoming was able to win the mythical collegiate basketball championship, because before Morrill's arrival here, the Cowboys had never played a team from the Big Ten. It was directly due to the efforts of the president that the units of the Army Specialized Training program were stationed here, as well as units of Naval Aviation cadets. These programs, without doubt, helped immeasurably to tide Wyoming over the rough spots of rock-bottom enrollment during the years of war thus far. . . . In the resignation of President Morrill, the University is losing one of its foremost backers. And the students are losing a real friend.

In a procedure contrary to tradition, Morrill himself gave the spring commencement address.

"I shall give up my work at the University of Wyoming with the most genuine regret," he told the students, and to trustees he commented on the "perfect understanding with the Board upon a plane of highest professional integrity." Few other Wyoming presidents had withstood such strenuous tests with such skill and good spirits.

The tests were by no means over. The crises of the post-war years carried much of the same frenetic tone as those of the war itself. Veterans replaced servicemen, and swarms of students came to crowd a campus that had been empty only a few months before. Inflation supplanted restraint, as the national economy fluctuated. International political instability gave rise to unnatural fears and "scares." To a great extent the University's new chief administrator faced the same dilemma as had so plagued his predecessor: How can one achieve "normalcy" when unpredictability is the rule?

The war in Europe had ended and that in the Pacific was about to be won when Morrill turned house and office over to George Duke Humphrey, formerly president of Mississippi State College and an acquaintance of Morrill's through their common activities in several national organizations. A man in his mid-forties who held the Ph.D. from Ohio State and possessed considerable experience in academic administration, Humphrey had few rivals for the position, and all of them failed to receive enough votes even to compete on the board's first ballot.

Anticipating a solid increase in enrollment (and indeed statistics for autumn quarter 1945 showed a rise of almost one-third in the student body as compared to the previous fall), Humphrey prepared to campaign for veterans' housing and building needs as his top priorities. In addition, he faced programmatic problems in terms of reestablishing curricula that had collapsed during the war and predicting where veterans' interests might lie. Faculty on leave and faculty in place were needful of salary adjustments as inflation caused soaring prices in the immediate post-war years. When he met with deans of the colleges for two days in February 1946, Humphrey was presented with specific budgets that called for an extra $175,000 to get through the second year of the biennium until April 1, 1947, by which time the legislature would have met again.

The administration watched with understandable misgivings as returning veterans swelled enrollment in winter quarter 1946 to 1,361, an increase of almost a third more than the autumn term statistics. Most importantly, these students had to be housed. In October, the federal government had provided fifty trailer houses for the use of veterans; but only slowly were these being made useable, for they had to be transported, remodeled, and installed through University funding. In addition, 39 prefabricated houses had been purchased through current funding — "exhausting all present resources," as Humphrey said. If predictions of a fall enrollment of 3,000 — including 1,000 married and 1,000 single veterans — proved accurate, and if all possible students with and without families were housed in emergency facilities on campus and in Laramie, the University would still need to provide additional space for almost 600 men. In desperation, new president and board pressed the governor for a special session of the legislature to cope with emergency needs. The special session (only the sixth in Wyoming history) was eventually scheduled for mid-April 1946.

It was Humphrey's first test before a Wyoming legislature, but his instincts and experience came through. On April 2 he wrote the speaker of the house on the University's needs.

The University is facing the most difficult period in its history. This situation exists for three reasons: 1) the increase in cost of living for members of the staff; 2) the inability of the University to secure new personnel because of the low salaries we have been able to pay, because of the lack of a retirement system, and because for the past few years graduate schools have been training very few students; and 3) the sudden tremendous increase in enrollment of veterans.

Copies of the University's request were sent to all county agents, home demonstration agents, and widely distributed to prominent citizens. In addition to statistics on veterans' housing, the proposal contained a list of 58 UW staff members who had resigned because of salary rates — although by far the greater number were not from the teaching faculty. The final request sought $137,000 to install federal units or construct housing for married and single veterans; $200,000 for new and returning faculty and staff; $138,800 for salary increases; a contingent emergency fund of $75,000; a power plant extension in the amount of $150,000; and a request for an act enabling the borrowing of money for self-liquidating loans to construct additional dormitory and cafeteria space.

Among Humphrey's notes is a list of the names of the University's "enthusiastic supporters" in the legislature. The president might well have added the name of Lester C. Hunt. Indeed, the governor's address to the legislature on April 15 was in the nature of an extraordinary plea. The governor recommended in favor of all proposed legislation.

The University of Wyoming faces a crisis in its career. The events of the next few months will set the pattern of the University for decades to come. . . . To appropriate less [than requested] would be to jeopardize the future of the University, and in the long run, of the State itself . . . We place a great deal of stress and apply our energies on the development of our natural resources — I submit, the greatest natural resource and asset in this State of Wyoming is the youth of Wyoming. The need is immediate. Shall we make adequate provision for our veterans to attend the University, or shall we be forced to limit the enrollment to the 2,000 students who can now be accommodated? I am confident your thinking is in harmony with mine, and there can be only one answer. Can we do less for those who fought for us than to provide facilities for the education they expect and rightfully demand?

The student newspaper headlined its support, calling to students that "This is your project!" Delegations of students attended legislative sessions.

The legislature responded by cutting the $75,000 emergency contingency fund, but by giving Humphrey everything else he needed: Funds were appropriated for erecting and improving federally-furnished housing; for new faculty and salary increases; to upgrade the power plant; and for the Natural Resources Research Institute. Authorization was granted for bond sales up to $535,000 for student housing. As before, the bonds were to be purchased as investments by the University Permanent Land Fund and retired gradually out of income from the housing itself.

Women's physical education - Archery, hockey, gymnastics and basketball, c. 1940

Nevertheless, the fall of 1946 brought another emergency situation. In spite of the legislative aid, housing was desperately short. In September, Humphrey reported to the board that faculty housing was inadequate to the needs of new employees, who were living in the men's residence hall or at the science camp while awaiting the remodeling of various "Butler huts" or apartments. The situation of the latter group was particularly touchy, since roads were wild and winter was approaching (the State Highway Department had agreed to keep the road open as long as possible), and at the summertime facility, wives had banded together to serve joint meals and to wash dishes. Students were equally hard pressed.

Lack of material and shortage of labor has so delayed contractors and University crews in the erection of housing units for veterans that it became necessary to postpone the opening of the fall term until September 24. By that date, all the Butler Huts for single men should be available, the 72-man dormitory will be completed, and enough of the row apartments will be finished to enable the University to house all students until the full building program is completed. Students will be crowded, and many married veterans will have to postpone, for a short time, moving their families to the University. All available living space will be used, temporary space in Merica Hall, lounging rooms and hallways in Hoyt and Knight halls, the gymnasium, study space in the Butler Huts, the East Cowboy Dormitory, etc.

In November, trustees decided to ask for more construction funding and to approach the next legislature for absorption of the previously authorized $535,000 bond issue (which had in stenographic error been scheduled for redemption in twenty years instead of thirty) into a new package which would not only permit construction of the proposed men's dormitory but would include an addition to Knight hall for women. Eventually the request came to include construction of a bookstore-art department building. The total request was $1,350,000. To the same board meeting, Professor H. T. Person of engineering presented the dramatic results of his salary study of North Central Association schools; Wyoming was well below average in all professorial categories.

The result was that president and board approached the legislature of 1947 with the largest request in the University's history. Based on the increasing number of students, the demonstrable need for salary increases, and the purchase of equipment to replace aging pre-war items, the request stood at $2.9 million for the main University, $356,000 for agriculture extension, and $170,000 for the operation of state farms during the next biennium.

This time the legislature was less generous. It cut the main University budget by more than $700,000 and agricultural extension by $60,000, thereby indicating its rejection of Humphrey's proposed salary increases. The state farm budget was slashed by almost two-thirds, and Humphrey was forced to agree to maintain only those farms at Archer, Afton, Gillette, and Torrington, and to abandon his plans to reestablish others. The president, who had already substantially reduced his budget in response to Governor Hunt's recommendations, eliminated requests for a bureau of business research, a model dairy, and retirement costs as planned.

Humphrey's greatest victory lay in pushing through the first of the big post-war building budgets. He received authorization to issue $1.4 million in revenue bonds to erect or add dormitories on campus. The legislature authorized appropriations for construction at state institutions throughout Wyoming and included therein an appropriation of more than $3.4 million for the University, to be utilized mostly for the education and agriculture buildings. Known later as a bricks and mortar man, Humphrey must have delighted in this first major construction program. In addition, although the sum was smaller than they had hoped, trustees were able to budget $95,000 for salary increases in the 1947-48 fiscal year.

In 1948, the University was again back at a special legislative session. Inflation had indeed not peaked and retreated, as the previous legislature had anticipated, so this time trustees were able to call on the cooperation of numerous other state agencies which found themselves facing equally devastating deficits because of "these days of wild inflation," as Governor Hunt called them. As early as December 1947, Humphrey wrote to Hunt anticipating trouble on the basis, he said, of the legislature's failure to appropriate the full requested operating expenses in 1947, plus the loss in income caused by an overestimate (or, as Humphrey said, "a drop") of student enrollment, and a 23 percent price increase, resulting in a loss of purchasing power and a desperate need to raise salaries again.

The University is not now in a position to meet the competition of other collegiate institutions and is experiencing difficulty in keeping at least a few of its good men. . . . The lowest paid associate professor on a nine-months basis at the University is paid $2,890 per year. At the University of South Dakota, the lowest paid associate professor receives $3,200; at the University of Idaho, $3,500; at the University of Utah, $3,685; and at the University of Nevada, $4,000.

He continued,

No further proportionate cuts can be made in the operating budget. Any such attempt now

would cripple every department of the University. If new revenue is not obtained by the University it will be necessary to eliminate educational activities, close down entire departments or colleges, discharge personnel, and restrict the educational opportunities which can be offered to the young people of Wyoming.

On April 25, Humphrey addressed a second letter to the governor and this time made it public as a "statement of financial problems of the University of Wyoming." Foreseeing an annual deficit for 1948-49 in the amount of $500,000 (including the main University; agricultural extension; and state farms and experiment station budgets), he reported that

In common with other departments and institutions of the state, the University finds itself in a serious financial situation because of greatly increased costs of operation. Increased costs of living are imposing serious hardships upon members of the faculty and other employees of the University. The increased cost of supplies and equipment makes it impossible to provide enough money for the minimum needs for expenses other than instruction. . . . No one is to blame for these conditions. At the time of the 1947 Legislative session, the Legislature and the state Administration were of the opinion that the peak of prices had been reached. In this opinion they were entirely justified, since there were indications at that time that costs would actually decrease during the biennium. Appropriations were based on the assumption that at least prices would not increase. It now appears that this assumption was fallacious, and it is inevitable that the state agencies and institutions, depending wholly or in part upon state appropriations, will find themselves in serious financial difficulties.

When a reluctant governor, this time pressured on all sides, convened the second special legislative session in two years (June 1948), Humphrey was ready with a 32-page report dealing with budgetary problems in detail, department by department, project by project, down to the most minor expenses.

At the special session, the governor virtually quoted Humphrey on his statements regarding inflation and the University's problems.

In academic circles there exists with respect to instructors and other faculty personnel the same shortage as exists in private business among

 150

painters, carpenters, electricians, or stenographers and office personnel. In consequence, Wyoming, because of its frequent inability to match salaries paid elsewhere, has lost to other institutions an unprecedentedly large number of its valuable faculty members; in fact the number is little short of alarming. . . . In the face of constantly mounting inflation, it is no more possible to run the University — or other state institutions and departments — on a budget made two years ago than it is for the businessman or the rancher to operate his establishment or the housewife to run her home on a budget drawn up on the basis of prices and wages of nearly a biennium ago.

The legislature's response was to appropriate an additional $376,000 for the University's use as operating expenses (including funds for agricultural extension and the operation of state farms), and $562,000 for the completion of the building projects (for the Colleges of Agriculture, Education, and the remodeling of Old Main) authorized in 1947. Owing again to inflation, the University revised its bond issue needs for the new dormitories and bookstore upwards to $1,600,000, and sought an appropriation of $268,000 besides. The legislature demurred on the issue of outright cash funding and authorized instead three bond issues in the amount of $1,850,000 — a policy that Humphrey later criticized as putting the University behind the eight-ball in terms of annual principal and interest payments.

By 1949, the immediate crisis of the post-war years was tempering. In this year, the legislature granted the main University $3.5 million for operating budget, specifying certain amounts for coal research, plus an additional sum for the Agricultural Extension Service, and enough funding to permit the reestablishment of state farms at Powell and Sheridan. The state also appropriated $400,000 to aid in the construction of War Memorial fieldhouse, the "downpayment" of which (in the words of the president) was to be made through alumni contributions and much of which would be financed through the issuance of revenue bonds in an authorized amount of $750,000. Although nearly 2,000 veterans were enrolled on campus in the 1947-48 academic year, the peak was over.

Enrollment in 1948 fall quarter began the downswing that would reach its nadir in 1953-54, when the number of fall quarter students stood at 2,291, almost 1,100 fewer than in 1947.

Humphrey seemed to enjoy politics, and in these first few years after the war, economic inflation and skillful lobbying turned the legislature toward generosity and led to considerable success. Not so easy of solution were some other problems which arose in the aftermath of the war. The surge of demand for college education led to a drive to eliminate the University's monopoly of public-supported higher education in Wyoming. Meanwhile, fears of international communist expansion brought about an intense and contagious "Red" scare, and Wyoming did not escape a challenge to the academic freedom its faculty sought to enjoy. Even the University's athletic programs — as dear to the heart of the new president as to the hearts of several trustees — stumbled and lurched as the administration tried to pull it to its feet after the long wartime hiatus.

The predictable instability of college football and basketball programs was greatly enhanced at Wyoming by the dismissal of Crane in 1941 and by the war years thereafter. Simultaneously with their firing of Crane, trustees moved to restructure the athletic program, adding fuel to the fire caused by the former president's conviction that his dismissal was in part due to the absence of a winning football team. In March 1941, the board separated athletic administration from the physical education department, placing the latter under the College of Education and taking the former to itself through a committee of four trustees. With Everett Shelton, who had led Wyoming to a conference championship in basketball in 1940-41, trustees signed a three-year contract renewal. Not so lucky was Okie Blanchard, who had been hired as football coach and director of athletics only the previous spring. Blanchard found his job as athletic director abolished; his duties as football coach cancelled; and his future assignment changed to dean of students, a position created especially for him. He stuck it out for more than a year, but in the fall of 1942 opted to leave the University for a high school coaching job. Once he was gone and contract problems averted, the student deanship was abolished and the athletic directorship was combined with football coach once more.

With Blanchard's demotion, Bernard F. "Bunny" Oakes was hired as football coach. Oakes also became acting athletic director in 1942, when the position was reestablished. That fall the board lost no time in devising a long and intricate "athletic control" regulation, by which responsibility for the troubled athletic administration was to fall, in order from the top, on the board, the University president, a "board of athletic control," the department of athletics, the ASUW senate, "alumni," and the Mountain States Intercollegiate Athletic Conference. The complicated system was simplified by the fact that trustees, in practice, tended to tackle all major problems themselves.

Oakes coached for two seasons at the beginning of the war (1941 and 1942) and brought Wyoming's team up from the bottom of conference ranks. In 1942, however, football was cancelled for the duration. In his position as acting athletic director, the new coach found himself supervising high school basketball tournaments, coaching occasional games for charity, and administering physical education programs for military men. His three-year contract was renewed in 1944 at a slightly lower rate ($4,500) until such time as football might begin again.

Right after D-Day, the trustees voted to reestablish the athletic program as soon as possible. When newly elected President Humphrey attended his first board meeting in August 1945, the war was over, and the president requested advice on the kind of program that the board desired. Clearly, the answer was vigorous and victorious. Oakes was present when the board enthusiastically voted to begin football competition again. Too late for the 1945 season, the coach concentrated on putting together a team for 1946: awarding athletic scholarships; trying to get the "boys" discharged from the service; and working with a new athletic director, Glenn "Red" Jacoby, who began service on April 1, 1946. But contract difficulties loomed. Early in 1946, the board offered Oakes a three-year renewal at $5,000, plus a bonus of $500 for each year he had served during the war, when both his service and salary had been reduced. Eventually, the bonus was declared unconstitutional by the state attorney general; Oakes refused to sign several contract offers; and it was not until late June (after months of negotiation and fraying tempers) that he agreed to a one-year offer of $6,750.

Unfortunately, 1946 was a bad year. The team was erratic and unsuccessful. Practice only began in September. Almost at once there were rumors about Oakes' status. In the homecoming game with Denver University, a last-second score evoked enormous controversy concerning both coaches and officials. Oakes's position was only damaged by a petition signed by most players and presented to Humphrey and the press in November. In the petition players tried to excuse themselves and the coach for their poor showing, and it is clear that Humphrey felt irritated not only at undue interference from the team but in his strong conviction that the coaching staff had inspired the petition. Oakes' days were numbered, and it is to Humphrey's credit that he quietly notified the coach in advance, wrote many letters of recommendation, and did his best to find Oakes a job. The football coach's contract came to an end in spring 1946.

In basketball, the situation was far better. Shelton coached the team through a whole series of winning seasons. Although basketball was dropped in 1943-44, the team came back third in its conference and won that conference in the 1945-46 season.

Shelton, however, provided his share of color. In December 1946, at a tense and brutally physical championship game with City College of New York at Madison Square Garden, just when in the last minutes CCNY surged forward from a tie to win the contest, the coach said (loudly enough to be overheard), "The Jews are getting away with murder tonight." CCNY Coach Nat Holman roared over to Shelton's seat on the bench, and when Shelton told him to move, shouted a violent response. Reporters from all the New York newspapers were there to pick up Shelton's statement.

Fur flew. The board and president began receiving telegrams even before the team returned home. It could not have been reassuring to have Jacoby wire that nothing had happened worth worrying about and that he would report later. Petitions poured in to the president's office. One card was signed by "Niggers and Kikes." An entire class of New York school children wrote letters protesting antisemitism. Veterans cried of Nazi tendencies. On the other side, much correspondence was

Coach "Ev" Shelton with players from NCAA championship team, 1943

received from local alumni defending the basketball coach. To his credit, Shelton came close to apologizing at a basketball writers' lunch, where he said that his remark was

purely descriptive. It had no racial or religious implications; however, if my remarks have caused any embarrassment or hurt anyone's feelings, I am sincerely sorry.

He was less successful in responding to Milton Gross, a sportswriter for the New York *Post*, who told Shelton that "We [Jews] don't like to be singled out." Shelton replied,

I told him that I was not singling them out, that we called them Indians when we played Indians, and we called them Chinamen when we played Chinamen, and when I played for Bethany College they called us Swedes.

The board finally issued a statement more or less defending Shelton's remarks and condemning the "language of base obscenity and vileness and depravity" used by the opposing coach. Wyoming's teams, trustees wrote, have included men of many religious, color, and racial backgrounds; the University was a "democratic institution" that brooked "no religious or racial intolerance." The team would not again appear in Madison Square Garden. After considerable national publicity, the storm in the athletic teapot died down. Still, Shelton was known to become overexcited on occasion, thereby continuing to evoke protests.

Of much more lasting academic significance, and still keenly remembered by those who fought its battles, was the controversy over textbooks that arose in 1947. In this, the age of Senator Joseph McCarthy and the "Red" scare, Milward Simpson was president of the board. From the pre-war years, as evidenced by his campaign against Senator Joseph O'Mahoney in 1940, he had been highly concerned about the infiltration of communist propaganda into the United States. His worst fears were confirmed at a meeting of the Governing Boards of State Universities and Allied Institutions held at the University of Michigan in the fall of 1947. Here Simpson and his fellow trustee H. D. DelMonte heard a speaker zealously warn of the threat posed by communist ideology to the American way of life, particularly through the medium of "subversive" textbooks — or even those that "did not teach our own principles and ideas of government." Simpson's report to the board on October 24 occasioned a resolution instructing Humphrey to "appoint a committee to read and examine textbooks in use at the University of Wyoming, in the field of social sciences, to determine if such books are subversive or un-American." Following instructions, the president set up a committee with Dean R. R. Hamilton of the law school chairman. On November 25, Hamilton asked all department heads to submit lists of textbooks required of students.

Faculty response was immediate and acute. The Wyoming chapter of the American Association of University Professors, with Professor Ruth Campbell chairperson, and urged on by Professor Fred Nussbaum, voted a resolution expressing concern for professional integrity and asked the trustees to reconsider their action. Following AAUP lead, the general faculty requested a formal hearing before the board and elected a committee of fifteen, with Professor T. A. Larson chairman, to state and support its position. Working rapidly, the committee of fifteen prepared an intricate report on the meaning of academic freedom in the hopes of persuading the board to affirm that principle; to rescind its call for a textbook investigation; or, at the very least, to define more carefully the terms "subversive" and "un-American" that were being widely tossed around.

Through the *Branding Iron* and a short-lived publication called *Common Sense,* an active element of students supported the faculty position. A student opinion poll, submitted to the president, found 261 opposed to the investigation with fourteen in support and four abstaining. Rumors circulated of a possible student strike.

Meantime, the press picked up the confrontation. Amid a rising tide of national publicity and inflamed opinions on both sides, few heads remained calm. Labor unions and chambers of commerce supported the board's position, as did a number of local newspapers, including the *Wyoming Eagle* (Cheyenne), owned and edited by board member Tracy McCraken. McCraken found himself in conflict with Erne Linford, editor of the Laramie *Republican-Boomerang,* which the trustee also owned. The *Christian Science Monitor,* Chicago *Sun,* St. Louis *Post-Dispatch,* and New York *Herald Tribune* were among papers that ran stories. Board members abandoned their usual discreet silence to write editorials, give speeches, and make statements for publication. Faculty — on the committee and off — were equally active. As the only non-tenured member of the committee of fifteen, Professor Gale W. McGee called the textbook investigation a "gratuitous insult" to faculty, who seemed viewed by the board as incompetent to select and interpret their own course reading materials. Several of McGee's students later admitted that they had been asked to report to the board about his lectures. Dozens of observers sent the president pamphlets and materials about communism that still remain in the files.

As chairman of the committee of fifteen, Larson was determined to see the issue decided calmly and reasonably in spite of the heat it had generated. The board had set January 24, 1948, as a hearing date, and all involved feared a hostile confrontation. The defusing initiative came from McCraken and trustee P. M. Cunningham, both of whom had favored the textbook investigation. Having contacted several members of the faculty committee of fifteen, McCraken arranged a meeting in Cheyenne four days before the board's hearing. Representatives of faculty committee and trustees sat down together. Together they agreed that the textbook investigations should come to an end and that academic freedom in principle should maintain.

CHAPTER EIGHT

On the same day, Simpson and Humphrey released to the public the report of the Hamilton committee. This investigatory group of deans and professors had examined 65 textbooks in question without finding any material that "falls under the denomination of subversive or un-American." Quietly chiding the board for its action, the committee asserted that it had been unable to agree on any clear definition of the board's terms. It specifically entrusted professors with pointing out in class any fallacious reasoning or biases they might discover in any assigned texts. Simpson and Humphrey declared themselves "happy" with the investigators' report. But meanwhile a petition circulated by an economics professor called on the board to go further: to rescind its action and to abandon any plans for future textbook examinations. One hundred and three faculty members signed.

The hearing before the board was not cancelled. Indeed, the faculty sensed victory and stood firm. On January 24, in a lengthy session, the board first heard and incorporated into its minutes the report of the Hamilton committee as previously released. Thereafter, the long document devised by the committee of fifteen and approved by the University faculty was introduced by Larson. Subsequently, it too was incorporated into the minutes. Herein academic freedom and its implications were carefully set forth and defined. Larson's own statement, thoroughly approving of the faculty stance, emphasized the need for mutual confidence and quiet reasoning. Trustees responded with a long statement in which they reaffirmed their commitment to academic freedom and their intention to govern the University under that concept as defined by the American Association of University Professors. The board acknowledged the faculty's point of view and the findings of the Hamilton committee. It agreed not again to challenge textbooks except under "extraordinary" circumstances.

Two days after the committee hearing, the board reaffirmed its statement that it would not "suffer or tolerate subversive teachings or practices within the university," but as long as investigatory action was not undertaken, no further argument developed. No single faculty member seems to have refused to sign the standard loyalty oath that caused such difficulties at other institutions. Professor Marshall Jones of sociology probably expressed the view of most faculty when he wrote that

we have gained a pretty fair settlement of academic rights and responsibilities in full as far as the faculty is concerned, plus some approach to an understanding of faculty rights and responsibilities by the Board.

The lesson of the episode, he suggested to Humphrey, was that faculty should have a greater voice in policy formation and that increased communication between faculty and board should become a matter of principle. To McGee, years later, the important thing was that the faculty displayed new cohesion and courage during the controversy. In fact, McGee thought, the faculty had "come of age."

Four years later, Simpson was still discontent. In spring of 1952, he requested of Humphrey a list of all the social sciences books currently in stock in the campus bookstore. To the president on March 26, 1952, he addressed a long and angry letter about the contents of one of them (in geography) and criticized the use of others — including a volume by John Dewey used in a philosophy class. Humphrey was calming and reassuring.

Really, Milward, I feel that we are very fortunate in that we have escaped the taints that some institutions have. I believe that I can handle any difficulties which you might anticipate quietly and effectively, as I have already done in certain cases. We are always on the alert and try to be especially careful in employing new people. Every faculty member who is employed by the University accepts the "Conditions of Faculty Service" approved by the Board of Trustees, which includes this statement: ". . . no one who advocates the overthrow of the United States Government or is a member of any organization advocating the overthrow of the United States Government shall be employed by the University of Wyoming." As I indicated, I feel sure that the three books you mentioned are being used in a way that would be entirely pleasing to you.

Drays' Cottage, faculty and staff housing, c. 1940

Simpson let the matter drop. But two years later he persuaded the board to give every University employee a government publication entitled "Permit Communist-Conspirators to be Teachers?" In 1962, Trustee Roy Chamberlain participated in a session at the Association of Governing Boards of State Universities entitled, "What Regents Should Stick Their Noses Into, and Keep Their Cotton Pickin' Hands Out Of." In response to Chamberlain's question as to whether regents should help select books and course materials, Humphrey answered, "Emphatically no."

While athletics made its comeback and faculty fought back the "Red" scare tide, the University was losing another battle of long-lasting financial and academic significance. As a perhaps inevitable effect of the war and the post-war educational expansion came the establishment of post-secondary institutions in other parts of the state. As early as 1945, the University lost its position as the sole public conveyer of college-age education in Wyoming. Legislation that year paved the way for a system of two-year or junior colleges, although exponents of a relocated agricultural college were less successful two years later.

For decades the University had fought to maintain its position as Wyoming's exclusive college on the grounds that division of resources would only make several poorly staffed and equipped institutions out of one good one. At first the problem centered around teacher training. During Crane's years, a shortage of teachers and increasing standards for certification brought acute pressure to establish normal schools in a number of locations. The University responded with a special teachers' summer school on campus; with "field" summer school classes (often sponsored jointly with the

State Department of Education); and with short courses and extension work. Teachers and their organizations persisted. One proposal would have added "normal" classes as a fifth year course at any state high school and required the University to accept such credit towards further work. Crane was especially irritated at the latter provision, for he regarded the granting of credit as the University's own prerogative and he believed the bill as introduced in 1927

> *lowers the standing of the State University because it is such a violation of all educational policies and standards. If continued, this policy will cheapen every diploma and every grade given by the University of Wyoming. It will endanger the institution's standing as an accredited institution on the list of the Association of American Universities.*

When a similar measure was introduced into the legislature in 1929 by the Wyoming Education Association, the dean of the College of Education complained that the bill

> *makes every high school accredited by the State Board of Education [into] a Junior College, as the University must give one year's credit in the regular work of the College of Education. This bill in spirit is contrary to the opinion of all persons who have studied the teacher training situation.*

Although the depression temporarily put an end to talk of educational expansion, more comprehensive bills surfaced in the late 1930s. In 1937, the senate (perhaps in response to Crane's long "brief") indefinitely postponed consideration of a proposed network of two-year or junior colleges. In 1939, a junior college bill was defeated in the house. There the matter stood until predictions for surging post-war enrollments once more inspired proponents of an enlarged statewide system.

In summer 1944, Morrill reported to the board that he had become aware of considerable agitation in Casper for a junior college to be constructed there. During the autumn, the president and W. C. Reusser, director of the University's extension services, got in touch with the Casper Chamber of Commerce, which was encouraging the junior college plan. They sat down with Earle G. Burwell, and other prominent Casperites, in an effort to reach a compromise. The exact content of their discussion remains unknown, but later correspondence indicates that the University representatives wanted the project for "junior colleges" to be exchanged for a program of "institutes" (which were apparently to represent extended high school vocational programs). The plan was "negotiated" only tentatively, for Morrill intended to request final approval from the trustees.

When the Casper committee published its brochure entitled "A Wyoming Junior College Program," the usually calm president was angry and, he said, personally embarrassed, for the brochure referred to "junior colleges" rather than institutes and hinted that the plan had already been approved by the board. Morrill complained of a

> *regrettable and disappointing breach of fairness and of the straightforward and ethical relationship which you are entirely aware I have sought to maintain with the Casper group in meetings with them and in the confidential discussions of our own Board of Trustees.*

Trustees responded by recommending a statewide system of vocational schools. In a brochure, addressed like the Casper publication to the legislators, the board proclaimed that Wyoming should not establish a junior college system, that "common sense says *no*," because

> *Wyoming is still at the hard job of building one first-class institution; Wyoming's limited population and resources cannot finance more than one; more colleges do not increase the proportion of students going to college; junior colleges are NOT required in order to meet Veterans' needs; junior colleges will duplicate, but with lower effectiveness, the work of the State University; public school vocational training, not imitated college work, is the crying community need; high schools should be aided to do a bigger and better job; junior colleges divide student enrollment, compete for resources and result in lowered educational standards.*

Protest was in vain. Two bills were introduced into the 1945 legislature, and although HB 10, proposing a state-financed Casper junior college, was defeated in the house committee of the whole, HB 83, providing that any school district might expand a four-year high school into a six-year institution financed by locally levied taxes, passed as considerably amended. Although it reflected the University's desire to utilize high schools as a base, the bill clearly anticipated a junior college system.

Casper Junior College was immediately established under the new legislation, and Morrill bowed to the inevitable. At the president's request, Dean Oscar Schwiering of the education college prepared a long report, stating the University's willingness to survey, consult, inspect, prepare bulletins, and offer other assistance to any high school district that anticipated adding a two-year college course. The board indicated that it would continue to give credit by examination for junior college courses; grant credit for any offerings jointly administered with the extension division; set up a special committee to check into individual courses; and grant credit immediately to any junior college recognized by the North Central Association. One of Humphrey's first acts as president was to attend, in good grace, the dedication of the Casper Junior College in August 1945.

The ceremony represented the end of a long era. Nevertheless, the University refused to give up. Plans for "University Centers" throughout the state began almost at once. When the legislature of 1947 failed to appropriate aid, Humphrey resorted to local financing as authorized by the act of 1945. The first result was a University Center at Powell, the fortunes of which are detailed in a later chapter.

The University was more successful in its efforts to defuse relocation plans for the agriculture college. In 1941, an effort by Sheridan legislators to relocate the agriculture college and its federal funds by calling for a popular vote was handily defeated. But because of the expansion in post-war college enrollment, the University had more cause to worry when the attempt was renewed in 1947. Moreover, if Milward Simpson was correct in his report to Humphrey, the "Sheridan people" had an eye on outside money so that once a location was adopted, the construction of buildings and purchase of equipment would present no problem. Simpson thought that Sheridan and Casper had a "hook-up" by which each supported each other's college-level enterprise.

Accordingly, Humphrey threw all his efforts into defeating the Sheridan bill. Presidents of other state universities were solicited for their opinions on separation of agriculture and general colleges; statistics were accumulated on Wyoming agriculture graduates and their accomplishments; financial estimates were provided; alumni and business clubs were approached; and legal opinions were solicited. Meanwhile, UW touted its proposal to set up a University Center at Sheridan instead and invited Sheridan leaders to tour the recently-established Powell facility.

As introduced into the house, the bill provided for the selection by vote of the agriculture college's location and for its operation as part of the University, with government vested in the UW board of trustees. It was reported out of committee with a Do Pass recommendation. Debate was heated but — in part through the hard lobbying of John Sullivan, Laramie legislator — the house voted in favor of postponement. Much of the success of the operation can be credited to the leadership of John A. Hill, appointed dean of agriculture in 1923. Hill lobbied tirelessly and stumped the state. One of the best known deans on campus, Hill earned his colors through his administrative ability; through the importance of his own program of research dealing with wool shrinkage; and with his easy-going, outgoing personality. Although the University won its battle, considerable bitterness remained.

The war had brought a crisis for Wyoming as for the nation, but the University — with the aid of Morrill's leadership — had faced difficulties and vexations with considerable confidence. The immediate problems after the war focused around construction, and here Humphrey found his forte. Pressures of enrollment led to the establishment of a long-delayed system of two-year or junior (the term later changed to community) colleges, while the athletic program barely staggered onto its feet and a faculty fought off a McCarthy-style textbook purge. Still, education in Wyoming had entered upon a new era. Expansion and opportunity were the slogans of the day. A feeling of optimism infected president and trustees. Humphrey's was actually to prove the longest administration in University history.

WILSON O. CLOUGH

t the age of 90, Professor Emeritus Wilson O. Clough — teacher, poet, historian — looked back musingly on his years at the University of Wyoming and realized that in no single year had he failed to publish some essay, book, poetry, or research. The total of his works comes to some fifty articles, twelve books, and poems uncounted.

This extraordinary man was born in New Jersey in 1894 and reared in upstate New York. His father was a Presbyterian clergyman. At Union College in Schenectady, he majored in English and philosophy, minored in history and Latin, and somehow found time to learn Greek, German, Old English, and French. His fluency lay in the latter, however, and he has translated a number of works from French for publication. It was in France that he served during World War I, and he stayed long enough to attend the University of Montpellier in Provence.

Afterwards, Clough attended several universities, earned his master's degree from the University of Colorado, and taught in a number of high schools before he came to Wyoming in 1924. Among the tales he still tells of these days, those of Leadville, Colorado, rank as most dramatic, for Leadville was a tough town of battles in the bars and violence in the streets.

Wilson Clough joined the University of Wyoming English department in 1924. From 1946-49, he served as its chairman. But by then he had also been secretary of the faculty and written both 50- and 75-year University histories. He was the first to hold the William Robertson Coe professorship of American studies. In 1957, his alma mater awarded him the honorary Litt.D. degree, and in 1961, UW honored him with the LL.D. degree as well.

Never a technician nor a specialist, Clough has always stood firm for education as broad, liberal, elite. The tradition of the liberal arts with its emphasis on classical education is man's means of passing on knowledge for its own sake to future generations, he wrote at age 82. Teaching, Clough said, is the "art and craft of persuading, coercing, cajoling, threatening, enticing, entertaining, outwitting, and disciplining others, usually younger, into the dawning of a suspicion that knowledge may be preferable to ignorance."

Wilson Clough still reads prolifically, although at 91 he has slowed down a little from his previous average of 100 books a year. The titles of his own works only begin to demonstrate the breadth of his interests: *Intellectual Origins of American Thought, The Necessary Earth, Academic and Otherwise, Brief Oasis, Past's Perishing,* and many others. This outstanding scholar has served the University and brought it his triumphs for more than sixty years.

Wilson Ober Clough,
professor emeritus, English

Chapter Nine

Buildings and Programs
1945-1964

The two decades after 1950 brought halcyon days to higher education in the United States. If the surge of veterans supported by the G.I. Bill flooded universities and colleges for the few years after the war, it also showed the way to hundreds of thousands of young men and women who came to regard higher education as essential in their development. Once the Korean War was over, the nation entered upon days of prosperity that permitted young people to attend colleges and universities at a rate never before imagined. To the majority of middle and lower middle class children — born, some of them, in the population boom beginning in the early 1940s — college education became not a privilege but a right. New institutions blossomed, and the junior college movement proliferated. Old institutions tightened their admission requirements against the flood or (in the case of public universities) expanded their programs into new and bigger fields. Young Ph.D.s crowded into shared offices as new faculty members, and old campuses, lost their identities in forests of high rise buildings and deserts of paved parking lots. Government and private foundations poured money into research projects for public and private needs.

In the burgeoning of higher education, Wyoming was never far behind. Although enrollment sagged by almost 1,000 students between the leaving of the veterans and the end of the Korean crisis, it began to grow again in 1952. By 1955, the University was enrolling 2,718 students in its fall semester. Thereafter numbers grew steadily: to 3,408 in 1957; 4,344 in 1961; and 5,370 in autumn 1963, the last year of Duke Humphrey's presidency. In 1947, 353 degrees on all levels were conferred; by

1962, the number awarded was 1,013. Off-campus programs almost doubled the number of students in any given year. Graduate students in 1949-50 formed 10.7 percent of Wyoming's enrollment; by 1962, in response to new programs and new technological advances, they represented 20.12 percent. If the baby boom of the 1940s was one reason for increased enrollments, it is also true that the percentage of Wyoming youth who chose to come to college nearly doubled between 1945 and 1962.

The number of faculty members increased as did the student population. In 1945, there were 218 full-time faculty; in 1955, 318; and in 1963, 474, although some of these counted agricultural or other research as their primary assignments. Academic programs, operating budget, buildings, endowment funds, community services, administrative staff — in all these areas, Wyoming, like its sister state colleges in the West, rushed forward. A newspaper clipping that President G. D. Humphrey kept in his files, stated that

Higher Education is bursting at the seams all over the country, and nowhere more than in the public colleges and universities.

Programmatic expansion began immediately after the war. As early as September 1945, Duke Humphrey called on deans and department heads to present to him in writing summaries of their immediate needs and future plans. The new president's request came like a cool drink of water after a long drought, for Crane had consistently opposed curricular expansion and the war had prohibited any major development during Morrill's presidency. Throughout the autumn of 1945, the University faculty on all levels labored at a survey of academic strengths, weaknesses, and necessities. Their reports aided Humphrey in becoming acquainted with his new institution. And, as they remain in the files, they are covered with notes and question marks in the president's handwriting.

160

These documents provide a fascinating survey of the University at the end of the war and the beginning of a new era. Deans John Hill for agriculture; Ralph Goodrich for engineering; O. C. Schwiering for education; O. H. Rechard for liberal arts (an appointment made by Morrill upon the retirement of P. T. Miller, after much consultation and deliberation); and R. R. Hamilton (recently returned from a Chicago firm) for law each presented long reports, frequently supported by many appendices. They delved into problems and formulated recommendations in terms of five-year plans. The summaries amount to a campus directory of academic programs, faculty, and hopes for the future.

If buildings and space formed a major theme for the Colleges of Agriculture and Education, bricks and mortar fell far short of answering all the needs of campus programs. Rechard's report from liberal arts — the largest college on campus — proposed the greatest number of curricular and organizational changes. He requested the transfer of the art department from the College of Education to his college, perhaps in preparation for the establishment of a school of fine arts in the future. He proposed the establishment of separate departments in geography, journalism, speech and drama, wildlife management, and perhaps bacteriology. He asked that business classes be placed in a new administrative unit. He endorsed the reports from former dean P. T. Miller recommending the establishment of a separate school of pharmacy and from Professors R. H. Denniston and Floyd Clarke on setting up a pre-medical curriculum.

Meanwhile, the dean of engineering proposed to add several new options in traditional degree-awarding fields. Law Dean Hamilton stressed the need for enough full-time law professors to meet standards set by the American Association of Law Schools, which had already postponed its accreditation inspection because of the lagging law program during the war. The school officially became the College of Law in 1945. Hill of agriculture proposed a new curriculum in veterinary medicine and the separation of the home economics department into a special division.

In February 1946, all deans met with Humphrey for two solid days to put their programs together. They universally endorsed each others' recommendations. The new president's notes indicate his enthusiastic support of expansion. In accordance with a previous faculty resolution, he had already solicited and received board approval to establish a formal graduate school.

Faculty plans were closely followed in the first flowering of curricular changes, 1945-55. Course revisions are too numerous to list here except in abbreviated form. The College of Education, for example, developed classes in audio-visual aids; a department of guidance; and new training programs—in-service teacher workshops as well as a nursery and kindergarten segment for the "Prep" school. In agriculture, a special range management program was inaugurated in 1947, and home economics was shortly separated into a separate division.

Within the College of Liberal Arts, many changes took place. In 1948, the departments of speech and drama, and journalism ("You know the interest of the Press of the State," Rechard wrote to Humphrey with his formal request) were established as separate units. In 1947, a professional curriculum in medical technology received college approval, joining already existing professional programs in geology, journalism, social work, and wildlife management. Physics added its professional curriculum in 1949. The professional chemistry curriculum continued. Proliferation of courses was such that in 1950, a faculty committee was appointed to monitor non-essential classes, course duplication, minimal class size, and other possible problems. In 1956, in accordance with a faculty recommendation, the board officially changed the name "liberal arts" to the "College of Arts and Sciences," in order more clearly to reflect the school's curricula.

Probably most important to the liberal arts college was an experiment in requirements to broaden the base of educational experience with a "general education" curriculum. Revised graduation requirements were officially put into effect in 1946-47, but classes that focused on a "general" education did not appear until 1948. That year, the liberal arts faculty began requirements (based in large measure on the Columbia University system) that approximated a freshman "core" program in Western civilization, fine arts and literature, biological science, physical science, and contemporary society. After several years of "careful observation of the new general education courses to evaluate their effectiveness," the faculty voted to abandon the plan.

Meanwhile, the campus was enriched by the founding of three new colleges. Having immediately after the war established a series of new vocational programs and an actual major in the field, the department of commerce, previously within the liberal arts college, was expanded into a full-fledged College of Commerce and Industry in 1947. Authorized by the trustees were four separate degree-awarding departments: accounting, business administration, secretarial science, and statistics.

In 1963, over the objections of that college's dean, M. C. Mundell, as well as the dean of liberal arts, and the president (who felt such a move should lie within the faculty's jurisdiction), the board transferred the economics department from liberal arts into the commerce college. The change was sponsored by Trustee John A. Reed, Kemmerer, who was concerned about finding an appropriate home for a major donation from alumnus John Bugas, and probably the economics department head, who sought what for him was a more congenial atmosphere.

The program in pharmacy was established as a separate school under Dean David W. O'Day in 1948. O'Day, Rechard reported, had

> done a very effective job of organizing and planning the work in pharmacy to date, and it is believed that he will do so with even more vigor and enthusiasm if he is given responsibility for its independent operation and promotion.

The School of Pharmacy moved into Merica hall, vacated by women students in favor of their new dormitory.

The founding of a school of nursing was more complicated. Nurses training had traditionally been attached to hospital schools, and from 1918-1931, the University had provided basic science courses for nurse trainees at Ivinson Memorial Hospital. In 1944, it did the same for the U.S. Nurse Cadet Corps. The recommendations of Professors R. H. Denniston and Floyd Clarke caused Morrill, and later Humphrey, to appoint a committee to study possible nurses' education on campus, a cause given impetus when the last hospital school in the

state closed in 1948. The enthusiasm of outside evaluators, the Wyoming Nurses' Association, the Wyoming State Medical Society, and others led the trustees to support a plan to offer two years of training jointly with one or more of the state's two-year colleges. In 1951, the legislature appropriated $61,000 for the project, to be established and maintained in cooperation with at least two schools and hospitals.

Immediately Humphrey appointed a committee to make a study and named as chairperson Mrs. Henrietta A. Loughran of the University of Colorado's nursing school. The 51-page Loughran report recommended that Casper Junior College, with Natrona County Hospital, be authorized to provide a two-year program; that the University, with Laramie's Ivinson Memorial Hospital, establish a similar two-year program plus a four-year curriculum leading to the B.S. degree; and that supplementary teaching units in various parts of the state provide specialty training: Cheyenne in public health and other areas, Sheridan in psychiatry, Rock Springs in rural nursing, and Basin in tuberculosis.

Location of the schools evoked immediate protest. When the board received the Loughran report, Trustee Harold Newton of Sheridan at once moved that his home county be accorded a full-fledged school. He argued that newly-established Northern Wyoming (later Sheridan) Community College (a "University Center") was accredited by the University while Casper Junior College was not and that Sheridan was planning to build a new $1 million hospital facility. Telegrams poured in from Sheridan, but also from many other localities, all with hospitals, all enthusiastic. Tempers ran high, and Mrs. Loughran's committee was at one time accused of approaching the issue "with a biased mind."

At first the board adopted the idea of three schools — Laramie, Casper, and Sheridan — but Humphrey insisted that funding was only sufficient for the minimal two programs which legislation required. Casper eventually was favored, although neither the dean of Casper Junior College nor many leading Casper citizens were enthusiastic about University control, as commanded by the legislature. Eventually (September 1951) an agreement was signed with the Casper college and approved by the board. Further problems arose when it was discovered that the program had to encompass three years by state law; the curriculum had to be revised to provide for a third year of nursing training on campus and in Cheyenne.

DUKE HUMPHREY

orn in Tippah County, Mississippi, six feet tall, a member of the Methodist Church, a Kappa Sigma, and a professional educator, George Duke Humphrey came to the University of Wyoming as its president in 1945. He remained longer than any other president before or since, beating A. G. Crane's previous record by a few months.

Humphrey was the son of a farmer, trader, and part-time politician. Just out of high school, he went to work as a teacher in a one-room Tishomingo (Mississippi) County school in 1915. Later he took degrees at Blue Mountain College (Mississippi), the University of Chicago, and Ohio State. As his Ph.D. dissertation, Humphrey wrote a history of American land-grant colleges.

Although he said later that he lost his heart to the West on a visit to Idaho before he was thirty, it was still a while before he moved. Instead, he worked his way up in the Mississippi school system from teacher to principal to superintendent, and in 1934 he was named president of Mississippi State. Active in many national educational organizations, Humphrey came also to be a friend to several important Mississippi politicians. Knowledge of his activities and perhaps his connections impressed the University of Wyoming President Lewis J. Morrill as well as the board of trustees.

Humphrey remained as president for nineteen years. During that time, his primary accomplishment was a building program that saw fifteen major campus projects completed at a cost of $20 million, not including the science center which was still under construction when Humphrey retired. Always sports minded — as a young president at Mississippi State he had worked hard to build a winning football team — Humphrey oversaw an athletic program that amassed seven Rocky Mountain Intercollegiate Athletic (Skyline) Conference championships in basketball and three post-season bowl games in football, plus numerous victories in the minor sports.

Duke Humphrey was a member of Scabbard and Blade and an honorary member of Phi Kappa Phi. In 1962, he was awarded the honorary Litt.D. degree from the University of Arizona. In all his years at Wyoming, he retained something of the South in his slight drawl, his personal demeanor, and his view of the world. Upon his retirement in 1964, he commented for the press on women's education; at a time when women were seeking enhanced professional opportunities, "Duke" saw women's education as "an education for the whole family . . . reflected in the cultural tone of the home, in the upbringing of children, and in the practical management of domestic affairs."

In 1964, amid persistent rumors that he might run for the U.S. Senate, Humphrey retired from the presidency. To one reporter, he said he had "an awful lot of pressure" to go into politics, and he admitted that he had never been comfortable trout fishing. Still, he had many consulting assignments in education; he planned to write a book; and his eyes were troubling him. Friends felt he never completely recovered from the trauma caused by the death of his wife, Jo. He never ran for public office, but he did maintain ties with political friends in and out of the state. He died in Laramie in 1973.

George Duke Humphrey,
fourteenth president, 1945-1964

To the great credit of Amelia Leino, hardworking head of the nursing program, the University *Bulletin* for 1952 announced the new curricula — both three and four-year courses — in glowing terms. Temporary accreditation was granted by the National League for Nursing; five years later, when the program became fully accredited, the department became a full-fledged "school." Success brought a third program — that which Newton had sought — as of July 1, 1957, when a two-year nursing training curriculum was established at Sheridan College.

Through the 1950s and into the 1960s, many special new programs made their appearance. The education college established student internships in schoolrooms throughout the state, although the program had to be financed in great measure by local school districts, since the legislature's immediate reaction was negative. Adult education launched a separate department of its own. Psychologists established a clinical program, and agricultural engineering became a cooperative effort of two colleges. Humphrey's plan to acquire a telescope through outside funding encouraged the program in astronomy, while an atomic reactor — one of only three in the Rocky Mountain area — spurred faculty and students in atomic chemistry and related fields. Briefly, agriculture tried a four-year curriculum in guest ranch management. A doctoral program in history — foisted upon an unwilling department by an insistent president — joined those in the "hard" sciences during Humphrey's last year. Summer institutes — among them the Institute of International Affairs, funded by the Carnegie Foundation and directed by Professor Gale W. McGee — enlivened a campus of green lawns and bright flowers, as did the creative arts workshops with their extraordinary series of guest musicians, artists, and writers.

In the late 1950s, campus was animated by the appearance of a number of exchange students from Afghanistan, whose education in agriculture and engineering was arranged through a federal government program. Beginning in 1953, the University sent faculty advisers to Kabul and elsewhere in Afghanistan under the auspices of a U.S. Operations Mission and the Royal Afghan Government.

The exchange project called for overseas teaching in vocational agriculture, but supplementary agreements added high school training in engineering, staffing of the agricultural and engineering faculties at Kabul University, and certain programs in agricultural research. More than thirty professors from agriculture and engineering moved to Afghanistan for varying periods of time on varying assignments. Few complained, although conditions were far from ideal: Buildings were often lacking in water or electricity; equipment was seldom adequate; and housing was difficult to find. Problems in communication and staffing were manifold, especially because the University frequently had difficulties recruiting personnel and the on-site mission staff frequently disagreed on policy. Politics, too, intervened. The program surged and wobbled; it was finally "phased out" in 1973.

Research institutes, too, expanded their operations. The Natural Resources Research Institute, inaugurated primarily for investigating Wyoming's mineral resources, offered services to mining corporations after 1943. The Bureau of Business Research, although at first denied legislative funding (1953), came into existence in 1955. With remarkable smoothness, the Agricultural Experiment Station continued its jobs. Only experimental substations (formerly called state farms) languished. They were seldom completely financed by the legislature, and Humphrey was convinced that legislators envisioned them as self-supporting commercial enterprises rather than experimental laboratories. Farms at Lander, Eden, and Lyman remained "inactive" and were rented to private individuals, but maintenance had to be continued and repair was a constant sore spot.

One program developed on campus after 1950 deserves special mention, for it not only brought the University its largest private endowment fund, but it eventually provided a model for nearly 24 other universities that aimed to duplicate the Wyoming curriculum. Nor was it without difficulties in itself, although Humphrey did his best to keep a tight rein of control. This was the academic program in American studies.

CHAPTER NINE

Some time in 1948, Trustee Milward Simpson put Humphrey in touch with his one-time neighbor in the Cody area, William Robertson Coe. A collector of Americana, Coe had at one time apparently offered his Western history and culture book and manuscript collection to the University, but Crane and the board had found it impossible to house the material in an appropriate manner, and as a result, the collection had gone to Yale. It was probably Simpson who approached Coe for a donation to the war memorial fund for the athletic fieldhouse. Coe's gift was a substantial $10,000 and in November 1948, Humphrey and Simpson flew to New York where they awarded the donor an honorary doctor of law degree. Thereafter Humphrey was careful to keep in touch.

That Coe's political and economic outlooks were conservative is probably to understate the case. From the beginning of their association, Humphrey continually emphasized to Coe his own patriotism and support. In the summer of 1949, he brought

Samuel Flagg Bemis, a professor of history at Yale University, to campus to give the commencement address. Bemis was one of the academics who enjoyed Coe's special confidence, and Humphrey carefully sent a copy of the address to Coe in New York. "You can see," he wrote in language that Coe understood, "that we are trying to bring to our students the principles on which America was founded and which should be perpetuated." President and financier thereafter entered into an exchange of views and printed materials on the merits of free enterprise and the dangers of socialism — an exchange in which each seems to have sought to top the other.

Although the Wyoming textbook crisis had come and gone, communist infiltration was still a hot national issue. That autumn, the University of Washington had dismissed its acknowledged communist faculty members. Calling the move to Coe's attention, Humphrey wrote that it would have "a tonic effect on higher education and has caused us

Bookstore building, c. 1950

to re-examine our ideals and objectives." Coe shortly provided Humphrey with a copy of a book called *Your Rugged Constitution,* the cost of which he underwrote for Stanford University Press. In the autumn of 1951, Simpson spoke to the Association of Governing Boards of State Universities on his fears of "foreign ideologies in our institutions of learning," a speech which Coe read and for which he expressed great admiration. Humphrey wrote admiringly of the Coe collection at Yale, and with James Babb, Yale librarian, considered the possibility of microfilming all or most of the materials so as to make them available at Wyoming. Both he and Simpson frequently stopped to see the elderly Coe in New York; after one of these meetings, Coe wrote Senator Frank Barrett that Humphrey "thinks right."

Early in their association, Coe described to Humphrey the course in American studies that Yale University had inaugurated, as based in part on the collection of Western Americana that Coe had donated to the Yale library. Humphrey responded with enthusiasm; he had often, he said, thought to begin such a course on the Wyoming campus and had plans in mind. Some time in the winter of 1949-50, the UW president made a special trip to Arizona, where the Coes were in residence, to consult with the potential philanthropist. Humphrey went well prepared. In his notes "For Talk with Mr. Coe" was included a carefully-drawn legal memorandum about the tax advantages of educational donations plus a strong statement about the contribution that capitalist free enterprise might make to the American educational system.

Adoption by large corporations and wealthy individuals of a plan for giving direct aid to public-supported colleges and universities — through endowments, scholarship, funds for providing needed buildings, and other kinds of support — could be very effective in overthrowing the dangerous threat of further control of our lives by a centralized and bureaucratic government. Certainly using for the purpose indicated a portion of the wealth which our system has allowed them to accumulate would be most worthwhile.

Leaving the conference on his way East, Humphrey was able to wire Simpson (in Cody) that

Conference Coe very satisfactory. Told me would help us substantially but did not say how or when. It will take time but he is very interested in University.

That the president added he was not sure whether the contribution "may or may not be a library" indicates the direction his planning was taking.

By early January 1950, the president was optimistic enough to appoint a faculty committee to work out one or more alternative American studies programs. To the group, headed by T. A. Larson, and including Professors L. L. Smith, H. H. Trachsel, R. E. Conwell, and Librarian N. Orwin Rush, Humphrey stated with assurance that Coe had promised a contribution. Perhaps at Humphrey's suggestion, Larson solicited — and received — some excellent suggestions from Bemis at Yale. The program suggested by the committee in its mid-February report encompassed a summer institute (with fellowships for high school teachers and appropriate visiting faculty); a winter program (student scholarships and guest lecturers); substantial additions to the library; and a special project for adult education throughout the state. The committee compiled a list of courses already offered on campus that might well become part of an American studies major and suggested a unique series of American heritage courses as core for the summer plan. The budget as proposed was $154,000 for five years. Humphrey was delighted; he at once sent the proposal to Coe. The philanthropist was cautious. Although he agreed to support one-fifth of the budget, he suggested that Humphrey look elsewhere for additional support.

In 1952, having sought in vain for the matching funds that Coe asked him to find, Humphrey sent Coe plans for a trial summer institute as devised by English and history faculty in a special proposal. The theme of the session would be American ideals, and a guest lecturer would teach a core course in the subject. Readings in American literature would be offered by Professor Wilson O. Clough and a class in history by Professor William R. Steckel, who would also serve as program director. Twenty fellowships would be awarded to high school teachers to cover their costs of attendance. Coe finally agreed to provide full funding in the amount of $4,000, provided the professors were "believers in our fight against State Socialism etc. and in the preservation of our American Way of Life and our Free Enterprise System." Humphrey responded:

I agree with you that the professors in charge shall be thorough believers in our American way

of life and militantly conscious of the danger of State Socialism. I assure you that Dr. Steckel and Professor Clough feel as we do about the creeping paralysis of State Socialism.

He suggested that Bemis of Yale be invited as guest lecturer, for "certainly no one can doubt his sincere belief in American institutions and ideals."

The 1952 summer pilot program in American studies was regarded by all as an unqualified success. Guest Lecturer David Potter, William R. Coe professor of American studies at Yale, substituted for Bemis, who had had to decline the invitation; Steckel and Clough contributed heavily and worked hard. Participating teachers, urged by administrators to evaluate their experience, expressed enthusiasm in letters to Coe and to Humphrey. At the end of the session, president reported to benefactor that

In my long experience as a school administrator, I have never had a conference, a short course, or a summer school in which I believe more good was accomplished than was accomplished in the Conference on American Studies.

Coe was obviously delighted. Without hesitation he pledged $10,000 for each of the following summers (1953 and 1954), always providing that Humphrey must have

assured yourself that [any lecturer] does not hold any of the radical ideas that you and I are interested in fighting.

Humphrey was willing, to the point that he rejected several suggestions for visiting professor before settling on those he deemed appropriate.

Once enthusiastic, Coe became more and more involved. He read with pleasure the carefully solicited thank-you letters from participating teachers. He financed a trip to Wyoming for Yale's librarian and a research trip to Yale for Wyoming's Wilson O. Clough, who was preparing his own book on the American heritage, based in part on his teaching of such a course over the years. He delighted in Steckel's publication of an article on the American studies summer program, and he contributed occasional sums for library books and clerical help. Through the medium of a "public relations" man named William Sauhering, whom most academics came to regard as self-centered and unreliable, he participated in planning and executing summer programs, offering advice and copies of *Your Rugged Constitution* for participants.

In the spring of 1954, Humphrey once again called on a faculty committee (Steckel, Clough, Larson, L. L. Smith, and Rechard) for an American studies proposal. The group suggested a program similar to that previously proposed, but added the necessity for library development, construction of an American studies building, and an endowed chair in the field. In spring 1954, Humphrey approached Coe to request a gift of more than $1 million. Coe was ill, and Simpson and Humphrey delayed their trip to New York. On the very day they arrived — April 22, 1954 — Coe officially wrote them that he planned to contribute $750,000. On April 23, securities and a check for $25,000 were in the mail. Final evaluation of the securities donated put their value (together with the cash) at more than $785,000. The estimated annual income from the grant stood at $40,000-$50,000.

President and trustees were elated. A "magnificent grant," the latter resolved in gratitude for Coe's generosity: "One of the most outstanding contributions that has ever been made to the perpetuation of the American heritage." Trustees gave special private thanks to Simpson and Humphrey for their efforts. With Coe's approval, the administration began plans for a new library building, "to be appropriately named," as Humphrey told their benefactor. In early 1955, the legislature authorized a bond issue to match the Coe grant in construction of a library, to cost an estimated $1.5 million. The legislators adopted a resolution of gratitude for Coe's "wisdom and generosity" and declared their intent that "the William Robertson Coe School of American Studies shall be developed through the years ahead to become a bulwark of the American way of life." Plans were made for the academic year scholarship program, and in autumn 1955, the American studies committee — after some debate about the desirability of bringing in an outside professor — voted the endowed chair to Wilson O. Clough. Three years later, Humphrey presided over the dedication of the new library and American studies school, with principal speeches made by Governor Milward Simpson, board President Clifford Hansen, and Arad Riggs, (a lawyer and friend of Coe's, who represented the Coe Foundation).

Saxophone section, Summer band clinic, 1945

Coe was not present, for he had died in March 1955, shortly after the legislature's commendation. By his will, he left the University an additional endowment of $1.8 million to support and develop its American studies programs. The account was to be administered by a national Coe Foundation, headed by William Rogers Coe (son of the benefactor) and a board, among whose members were both Humphrey and Riggs. Among the foundation's charges was the establishment at other institutions of summer refresher institutes of American studies based on the Wyoming model and dedicated to "meeting the threat of Communism, Socialism, Collectivism, and Totalitarianism and other Ideologies opposed to the preservation of our System of Free Enterprise." The Wyoming program seemed permanently guaranteed and generously financed.

American studies was unique in its financing and administration; problems incurred in this program were of a special kind. In other areas, the constant multiplication of courses and curricula brought different sorts of dilemmas and vexations. After all, such notable expansion — especially after many years when gains could be measured in inches — seldom occurs without some difficulty, and problems inevitably arose.

Some predicaments might be termed out-and-out jurisdictional disputes. Who was to direct, for example, the students enrolled in the College of Arts and Sciences who wished at the same time to earn accreditation to teach through the College of Education? As early as 1948, Rechard and Schwiering got into a tense argument, during which the education dean (supported by signatures from his staff) angrily told Rechard that he could not guarantee practice teaching to students not majoring in his college, while Rechard contended that liberal arts graduates who took the requisite education courses should be certified and placed as teachers "without prejudices because of the source of [the] degree." Allan Willman, head of the department of music, was involved in a continuing crisis along the same lines, for music education majors were particularly needful of those special skills taught exclusively in the music department. The series of formal agreements signed later by Rechard and Harlan Bryant, who became dean of education in 1954, hardly solved the problem. In 1959-60, A. J. Dickman, head of the foreign languages department, became involved in an even more unpleasant debate with Bryant and Professor Bernadene Schunk (education) about the competence of their mutual students.

Education was involved, too, in an equally complex dispute with the department of intercollegiate athletics (Glenn J. "Red" Jacoby, director) about the focus and purposes of the men's and women's physical education courses. In 1950, the trustees asked Humphrey to investigate and seek "better harmony." After a good many exchanges about equipment like towels and baseballs, Bryant agreed that Jacoby should take over direction of physical education. The new department became known as the "Division of Physical Education and Intercollegiate Athletics." Jacoby was assisted by R. D. Watkins.

As faculty and staff increased, personnel problems also arose. These were probably at the bottom of the board's request for special reports from the heads of the departments of history and English in mid-1946. T. A. Larson reported with no difficulty on why several individuals had left history department employ — most of them, like eminent Russian historian A. Lobanov-Rostovskii, for positions of greater salary and prestige. In English, the problem seemed to revolve around the policies of a recently-retired department head and the "troubled political atmosphere" that some faculty traced to Crane's single-track phobia about radio broadcasting courses, then administered by the English department. Professor Wilson O. Clough's description of his philosophy as new head of the department — as compared with the beliefs of the previous head — is a masterpiece deserving of publication in its own right. Clough wrote:

In general, my "philosophy" for the department is neither revolutionary nor dramatic, but one, I hope, of recognition of the practical aspects of the annual problem, changing but little from year to year, as far as the newcomers are concerned. We deal first with human beings; and literature is not a mystic shrine but a form of experience, a normal part of maturing. . . . I have no final statement of a philosophy. Any such statement is a map only — not the voyage nor the achievement — and I am dubious of premature conclusions.

In 1951, the entire liberal arts faculty seemed beset with unease about its rapid expansion and in particular about its sponsorship of career-oriented curricula. That year Rechard appointed a "Committee on Aims and Purposes," which took more than twelve months to devise a long report on goals, requirements, professional programs, service functions, research, and other matters of faculty concern. L. L. Smith of the English department was chairman. The committee called for maintaining traditional values as compared to "utilitarianism" and expressed the special hope that professional programs would be continually reappraised to determine their breadth in values — "social, moral, and intellectual." Although the faculty had experimented with general education and returned instead to a traditional curriculum, the committee warned that "worship of facts" should not replace studies "that lend themselves naturally to judgments and evaluations." Rechard sent the Smith report to Humphrey, who complimented the committee on its work. Still, the nature of professional programs in the college remained a point of debate and concern.

Perhaps the gravest problems in rapid curricular expansion lay in maintaining a hard core of quality and strong standards. No one wanted watered-down courses or weak requirements, but new programs took time to build; in their early years, they often fell behind national standards in terms of personnel, equipment, library, or facilities. One measure of quality lay in formal accreditation by recognized national and regional organizations. Such accreditation was periodically reviewed and always required enormous self-study and self-appraisal.

Since enrollments and offerings were generally small, few new programs were accredited without some difficulty. The professional chemistry program in arts and sciences and the College of Commerce and Industry programs were denied accreditation the first time around because of cramped facilities and faculty standards (including salary rates). The American Association of Collegiate Schools of Business, Humphrey reported to the board,

withheld the accrediting of the College of Commerce pending reduction of teaching loads and the building up of staff to a point where approximately fifty percent of it shall have the equivalent of a doctor's degree,

while the American Chemical Society refused recognition to the professional curriculum because of

a lack of adequate space for labs, lecture rooms, and faculty offices, a burdensome teaching load, low salary schedule, and lack of separate library.

Although nursing was accredited shortly after the college was founded, troubles accumulated a few years later.

In 1941 when the accreditation team from the Engineering Council for Professional Development inspected campus facilities, it found laboratory equipment badly wanting in civil and mechanical engineering and appropriate faculty lacking in the electrical field. The publication of these criticisms before the final positive decision was announced called forth considerable administrative irritation. It was eighteen years before H. T. Person, then dean of engineering, wrote Humphrey that accreditation could be achieved in two more of the college's programs, but that for certain other options, it would be wiser to wait. Meanwhile, although the College of Pharmacy had been duly accredited, national standards, as determined by the American Council on Pharmaceutical Education, demanded that it develop a five-year program by 1960 if it sought to have accreditation renewed; such a change was adopted on schedule.

In regard to accreditation, the law school had special difficulties. Since 1923, it had been accredited by the American Bar Association and held membership in the American Association of Law Schools. But it continued to enroll a relatively small number of students and had trouble maintaining the faculty and facilities that the ABA

required. During the years of World War II, faculty and students declined in such numbers (as in many other similar schools) that the ABA postponed its accrediting visitation.

Another crisis arose in 1956, when the chairman of the ABA inspection committee reported that the law school needed at least one new faculty member, a larger budget for the library, higher salaries, and funds for research assistance. Although the request for the 1957 legislature had already been prepared, Humphrey immediately approached the governor, who agreed to an amendment on the law school's behalf. In the interim, however, the investigator's report was released to the press and given considerable publicity. Humphrey was angry at the report, which he called "unjustified criticism," biased, and unrealistic. He was even more furious at the publicity, which he publicly blamed on the investigator (who had not insisted on the confidentiality of his memorandum) and privately blamed on Dean Hamilton (who had released the story without permission in the hopes of commandeering the necessary funds for accreditation). The legislature repaired the damage with increased funding, and in 1962, when the ABA and the American Association of Law Schools again inspected the school, it was "generally rated excellent," in Humphrey's words. Meanwhile, the incident occasioned a University news release listing the 23 national and regional organizations in which the institution held membership or which approved or recognized its programs.

Enlarged, enriched academic curricula called for money, especially if high quality standards were to be maintained. Acquiring funds was a University president's special charge. The vast expansion after World War II sent Humphrey to the legislature with ever-increasing demands. If the president was often content to leave academic matters in the hands of deans and faculty, he always kept legislative business strictly in his own control. Herein lay Humphrey's forte.

Like Crane, Humphrey worked hard. He checked and rechecked budget items proposed by deans and his financial staff, often calling on them for careful explanations. He stumped the state to sell the University's program to the leading citizens in twelve communities. He was always prepared with statistics and arguments for the special University meeting with the committee on appropriations, and he took thereto board members and such fiscal aides as might be needed. He knew virtually all the legislators personally and kept his finger on their pulses throughout the budget-setting process. Unlike Crane, Humphrey was an easy mixer, at home in Cheyenne's Plains Hotel, in the governor's suite, or in any smoke-filled room. One of the governors with whom he worked has called him a consummate politician. Although it is not true that the legislature always gave him exactly what it wanted, it is accurate to say that his efforts to achieve funding for University projects generally met with success.

From the very first, Humphrey pushed for increased operating budgets. In his first five years in office the president steered the University request through four legislative meetings — two regular and two special sessions — with increased appropriations from year to year. By 1951, the main University "contingent" appropriation (supporting all but special projects, construction, agricultural experimentation, and agricultural extension services) stood at $4.5 million as approved. It had not, Humphrey reported to the board, been the best of years, because of the uncertain international situation surrounding the Korean War. There was, he said,

an uneasiness in the minds of the members of the Legislature because of the unsettled national and international conditions, which made it almost impossible to foresee with any degree of certainty what will happen in the next few years.

From the University's original request, the legislature had cut almost $500,000, and faculty salary increases, for which Humphrey had argued, had to be restricted to less than 2.5 percent. In 1953, trustees carefully pared their biennial request to about the same amount (near $5 million) that they had requested in 1951, and the legislature reacted similarly in cutting about $500,000 from the main University contingent fund. But thereafter, the appropriation began to climb, reading $6,610,468 for the main University in 1959; climbing to more than $9.5 million in 1961; and increasing in 1963 by more than $1 million for the biennium.

A special footnote must be added: Throughout this period, the legislature — and particularly its appropriations or ways and means committee — assumed ever more control over the UW budget and asserted ever more positively its right to determine exactly how University funds were spent.

Back in Crane's days that had seldom been the case. Of course the president always took to the legislature a budget proposal showing that the total amount of the mill levy was necessary, and the board always presented to the governor a full accounting of how the money had been spent. Still, legislative supervision was minimal, and even when the mill levy vanished and every biennium brought a special appropriation, the "main University" item was carried without strings attached. Only occasionally were funds earmarked for special purposes. Instead the appropriation was usually divided into allocations for the main University; agricultural extension; agricultural substations; and a few special projects, like the interstate medical training program and the statewide nursing program. In 1953, Humphrey remarked approvingly on the system.

Generally, the appropriation is not restricted, and this is extremely desirable. At times the Legislature earmarks a part of the appropriation for specific purposes; and this practice often makes it impossible for the university to charge expenditures against the various revenue funds in the most effective manner, or at the most effective times.

The president spoke too soon. During that very session the practice changed, perhaps through the influence of Keith Thomson, legislator from Cheyenne, who in a violent interview with Humphrey accused the trustees of misappropriating funds and contended that the University's budget presentation was deliberately designed to confuse rather than clarify. When the ways and means committee cut the University request, Humphrey asked for an explanation and got more than he anticipated. On March 2, 1953, the committee informed the president of exactly how it "felt," "believed," or "suggested" that University moneys be spent, and indeed the letter spoke not just of the legislative appropriation but of the University's total budget, which contained funds received from many different sources. Humphrey drafted an irritated letter, but it is possible that he never sent it.

University sorority, c. 1950

Four years later, Milward Simpson, as governor, requested a careful explanation of his friend Humphrey's proposed budget. The president found himself justifying salary increases for the law school; explaining how scholarships were awarded; defending the maintenance of emergency funds; and supporting the level of student fees—among 25 other specific items. That same year the ways and means committee proposed that all University funds be handled by the state treasurer and expended through state vouchers, a measure that met defeat, in part because of Governor Simpson's efforts. Still, an official act set limits on the salaries of the University's director of finance and its superintendent of buildings and grounds.

To the board Humphrey reported that the ways and means committee had hinted that emergency funds were being used secretly to inaugurate programs that the legislature would then be obligated to continue, and that some legislators were certain there were "hidden items" in the budget itself. In 1959, when cuts in the budget request caused the board to increase tuition fees, Powell Legislator Richard Jones protested that

this move in effect defeats the intention, as I saw it, of the Ways and Means and the entire Legislature to hold the expenditures of the Main University at their recommended figure.

In some exasperation, Humphrey got the co-chairman of the committee to state in writing that he had expected such a fee increase. Still, the committee insisted that its detailed breakdown of recommended appropriations "serve as a guide to University officials in preparing operating budgets." In vain the president complained and protested.

Perhaps in an effort to establish clearer lines of control, Humphrey changed the form of the budget presentation in 1961, emphasizing as he said "function and performance." His request for the "general University" included items for resident instruction, organized research, educational services, library, general administration, plant maintenance, and capital outlay. The move could hardly be called successful, if less legislative intervention was what the president sought. The ways and means committee still insisted on having a statement of funds outside of state appropriations that might be budgeted. Within the new "functional" categories, it further broke down totals: salaries, salary increases, part-time wages, contractual, travel, supplies, equipment, fixed charges, and others. It recommended in each instance how funds should be handled, down to such matters as weatherstripping, the rodeo team expenses, and construction of a handball court. The same situation existed in the session of 1963. Having expanded its needs and services, the University found itself putting increasing efforts into itemized accounting at legislative behest, even though accounts were still audited and detailed annual reports of expenses were regularly presented, according to law.

In his building program, Humphrey was more easily successful, perhaps because although construction had to be approved by the legislature, most funding actually came from special sources, and legislators seldom had to dip into the general fund. Like Crane, the president gloried in bricks and mortar. During the Humphrey administration, central campus took the form it has today; in addition the University acquired its first high-rise dormitories, and its present (though then smaller) football stadium and fieldhouse. Like Crane, Humphrey utilized imaginative and complex financing to raise campus structures. In many ways, Crane's early policies laid the basis for the later president's construction successes.

Humphrey, too, funded building through the issue of bonds — legally not subject to voter approval — to be purchased by the state of Wyoming and retired (whenever possible) from income generated by the building. By law of 1920 and subsequent amendments, the University was guaranteed nine percent of the first $4 million paid to Wyoming by the federal government as the state's share of oil royalties earned on federally-owned Wyoming lands. In 1951, Humphrey proposed and won support for a bill which also granted to the University (by means of a University building excess royalty fund) nine percent of any royalty received by the state in excess of $4 million a year. Such funds were earmarked for construction. On these foundations bricks and mortar were laid. Beginning in 1950, there was scarcely a year in which some new campus edifice was not rising.

Most campus building projects were completed with minimal contributions by the state. In the early 1950s, oil royalties financed the construction of a law school building, an addition to the geology building, a home for the physical plant maintenance and repair department, and certain minor projects like construction on the dairy farm. Revenue bonds were issued for dormitories (Wyoming hall, additions to Knight hall), married student housing, new sorority and fraternity houses (built with the assistance of University loans on the mall planned by Crane), and the War Memorial fieldhouse and stadium — in all instances bonds to be retired out of future revenues from the construction itself. In the case of the stadium, donations of more than $200,000 (well below the amount predicted by the public relations firm hired to consult on the campaign) were instrumental in persuading the legislature to authorize the issuance of revenue bonds to help. Throughout these years, only the education and agriculture buildings were completely financed from the state general fund, although the stadium was given a $400,000 boost.

In 1955, the whole carefully-structured edifice came close to toppling. What happened was that the income from which bonds were to be retired (on a carefully devised schedule) turned out to be much less substantial than had been anticipated. In the eight years between 1945 and 1953, Humphrey wrote in his legislative report, nearly $9 million had been invested in permanent structures, of which $2.6 million had been raised through the sale of "self-refunding" bonds. Payments for securities issued during the Crane administration also had to be met. The president admitted that bonded indebtedness was too high, a situation for which he found the legislature partly to blame, because on two occasions it had increased the total amount of authorized bonds in order to avoid appropriations (as recommended by University officials) from the state general fund. In another instance, a strike had delayed the opening of a new men's dormitory and caused a set-back in collection of necessary fees. Humphrey wrote:

> *The result was unfortunate. Large payments upon principal and interest became due prior to the occupancy of Wyoming Hall. . . . The profit margin at the Hall is much too small to make two bond payments in any one year, so the Hall has been under a debt handicap from its very inception.*

Indeed, Wyoming hall was a year in arrears in payments into the bond retirement fund. The University as a whole was obligated in the sum of $2.5 million annually for principal and interest payments and was falling behind at the rate of $150,000 per year.

Humphrey had a solution. He proposed a massive refinancing plan. His suggestion was that outstanding bonds for five previous projects be recalled and refloated through a new issue of $2.3 million in revenue bonds at two percent for twenty years. The average annual cost of principal and interest payments would be lowered to an amount that Humphrey estimated could be repaid out of local income and annual oil royalty funds. Since the state treasurer had purchased the previous bonds as an investment for state funds, recalling would cause no legal difficulties once approved by the legislature. First to the board (which took hours of its time to debate exact amounts of principal, interest, and duration) and then to the legislature of 1955, Humphrey successfully argued his project.

The results were more spectacular than trustees anticipated. The 1955 legislature authorized the consolidation of the outstanding bonds into new bonds in the amount of $2,327,000, to be issued at a suggested interest of 3.5 percent for a period of twenty years. At the same time, it included in the bond issue Humphrey's new requests of $384,000 for married student apartments and $600,000 to match Coe's donation for a new library. The total of $3,461,000 in principal, plus interest, was to be paid off from local income and the oil royalty funds.

Out of the woods of past indebtedness, an elated president moved forward with an armload of new construction plans. Bond issues came thick and fast. Funds for the William Robertson Coe library were increased when the board opted to use part of Coe's legacy to match extra money set aside by the legislature. The library construction project was thus guaranteed at least $1.5 million. In 1957, the legislature authorized the board to issue another $625,000 in bonds (to be purchased as usual by state funds) for an addition to the Wyoming Union, although protests from local hotel keepers caused trustees to cancel their plans for a number of guest rooms on the top floor. The same legislature authorized a bond issue of $650,000 for a new engineering building, for which an additional amount of $209,000 was to be added from the University Building Improvement Fund (oil royalties); Vice Admiral Emory S. Land had already pledged $50,000 toward construction, and the oil and gas industry agreed to provide $500,000 for equipment. Two years later legislators agreed to another huge bond issue of $11,743,000 to finance three dormitories (one with cafeteria), an infirmary building, a new building for the College of Commerce and Industry, another module for the service building, additional married students' apartments, and a considerable intramural and intercollegiate athletic area. Never mind that the state was unable to purchase all of the bonds involved; that considerable difficulty was encountered in selling the bonds through private brokers and agencies; and that the interest rate had been raised to four percent.

In this rocketing increase of debt, the legislature demurred on only one small point. In 1959, Representative Frank Mockler introduced a special amendment to the enabling act that provided that no building be erected ("whether it be financed by a State appropriation, oil royalties, gifts, bequests or any other means") in the quiet corner of campus (bordering Ivinson and Ninth Streets) where trustees had proposed to place the new women's dormitory. Nellie Tayloe Ross hall, named for the first woman governor, had to be relocated on a corner of the campus mall called Prexy's Pasture.

In 1961, Humphrey embarked on the last of his great building projects with what was at first planned as a single building to house the physical science departments. Under the direction of a series of faculty-staff committees, the plans rapidly expanded to include an $8 million science center, the remodeling of several dormitories for other purposes, and the addition of at least one new residence hall. The board demurred at the president's plan for a mammoth reissue of outstanding bonds, in part because of legal problems involved in redeeming the old series. A good many problems arose in planning finances, especially since the bonds from 1959 were still in the process of sale; the University Building Improvement Fund had been committed for many purposes through 1965; and capital outlay and debt service (as indicated in the University's legislative request in 1963) totalled more than $2 million per biennium. Still, trustees approved Humphrey's plans; the age of technology and science demanded that the University not be permitted to fall behind.

The science center — officially named the George Duke Humphrey Science Center — became the president's favorite construction project. "Frankly," he wrote to the editor of the Sheridan *Press* in 1963, "I feel that the proposed Center is about the most important request I have presented to the Legislature in my years at the University." As a member of the board of the National Science Foundation, Humphrey was aware of possibilities for foundation and government assistance, particularly from such science-conscious institutions as the Atomic Energy Commission, the National Aeronautics and Space Administration, and the National Institutes of Health. In early 1963, he wrote to presidents of all Western state universities inquiring about their science facilities and their universities' science funding. Press releases on new scientific discoveries and programs were distributed throughout the state, and Humphrey stumped all counties as usual.

In 1963, the legislature approved the president's plans and endorsed a bond issue to remodel dormitories, construct a new residence hall, and build the proposed science center. The total issue reached $5,734,000 for all projects. In addition, a second issue in the amount of $1 million was to be devoted to married student apartments. These construction bonds were to be redeemed over the years through dormitory and housing profits and from those funds in the excess royalty accumulation not previously committed against prior bonded indebtedness. Two years later, the legislature added bonded indebtedness in the amount of $4,210,000 to cover further science center construction; to add a classroom building; and for miscellaneous other projects, this time with bonds to be repaid from the University Permanent Land Fund, primarily oil royalties from early federal land grants.

The location of the science center was not easily determined. Recognizing the advantage of situating the complex as close as possible to related facilities in engineering, agriculture, geology, and the health sciences, trustees eliminated a number of potential sites and settled (February 1965) on the west end of Prexy's Pasture, immediately east of the arts and sciences building. That a concerned president carefully leaked the decision to the Laramie *Boomerang's* editor, who in turn revealed it to the world at large, accounts for the survival intact of the central campus square. Storms of protest battered the trustees from around the state — from alumni, students, legislators, and others. Reconsidering, the board opted instead to locate the center west of the arts and sciences building, although several structures would have to be removed from the area. In rationale, Harold F. Newton, board president, cited among other factors the importance of the "continued beautification of a growing university." In 1971, the legislature passed a law banning construction on Prexy's Pasture forevermore.

Financially, the president took a gamble, and if he personally won the throw, he mortgaged the University well into the future. The debt incurred for building construction was scheduled for annual repayments into the 21st century. The annual interest and capital payments at the time Humphrey left office totalled more than the complete bonded indebtedness of the University in 1949 ($2,201,000). But oil royalties were increasing, enrollment was growing, and increasing numbers of faculty crowded offices, library, and laboratories. It may have been prophetic that in 1962 the University had to require out-of-town freshmen to live in recently-built dormitories that might otherwise have stood partially empty. Within twenty years, classroom, library, and office space was at a premium, in spite of remodeled facilities in the center of campus and additional buildings on its outskirts. Humphrey's bricks and mortar provided no permanent solution to the University's need for space.

One further note should be appended before this chapter on expansion comes to an end. As increasing numbers of students flooded campus, a call arose for higher education in other sections of the state. One community college — that located at Casper — had been founded in 1945. Other communities sought similar institutions. Fearful for its own budget and for the size of its student body, the University was less than enthusiastic. Indeed, of all the problems left to Humphrey by the Morrill administration, none was so difficult of solution and intricate of analysis.

Since the administration was not eager to endorse the construction of rival, independent two-year colleges across the state, it devised its own plans. The first suggestion — that "branch" or University Centers be set up in the far corners of the state — sustained a blow when the special legislature in 1946 failed to endorse the requested appropriation for teaching faculty and even went so far as to order that no "center" instruction be financed out of University funds. Humphrey countered with a second plan. By autumn, he was able to report to the board that voters in the Powell school district, located in the far northwest corner of the state, had approved by a margin of 75-1 a 1.32 tax mill levy for a two-year "University Center." The mill levy, plus money from the school district budget and fees to be collected from students, would suffice to pay faculty, equip offices, provide clerical and janitorial help, purchase supplies, and maintain a small library budget. The University would furnish supervision (through its regular extension division), aid in selecting personnel, and grant University credit for approved courses. All financial accounting, including the issuance of payroll checks, would take place in University offices. To the board, Humphrey was highly enthusiastic.

It is thought that the movement for establishing Centers is one which will do more than almost any other program toward broadening the base of education and spreading the influence of the University over the State,

he reported.

Indeed, no sooner had the Powell University Center opened its doors than Humphrey received a request for a similar institution from a Sheridan agricultural college committee, adjunct of the Sheridan Chamber of Commerce. After a year of negotiation, the board met (January 1948) in Sheridan to celebrate another new agreement.

These two-year programs, together with the one soon established in Goshen County, were devised for three groups of students: returning adults, those who planned to transfer elsewhere (probably the University) after their sophomore year, and terminal students. Strong emphasis was placed on vocational education for those not planning to continue: Courses were offered in agriculture, education, commerce, engineering, in addition to the traditional liberal arts. For some time, the plan worked smoothly, and Humphrey was able to report in 1949 that local authorities were "living up to their agreement with the University in respect to finances in a very fine way."

Still, ties were slender, for the University provided little or no cash but primarily services to the established centers. In 1948, to the special legislative session, Humphrey carried a request for "deficiency" financing of the center programs in the amount of $32,000. In a fit of good spirits, the legislature approved, but at the following session (1949) a similar appropriation, to be included in the University budget, was blocked and the administration told again that it might not invest University funds in center teaching. Although W. C. Reusser, head of adult education, urged the centers to continue their programs through local resources and although they tentatively agreed, it did not take local authorities long to recognize that the University's role might easily be dispensed with if no actual money was forthcoming.

For some time the administrative relationship between the so-called centers — by 1959 all calling themselves community colleges — and the University remained abysmally unclear. Reusser himself, as dean of adult education and community service, found it hard (he reported) to answer questions. Were the community colleges part of the University? Their courses were approved by UW; their entrance requirements, scholarship standards, and course requirements were similar; and instructors had to be approved by the University board for appointment. But in that case, did tenure status at Sheridan enable faculty to transfer to campus should positions be phased out? And if the community colleges were indeed University branches, why was there argument (especially with R. E. McWhinnie, registrar) about the number of units that could be transferred towards a campus degree? What exactly was implied by the annual University accreditations? None of these questions proved easy of solution under the joint administration — although community financing — of the two-year institutions. Even Casper Junior College — independently established and never administratively dependent on University resources — found itself embroiled in the controversies evoked by its inclusion in all the "community college" legislative regulations. Legislation of 1953 and 1955 only served to define a few terms; actual relationships were left to negotiations and to the Community College Commission, established by law in 1951.

The problems became acute in 1956, when citizens in both Riverton and Evanston proposed to establish two-year or community colleges. Humphrey met with heads of the current institutions, and all agreed that proliferation of colleges could only mean inappropriate division of resources; they were ready to propose to the legislature that no more than six community college districts be authorized. The board's expressions of concern caused Governor Simpson to suggest a possible constitutional amendment limiting the number of institutions and restricting their programs to two years — a slap at Casper's college, where a four-year program was already being discussed. His plan received only lukewarm support among trustees who pointed out that such an amendment might take years to enact.

By December 1956, with the legislative meetings only a month away, the community college deans and University administration came to an agreement about legislation to be sponsored: This included an increase in the tax base legally necessary for establishing two-year colleges; an appropriation of $130,000 to be administered through the University; and a possible constitutional amendment such as the governor had proposed. However, Casper and Sheridan deans reported opposition in their districts. A chagrined Humphrey told the board in January that without his prior knowledge, legislators from the two districts had introduced bills asking for a substantially higher and independently administered appropriation. A meeting of members of the board of education, the University, the ways and means committee, and representatives from all the community colleges failed to produce agreement. The

176

legislature of 1957 accordingly did not endorse any constitutional amendment; instead, it contented itself with minor revisions in the operative laws. It did, however, provide $80,000 for community college operation and authorized the University to act as administrator. Bitterness and backbiting continued. As the student newspaper put it,

> Some legislators in the Casper and Sheridan vicinity were extremely critical when it came to the University and its relationship to the junior colleges. . . . The University and the officers of administration are, it is apparent, bearing the brunt of a feeling that UW did little to support the junior college legislation.

Reusser was upset because the head of Northern Wyoming Community College (more commonly called Sheridan College) regularly referred to himself as "president." In the agreement signed between the University and the new Eastern Wyoming College, the University reserved to itself control of many academic policies. The president of the Eastern Wyoming College board of trustees wrote to Humphrey in somewhat pathetic vein:

> As you undoubtedly know, we have struggled for the establishment of a Junior Community College at Torrington for the past ten years, and there have been times when we did not know whether the doors would remain open or not, and there have also been times when we felt that those under your command had not been very favorable toward us. As you also know, we have thrown our support back of the Trustees of the University of Wyoming to be the governing body for higher education in the State of Wyoming, instead of splitting the authority and approval as Casper, along with Sheridan, would liked to have done. . . . We sincerely feel that you will do everything possible for us, but our experience with others we do not feel has in any way assisted us in establishing a Community College at Torrington.

In 1958, faculty for the community colleges were listed in the UW *Bulletin* under the division of adult education and community services. But Sheridan College proposed a new agreement with the University that would mean, Humphrey claimed, "almost complete withdrawal by the college from cooperation with the University."

Art class sketching assignment, c. 1955

Throughout this year and the next, tempers really flared. In late 1957, Dean Maurice Griffith of Casper Junior College approached University Trustee J. M. McIntire to suggest that the third-year nursing residency program be attached to the Casper institution instead of to the University. "You will find Duke uncooperative," he wrote,

> on this as he is on anything else that would give additional educational opportunities to Casper. . . . I hope, however, that he will see this as an educator and not as a Laramie partisan so there will not be needless division of students between two programs in nursing.

McIntire was perhaps indiscreet in showing the letter to Humphrey who responded promptly to the "uncalled-for attack." Caught in the middle was nursing dean, Amelia Leino, who was forced to defend herself in one long document after another from Griffith's claim that she was incompetent and "antagonistic" toward the Casper nursing faculty. Defending Leino, Humphrey got involved, too, in a nasty correspondence with J. C. Carr, administrator of the Casper hospital.

Once the anger raged, the battle was joined. By August 1958, Richard E. White, dean of Sheridan College, was ready to side with Casper on the suggestion that the University's board of trustees not be accorded any special position in the administration of community colleges and thus Wyoming higher education. Humphrey responded:

It seems rather obvious from your Board's action that you are concerned with getting help from the University only until things are worked out in accordance with your ideas, and then the University can go its way and you will go yours. . . . Whenever we advance any suggestions, they are immediately questioned by you as indicating a desire on the part of our Board to control the junior colleges. Never has the University Board mentioned the word "control."

To Richard Redburn of the Sheridan *Press,* the president added:

Does it mean nothing to the community colleges that the University is willing to give them the benefit of its years of experience, to lend them its prestige in getting their programs accredited? It is difficult for me to understand why some of the people connected with the community colleges do not trust the University.

Mistrust, of course, mounted. Humphrey's cause was not abetted by Governor Simpson, who in the fall of 1958 suggested a special board for community college administration, or by Governor-elect J. J. Hickey, who publicly spoke out against proliferation of two-year colleges but gave strong support to the existing institutions.

In 1959, the legislature solved the problem by virtually establishing two-year college independence when it restructured the Community College Commission to limit University representation and authorized the commission to act as the sole administrator and distributor of all legislative aid to community colleges. Still, legislators urged statewide cooperation and made it clear that any college supported by the state must be accredited annually, either by the University or by a regional association.

With this law, the University's efforts to maintain a hand in community college administration came to an end. True, for several years faculty teams continued to investigate and accredit two-year institutions, until such time as the North Central Association Accreditation team was called in. By board policy, University representatives met frequently with the Community College Commission, and consultations continued on course coordination and the award of credit. General administrative independence was accompanied by increased state and federal funding. By 1961, the Community College Commission was receiving more than $500,000 each biennium from the state treasury plus regular federal support for its vocational education programs through the Smith-Hughes Act. In 1963 — Duke Humphrey's last legislative year — the appropriation climbed to more than $700,000.

In retrospect, the expansion of the higher educational system throughout the state seems almost inevitable. The same pressures that made for expansion on campus exerted an influence on other communities. With the geographic breadth of Wyoming, the emergence of new two-year colleges was preordained, and not even the University's vigorous attempts to extend its programs into the far corners of the state could substitute for the locally-financed institutions with local control. That what began as University Centers should evolve into community colleges was actually written into the original charters, by which the University provided little but guidance. That these colleges in turn should become totally independent was unavoidable too. The best that the board of trustees might expect was the kind of cooperation that eventually evolved through the Community College Commission and — much later — the provision of such supplementary programs on a local level as would enable many non-traditional students to complete their degrees at home. The quarreling and backbiting of the 1950s did little to enhance anyone's prestige.

With the huge expansion of college programs, University financing, and campus building came a need for more efficient administrative procedures, faculty self-rule, and enhanced student activities. To these functions of expansion between 1950 and 1964, the following chapter is devoted.

BASKETBALL

orty-two years after the memorable basketball season of 1943, the fans were still talking about it. In March 1985, inspired by the contest between Georgetown and St. John's in the National Collegiate Athletic Association's semi-final round, the Denver *Post* published (and the Laramie *Boomerang* reprinted) an article about "way back when." In 1943, the Cowboys had defeated both teams. Wyoming not only beat Georgetown for the NCAA championship, but the Cowboys went on two nights later to defeat St. John's, the winner of the National Invitational Tournament. Basketball fans celebrated in the streets.

But basketball has often led Wyoming sports fans to victory parades. In its very first game, the Wyoming team of 1904-05 swamped a "town" team by the score of 17-8 — hardly a big point

Men's basketball team, c. 1900

gainer, but then they were only beginning. Back in the days when John Corbett was coaching all sports, the team posted a 7-2 season (1918) and followed with 10-1 (1919).

The real excitement came in the mid-1930s. Fans who "remember when" still get a gleam in their eyes when they speak of the victories amassed by Coach "Dutch" Witte. After nine years, Witte's record was 134 wins to 51 losses, plus two championships in the Rocky Mountain Intercollegiate Athletic (Skyline) Conference (1932 and 1934).

In those days, Wyoming was in the Skyline's "eastern" division, and its greatest rivals were the "western" division Utah schools. In 1931, a fast-hitting Utah team defeated the Pokes in two of the three conference championship games. 1932 was a different story, as Cowboys, with the aid of the coach's brother Les Witte, who was on the first team, won two out of three against Brigham Young to take the conference title. Three-inch *Branding Iron* headlines spread the news to fans as the team "crashed into the limelight" for "the greatest basketball season in the history of the University."

If the sportswriter was wrong, it was only because the best was yet to come. Although the Skyline title eluded the Cowboys in 1933, the following year they made up for the loss. In games often played "before a frenzied mob which filled the big Wyoming gym to the corners," Witte's team won 26 and lost 5. In the final series for the Skyline championship, again played against BYU, basketball fever reached its heights. Wyoming took the first victory by a handy 43-38. In the second game, the team trailed by 12 points with 12 minutes remaining, but in a cliffhanging overtime, it beat BYU 47-44. The final game, too, saw a Cowboy victory.

In these days before the organization of the national collegiate basketball championships, Wyoming was invited to a Tulsa, Oklahoma tournament following the regular season's play. Playing eight games in ten days, the Pokes slumped in the end to lose their last three. In some games, the first five played all the way. In the contest with the Tulsa Oilers, Wyoming's leading point gainer played throughout with a sprained ankle. When the team came home, 4,000 cheering fans met them at the train.

In recent years, basketball has not lost its punch. In his first five seasons, Coach Jim Brandenburg had an overall record of 96-48, and Wyoming won two Western Athletic Conference championships.

Chapter Ten

Faculty, Students, and Administrators, 1945-1964

As students flocked to campus in the post-war years, faculty, too, increased in number, and rapidly-employed young professors identified their careers with the University's prosperity and its future. Staff burgeoned, and organizational chart followed chart as administrative officers appeared and disappeared or shifted from one function to another. The growth pains of an expanding University called for a new set of procedural and structural regulations to replace the scattered rules of previous decades. Important definitions of faculty rights — freedoms for academics, both in and out of the classroom — were debated at Wyoming as at other institutions throughout the country. If students felt restive under some old constraints, they could hardly help celebrating — along with alumni, faculty, trustees, and others — when President G. D. Humphrey fulfilled long-standing ambitions through a series of winning coaches who finally put Wyoming on the athletic map.

Wilson O. Clough estimates that between 1945 and 1947, more than 150 individuals were added to the teaching faculty, although, of course, some ranked as replacements for resigning or retiring predecessors. Many new faculty remained for years, or a lifetime. Still, turnover in these post-war years reflected chaotic conditions; not for some time did the faculty seem to settle in more permanently. Even then, the comings and goings — particularly among the ranks of instructors and assistant professors — caused many a headache for colleagues and administrators. Not until 1950 could Humphrey report "stabilization in faculty employment."

Returning faculty had special problems; included among them were men like Robert H. Bruce, T. A. Larson, Allan Willman, and A. J. Dickman, to name only a few. They had served their country during the war; to what would they return? Where would they stand in relation to promotions and tenure? What would be the status of their salaries?

In 1943, Dickman wrote to Fay Smith from "overseas" to raise the issue of

the salary increases and advancements of those who chose to remain at home. Will that mean that we, who are away, shall not benefit of those adjustments when we return, since the accepted procedure has been that those returning from leaves of absence come back at the salary they received when they left, and shall we be penalized because we did what we thought was the best and most honorable thing?

Nobody knew, and no formal policy seems to have been enunciated. Instead, deans agonized over individual adjustments and scrambled for the dollars to make them.

Thus personnel new and old had to be evaluated for rank and title; formal offers had to be advanced to them; tenure as well as salary had to be resolved. Considerable turmoil accompanied the procedure. Humphrey had not been long in office before it became clear to him that even the simplest coordination of campus operations was endangered by a lack of precise knowledge of procedures, rules, and responsibilities.

Indeed, no careful compilation of University regulations nor any codification of rulings in force had been in operation for decades. Such a document seemed superfluous during the quiet Crane years, and Morrill had simply had no time during the war. Although the body of regulations constantly expanded and was often altered, no single reference source existed.

That four historians could maintain an abiding commitment to their profession — through research, publication, and service in many national organizations — and yet devote a century and a half to their institution and its students demonstrates a dedication that has caused generations of alumni to look back with both fondness and awe on their U.S. history and Western civilization classes.

Laura White was a beautiful young woman when she came to the University as an instructor in 1913. Born in Bloomington, Illinois, she had received her bachelor's degree (1904) and her master's (1912) from the University of Nebraska. A year after her arrival, her colleague and department head, Agnes Mathilda Wergeland died, and White found herself at the age of 26 head of a one-woman department. In 1917, she earned the Ph.D. at the University of Chicago.

Like many women professors of her generation, Laura White never married. Had she done so, she would have lost her position and perhaps her profession as well.

Instead, she opted to devote a lifetime to her career and her University. She belonged to Phi Beta Kappa and was instrumental in bringing a chapter of that honorary association to Wyoming. In addition to many articles, she published two books, both biographies of U.S. political figures. In 1944, she was elected to one of the highest honors accorded to historians even today when she became a member of the council of the American Historical Association. She continued as head of the history department until she became seriously ill. She died on July 29, 1948.

White brought a second member of the small department to Wyoming in 1925. He was Frederick L. Nussbaum, historian of Europe, who together with his wife Cecil became a "leader in Laramie's intellectual life" until his untimely death in 1957. Nussbaum had earned his undergraduate degree at Cornell, received the Ph.D. from the University of Pennsylvania, and taught at Northwestern, Temple, and the University of Southern California before he took his permanent place on the Wyoming faculty.

Winner of the prestigious Herbert Baxter Adams prize for his first volume on the French Revolution, Nussbaum went on to write twelve articles and two more books, one of which became a volume in the important History of Modern Europe series. In his work, wrote T. A. Larson in 1959, Nussbaum laid low national boundaries in order to seek out a common European civilization and culture. He was not a specialist but a generalist, a believer in broad liberal education, who crossed freely from one academic discipline to another. In creative scholarship, Nussbaum found (he said) the high moments, the significant rewards of a teacher's life.

Scholar and teacher, Nussbaum enjoyed the life around him. He served on the board of editors for the *Journal of Modern History,* he delighted in taking part in faculty plays, and he ranked as a brilliant conversationalist who loved good talk. In his lectures, he made a point of thinking aloud, and good students learned to think in his classes.

T. A. Larson (retired 1975)

It was to replace Nussbaum, who was researching in France that year, that T. A. Larson first came to the University of Wyoming in 1936. Larson was a historian of early modern England. Born in Nebraska, he had earned his bachelor's and master's degrees at the University of Colorado. His master's thesis concerned church and state in fourteenth century England, and his Ph.D. dissertation (Illinois, 1936) was on crown and clergy in the reign of Edward III. Upon Nussbaum's return, Larson spent a year working in England and published his first article in the prestigious *English Historical Review.* Called back to Wyoming the following year to substitute for Laura White, he accepted an offer to stay and agreed to work up a course in Wyoming history to replace that taught by Grace Raymond Hebard until her death.

Several thousands of students flocked into Larson's course in Wyoming history. He supervised eighty M.A. theses and six Ph.D. dissertations — the first in the history department's doctoral program. He served as department head from 1948-1969, directed the School of American Studies for ten years, and held the William Robertson Coe chair in American studies. Among his many articles and four books is the *History of Wyoming,* published in two editions (1965, 1978). He was a founder and president of the Wyoming State Historical Society and president of the Western History Association, in addition to many other positions. For four terms following his retirement in 1975, Larson served in the Wyoming legislature and became a member of the important appropriations committee. In 1984, the University awarded "Mr. Wyoming" its highest honor, the LL.D degree.

While Larson lectured in Wyoming history, William R. Steckel taught the U.S. history survey, and particularly its colonial sections, to two generations of Wyoming freshmen. A Harvard graduate with a Ph.D. from Stanford University, Steckel earned a professional prize for his dissertation on colonial Pennsylvania publisher and journalist Christopher Sauer. In 1937-38, he served as private secretary to the American ambassador in Denmark, a position that whetted his appetite for travel in future years all over the world. The first director of the American studies program on campus — a program that later became a model for similar summer institutes all over the country — Steckel resigned the position in 1956 in order to accept a year-long Fulbright lectureship in Germany.

Co-author of a multi-volume work entitled *Patterns in American History,* widely used in college classes, he served as a visiting professor at the University of California, San Diego, in 1968. In 1979, President Edward Jennings tabbed him to be acting vice president for academic affairs.

William R. "Bill" Steckel (retired 1980)

Like Larson, Steckel steeped himself in community activities. He served on the Laramie City Council, as mayor of the city, and on the executive board of the Wyoming Association of Municipalities. He has been active in politics and in his church. In retirement, he continues to organize educational institutes and to work on his favorite project, the history of the West Indies. To the many students who remember him, Steckel remains an example of an academic who devoted himself to community and to institution. Like his three predecessors, he is a historian who cares.

Board resolutions could change policies and personnel, but only a secretary's good memory might set them in order. During Morrill's administration, for example, all deans were required to serve on twelve-month appointments, with four weeks of summer holiday. In June 1941, the board ruled that its own deputy treasurer would become purchasing agent, thus quietly depriving E. O. Fuller (transferred to full-time management of the bookstore) of his position. At the same meeting the offices of board secretary and University comptroller were combined and turned over to Fay Smith; the personnel office was abolished; and the special student welfare office was ended and its responsibilities assigned elsewhere. In 1943, Morrill encouraged the Faculty Advisory Committee to set up its own bylaws, which it promptly did; these were approved unanimously by the faculty and thereafter included in the bylaws of the board.

Meantime the faculty itself met regularly to determine policies on academic curricula and students. Student organizations and departments had their own rules of procedure. Some minor questions were resolved by presidential memorandum. By 1945, documents establishing rules were scattered and difficult to consult, since minutes of departments, faculty, board, and miscellaneous campus organizations comprised many large, unindexed volumes or notebooks. The new president himself was hard put to determine how things stood.

It was under such circumstances that Humphrey commissioned what was called a "University Developmental Study" in 1947. He made its purposes clear.

The rules and regulations established by action not formally embodied in the By-Laws of the Board have never been brought together and codified at the University of Wyoming although the matter has been the subject of Board discussion upon a number of occasions. It is practically impossible, therefor, for a Board member, an administrative officer, or anyone else to determine with certainty whether a Board rule exists . . . except as officers recall Board action or as the rule becomes embodied in normal practice and is thus assumed. . . . Examination of the minutes of the Board, of the University Faculty, and of many other committees from the beginning of the University, indicates that not only are Board rules difficult to discover, but also that important aspects of general legislation

. . . have never been covered by Board action. . . . Reports of Board Committees, of the President, of the Faculty and its committees, and of other agencies, which embody proposals of legislative character . . . are not embodied in the minutes of the Board and are preserved in the scattered archives of a multitude of agencies.

To coordinate this endeavor Humphrey appointed a committee of Professors Robert Bruce (chairman), Ruth Hudson, and Walter Reusser. For the final review he brought to campus Arthur F. Klein, retired dean of education from Ohio State University. The result was a mammoth compilation often referred to as the Klein report.

In 1947 and 1948, almost all of the faculty devoted hours of effort to the Klein report. In so doing, they undoubtedly far exceeded the charge that the president had anticipated, for they not only reviewed, as Professor Richard Hillier later wrote,

every branch of University activity and concern but also analyzed the social, political, and intellectual needs of Wyoming as well as evaluating its physical and industrial resources. Their conclusions and recommendations filled scores of reports, the most important of which were preserved in five bound volumes . . . with a total of more than six hundred pages.

Among the many side-results of the Klein report was a history of the University, prepared by Ruth Hudson. There was also a faculty and staff manual, written by a committee with Professor Wallace R. Biggs chairman. It contained summary entries, arranged alphabetically, on nearly 100 topics and was designed in such form that future rules incorporated by the trustees could be added.

In its final form, the Klein report provided a broad-based set of University regulations, predecessor to the present Uniregs. The report is divided into a number of sections, depending on the origins of rules and regulations set forth. First came the bylaws of the board of trustees, prepared mostly by Klein himself, and based primarily on the constitution already in effect. There followed board rules, under the general title of University regulations; thereafter the regulations originating in the president's office and approved by the trustees; thereafter rules and regulations of the University faculty; and finally, rules and regulations of the various colleges and special administrative divisions. Although the original plan was to include departmental regulations and various office manuals, it does not seem that these were incorporated into the final report.

Among the matters covered in various regulations that demanded board approval are such problems as the general organization of the University; the structure of the president's division (which included not only administrative functions but the library, the military departments, science camp, and the Natural Resources Research Institute); the function and structure of various presidential advisory bodies, of the colleges, and of other units; conditions of faculty service; degrees and diplomas; and material on students, such as fees, admission procedures, and so on. Most of the regulations were items that called for trustees' approval, including (for example) such matters as student discipline, educational program requirements, financial responsibilities, and faculty promotions in rank. In no way can all the material be summarized here, but several items are worth noting.

The Klein report did little to change the structure and function of the board of trustees, but several provisions — probably engineered by Humphrey himself — are worthy of comment. By the new board bylaws, the post of paid secretary and comptroller of the trustees was eliminated. Thus did Fay Smith lose his position of power, for although he was transferred to the position of land surveyor, he was shortly required to retire. The new board secretary was a member of the board, with Humphrey's previous Mississippi State assistant, Miss Tom Womack, listed as deputy secretary so that she might actually record the minutes. A parallel provision governed the trustees' treasurer, and the deputy board treasurer also became the highest permanent University financial officer.

Another immediate requirement of the Klein report was that each college officially adopt a series of rules and regulations of its own. This, too, occasioned great faculty labor; but during the next several years, college and division regulations were gradually presented to the board, approved, and incorporated into the University rules.

"Conditions of faculty services" included items from a "personnel policy" memorandum drawn up by a faculty committee. Although proposals for automatic annual salary increases and cost of living adjustments were eliminated, procedures and policies on sabbatical leaves became part of the report. The "conditions of faculty service" included the American Association of University Professors' statement on academic freedom as published in 1940 and thereafter approved by the board. Promotion provisions were also drawn from previous board regulations, as was approval of the "limited service" retirement plan. Under the "faculty rules" proposed by a committee of R. R. Hamilton, O. H. Rechard, and A. J. McGaw, was a suggestion for a faculty senate that was subsequently rejected by an all-faculty vote. There was also a proposal for the appointment of a vice president for instructional matters, a suggestion approved by the faculty but vetoed by the board.

With the aid of the many faculty committees that worked on individual segments of the Klein report, the new document clarified and codified much legislation of concern to the faculty as a whole. Prominent was the definition of academic tenure in rank. The lengthy regulations proposed by the faculty committees of 1938, and finally approved by the board in 1944, were — after some revisions by a faculty committee — incorporated into the new regulations. Permanent tenure was defined as granted by the board upon the advice of a series of administrators: first department heads, then deans, then the president's advisory committee. Careful review was required following a probationary period. Humphrey regularly brought each individual tenure, reappointment, promotion, and resignation decision directly to the board with the recommendation of the committee involved. The board seldom argued the decisions as presented. In 1953, after some question as to the timing of the tenure decision, the board approved a regulation that permitted a tenure decision after the end of a three-, four- or seven-year probationary period. In 1958, at the request of T. A. Larson and the president's advisory committee (faculty representatives from each college), trustees set the limit at four years.

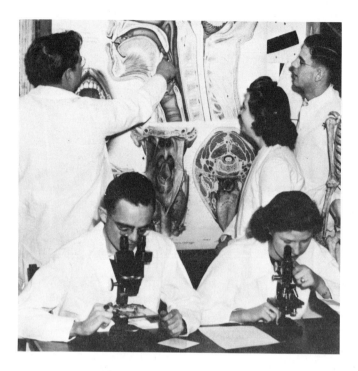

Anatomy lesson, College of Nursing, c. 1955

Meanwhile, the board solidified its stand on granting no tenure to married women but soon eased its definitions of nepotism in 1952 (and again in 1960) — very probably following violent complaints of A. J. Dickman about the treatment of his wife. At the request of L. L. Smith, who was promptly made chairman of a committee to investigate and recommend, policies on sabbatical leaves were revised (1952) in accordance with Klein report recommendations. Thereafter, faculty on one-year sabbaticals were granted half (instead of 40 percent) pay.

The faculty's role in University governance was prescribed in the report. New appointments had long since been initiated at the departmental level except for those in administration or those of dean-level rank. Even in the latter instance, formal and informal faculty consultation was customary, as exemplified by Morrill's procedure in replacing P. T. Miller, dean of liberal arts (spring 1945), and Humphrey's similar consultation in seeking a new arts and sciences dean in l961. Faculty were often called in to give opinions on retirement; here individual cases were individually judged, for frequently senior staff — as witness O. C. Schwiering, Fay Smith, Walter Reusser, and A. L. Keeney — were reluctant to give up their posts. On occasion, however, a high administrative position was filled with someone approved strictly by board and president, with no apparent faculty consultation.

One grave problem for faculty members was frequently addressed but never solved. The level of Wyoming salaries when compared with the regional and national average remained consistently low. Presidents could not help but be aware of this gap, brought home when faculty left for better-paying positions. As early as wartime 1943 Morrill complained to the board about the comparatively low level of faculty salaries at a time when the cost of living was steadily increasing. Under such circumstances, he told the board, "the question of staff morale . . . is critical." During his brief tenure in office, this president raised twelve-month salaries above the nine-month level, a move that brought him particular approval from such colleges as agriculture, where year-long duties were the pattern. In 1944, Morrill was responsible for small increases for "some" faculty members in the amount of approximately four percent. The addition of new faculty and the return of former faculty caused confusion in the matter of comparative salaries immediately after the war. In connection with the Klein study, a faculty committee attempted without success to set salaries by ranks and proposed cost of living increases.

Humphrey's biennial request to the legislature almost always contained a request for salary increases, as recommended by faculty and administrative committees. In 1950, the budget permitted a small increase; a chart in the files indicates that assistant professors received an average pay raise of only $48 per year. Another committee — this time Rechard, Forrest Hall, and Lawrence Meeboer — was set to survey the situation. Its findings showed that Wyoming nine-month faculty earned an average of $3,361 - $4,930 per year in accordance with rank and that all instructors were well below an "average standard scale." Humphrey managed a "standard of living" increase in 1952, but a larger raise went down the tubes in 1955, because of legislative disapproval. There followed a mammoth administrative effort. A series of press releases pointed up faculty accomplishments and why faculty had left the University. Editorials in the student newspaper called on the legislature to increase wages in order "to hold well-qualified staff members and attract good young people to the teaching profession." Humphrey told the board that he would seek increases of fifteen percent and ten percent (in that order) for the two biennial years, 1957-59.

Since merit calculations frequently determined distribution of salary funds, the president set up another committee, (Verna Hitchcock in home economics was chairperson) to define merit for salary considerations. In their report (1956), Hitchcock and her committee stressed five categories for distinguished service: teaching effectiveness, productive scholarship, University and college service, public service, and professional activity. Accompanying the report are statements from deans and committees from each college, with that of the arts and sciences committee (T. A. Larson, chairman) providing the most thoughtful analysis, including discussion of the usefulness of student teacher ratings and provision for instances in which deans and department heads might disagree on an individual's merit rating.

This time, all was not in vain, for although the legislature of 1957 reduced the salary increase fund by one-fourth, faculty, staff, and laborers received increases of up to sixteen percent. More committees followed (a dean's report was compiled in 1958 and in 1962 John Chalmers was chairman of a committee that presented another comparative study), with the result that merit increases were again scheduled in 1959 and 1962, in spite of opposition from some members of the board and from Governor Jack Gage.

Perhaps more important to faculty in the long run was the problem of fringe benefits. No continuing situation had caused more difficulty through the years than the search for an adequate faculty retirement system. Committees had worked on retirement off and on since 1925, but as late as 1947 the only plan in legal effect was a "limited service" scheme, whereby faculty were rehired after official retirement and paid for a reduced schedule of assignments after the age of 70 (lowered to 65 in 1946). Plans for systems to which the University might make financial contributions over and above an employee's years of service had been consistently vetoed by governors or declared illegal by attorneys general. In 1943, when the Wyoming Education Association introduced a teachers retirement bill similar to one previously vetoed by Governor Nels Smith, the University's retirement committee demurred of participation, since it believed the faculty would prefer "limited service" with pay to any program calling for regular faculty contributions into a retirement fund. A year later, however, Schwiering (who was active in the WEA) and others agreed that University faculty should participate in a state employees' retirement plan similar to one adopted by the board in 1939 and declared illegal then by the state insurance commissioner.

This state system, providing for a five percent contribution by faculty and University alike, necessitated a legislative appropriation of nearly $100,000; finally, in 1947, the legislature agreed. Four years later, the plan was revised when all employees — including faculty and staff — were placed under the federal social security system. Hours of complicated reckoning went into the board's response, but trustees (with the enormous assistance of financial administrators) worked out a system that provided equivalent benefits for years spent under the "limited service" option and added social security benefits to the regular state retirement. Actually, the policy was so complicated that each case had to be separately considered by the board and it was never (as the president's advisory committee freely admitted) clear or widely understood. What was apparent was that retirement funds remained grossly insufficient; through the 1950s and 1960s, faculty who retired found themselves trying to live on a pittance.

Problems arose also as to the appropriate age for retirement. In 1954, the American Association of University Professors' local branch (in a letter signed by Professors Glyn Thomas and Donald L. Blackstone) asked that the retirement age be fixed between 67 and 70 in accordance with AAUP recommendations, but the faculty retirement committee opted to leave things as they were — that is, with the retirement date to be determined on an individual basis by the president's advisory committee and the board of trustees. In 1947, a modest group health insurance program was inaugurated, but trustees did not budget for University contributions, so the faculty paid. As late as 1963 the legislature refused to contribute moneys to any life insurance program. Thus while some institutions compensated for lower salaries with fringe benefit plans, the University remained far behind on both scores.

Meanwhile, increasing enrollment and a growing faculty, together with the greater complexities in accounting, the multiplying different budgets, the building programs, and the increased size of physical plant, all commanded an enlarged administrative force to cope. At first, Humphrey's appointments seemed merely to involve substituting individuals of his choice for those who had held power under preceding presidents. He began by placing his long-term secretary in the position of deputy secretary to the board. When Fay Smith's term as board secretary and comptroller was terminated, L. G. Meeboer moved into place as the board's deputy treasurer, but was given the titles of assistant comptroller and purchasing agent as well. Soon Elliott G. Hays was acting as Meeboer's assistant and taking over the latter's duties when Meeboer was given special assignments in the building program. An increase in staff became apparent. Special offices were established for budget, auditing, personnel, and even the accumulation and analysis of University statistics for budgetary, audit, and other purposes. The maintenance and repair of the University's physical plant became so complex as to require a special supervisor, and soon there was also a staff personnel manager.

By the mid-1950s, the number of administrative departments had therefore burgeoned. In addition to the traditional special accounts for the trustees and for the president's office, the budget listed special categories for the offices of alumni relations, athletics, the dean of men, the dean of women, the land coordinator (merged into "Studies and Statistics" when Fay Smith reluctantly retired in 1954), the news service, related student services (the registration and records, and admissions office), student health, student personnel and guidance, studies and statistics, the business office, buildings and grounds, physical plant improvements, ROTC, Wyoming Union services, and to cap it off, "miscellaneous."

Humphrey continued to make ad hoc changes not only to streamline operations but to benefit from the talents of particular individuals he appreciated. In 1956, he established a separate information service, which took over such assignments (previously separate) as news releases, publications, radio programming, and eventually field counseling with potential students throughout the state — a task previously handled through the admissions office. Hal R. Taylor became director of the service, and the following year agricultural information (Taylor's own specialty) and athletic publicity were added to the new service. When Taylor left in 1958, Humphrey promoted Harold Benn (previously an assistant dean in the College of Agriculture) to the position and made him executive assistant to the president as well. Benn worked well with Humphrey: The president called him "one of the most dependable, efficient persons I have ever known" and wrote that "In his quiet, unassuming manner he is able to secure full cooperation from those with whom he works." Three years later there was a new director of information, but Benn remained as the president's executive assistant.

By that year, the budget shows a special account for the internal auditor and another for the mail service. Organizational charts published by the division of studies and statistics ran to many pages. The division of finance and budget (office of the deputy treasurer of the board) encompassed offices of accounting, payroll, cashier, property, purchasing, student organizations, auxiliary enterprises, and seven further sections that came under the heading of buildings and grounds. The internal auditor was responsible for systems, auditing, advisement on management and accounting, plus the records retention program. "Studies and Statistics" contained an IBM bureau for processing and service which supervised University lands. The office of student personnel and guidance handled such matters as testing, student employment, veterans relations, and a study skill center. That the legislature was irritated at administrative proliferation seems to be indicated by its efforts to fix the salaries of certain University officials on several occasions.

In 1961, Humphrey went to the board with a plan for administrative reorganization. He thought, he said, that the University was becoming too large for the current system, and he proposed a series of screening officers to act as liaison between himself and lower-echelon officials. Originally he suggested the appointment of three vice presidents — for academic affairs, finance, and what he called nonacademic affairs, or student and miscellaneous administration. He then changed his mind to suggest four divisions: academic, student, business and plant affairs, plus the information and special services section already functioning.

For a year president and board considered. The final plan, presented by Humphrey to the board in March 1962 in a 37-page report, suggested a series of executive assistants: the already present executive assistant to the president (Benn's office); plus other assistants for student affairs (including the "related student services" performed by the registrar); business and plant affairs; and information and special services (alumni relations, data processing, physical education and intercollegiate athletics, the library, and statistics). Only the section for academic affairs would immediately merit a "dean" at its head, and John Chalmers, then dean of arts and sciences, was shortly appointed to the position. Opting to move slowly, the board confirmed Meeboer as head of business and plant matters, his current assignment; added a new executive assistant for information; and (a year later) employed William "Bud" Davis, as executive assistant for student affairs. Meantime, Robert Prahl handled buildings and grounds. Robert G. Arnold became plant engineer, and a supervisor of housing was added to the administrative potpourri.

It would have been astonishing indeed if all these offices had worked together in efficiency and harmony. Sometimes they did, but often they did not. Humphrey did not care for Chalmers as academic dean; shortly after the appointment it was clear that the president became restive with Chalmers' independent stance. When the dean resigned for another position, Humphrey immediately, in mid-summer and without a search, appointed James Ranz, previously University librarian, to the post. Ranz was, the president told the board, "one of the most effective administrators the University has had during the time he [Humphrey] has been at Wyoming." That was sufficient for the trustees. Relations with the alumni office involved the board in a series of difficulties, most of which vanished when F. Richard Brown was appointed as executive director in 1960.

The office of related student services — registration and admissions — presented recurrent problems, especially during this period when a transition to computerized forms was essential. The registrar's office was a natural focus for student discontent as well. In 1958, the *Branding Iron* accused the registrar of playing favorites by distributing registration books in advance to his own fraternity. R. E. McWhinnie calmly wrote to Humphrey that

the situation is motivated by fraternity jealousy and complicated by irresponsible campus journalism.

Pressed to investigate, Forrest Hall reported that registration costs per student had increased as the number of students went up, even though a data processing office had taken over many duties since 1950. In spite of McWhinnie's insistence that the problem was one of inadequate staffing, an outside expert was eventually called in to check registration procedures. Although the report was generally kind, firm suggestions were included about punched card and data processing approaches, and the board appointed a faculty committee to monitor registration procedures. During the same period, the admissions office was accused of being snappish with potential students, and considerable controversy resulted.

These small grievances reflected more than anything the particular inclinations of administrators, especially in relationship to Humphrey and Humphrey's sense of his presidential responsibilities. If any individual constructed a base of power for himself, if he became too independent or overly sympathetic to a viewpoint critical of the administration, his tenure was usually brief. If particular personalities conflicted with that of the president, these individuals usually found themselves in isolated positions or seeking jobs elsewhere. For all his surface geniality, Humphrey ran a taut administrative ship, on which each oarsman was required to stay in cadence.

Such coordination was much more difficult to achieve among faculty members. Many of them came to Wyoming with a dedication to independent thinking that bordered on feistiness, with principles gleaned from very diverse backgrounds, and with integrity that caused them continually to speak out about their own beliefs. In the climate of the 1950s and 1960s, few if any Wyoming faculty could be considered radicals and the campus was never shattered by the kinds of political disputes that sundered the faculties of other U.S. universities. Still, many took sides and assumed stances that were anathema to the trustees, who — Republicans and Democrats alike — were generally substantial and conservative citizens.

Some of the protests were short-lived or concerned with individual episodes, but nevertheless they lent credence to the conservative nature of trustees, administration, and sometimes faculty as well. A professor of political science was denied a sabbatical leave on which he intended to study the origins of the Communist Party in Sweden.

Although he remained a popular teacher, he thereafter found his relationships with president and department head progressively deteriorating and, he contended, his promotion delayed. When he left for another campus in 1963, the *Branding Iron* protested his case as an example of a "certain lack" of academic freedom. In 1951, one of the deans became alarmed when the University was listed in a national journal as an institution in which "socialism" was taught; and a few years later editor Russell Kirk, neo-conservative, raised considerable fuss in *Modern Age* when he discovered that the University library classified his journal as "propaganda." Trustees apparently did not protest when, in 1949, Professor Gale W. McGee invited a Soviet embassy official (along with anti-Soviet Russian former premier Alexander Kerensky) to campus for an international affairs conference. "Our own ideas are so strong," McGee wrote, "that we should not fear to compare them with those of Mr. Stalin." Ten years later, however, the board refused to condone the inviting of the Soviet ambassador for a similar summer conference. In 1958, the local branch of the American Association of University Professors sent Humphrey some materials decrying the federal loyalty oath, but the president was unimpressed; the loyalty oath once required by the University of all its employees quietly slipped out of use at some uncertain date.

Two political issues seem worthy of special mention here, in that they caused substantial difficulty for faculty and administration and the results of their "solutions" seem comparatively long-lived. One problem concerned the right of the faculty to run for high political office; the other focused around the limits of academic censorship where donated money was concerned.

As early as 1950, the board became concerned about faculty members who might opt to run for public office and directed Humphrey to design a ruling that such individuals be required to resign at the time of filing for candidacy. Rumors may already have been circulating about the potential U.S. Senate candidacy of Gale W. McGee, history professor (later senator and ambassador). Bolstered by a call from Republican Governor Crane asking the trustees to formulate a policy, Humphrey drafted a resolution which the board adopted in June 1950.

Since a college or university provides a sanctuary for faculty members subscribing to the principles enunciated by the American Association of University Professors in respect to academic freedom and the granting of continuing tenure following probationary service, the Board feels that the same protection provided the faculty member should also be given to the University by members of the academic staff. . . . In the event the staff member is defeated there will be no prejudice on the part of the Board toward his reemployment should his services be needed by the University.

Trustees moved too fast, however, for Tracy McCraken — Democratic newspaper publisher from Cheyenne and perhaps the most influential member of the board — had not been present at the meeting. At his request, and following a lengthy discussion, the board agreed to reconsider and "make a further study of the subject, though the faculty had not requested it." Although the matter seems to have been set aside for almost a year, the chairman of the trustees in 1951 appointed a committee to investigate policies at other universities to determine whether a candidate must resign before the campaign or might simply take a leave of absence (without pay) during the campaign period. The committee's report did not influence the board, for most University deans consulted had endorsed the policy of temporary leave rather than out-and-out resignation. Humphrey stood firm for requiring a candidate to sever his University ties at once. In its morning session on December 14, 1951 (with McCraken again not present), the board voted for resignation; when McCraken arrived that afternoon, he pointed out a procedural error in the ballot-taking that caused the vote to be tied and the issue was once more tabled.

While McGee built bridges, trustees opted to remain aloof, as if reluctant to open a Pandora's box. In 1954, when McGee and others received a $40,000 grant from the Carnegie Foundation for a summer Institute for International Affairs, the board commended the effort and attached its member J. R. Sullivan to the committee in charge.

Ross hall excavation, c. 1959

When McGee then proposed to direct a European tour, trustees debated at length but ended by endorsing the plan and commenting on the "initiative and leadership" it demonstrated. By 1955, McGee's progress towards the senatorial nomination was marked by speaking engagements in all corners of the state; Humphrey (and perhaps the board) approved an agreement among professor, department head, and dean strictly defining a policy on "commercial speaking dates." In spring 1955, the board approved McGee's request for leave without pay to serve the U.S. Senate Judiciary Committee as a research counsel, a position procured for him by Democratic Senator Joseph O'Mahoney. Trustees must have hoped for a peaceful interlude, although they spent some effort demonstrating to the press that McGee was working for the committee rather than the Democratic senator himself.

Nevertheless, the fat was in the fire. Political problems were only compounded in McGee's absence, for at the end of summer term 1956, Professor Jerry O'Callaghan, McGee's replacement in the history department, announced his candidacy for Congress on the Democratic ticket. Although Humphrey repeated over and over that O'Callaghan was no longer in the University's employ at

the time he announced his decision, nobody seemed to listen. Attacks began but did not stop with Reuben Anderson, head of the Wyoming Farm Bureau Federation, in a letter to Humphrey dated September 9. In its meeting two weeks later, the board almost came to blows about an angry tirade by Trustee John A. Reed, Kemmerer, in which he

stated that he felt the University should be kept on a non-partisan basis and that in his opinion the History Department faculty was made up entirely of a left-wing partisan group. He mentioned the fact that one member of the History faculty, who served during 1955-56 on a supply appointment, has announced his candidacy for the U.S. House of Representatives on the Democratic ticket and that another member of the faculty of the Department was using his affiliation with the University to gain publicity for himself preparatory to becoming a candidate for office on the Democratic ticket. He also expressed his feeling that too much attention was being given to Russia in the classes on American history and in addresses made by a faculty member of the History Department.

McCraken and Velma Linford, state superintendent of public instruction, hurried to the historians' defense, and other trustees expressed their disapproval of the term "left wing."

The defeat of O'Callaghan and victory of the Republican candidate, Keith Thomson, hardly calmed the seas. Anderson was back at the attack immediately after the election — this time with considerable publicity on all sides. Republicans cited the Hatch Act that barred government employees from political activity; Democrats held up as examples Senators Wayne Morse (University of Oregon law school), Paul Douglas (University of Chicago), J. William Fulbright (President, University of Arkansas), and even Woodrow Wilson from Princeton. Editorials — like that in the student newspaper on November 16, 1956 — insisted that running for political office was a right of which no one should be deprived. Alice Stevens, wife of a speech professor, attacked Anderson in a Laramie *Boomerang* column, and Anderson's response to Humphrey was so angry that the contrite author wrote the next day to ask the president to destroy his letter.

To the board meeting in December 1956, Humphrey brought a long and careful report. He reviewed the trustees' previous action — or inaction — on the problem of political candidacy, cited pertinent statutes, and isolated issues. The resolution he presented had been drawn by law Professor E. George Rudolph, now legal adviser to the board. In the midst of long discussions, Congressman-elect Keith Thomson requested and obtained a hearing. Victory had not dimmed Thomson's anger. His objections to the board's lack of policy in regard to faculty political candidates was only part of his complaint.

Mr. Thomson stated that he had not been "entirely happy for some time with the educational situation at the University." He stated that he had the "continual feeling that education at the University is going backward instead of forward." He referred specifically to the College of Law, which he implied had deteriorated greatly in the years since World War II. . . . He added that he had no solution to propose but that unless something was done to correct the situation his children would not attend the University.

At this meeting the board finally adopted a policy requiring faculty candidates to apply for leave of absence without pay when they filed for public office, such leave generally to continue throughout the fall semester. Thereafter, victors would be expected to resign and losers to resume their duties. McCraken was among those in favor; Reed voted firmly against.

The adoption of a policy — in the wake of a Lusk *Herald* editorial calling for McGee's resignation — solved some but not all of the problems. When McGee announced his candidacy in the spring of 1958, supporters and opponents lined up firmly, both on the board and off. Reed remained McGee's sharpest critic among trustees; although others may have been equally opposed to his candidacy, most preserved an impartial public stance. As early as October 1957, Reed wrote Humphrey that he believed the board had played into McGee's hands in granting him leave to work with the Senate Judiciary Committee — although "innocently and with no intention whatever to promote him for public office." After considerable question on campus and off, Clifford Hansen (later Republican senator and Wyoming governor) took it upon himself to investigate McGee's teaching load, only to find that he had a heavier load of students than anyone else in his department. As history department head, Larson was summoned before the board to report on McGee's absences from campus; he showed the trustees an agreement similar to those of previous years in regard to classes missed and substitutes to be hired.

In May 1958, Reed wrote Humphrey again complaining about McGee's speaking in Kemmerer on a Friday evening. Humphrey's response was calm but hardly supportive.

Please be assured that I am not trying to justify Dr. McGee's actions;

I am, however, giving you the facts. I have no doubt that the meeting in Kemmerer on May 9 was "a straight partisan political meeting." However, John, it seems to me that I have made my position quite clear, and since it was the Board's action that made it possible for Dr. McGee to carry on the way he has, I believe anything that is done about the situation must also be action of the board.

Reed was not placated. When McGee requested leave, Reed was unable to attend the board meeting but wired his opposition; nevertheless the board approved McGee's request. Even in July, Reed wrote to Humphrey that he "always questioned the integrity of Dr. McGee with respect to the time he devoted to the University as an instructor." Throughout the summer, he pestered the president with questions about McGee's summer pay from the International Affairs Institute budget, and Humphrey looked up all the old vouchers in order to demonstrate that nothing was out of line. Finally, Reed complained bitterly about the "pink" politics of the speakers that had been selected for the institutes; he had to be reminded by Humphrey that Sullivan, a board member, regularly sat on the committee that made such decisions.

Although the board's clear desire was to keep the University out of politics (and in Reed's case, out of Democratic politics), McGee's early support came from faculty friends. The situation was often delicate. Once a member of the English department made the tactical error of soliciting campaign funds from his faculty peers through a notice printed on a University hectograph machine and distributed in departmental mailboxes. The indiscretion was reported to Humphrey, who — with agreement from Hansen, then chairman of the board — interviewed faculty from history and English, all the deans, and several administrative officers in an effort to unearth any other similar episodes. He found nothing. McGee himself said he would not have sanctioned the problem memorandum, and the saddened perpetrator apologized. Even the board agreed that the incident seemed trivial, and Humphrey settled for reading the trustees' regulation about partisan politics at the spring faculty meeting. McGee was questioned for his use of Knight cafeteria (open to faculty for general entertainment) for a faculty dinner of possible political import.

The truth was that McGee's campaign brought everybody into the act. As early as spring, Teno Roncalio, state Democratic chairman, confused the issue by attacking the University in a series of publicly "proposed" platform planks. Roncalio suggested that football, highly supported by Republican Governor Simpson while he served on the board of trustees, be de-emphasized and that the Democrats request a "long look" at the classroom to determine why the University was not

growing in prestige, in size, or student body, and in proportion to the other universities of the Rocky Mountain West.

He suggested that the board be reduced from the twelve members legalized by the legislature in 1951 — a creation "of a prior Republican governor [Frank Barrett] only to build his personal political fences in Wyoming." Roncalio's assault brought angry statements from trustees, governor, and the faculty branch of the American Association of University Professors — groups that seldom acted in consortium. Even the candidate spoke out, and McGee publicly told his party to stay away from the University, which was, he said, "off limits" for partisan politicking.

During the fall, the student newspaper leaped with delight into the political arena. Many issues were filled with discussion of the campaign. Both Young Democrats and Young Republicans on campus boasted of tripled membership. Senator Wayne Morse came to speak for McGee, while Senator Karl Mundt appeared for Frank Barrett, McGee's opponent. Vice President Richard Nixon made a special trip to Cheyenne. The *Branding Iron* left-handedly endorsed McGee's candidacy with its statement that if he lost, the board might set a stricter policy on faculty politicking.

Faculty became involved. Professor Ralph Conwell of economics led the Republican faction, while the McGee side was dominated by his history department colleagues T. A. Larson (head) and W. R. Steckel. Larson's public endorsement and support of the candidate led him into an exchange of strong letters with Reed, who called Larson biased and ended by writing that "I am sorry about the whole situation so far as the University is concerned." That was shortly after the November elections when McGee won the Senate seat. Thereafter, the regulation of faculty running for political office faded as an immediate issue.

At about the same time, however, the crises evoked by the American studies program were reaching a peak. From the beginning it was apparent that Coe's strictures about the political nature and content of the program went against the grain of faculty commitment to academic integrity. In 1950, when the faculty committee headed by Larson was assigned the task of suggesting potential summer lecturers, Humphrey made it clear that the political beliefs of those invited must coincide with the benefactor's concept of Americanism and the free enterprise system. Quietly, Larson made a few substitutions among the highly-respected professors on his list.

But the Larson committee was reluctant to adopt restrictive covenants. In a long letter to Humphrey, Larson pointed out that both Wyoming faculty and committee were "conservative, a good deal more conservative than most college faculties," and would undoubtedly "stoutly defend" the free enterprise system. But one could not tell lecturers what to say, and a University must always pursue the truth. Rather than stating that he is giving a course to defend free enterprise, a professor should

look at the facts with his students, and then draw conclusions from the record. The American Studies Committee feels that the facts do warrant the conclusion that the free enterprise system has contributed magnificently to making life worth living in the United States, but even so it feels that the student should be permitted to reach that conclusion for himself in the light of the full evidence.

The immediate problem of selecting summer lecturers that year was solved by inviting Samuel Flagg Bemis, whom Coe knew and admired, and — when he could not accept the invitation — by substituting David Potter, also from Yale. For the next few years, summer visitors were carefully screened by the president on the basis of their experience, their associations, and their current academic institutions.

After Coe's death, the problem became not better but worse. The Coe Foundation was equally — or perhaps more — concerned with politics and committed to a course more conservative than that of Coe himself. One particular episode demonstrates foundation policies. Following through on plans that Coe had approved before his death, the UW American studies committee, aided by the executive secretary of the American Studies Association and other nationally-known figures, began with enthusiasm its planning of a high-level summer conference on American studies programs, to be financed by Coe's final special gift of $10,000. A list of eminent professors and other potentially interested individuals was drawn up by the local committee and particularly Steckel, the American studies director. In March 1955, Humphrey inspected the list and eliminated a number of names on political and other grounds, after carefully checking in biographical dictionaries. Invitations went out. Then suddenly, within the matter of a few weeks, the conference was cancelled at Humphrey's orders. To the board in early June, the president offered his explanation. The Coe Foundation trustees, he said,

felt that the entire Conference as Mr. Coe had approved it should be held or it should not be held at all. Also, he pointed out that the Trustees of the Foundation had questioned the loyalty to American principles of one or two of the persons to whom tentative invitations to the Conference had been extended. The Trustees [of the University] expressed concern that any person of questioned loyalty had been even tentatively invited to the Conference, and it was the consensus of the Board that the American Studies Committee on campus should submit to the President the proposed list of invitees for any future conference, that the President should check with the Un-American Activities Committee on every person listed and then submit the names of those selected to the Coe Foundation for approval before any invitations are extended.

Steckel was angry and mortified, but the invitations were duly rescinded. From correspondence between Steckel and Louis D. Rubin, executive secretary of the American Studies Association, it seems clear that William Sauhering — who was doing little but touring the country as a self-designated representative of the Coe Foundation — had muddied the waters, perhaps with the aid of Coe's unusually powerful private secretary, now on the foundation board. Both Humphrey and Steckel raised enough of a protest to William Rogers Coe, the benefactor's son and a Coe Foundation director, as to have hopes of extinguishing Sauhering's influence and activities.

194

Humphrey remained deeply involved with the Coe Foundation as a member of its board and as sponsor of what had become a model summer American studies program. After the humiliating conference cancellation, the president consistently checked potential summer guests with the House Un-American Activities Committee — and sometimes with other similar organizations — through the intervention of a New York lawyer named Arad Riggs, who also served on the foundation board. Many notable professors were approved by Riggs, but the files contain documentation on many who were rejected because of their participation in a suspect organization or their signature on a protesting petition.

When in the autumn of 1955, Humphrey proposed to the foundation that twenty young faculty members from across the country be financed to visit and inspect the model summer program, the foundation's response seemed lukewarm, and Humphrey turned to David Potter, Coe professor at Yale, for support. Potter listened, but then put his cards on the table. He could not participate, he wrote Humphrey, for

> *if I followed the sense of that meeting, I could not put on the list such names as Henry Commager, Merle Curti, Walter Johnson, Basil Rauch, and other reputable historians who have been conspicuously "liberal" or New Dealish (This is not a question of pro-Communists, whom I would certainly wish to exclude). . . . I have been disturbed for some time by the undercurrents of suspicion concerning the conditions which Mr. Coe attached to his gifts, and while I know that these suspicions are not justified, still I have feared that they might do just as much damage as if they were.*

In response, Humphrey hoped for a general "reconsideration of the entire program" and bitterly attacked the "sniping and unethical procedures of Sauhering during the past few years." Quietly, however, the inspection plan was dropped.

In the spring of 1956, Steckel requested a leave of absence to accept a Fulbright lectureship abroad — an offer similar to one he had declined at Humphrey's request the previous year. By now, the constant political pressures had obviously caused him to lose faith. He wrote:

> *I do not know whether I want to continue as director of American Studies. At present my inclination is to resolve this question in the*

> *negative. . . . Should continuity in the office of director of American Studies during the coming year be deemed a vital consideration, I feel strongly enough . . . to resign that office to make the institutional and personal gains which seem to me more important.*

In irritation the board voted to accept Steckel's resignation and to find another director who would work "enthusiastically and wholeheartedly."

Steckel's replacement had no easier time. He was Professor Robert H. Walker, whom Steckel had recruited to join the growing program in 1955. Assuming the directorship in July 1956, Walker began with enthusiasm but soon felt the strictures placed upon him. Walker disliked the investigation of visiting faculty's political activities and found it depressing. Besides, the inefficient, bureaucratic process was so long and cumbersome that Humphrey had begun submitting lists of twelve or more names at one time. Friction between Walker and Humphrey also developed over curricula, and Humphrey's files contain Walker's list of courses that might constitute an American studies major as covered with the president's notes: "no" and "not enough on constitution," and "poor" constitution. Walker's suggestions for an enlarged advisory committee were rejected by the president, who said the committee as it stood was "very pleasing to the Coe Foundation," although that did not keep Humphrey from reconstituting the committee in his own way. In 1958, Walker found a major proposed course dropped without explanation from the *Bulletin.*

It was no surprise to the director to discover that Humphrey, apparently with the American studies committee's concurrence, did not plan to reappoint him after the 1958-59 academic year. In a long final interview, Humphrey (according to his own notes) told Walker that "his was a maturing but not a matured philosophy of what an American Studies program should be."

> *I told him also that I should have selected a man like Gabriel or Potter in the beginning and that if I had been able to look ahead far enough I would not have given the directorship to men as young as he and Dr. Steckel are. I complimented him on his interest and growth.*

Steckel was then 43; Walker 34. In February, Walker officially resigned, simply stating that "After the termination of the present academic year, I will no longer be interested in employment at the University of Wyoming." Privately he wrote of the program that "Every effort has been made to cater to the nationalistic and patriotic whims of the Coes."

As new director (July 1959), T. A. Larson had more success. Humphrey knew and respected him. Some of the tensions had ebbed from the political atmosphere as the Coe Foundation became less energetic in its expansion. Long lists of agreeable visiting faculty had already been compiled. As a much tested administrator, department head, and committee chairman, Larson had the experience and the temperament to steer the program on a quiet and steady course, shoals and rapids notwithstanding.

In spite of the difficulties of managing the Coe endowment, trustees never opted to provide guidelines for gifts with strings attached. In other donations, the University was luckily granted a freer hand. For example, John S. Bugas, prominent UW alumnus and Ford Motor Company official, bestowed considerable funds on the economics department, but was concerned only that his gift not be used for a "bricks and mortar monument" and that if it served to endow a professorial chair, the professor should be a "person of distinction" and not a member of the "lunatic fringe." After 1959, the University made a concerted effort to solicit gifts from corporations and individual alumni, and substantial funds were gathered, with pledges of future interest from others. A University development fund, set up as a separate non-profit operation in 1957, became the University of Wyoming Foundation in 1962.

Meanwhile, student life had returned to normal patterns, and seldom were politics of more than passing concern. If the first five years after World War II had produced what the president once called "post-war restlessness and a tendency to assertive individualism," campus soon resumed its pre-war serenity. One new but "pleasant" condition existed, Humphrey reported.

The children of married veterans [and later students] living in University housing units were very much in evidence; they added refreshing variety to campus lie and evoked frequent surprise and laughter. Contests for beauty queens and kings among the babies became as important and as exciting as those among the college girls.

After 1958, Wyoming students went their way with little care for politicking (at least judged by the pages of the *Branding Iron*). True, the electoral campaign of 1960 awakened considerable interest, especially when Henry Cabot Lodge (Nixon's vice presidential running mate) and Ted Kennedy (whose brother was about to be elected president) both spoke on campus for their respective parties. Three years later President John F. Kennedy appeared to talk about natural resources and their development, an event that attracted some 13,000 people. But the student newspaper still gave considerable space to "Beatlemania," particularly as to style of dress and "unusual haircuts;" the "twist" was going strong; and folk singers of all styles drew great student following. In May 1961, shortly before final exams, 500 students chanting "we want panties! we want panties!" attacked women's dorms and sorority houses — an episode that generated far more excitement than the exchange of letters in the *Branding Iron* regarding "apathy" towards communism. On the whole, campus activities were still led if not dominated by fraternities and sororities. To counteract the situation, an independent students association was founded in 1962, but whether it was truly a "political and service" rather than a social organization remains uncertain.

The 1960s were expansive years on the whole. Students were steadily increasing in numbers and seemed to be maintaining their general prosperity. In 1958, enrollment totaled 3,400; in 1962 it was 4,350; and in 1970 it rose to 8,500, a figure that eclipsed by almost 1,000 the prediction of seven years before. Fees continued to be low, as promotional material frequently pointed out — in 1955, registration per semester cost $100 for a Wyoming student and $205 for anyone from outside the state. Ten years later, tuition for an in-state student was still only $153 each semester. In 1963, the

Annual student steak fry, c. 1958

board was delighted when the legislature appropriated $70,000 to add to existing scholarship programs which supported up to twenty percent of campus students to some degree. These large ($1,000 per year) new scholarships were slated for "superior" Wyoming high school students and designed to stop the "continuing export" of top-level students to other universities. Recruiting efforts continued in the state's high schools and in 1962-63, the field relations counselor contacted more than 4,300 graduating seniors at high schools throughout the state with information about the University and its programs. If temporary declines in enrollments had caused the trustees some concern in the early 1950s, the consistent rise thereafter was good news all around.

On occasion, criticism surfaced about the number of out of state students, whose tuition never completely covered educational costs, but Humphrey reported in 1962 that the number of enrollees who were not from Wyoming stood at 29 percent and seemed to be declining. Many such students were graduates seeking advanced degrees and special training. Between 1949 and 1959, enrollment in graduate studies tripled its rate of growth; and by the latter year graduate students represented 14.3 percent of total University enrollment.

Problems of ethnic minority education seemed remote, but in 1951, having examined recent statistics, the editor of the student newspaper questioned whether the University was "fulfilling adequately its responsibility for educating women" and suggested a re-examination of campus offerings with women's interests in mind. Several years later, after the enrollment of women had badly declined, Humphrey appointed a committee with Professor Ruth Hudson, chairperson, to investigate. The committee had some positive recommendations — like a reevaluation of the advising system, the addition of women faculty as role models, a few additional courses, and cooking facilities in dormitories — but on the whole concluded that the problem was nationwide and that motivating women toward college attendance was actually a sociological task. It was with considerable fanfare that the University graduated its first woman electrical engineer in 1961.

Among UW students, many were superior achievers. In the president's report for 1962-63, to take only one example, Humphrey was able to list four students who had received Fulbright awards; one who was granted a Woodrow Wilson fellowship; a master's thesis that won a national prize; plus sundry scholarship cups, nursing test scores, design competition awards, vocal music auditions, and other accomplishments. Still, great concern was frequently evinced about the number of student withdrawals and scholastic failures. In 1956, the president raised the issue at a faculty meeting and received numerous thoughtful comments from professors on campus.

Faculty called attention to a variety of problems. Some thought that high schools were reneging on their responsibilities, particularly in regard to core subjects. Others believed that better academic counseling would turn unqualified students away from classes for which they were unsuited or unprepared. L. L. Smith of the English department wrote that "failure is almost inevitable" under an open admissions policy which drew into college a larger and larger percentage of high school graduates — "students who, a generation or so ago, might not even have reached high school." It was, Smith thought, not so much the high school curricula but

the social and economic prestige built up about a college education, and, of course, the fact that money for sending one's children to college can, apparently, be found.

Practically, Smith said,

I do not believe there is any hope in thinking of more selective admissions standards, for it seems to me that this is an untenable position in light of the University's relations with the people of the state and the broad basis of public support that makes a state university possible. . . . Some relief may come from junior colleges and university centers, but this will involve sharing a responsibility rather than avoiding one. . . .

One phenomenon widely credited with interfering with student scholastic excellence was the broad scope of extracurricular activities. In fact, Trustee Clifford Hansen once brought the matter up at a board meeting, and Dean M. C. Mundell (College of Commerce and Industry) once wrote Humphrey about a student whose "reasonable" abilities had been totally distracted by a long list of social commitments. Humphrey duly complained to the deans of men and women. Nevertheless, there is nothing to show that extracurricular fun was ever officially limited. Student handbooks listed a wealth of possibilities: campus movies, bowling alleys, wild game steak fries, the dean of women's tea, the traditional Engineers' Ball, tugs of war, homecoming, bonfires, the Iron Skull Skid, winter carnival, sweater queen contests, rodeo, the Inkslingers' Ball, the military ball, theater and musical productions, sororities, fraternities, clubs, intramural sports, and Religious Emphasis Week. No one could lack for something to do and somewhere to go. The most serious of the student undertakings lay in the Associated Students of the University of Wyoming (ASUW), with its officers and senate; the official constitution for this organization was periodically approved by the board of trustees, sometimes with amendments. However, even the ASUW president once bemoaned the failure of the organization to "concern itself with issues of some magnitude." The *Branding Iron* and the *Wyo* (yearbook) were long established campus institutions, and occasionally humor magazines would make an appearance — one such called *Snipe* termed by Milward Simpson "suggestive, low and smutty," was suppressed by the board in 1953 after a short and perilous existence. On the other extreme, a group of students for some years attempted to collect donations for a non-denominational chapel on campus; the plan eventually failed for lack of money.

The principle that the University stand *in loco parentis* died hard but at least began somewhat to fade by the early 1960s. True, the administration maintained concerns and controls. In 1952, trustees refused to permit the *Wyo* to run advertisements for whiskey, but they did say that tavern ads were all right if "their products" were not mentioned and "their patronage . . . not invited." In 1954, when a national magazine listed Laramie as one of a number of "cities of vice," the board agreed and strongly urged the city to clean up for the sake of student welfare and parental peace of mind. Once the veterans were gone, as the *Branding Iron* pointed out, the "return to normalcy" produced a noticeably younger student body. If dormitory girls were allowed a special late night (1:30 a.m.) for homecoming in 1956, plus a "honors" sign-out system the following spring, the boom was lowered on freshman women with a series of regulations. This caused the *Branding Iron* to border its front page in black and to write that the "new plan could not be too far from Cotton Mather's Puritanistic attitude," a scholarly reference such as editorials did not always contain. But even the student newspaper urged students to forego Levis and dress better in the classroom, and the University student handbook made prim suggestions about what to wear when — frequently including admonitions about polishing shoes. In 1961, the *Branding Iron* ran an article about "feminine smoking habits" with the aim of showing men and women alike how a female smoker might "create the impression of a lady."

By that time, however, student attention had come to focus around one extracurricular activity above all, and polished shoes were hardly in question. Football in Wyoming had barely ranked as a living sport before Duke Humphrey became president. In the marvelous early years from 1893 to 1903, as ordinarily coached by some faculty member, Wyoming footballers posted a good many winning seasons. However, a season consisted of one or two games, and the team's antagonists on the field often included such ad hoc opponents as Cheyenne businessmen, fire stations, traveling teams, and local high schools. By 1903, when more formal schedules were set among Colorado, Nebraska, Montana, Utah, and Wyoming teams, Wyoming's winning seasons fell to two in a decade (1904-1914). During the years of John Corbett's colorful coaching (1915-1923) and his major expansion of intercollegiate athletic programs, UW

posted only one tying season and lost seven. Although the board brought in several highly-touted coaches in the years between the wars — Lonestar Dietz (Haskell Institute), 1924-26; George McLaren (Pittsburgh), 1927-29; John R. Rhodes (Nebraska), 1930-32; Dutch Witte (Nebraska), 1933-38; Joel Hunt (Texas A&M), 1939; and Okie Blanchard (Wyoming), 1939 — among all of them, the team managed only two winning seasons. Crane was uninterested in football, and his attitude played a major role in his dismissal by an athletic-minded board in 1941. When new coach Bunny Oakes (Illinois) failed to turn the tide either before or immediately after the war, he, too, was dismissed (as has been mentioned) in 1946.

The upturn of the football program may well be credited to Glenn J. "Red" Jacoby, hired as athletic director in 1945, just before Oakes' hopes for a winning post-war season were dashed. Whereas in the past, the board had taken upon itself almost every detail of athletic program management, anyone reading board minutes can sense the increasing confidence in Jacoby's judgments among the trustees. Jacoby worked well with Humphrey; he was an unusually efficient manager in terms of his own budget and department; he gained such respect with the board that close observers credited him with supervising, not just coaching appointments, but the expansion of athletic facilities and physical education programs in general. In 1954, trustee Chairman Tracy McCraken praised Jacoby as "the best there is."

Bowden Wyatt from Tennessee, appointed to replace Bunny Oakes in the spring of 1947, immediately improved the team's performance, but it was several years before he could boast of a winning season. In 1947, the board went out of its way to reaffirm its confidence in a coach whose record was four wins and five losses. The following year, Wyatt did no better, but in 1949 he began to roll. 1950 was a great Wyoming year, for the team not only won every game on its schedule but defeated Washington and Lee in the Gator Bowl by a score of 20-7. In the next two years, Wyatt did not lead the conference, but nevertheless Wyoming football could boast of winning seasons. In 1952, both Wyatt and Jacoby got new contracts, and all indications are that the board would have awarded them something like tenure, should such a practice have been possible.

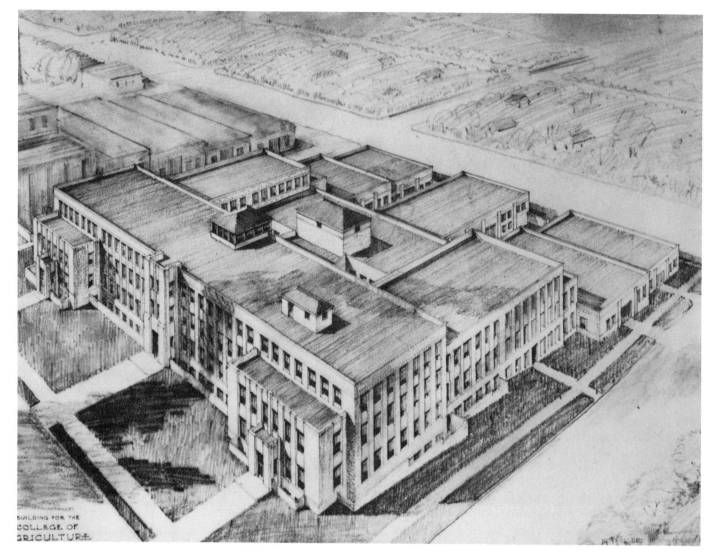

Architect's rendering, College of Agriculture, c. 1950

The years 1952-53 were fraught with other problems. In March 1952, Humphrey almost got in trouble with the board through an identification — prominently quoted by the Alumni Association president — of his attitude with the recent recommendation of the Committee of the American Council on Education, which had called for the de-emphasis of college athletic programs. Before the board, McCraken demanded an explanation, and Humphrey at once asserted that Wyoming had seen no overemphasis on athletics. He cited the scholastic record of the athletes, the number of

athletic scholarships, and the lack of relevance of the ACE resolution to Wyoming in particular. The board minutes read that

after some discussion, Mr. McCraken stated that he felt the Board of Trustees should go on record as believing that at the University of Wyoming and in the Mountain States Conference, athletics is not and has not been overemphasized, and as being opposed to any action that would tend to curb the present effective program. He stated also that he felt President Humphrey should be authorized to make a statement to the press including the Board's position on the matter.

The motion passed.

Still, the problem was by no means so simply resolved, especially when the question of athletic scholarships became a scandal in the North Central Association of Colleges and Secondary Schools, on the statute books of which stood an old ruling that virtually outlawed athletic scholarships and financial aid. When public exposure of numerous such grants at football colleges throughout the country led to a review of the ruling involved, presidents of all athletic-minded institutions (including Wyoming) vigorously protested that the regulation was out-of-date. Wyoming, Nebraska, Missouri, Oklahoma, Colorado and other schools were particularly singled out by the NCACSS, which had set up a board of review to protect the "conception of intercollegiate athletics as an amateur, educational activity." Eventually the organization dropped its complaints and the rule was modified. But regulations for athletic scholarships and prerequisites continued to provoke difficulty. In 1955, Jacoby reported to Humphrey on his disapproval of new Mountain States Athletic Conference (Skyline) rules on athletic scholarships and employment, and in 1956, the athletic director was forced to devise a series of regulations governing recruiting, about which he informed all coaches.

Meanwhile, football coaches came (and went) and with them a series of championship games. Bowden Wyatt's decision to move to Arkansas in January 1953 not only led Humphrey to burn long distance phone wires communicating with his University of Arkansas president-friend, but called forth considerable irritation on the part of the board. Wyatt had given no notice of his application, and the board testily admitted that although the coach had "done a splendid job for the University, the University has also done a great deal for Mr. Wyatt." Release from contract was a foregone conclusion — in that keeping a bitter coach guaranteed a losing team — but the board in its press release could hardly control its annoyance for Wyatt's "apparent disregard for the sanctity of his contract, which still had approximately nine years to run."

Jacoby accordingly screened 150 applications and presented nine to the board, with his personal advice that the trustees hire William Phillip Dickens of Tennessee, for he met an important Jacoby criterion in that he had "not passed the pinnacle of success but was instead struggling to get to the top." Dickens was willing to accept a salary from which the board deducted $75 a month for investment in bonds that would be turned over to Dickens if he stayed for the requisite three years but accrue to the University if he did not.

These upward years were filled with football excitement. Dickens coached the team through four winning seasons, including a 21-14 victory over Texas Tech in the Sun Bowl in 1955. Tensions began to rise as early as 1954. In that year, Humphrey furiously protested the officiating — "the worst in the history of football in the Rocky Mountain region" — at the UW homecoming game with Utah and urged the conference commissioner to get rid of the officials involved. A worse protest was launched the following year regarding the Denver game, lost by the University at an official score of 6-3 on a last minute field goal strenuously protested — and never acknowledged as legal — by the Wyoming team and its fans. It had seemed to partisan observers that the play had been whistled to a stop. In 1956, the team again won the conference championship, although excitement reached such a peak that even the *Branding Iron* protested the fans' "attitude toward sportsmanship." The winning season brought a $2,500 bonus from the board to the athletic department, with $600 earmarked for Coach Dickens personally. Neither the bonus, nor the fact that the board had (in 1956) ceased to withhold anything from the coach's salary, kept Dickens from accepting an offer from Indiana in early 1957. In spite of the negative vote of three trustees and the publicized irritation of McCraken, Dickens was duly released. The *Branding Iron* promptly ran a cartoon portraying the University as a "Prep School for Coaches."

Dickens' replacement, Robert S. Devaney from Michigan State (with $75 of his monthly salary duly withheld pending contract fulfillment), scarcely slowed the tide. Devaney led the team through five winning seasons and a Sun Bowl victory over Hardin Simmons (14-6) in 1958. Leave aside the "incident" that occurred in a Denver hotel after a squeaky loss to Denver University in the last game of the season. This incident apparently involved two football players, two coaches, a house detective, and the police, and caused "widespread unfavorable publicity" but was indignantly reassessed by the board in a statement calling for an apology from DU officials and Denver authorities. In 1959, Devaney collected a bonus, and in 1960, an increased budget and the end to the withholding clause of his salary contract. His move to Nebraska in early 1962 was the cause of great anger among the trustees. Devaney had not given prior notification; he and his staff had slipped away to Nebraska for extended negotiations; the board feared the former coach's potential for "stealing" Wyoming's best players. In the end, trustees furiously billed the Nebraska director of athletics for $3,799 to cover telephone calls, salaries for the month of January, and certain of Devaney's paid household expenses for the period he was gone. They need not have worried. Lloyd Eaton, Devaney's assistant who was appointed head coach at once, was to start slowly (a 5-5-0 season in 1962) but end by heaping even more glory on the team.

Compared to the ups and downs of football, other sports at Wyoming seem stable and quietly successful. In basketball, UW compiled an extraordinary record. During the twenty-year tenure of John Corbett as coach (1904-1924), Wyoming played only 144 games, and although most of them were losses, Corbett compiled a series of winning seasons after World War I. Both Stuart Clark (1924-30) and Willard "Dutch" Witte (1930-39) coached consistently victorious games; spectators long remembered White's extraordinary season of 26 wins and three losses in 1933-34. Everett F. Shelton was at the controls after 1939, and during his 19 years as basketball coach, Wyoming won 328 and lost 200. He had some big seasons, including victories over Georgetown in the NCAA championship and (in a special playoff) over St. John's, winner of the National Invitation Tournament, in 1943. There was also a 22-4 season in 1946-47, and a 28-7 in 1951-52, to mention only a few. Shelton's team went to the NCAA tournament in 1941, 1943, 1947, 1949, 1952, 1953, and 1958, although it only carried off the honors once (1943). By 1952, Shelton had turned 53 years of age, and the six-year contract tendered him by the board contained a clause that on mutual agreement, he might be relieved of active coaching and "assigned other University duties compatible with his experience, age, and physical condition." It is noteworthy that he was still conducting himself with vigor (one

board member suggested that he "be more careful" with his language and his actions at basketball games) and that he continued to post winning seasons through 1955, but by 1957 the losses were mounting and the board proposed to buy his contract out. The trustees actually kept the coach on until his resignation in 1959 to go to Sacramento State. His successor, William M. Strannigan, had a few bad years, but by 1964 basketball was entering on a series of winning seasons again.

Meanwhile, other sports compiled creditable and sometimes excellent records of their own. Although they never ranked as money-makers, programs in boxing, wrestling, fencing, and gymnastics were initiated by Corbett after World War I. In the 1930s and 1940s, Wyoming added swimming, skiing, track, golf, baseball, and tennis, often coached in their infant years by faculty members. Such sports as golf and baseball faced particular trials in the Laramie climate, but others — wrestling, skiing, and swimming — won (and continue to win) laurels for the University. Besides its football and basketball victories, Wyoming took twelve wrestling championships, four baseball pennants, two titles in tennis, and one in swimming during the 24 years of the Mountain States (Skyline) Athletic Conference.

In 1960, the conference began to fall apart as several schools withdrew to slow down their athletic programs and others to move to larger conferences. Blessed with a winning football team and a new basketball coach, Wyoming's trustees resolved not to "lessen" or de-emphasize the athletic program but to make every effort to keep moving forward. As a result, the next several years saw Jacoby, with Humphrey's backing and assistance, working hard for the foundation of a new conference. Even the trustees were enlisted in an effort to interest the Utah universities. The result was the Western Athletic Conference, consisting of schools in Wyoming, Arizona, Utah, and New Mexico. Five years later, Colorado State and Texas-El Paso joined the WAC. When the Arizona schools left in 1976, San Diego State, Hawaii, and later the Air Force Academy became members.

CHAPTER TEN

By 1964, Wyoming athletics had found a place in the sun, but that was only one of the changes of Humphrey's years. The president had come to campus at a time when academic institutions all over the country were bursting at the seams. In two decades enrollment substantially increased. Academic curricula and programs blossomed in almost every field. Community service and Wyoming-oriented research achieved such distinction that complaints were few and far between. New young faculty added zest to campus. The physical plant changed radically with the addition of $20 million in new buildings. For some of these advancements, Humphrey — on the brink of his retirement in 1964 — might take almost personal credit, although he was always aided (particularly in finances and athletics management) by a hard-working and dedicated staff.

As for himself, an evaluation of his personal impact and personal goals is difficult, for George Duke Humphrey was a different man to every group with whom he had close contact. There is no doubt, to begin with, that he worked hard in political — and particularly legislative and gubernatorial — relations. With his colleagues and those superior to him in authority, he was friendly, easy, and even charming. He developed powerful connections through the trustees — two of whom went on to become governors while he remained at the University's helm — and he made the most of them without seeming to try.

As a politician, he was superb. Perhaps his status as a Southern Democrat helped, for he was able to act the Democrat with liberals and play the conservative with Republicans, maintaining a solid friendship with men of both parties. But for the sake of political balance, he could even become humble. A case in point lies in his relationship with J. J. Hickey, Democratic governor elected in 1958. During the 1959 legislative session, Humphrey and Hickey began on opposite sides of the fence, for Hickey slashed the University's appropriation request by $1.5 million and Humphrey responded with something close to threats, suggesting that the University might well have to eliminate colleges or departments, double or triple fees, and put a cap on enrollment. However, Hickey, a Democrat, surprised the press with his appointment of three Republicans to the board of trustees in an apparent effort to keep the twelve-man board equally apportioned.

In the files is a note from Humphrey to Hickey dated March 3 and marked "personal and confidential." Humphrey wrote:

Knowing of your interest in, and your love and devotion for, the University, I feel I should write this letter.

Our communications seem not to have been very good since November. I am not sure just why they have not been. Perhaps my dedication to the University and my sense of dedication to the young people of the state have made me overenthusiastic in behalf of the University's interests. In any event, I am anxious that our communications should be improved and assure you that I will do my part to bring about this improvement. . . . I hope that we will be able to work together in such a way that the University, in which we are both interested, will continue to grow and expand as the state goes forward in its development.

To which Hickey responded:

There is no one but who admires you for your efforts in behalf of the University. We, who have a deep devotion for the University, have no fear for its continued progress under your hand. . . . I know that our association in working together for a greater Wyoming and a greater University will always be pleasant.

Humphrey considered politics as a career, for politicking was his forte. Apocryphal though it may be, the story that he flipped a coin with a Mississippi colleague to determine which would enter the senatorial race says something of Humphrey's ambitions. Near the end of his career, he was frequently rumored as a potential U.S. Senate candidate. The student newspaper publicly speculated on the topic, and in the files is a letter from Senator Milward Simpson (dated June 21, 1963, when Humphrey was slated to retire) on which Simpson penned at the bottom: "Duke: Run on Dem. ticket for U.S.S. M." Frustrated political ambitions only made Humphrey enjoy political contacts; they never caused him to forget his job. Years after he retired, he regularly appeared in Cheyenne in the offices of legislators or of Governor Stan Hathaway to lobby for some University cause.

With trustees, Humphrey worked equally well. Although conflicts occasionally developed — particularly on hot political issues — the president was generally adept at pouring oil on any troubled waters. Although trustees occasionally refused to adopt his recommendations, they more usually agreed with him; in any case, he seems to have abided by their decisions. In the 1950s, Trustee Tracy McCraken clashed frequently with Humphrey on McGee's Senate candidacy, but through the years John Reed's opposition to McGee seems to have caused the president even more trouble; in any case, he clearly weathered both storms.

Later with Milward Simpson, Humphrey developed a very special relationship. Their close association brought a kind of affection between them. In 1951, when Humphrey had been ill for several months (causing Simpson, as chairman of the board, to substitute for him during commencement exercises "without lousing them up too much," as he put it), Simpson took almost a paternal tone, urging the president to take it easy and rest. He added:

The Board is willing to share the burden with you. We expect you to bring all your problems to the Board and let us help in solving them. There is no use of your trying to protect us from vexation. . . . We're particularly interested in your well-being and we want you and your family to be happy there at the University. You can't be happy when you're worried, and you can't be happy when you're not well.

Humphrey was puzzled at Simpson's reference to problems he failed to take to the board.

Certainly I could not ask for a better Board of Trustees than I have. Please be assured that I shall never try to keep anything from you in which I think you would be interested or which would concern the Board in any way. If in the past I have failed to tell you anything which I should have told you, my mistake has been one of the head and not of the heart. . . . I appreciate more than I can tell you having as Chairman of the Board a person with whom I can discuss in all frankness any problem that arises, and you have been a tremendous help to me. . . .

Simpson responded reassuringly.

I just feel that you're working at too great a rate of speed. . . . I can't help but feel that perhaps I'm falling down in some way and the burden is getting greater and greater upon you. . . . I'll always be the same frank friend of yours in the future that I have been in the past, and I trust you will do the same with me. Now, go ahead and get well, and I'll see you whenever you want us down there.

Not everyone felt so affectionate towards Humphrey, and he developed few close friendships among faculty and administration — perhaps the greatest exception being Jacoby, whom he always respected. Mostly, he cut a larger swath off campus than on. For one thing, in the administrators around him, he preferred quick men, who did what they were requested thoroughly and silently. With people below him in rank, he was generally reluctant to consult, and if he did so, he usually made up his own mind and issued his own commands. Executive assistants were called on less frequently to make decisions than to prepare reports, handle problems discreetly, and brush lint off the presidential shoulders before legislative sessions. Humphrey would have been the first to admit his need for their assistance, but he always disliked signs of independence. Loyalty and obedience were the traits that he most admired in administrative office.

Although he paid due respect to memoranda from deans and department heads, Humphrey treated young faculty as personal employees. From them, he demanded utter loyalty, and (particularly in his later years) he became extremely sensitive to any rumor of faculty criticism of his administration. Young faculty remember being called to task for coffee-shop remarks, and sometimes for remarks never actually made. Humphrey did not hesitate to call in any faculty member who became eligible for tenure, and it seemed to many of them that he made more than necessary inquiries into their politics or their backgrounds. Faculty found themselves punished rather than praised for initiative and independence, particularly outside of the classroom. As early as 1948, two young political scientists who had worked with the legislature's interim committee and sought to aid certain associations, like the Wyoming Association of Municipalities, cited the president's disapproval and refusal to consult with them as one cause of their resignations. Duke Humphrey was considered by many faculty to be a "bricks and mortar" man, who demonstrated little understanding of academics and cared less.

Widespread among faculty was the belief that the University was being run like a Southern plantation. Years later, a prominent alumnus spoke to the aura of remoteness and even secrecy in the Humphrey years — something that legislators, too, had commented upon.

A board of Trustees, insulated from criticism, as it was during the Humphrey regime, and operating in secrecy, works at a disadvantage.

And further:

. . . one of the great failings of the people who have guided the destiny of the University over the past 20 years has been their total disregard of the benefits of letting the public know the University's problems.

Construction of Biological Sciences building (left) and Physical Sciences building (right), 1968

Duke Humphrey served the University for nineteen years, and he was pretty sure he knew how to run things right. Trustees echoed his confidence. He received from them regular, though not excessive, salary increases; and in 1952, his contract was renewed for ten years. In 1960, he was being courted by the Western Interstate Commission for

Higher Education as a candidate for its directorship; he told the trustees that he would prefer to stay at the University until retirement and thereafter perform in some special capacity — as a consultant, or perhaps as administrator of the American studies program, because of his close relationships to the Coe Foundation. He turned 65 on August 30, 1962, and the board gladly granted his request to stay at the helm until the following July 1 (his normal retirement date), particularly since the building program was (as usual) in full swing. In January 1963, after an executive session, trustees unanimously requested another year of his time. They suggested that he remain active until July 1, 1964, and thereafter, until the age of seventy, serve as administrator of the School of American Studies, consultant to the University, and professor of higher education.

George Duke Humphrey's formal retirement occurred as scheduled with considerable fanfare and recognition. Thereafter he made his headquarters in an office in the American studies wing of the library. He continued his interest in University affairs, reported frequently on Coe Foundation policies, and prepared special reports on such matters as a proposed business history center. He was somewhat distressed when trustees insisted on his complete retirement at the age of seventy (as of June 30, 1968), but still grateful that he might retain his office space as long as he wished. He died in Laramie on September 10, 1973.

Chapter Eleven

Students in Rebellion
1964-1972

he decade of the 1960s was a time of student activism all across the country. For one simple thing, students were growing up; young people were coming of age earlier and more vigorously than before. The old restrictive regulations on dress, habits, and living conditions came to be resented as anathema by a generation aware of its strength and competence. More importantly, young men were being asked to serve in the military in an unpopular war, and on campus after campus across the country "peaceniks" demonstrated while more aggressive types took violent action against the military and industrial establishments. Finally, as a corollary to all the above, students came to consider great social problems as part of their own world and personal responsibility. In the 1960s and the 1970s, that meant questions of war and peace, educational philosophy, minority rights and privileges, and such eternal problems as civil rights — freedoms of speech and association. Although the University of Wyoming campus never saw the extremes of the new movements, it experienced its share of protest. Reading the documents today sets one back into a different world.

As it happened, the late 1960s saw a series of presidents come and go just at a time when student protest was accelerating across the country. Four presidents assumed the office in rapid succession between 1964 and 1968, and only the last of them was to endure more than a decade. Continuity in administration was maintained by vice presidents and presidential assistants and, of course, by the University trustees, into whose laps fell problems of presidential appointment as well as concerns about radical student activities.

Well before Humphrey retired, the trustees began considering how they would conduct their search for his successor. One can well imagine

their worries, for Humphrey had served so long that no board member was practiced in the selection of presidents — although all were soon to become so. As early as spring of 1962, when it seemed possible that the presidential search would be conducted the next year, trustees considered procedures. The American Association of University Professors had proposed that the local chapter name a faculty committee with which trustees should confer. Humphrey supported the committee concept, provided that staff was included too. Trustees were reluctant to abandon control, and in April 1962, they changed their own regulations to provide that the board would appoint a committee to advise in the selection process, including thereon both faculty and staff.

The suggestion that the committee might be appointed, rather than elected, called forth protests by the AAUP. In April, the faculty as a whole uncertainly postponed discussion. In the course of the year 1962-63 — which, it turned out, was not Humphrey's last year in office after all — faculty and trustees reached a compromise, and the latter agreed to select its advisory committee from a panel chosen by the faculty. A panel of names was finally presented to trustees in October 1963, and after some suggestions added by the board, the final committee was appointed. It included Dean H. T. Person of engineering as chairman, with faculty representatives from the Colleges of Agriculture, Arts and Sciences, Commerce and Industry, and Education, plus "Red" Jacoby (athletic director) and Elliott Hays (presidential assistant for finance and deputy treasurer of the board of trustees). Humphrey expressed the hope that

the Trustees . . . would give the committee an opportunity to be of some assistance in the selection of a new President. He pointed out that, although the final selection must rest with the Trustees, the faculty and staff would be vitally concerned with the selection also, since they would have to work closely with the new President.

CHAPTER ELEVEN

In a flash of foresight about possible troubles,

Dr. Humphrey pointed out that the Trustees would not be able to keep a good man in the presidency for very long if there were too much interference on the part of the Trustees in the administration of the University, and he suggested that the Board adopt a theory similar to his theory of administration — that is, one of setting policies, adopting rules and regulations, telling the President what would be expected of him, and then giving him a free hand.

Whatever the board's reaction, one senses that this last lame-duck year (1963-64 — when, although the president had turned 65, trustees had agreed to his staying in office) was not the happiest of Humphrey's career. Although the long-term president remained the public representative of his institution in Washington, D.C., at the legislature, and throughout the state, his personal influence at home began to wane. For the first time, trustees seemed to be aware of Humphrey's age. In 1963-64, in a procedure not common in the Humphrey years, the board circumvented the president and designed the annual budget itself in direct consultation with the deans. It was a source of concern to Humphrey that all was not well with the financing of his favorite project, the science center. Indeed, Humphrey, who was on the board of the National Science Foundation, had considerably overestimated the level of federal funding that might be available to assist in construction, and had Congress, in a new awareness of the need for modern technology and equipment, not passed a law providing matching funds for campus buildings, the entire plan might well have been in jeopardy. Nor do documents indicate that Humphrey was carefully consulted about his successor, although early on he presented the trustees with suggestions for institutions to which they might write.

By December 1963, the trustees had narrowed the field to a panel of nineteen, at which point they consulted their faculty committee for advice. At the committee's suggestion — although after "consideration of other candidates" — the field was reduced to four finalists, with whom interviews were conducted by board and committee in mid-March 1964. Called in for a final evaluation, Person told the board that any of the four candidates seemed appropriate to the committee. Still, the trustees hesitated: On a secret ballot, John T.

Fey, president of the University of Vermont, received a majority vote, but the motion to grant him the position was nervously withdrawn in favor of a call for further "investigation of Dr. Fey's background." It seems likely that the trustees were concerned about the candidate's policy of de-emphasizing intercollegiate athletics at Vermont. If a final investigation proved positive, board members Harold Newton and Robert McCraken were to contact Fey with a firm offer. That proved to be the case. Fey came to Wyoming with a five-year contract beginning at $25,000 a year.

No individual could have been more different from Duke Humphrey than was Jack Fey. Sophisticated, vigorous, and young (47), Fey immediately created a positive image of strong and outgoing leadership. If Humphrey's forte lay in political manipulation and one-on-one persuasion, Fey liked openness, frankness, and ebullience. He was a man of immediate popularity with faculty and administration, and he won friends all around him. If Humphrey had entertained any thoughts of influencing the new administration — and in his last year he had made two major appointments, those of vice president for academic affairs and dean of arts and sciences, both of which might have afforded him opportunities to influence decision-making — he was not to succeed, for Fey's character and leadership won him supporters from the start.

At his inauguration in December 1964, the new president sponsored a symposium on the role of scholarship in an age of science. Praising Humphrey for his foresight, he made it clear that his own long-range plans included the encouragement of scientific research, an enhanced graduate program, and the goal of nationally-recognized excellence. Among his early appointees was a director of research development, a position accepted by R. H. Denniston from the zoology department. But even more vigorously, the new president spoke for the need for broad and liberal education to encourage the "capacity for making intelligent decisions." He spoke frequently of the library as a tool for the fields of history and English much as the science center would promote what he hoped might be an outstanding research program. Among his greatest admirers were faculty and dean from

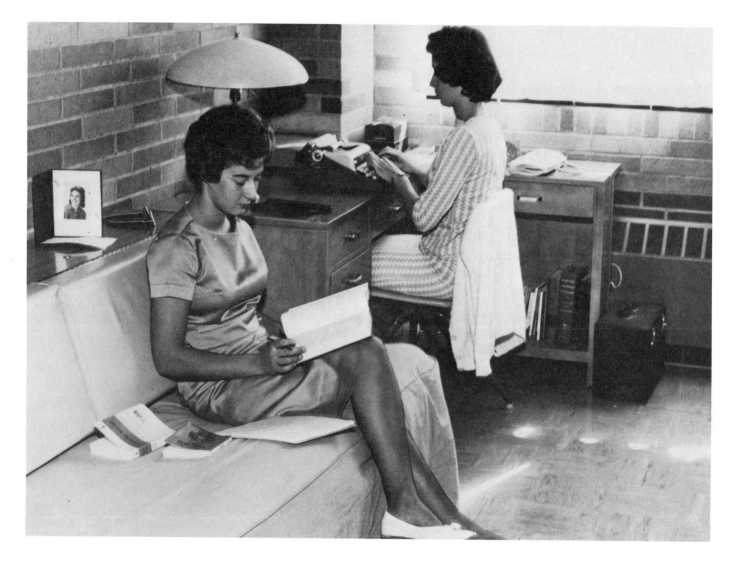

Ross hall roommates, c. 1962

the College of Arts and Sciences, which Fey saw as the key to the University's future. At last, the college dean said later, arts and sciences was to develop programs and research on its own, rather than to act primarily as a "filling station" to "service" professional schools. During Fey's administration, a University professor for the first time was hired at a salary of more than $20,000; he was Derek Prowse, head of the physics department, an internationally known physicist brought in to build a physics research program. Most important of all, said the president,

> *is the seeking, the curiosity, the skepticism which is a prerequisite to learning,*

and the emphasis on change which such seeking evoked. With Fey in command, faculty and administration looked with reborn enthusiasm toward a new era.

Unfortunately, it was not to be. Less than a year after his inauguration ceremonies, Fey tendered his resignation to the board. He was leaving academe for "a challenge in a new field" as president of the National Life Insurance Company. The student newspaper reported "bewilderment and confusion" at the announcement, but Fey emphasized that he was leaving without rancor. "I was enthusiastic about UW when I came here," he told the *Branding Iron,* "and I am just as enthusiastic today." Typically, he spent his last few months in long-range planning, particularly seeking special support for the College of Arts and Sciences. One alumnus wrote to the departing president,

> *You will be missed by more people than you may realize. A lot of us considered Jack Fey to be the "white hope" of our State University.*

208

Thus it came that in spring 1965, the trustees had to try again. This time the advisory committee chairman was James Ranz (academic affairs). It was composed of representatives of all colleges plus Lawrence Meeboer of the finance office. Letters went to all kinds of educational institutions and organizations. By February, 111 applications had been received, and the number of candidates was narrowed by the trustees to 57. In its formal instructions to the faculty-staff committee, trustees asked it to narrow the list to twenty. They also told the committee that the candidate must be between 35 and fifty; should have a doctor's degree; and must be a person of high integrity with experience in finance, teaching, and administration. They reminded the committee that

In addition to academic excellence, successful intercollegiate and extracurricular programs are important to the growth and morale of our state university,

perhaps a reference to Fey's view about the role of college football and to the fact that no athletic representative was serving on this committee at all.

Board and committee did their work carefully. The first list of candidates contained a number of outstanding individuals, several of whom were to go on to positions of considerable reknown. Unfortunately, many of these candidates withdrew from the competition, and the list was decimated. By mid-March, the "A" list contained nine names, including two local candidates — Ranz, who had resigned chairmanship of the committee to become a competitor, and Frank Trelease, dean of the law school. After a special meeting in Cheyenne on March 18, to which faculty committee members John Senior and John Miller were invited, the board made it clear that it would check out additional "selected individuals." The final interview list was again decreased by withdrawals. By late April, there were five candidates, including Ranz.

In mid-May, at a special session in Casper, trustees determined to offer the job to John E. King, then president of Kansas State Teachers College at Emporia. King's name had been added to the list by trustees when the original candidates began to withdraw. The faculty committee protested vigorously — it had hoped for a man with Fey's background in arts, sciences, and sophistication. King was a teachers' college product, little known in academic fields. King was given a five-year contract, to continue through June 1971. As he shortly resigned to move elsewhere, Professor Senior cited the selection as a commanding reason for his departure.

Problems developed almost at once. King's manner in public was friendly and folksy — what one of the deans most closely involved has called "country." His warmth was well-received by citizens around the state and by students on campus. Touring Wyoming communities, the president emphasized his pleasure at the sweep of the landscape and the romance of the plains, which he obviously appreciated.

In the office, he was less congenial. Staff who worked most closely with him remember being bawled out like children, threatened with dismissal, or humiliated (as one of them said) not only in administrative conferences but in public. The new president's reactions were immediate and often intemperate — for example, when at a high-level meeting, the president offered to take a dean (who was considerably larger than he!) "behind the woodshed." To make things more difficult for the staff around him, King's apparent lack of acquaintance with, and seeming disrespect for, established routines left his colleagues jittery, for he did not hesitate to override committee decisions, and he occasionally laid responsibility for what he deemed an error (the use of the word "sex" in a *Branding Iron* advertisement) where it did not belong (the committee of deans). Like Crane, the president was a man of stern and rigid moral standards that were difficult to enforce on a college campus of the 1960s.

In contrast with his predecessor, the new president did not impress the deans with any appreciation for basic research. Nor did he press for enhanced scholarly achievements or high-level credentials for faculty; one dean remembers being told to seek professors at community colleges, for King refused to endorse the appointment of Ph.D.s. Needless to say, the arts and sciences faculty were among the first to mourn Fey's departure. King's immediate assistants did so too. Accustomed to a president whose memory was almost photographic and who could recite budget figures without even consulting his notes, administrators working with the new president still remember their alarm when King seemed more at ease approaching the pre-legislative meetings armed with anecdotes instead of figures.

King faced his first legislature in early 1967, and here lay his ultimate undoing. Apparently he relied on a "country" homeyness and a general geniality to carry him through. In his trips through the state, according to one source, he demonstrated little knowledge of special Wyoming conditions, particularly in stock growing and agriculture. At the legislature he appeared without doing his homework on statistics and programs, so that he lacked specific knowledge of many budget requests; nevertheless, he had no inclination to lean on assistants for advice. The budget request was ambitious, for King asked for 71 additional faculty members and a $7 million increase in the "resident instruction" area. In an ill-advised moment, he promised to raise $1 million from private sources for a new student union building. Faculty members were reported angry and ready to leave: Several — like Benjamin Tilghman, head of the philosophy department — resigned. During the legislative session, several deans received private telephone calls from a presidential assistant urging them to speed to Cheyenne without fanfare to confer personally with leading legislators in order to save their programs. Results of the session were not a disaster for the University (as has been portrayed), because funding increased in most areas. However, King's budget was $5 million short of realization. The disaster was his.

By the end of February, leading deans and administrators — including the vice president for academic affairs — were sensing universal chaos. Problems with the legislative program, recurrent differences in educational philosophy, and the cavalier treatment afforded them by the president finally united them in what was for some a reluctant revolution. In mid-February, at the instigation of several deans and with strong support from several others, the academic deans and other leading officials met in a private home to compare notes and air grievances. Unity was essential, and several among them were at first hesitant to intervene, but eventually all agreed that change was necessary. In a letter presented to the board of trustees at its meeting on February 24, the deans expressed (according to the minutes)

their complete lack of confidence in the academic philosophy and administrative ability of Dr. John E. King, Jr.; their great interest in the future of the University and willingness to serve in any capacity other than that of president; their desire to meet as a group with the board. . . .

One dean stated later that their joint disavowal of presidential ambitions was to make sure the board understood that no single one was acting out of hope for personal gain.

At the board meeting, trustees agreed to the deans' request for an audience. The next day, the board heard the deans, one by one, explain reasons for their rebellion. Several of them expressed an intention to leave if the president was not dismissed, and similar feelings among the faculty were cited. In the high tension, Amelia Leino, dean of nursing, was unable to control her tears. President King sat and listened. Trustees heard the deans out, sent them away, and pursued their discussions in an all-day executive session. When they emerged, they had drafted a letter to the deans, resolving firmly that

the Deans be advised that the Board has taken no official action on their letter; that the Board urges and expects the deans to make every effort to cooperate with the President in resolving their differences; and that they attempt to obtain the cooperation of their Faculty and Staff, all in the best interest of the University.

The day was Saturday, but the deans got the message. In what must have been anger and frustration, several of them released the text of their letter to a local radio commentator.

Meanwhile, trustees headed for home. On Sunday, discouraged deans conferred by telephone, many presuming that all that remained was to compose their letters of resignation. Eventually, Frank Trelease, highly respected dean of the law school, was persuaded to act as spokesman and call a local attorney who served on the board of trustees. To his surprise, he found that the board had not taken seriously the deans' threats of resignation. It fell to Trelease to clarify the situation and, on request, to telephone another out-of-town board member. The next day board Chairman Joe Watt hurried to Laramie, calling trustees back into session. That day, King submitted to Watt a letter of resignation, with the suggestion that Watt use it however he saw fit, "as a hole card." It would be difficult, the president wrote, to continue without the support of the deans. He officially requested certain financial considerations should his five-year contract be cancelled.

CHAPTER ELEVEN

Negotiations continued through the following day. One might suppose that the five new board members, who had no stake in the previous presidential gamble (against the advisory committee's protest), made their voices heard. At a meeting finally called on March 1, the board opted "with regret" to accept King's resignation, and a committee quickly negotiated a financial settlement. The board thanked King for his "fine spirit and attitude in this critical period," and the governor pointed out to the press that he "did everything possible to make it easier for the Board of Trustees. He's a man of great character." King in turn accepted fate without apparent rancor. In all published interviews, he expressed only warm memories for his tenure at Wyoming, and to Watt he wrote:

Good luck to you and the Board. I am not bitter about this and do not intend to let this situation keep me from trying to be useful. You can depend on me to be dignified in the comments I make. You are as good a Board of Trustees, including old and new members, as I have ever worked with.

To King's suggestion that the board hire one of the deans as an acting president, trustees demurred, as indeed the deans had requested. Instead the board followed the deans' advice and offered the temporary position to highly respected H. T. Person, long-term dean of the College of Engineering, who had retired from that post in 1964 at the age of 61.

Public outcry at this unprecedented event was almost inevitable. Trustees, deans, and president alike agreed to keep mum and released no statements to the press, with the exception of the text of the deans' letter, which only added fuel to the fire. King had acted nobly, and for his benefit and the good of the institution, everyone abided by the pledge of secrecy.

As so often, however, discretion only led to greater problems. Rumors circulated and protests multiplied. Newspapers across the state, talking "great shock" and "complete surprise," complained openly of the news blackout, and criticized the "attitude of silence" that gave rise to "damaging rumors," which, claimed the Sheridan *Press,*

will inevitably find Wyoming people saying, "if they can't get along down there, I'm not going to send my boy there."

What does the future hold for the University of Wyoming, asked the Laramie *Boomerang,* commenting on the sequence of four presidents in three years. The *Branding Iron,* which had mourned the loss of a new student union through King's casual commitment to raising $1 million, now mourned the departure of the president in equally heartfelt terms.

Thank you [Dr. King] for taking a special interest in the student as an individual human being who has a right to personal consideration from the president of the University no matter how busy that president may be. . . . Thank you for taking away some of the cold, impersonal atmosphere which is the curse of most universities that have forgotten that they exist to teach people rather than to shuffle IBM cards. A good many students appreciated having a president they could talk to and we won't forget it for a long time.

Among all the worries and complaints, only a few professors came forth to support the deans. John Senior, against whose advice King had been hired, launched "a pointed attack" on modern college administrators at a campus literary meeting, and a week after King's dismissal a couple of chemistry professors defended the deans, who, they pointed out, had

served the University an average of 22 years, and therefore would not take the action they took lightly, or against what they felt would be the best interest of the students and faculty.

Through all the calls for explanation and the demands for the end to secret sessions at trustee meetings, those involved kept their silence.

One reason the University weathered the immediate storm lay in the reputation of the new acting president. Person was widely known and universally respected across the state. Well acquainted with the University from his many years as engineering dean, he brought to his new office considerable administrative and financial experience. For picking up the pieces and setting the ship back on course, no better man could have been found.

Only one minor difficulty marred Person's ten months in office. When he was approached by trustees to become acting president, Person had told them of his financial interest in and relationship to the J. T. Banner Co., a Laramie firm which frequently bid on University architectural and engineering contracts. Person advised that he would be willing to sell his interest and resign his position (as a director and vice president) in the organization, but he affirmed that he would be unwilling to become president of the University if his presence would prejudice the board against accepting the company's bids.

Assurances were exchanged, and Person immediately divested himself of the stock and resigned as an officer. Unfortunately, apparently because of oversight, his name reappeared as a company officer when the Banner firm reregistered as a corporation in July 1967. On recommendation of the board's building committee and apparently without Person's participation, the Banner bid for architectural design of the fine arts building was accepted by trustees just before Person's term in office ended, and almost at once a complaint was registered through Harry Roberts, state superintendent of public instruction and ex-officio member of the board. Trustees anticipated trouble, and Watt requested an opinion from the board's legal adviser. Joseph R. Geraud's opinion fully and categorically exempted Person from "conflict of interest."

Nevertheless through the next year, a University alumnus, Jack Rosenthal, owner of a Casper television station, sparred with trustees and president alike on the awarding of the contract and the board's unwillingness to open its records. Only after Trustee H. A. True, Jr., sought out Rosenthal in Casper in October did Rosenthal agree to let the matter drop. He still objected to the board's lack of openness with the public. By then, Person had stepped down. In appreciation of his work, trustees awarded him the title of president (rather than "acting president") retroactively, and at his final board meeting, they gave him an unprecedented standing ovation.

Meanwhile, the business of selecting a new president began again. This time, the board agreed to an advisory committee elected by the various colleges (one member from each) and then appointed thereto Robert H. Bruce, graduate dean, as chairman, "Red" Jacoby to represent the athletic program, and Elliott Hays from the fiscal administration. Trustees still had on hand the vitae and recommendations for a number of candidates considered in 1966. Educational institutions throughout the country again were contacted. To a special board meeting in July, Bruce presented a list of nine candidates, and the board selected four for special interviews. Although again several candidates seem to have withdrawn and others were invited for interviews to replace them, the procedure went on the whole smoothly, Bruce was consulted at each meeting, and four candidates remained on to the final list.

In September, after a number of meetings, a committee of three was set up to check especially on William D. Carlson, chairman of the department of radiology in the nationally-recognized veterinary school at Colorado State University (Fort Collins). The committee reported back enthusiastically. Undoubtedly it was influenced by Carlson's attachment to the Rocky Mountain area, which did not preclude his resigning but made it perhaps less likely. Several of the selection committee members seem to have known the candidate personally. Senator Clifford P. Hansen conveyed strong recommendations for Carlson from his friend Senator Gordon Allott, whose Colorado campaign Carlson had helped to manage; high political connections were always assets in University presidencies. Carlson's experience included scientific expertise and administrative experience as department head. He had even once sought to play college football, but was rejected because he was not big enough. The board had reason to be pleased with its choice, and this time the faculty committee did not object. Carlson was given a five-year contract. He assumed office on January 1, 1968.

It was Carlson who bore the brunt of the wave of student activism and discontent that struck Wyoming several years later. For some time, the University campus had maintained its cool. The first manifestations of the new social conscience grew up in the South, where in the early 1960s, a civil rights movement was underway. The UW student newspaper took frequent note of events in the

212

autumn of 1962 and commented particularly on the effect of legislation on the University of Mississippi, center of the Southern controversy and located in Humphrey's home state. Although the *Branding Iron* supported the views of the National Association for the Advancement of Colored People (NAACP) in terms of campus integration, its editors were not convinced that "forcing the issue" would make for a permanent solution to the black student problems of the South. During demonstrations on the Berkeley campus a few years later, student editors became a little bolder.

We should not condone these demonstrations yet in a sense they attest to the growing maturity of today's college aged adults. Call it rebellion, call it radicalism. Nevertheless, it's a sign of an awareness of the world.

The Wyoming student, the editorial contended, was

less concerned with civil rights, Communism, and poverty than his big-city counterparts — but not at the expense of his maturity. The maturity is here . . . but somehow still shrouded by an aura of apathy.

The newspaper in 1964 and 1965 constantly complained about poor attendance at cultural events. "Provincialism could be the academic death of this University."

Still, elements of the radical and counterculture slipped in. In spring of 1965, a group of concerned students founded an organization they called the Student Nonviolent Coordinating Committee, although they never affiliated with the national SNCC. About forty became charter members, and the society listed two faculty sponsors. Its proclaimed goal — the elimination of discrimination on campus — was almost at once attacked in a letter to the student newspaper. There was little discrimination, the writer stated, SNCC was only "creating a tidal wave in a peanut pond," and the organization should disperse. Within a few months, SNCC changed its name to the Student Committee for Civil Liberties and devoted its efforts to changing coed dormitory hours. In early 1966 it died; it "suffocated from non-involvement," as the *Branding Iron* put it.

A few other efforts were made to assimilate Wyoming students into the world of their out-of-state contemporaries. The campus ministry sponsored a weekly coffeehouse, including an "alternative" bookstore off-campus. Mortar Board honorary held a seminar on the Vietnam conflict, and some concern about the draft was apparent in the student newspaper. Occasional speakers came to campus to discuss and describe social injustice: Corky Gonzales, a Chicano activist; representatives of the Black Panthers; and members of the Students for a Democratic Society. Students, wrote the *Branding Iron* editor in spring 1966,

have heard the Lettermen and Kingston Trio. . . . But they have not heard Bob Dylan . . . or Martin Luther King. And they probably never will.

Still, a few students joined the "hippie" counterculture. Some were arrested for peddling drugs, others (21 and over) lived in suspicious off-campus digs, and some took to wearing long hair or ankle bells. As late as 1967, the University had not developed a specific disciplinary policy for drug possessors. An astute observer might have taken alarm at the number of bomb scares (21 between 1966 and 1969); false fire alarms (although many seemed to have been set by one individual); or the declining student interest in fraternities. In 1964, a total of 800 went through fraternity "rush." In 1968, the number was 250, and the fraternities were trying to change their image for a student body "more sophisticated, more alert, more aware of the world." Still, all in all, most students were more concerned with drinking at football games and exhorted each other to better conduct. While, as one Cheyenne newspaper article put it, "Unrest Troubles Most Major Universities," the University of Wyoming campus remained an "island of tranquility." Carlson said the same, and he credited the absence of conflict to luck — as well as to a "fine, enthusiastic student body" and a "responsible, dedicated faculty and staff."

The change in the direction of activism and protest came gradually, beginning in the 1968-69 academic year. By then Vietnam was becoming an acute issue, and a student peace movement had been organized. In early 1968, several dozen students picketed interviewers on campus from Dow Chemical Corporation; several signs were ripped down by men in athletic jackets, but no person-to-person violence erupted. Several professors debated the issues of the Vietnam war, and an English professor took the lead in advancing the views of the "doves." By early 1968, the ASUW senate produced a "bill of rights," based on the protection of civil liberties — freedom of speech, press, protection from illegal search, etc. — as compiled from several documents devised by national organizations during a senate "retreat." Passed by the senate, the bill was to be presented to the administration for approval the following year. Meanwhile, there was considerable concern in the *Branding Iron* over what the editors called an increasing "cowboy-hippie chasm."

At the end of spring semester 1968, the special event "Shake the Nation" aroused considerable campus interest; it was billed as folk singing, "bitch-in," "love-in," "teach-in," and above all discussions on Vietnam designed to "arouse students' interest concerning contemporary issues on and off-campus." Some months later there were rumors that the Students for a Democratic Society had agitators on campus and were actually planning to take over a building; the police chief had noted the presence of many "strange people" around. In August 1968, Carlson participated in a panel on student unrest at a meeting of the Western Interstate Commission on Higher Education in Hawaii. He was able to report with pride that the Wyoming campus was quiet, and his remarks were followed by an article in a Honolulu newspaper by a reporter who visited Laramie and found Wyoming a "welcome haven."

> *There wasn't a pop-art "peace" poster, a free speech merchant or a draft card burner in sight. . . . "Student power?" grinned one [student]. "Sure, we've heard of it. But not here. That stuff's for kooks." [And another:] "We don't need strikes and sit-ins. We have an effective student government and close cooperation with both administration and faculty."*

Still, the reports of Communist influence, "militant disruption," and "infiltration" which Carlson had heard from his panel colleagues were scarcely reassuring. At the beginning of fall semester 1968, the president began preparations for trouble. Calling a meeting about student disorders, he asked faculty members to volunteer to act as trouble shooters in case of the threat of violence. A number stepped forward, including several with reputations as radicals. By October, Joseph R.

Geraud, as student affairs officer and legal adviser to the trustees, had devised a set of procedures to follow in case of student disorders, procedures featuring volunteer faculty who would go to the scene and be the first to attempt negotiations. A proposal to have another "Shake the Nation" alarmed one of the past faculty sponsors of SNCC, who affirmed that his sponsorship of both that organization and the previous "Shake the Nation" were actually measures "to control the activities — unobtrusively control them, of course — and prevent any extreme demonstrations." Taking credit for "killing" SNCC because he "did not approve of its aims or its personnel," this faculty member wrote that he was particularly concerned about outside radicals.

> *I am convinced that outside people could have a very bad effect on our basically sound students because our students are — "trusting" is the only word I can think of — and assume that people with whom they deal are honest and people of integrity.*

Carlson called him in, especially, to discuss problems.

In the spring of 1969, a number of young faculty members led a boycott of the annual military ball and proposed instead a peace ball with "progressive music" "in an atmosphere that is congenial with peace, not war, love not death." Within a five-day period in late March, the police received three bomb threats, and after one call someone tampered with the gears in a city fire engine which then crashed into three parked cars.

At the annual Governor's Day review of ROTC units in May, a March for Peace was sponsored by the Student Peace Union, which invited Carlson and some other administrators to sit on the lawn and talk things over. Carlson said he would be happy to meet any other time, but he was tied up with the governor. The peace march occasioned angry reactions from citizens in Laramie and around the state. One telegram specifically accused the president of permissiveness:

> *Your decision encouraging a demonstration against ROTC at my state University is to me deplorable. ROTC has supplied over 60 percent of officer personnel for our armed forces. Historically oppositions to it are irresponsible and anti-American.*

CHAPTER ELEVEN

Student peace marches, on campus and the nation

A well-respected Laramieite expressed "utter dismay and deep disappointment over the display which took place on the University Campus," particular distress that "certain faculty" had announced support and encouragement, and "deep disappointment and real concern for the kind of guidance which is being given to many of the students of the University." ROTC had changed from a required to a voluntary program in 1965 at Fey's instigation and upon the report of a special committee, a faculty vote, and the approval of the board of trustees. It remained a symbol of the military and the war in Vietnam. In mid-October,

it again became the brunt of posters during a campus march on the occasion of the national Vietnam moratorium.

In that month, too, the first major problem of the decade erupted. Oddly, it had to do with minorities, the small numbers of whom on campus could hardly have led officials to anticipate trouble. The Wyoming campus had not been any kind of a gathering place for native Americans, Chicanos, or blacks, with the exception of those who were recruited on athletic teams.

"DOC" KNIGHT

While my formal training in geology was limited during my undergraduate years," wrote Samuel Howell Knight in 1974, "my informal training was exceptional." Of course, "Doc" Knight began with great lineage. His father, Wilbur C. Knight, was the University's first geology professor, accepting his appointment in 1893, a few months after Sam was born. Although Wilbur Knight died when his son was only ten, Sam had taken to hanging around the science hall, and as a young boy he traveled

Samuel and Everett Knight, 1900

*Samuel Howell Knight,
geology professor, c. 1925*

across Wyoming with William H. Reed, then curator of the miniscule geology museum. Covering twenty miles a day by wagon over rough Wyoming terrain, Sam and Reed hunted fossils, observed rocks, and poked through Como Bluffs, an extraordinary deposit of dinosaur bones. After Sam graduated from Wyoming, he enrolled for advanced work at Columbia, where he was pleased to discover that his background in the field was far more comprehensive than that of many of his contemporaries from larger universities.

An intelligence officer in World War I, Knight was one of the first to use terrain analyses in warfare.

"Doc" Knight began his teaching career at Wyoming in 1916. Thereafter he became head of the geology department, state geologist, and curator of the geology museum. By 1953, when the University awarded him an honorary LL.D. degree, he had built a department with a national reputation.

To his students — perhaps 18,000 of them — he was the man with the chalk-talk — a series of blackboard sketches that he drew free-hand with both hands in colored chalk to accompany his lectures. Possessed of an extraordinary talent for three-dimensional visualization, Knight became nationally known for his unique drawings and was twice a distinguished lecturer for the American Association of Petroleum Geologists, which made him an honorary member.

"DOC" KNIGHT

Samuel H. Knight, office at science hall, 1916

Sam Knight knew from childhood that Wyoming was one of the greatest collecting grounds for vertebrate fossils in the country. Collecting was one of Knight's joys, and even with patchwork funding, he managed to develop an outstanding research collection of vertebrate fossils. Beginning with a small display area, Knight built his beloved geology museum, with its huge central brontosaurus, the bones of which had been collected at Como Bluffs, and the laborious assembling, mounting, and reconstructing of which Knight performed with his own hands. Later he took on another project. Based on a small model he constructed himself, he built the 45-foot tyrannosaurus rex — the huge, weathered beast that greets visitors to the geology museum.

Knight belonged to Wyoming. "As far back as I can remember," he wrote, "the campus, the surrounding plains and encircling mountains had such firm hold on me that I never wished to live elsewhere." Four generations of the Knight family have been (at least for a time) Wyoming geologists. His mother was Emma Howell Knight, dean of women from 1911-1921, for whom Knight hall dormitory was named. Sam was chairman of the Alumni Association, served on many athletic committees, and had a homecoming parade dedicated to him with the theme of "Two Million B.C." In 1974, when the geology building was officially named for Samuel Howell Knight, the geology-minded family all gathered for the celebration. Sam Knight died in Laramie in February 1975. The University of Wyoming was then 87 years old. "Doc" had been part of it for 82 years.

Only a few episodes with racial repercussions might be cited in the University's recent history. In 1961, the Wyoming Advisory Committee on Civil Rights came to investigate an unidentified charge that the University discriminated against blacks. "I have no idea what the committee is talking about," wrote then President Humphrey. "It's kind of like a gestapo." Minority students were "discouraged" from entering the University, the committee found, on the grounds that the campus would provide them only a "limited social life." Pressed to make a more positive statement to set the record straight, Fey issued a firm commitment to non-discrimination and the tradition of "equality for all," in 1965.

A few sources for minority dismay continued to exist throughout the late 1960s, and the student newspaper made a point of reporting on them. The "lack of social acceptance" of blacks was deplored by the *Branding Iron* in 1966. During the same year, a minor controversy over interracial dating made the newspaper's pages. Anti-black policies in town housing, restaurants, and the fraternity system led to sporadic complaints. In 1968, the *Branding Iron* reported on the boycott of the "Campus Shop" on the grounds of discrimination and urged the University to take strong action against individuals and organizations involved in similar tactics. In the academic year 1968-69, a movement on campus favored the incorporation of black studies into the curriculum, and that spring saw Professors Roger Daniels (history), Thomas Brockmann (anthropology), and Robert Hemenway (English) presenting a series of lectures on black culture. That spring brought a nasty episode when several blacks spontaneously attacked an intramural game referee who they said called them niggers. The students were charged with assault and suspended. Carlson had to explain to the Cheyenne NAACP.

The Black Student Alliance (unaffiliated, it claimed, with any national organization) was the first of the minority student groups to claim a place on campus. Recognized by the ASUW as an official campus association in April 1969, it found a faculty sponsor in Daniels and an articulate leader in a black graduate student named Willie S. Black. The BSA cooperated with the *Branding Iron* in identifying and publicizing cases of discrimination. In part because of its existence, Carlson set up a committee which included Black, other student leaders, six faculty members, and several administrators. This committee was to make recommendations in order that the "educational programs and student life on campus be so structured and so organized that minority groups on campus are able to derive maximum benefit from them." No doubt he was also inspired by the example of Lloyd W. Eaton, whose memo to "Red" Jacoby earlier in the year had suggested a special recruiting effort to bring black girls to a campus where there were 33 male black students (including 22 athletes) and only four black women. Special minorities recruiting was begun by a student committee (consisting of three blacks and four Chicano students) the previous summer, as financed by an appropriation from the board of trustees.

No trouble might have erupted at all had 22 athletes — including fourteen on the football team — not have been black. Athletics not only brought blacks together as a group, but served, too, as the focus of much campus, alumni, faculty, and administrative attention. In the fall of 1969, Wyoming had one of the "winningest" football teams in its history. Eaton was coach. Beginning in 1962, he set Wyoming football on the national map with a series of winning seasons, capped with bowl games in 1966 and New Year's Day 1968. For a bleak moment in early 1969, it seemed as though Eaton might move on, but Carlson (authorized by the board to give him "carte blanche" so "we wouldn't lose him") persuaded him to stay. His winning slogans of hard work, skill, sportsmanship, and discipline kept hopes high, as did his three-year record of 27-4, one of the best in the country. Coming off a Sugar Bowl post-season game, Eaton ranked as a state and campus hero.

But on October 16, 1969, two days before the scheduled football game with Brigham Young University, a letter from the BSA was hand-delivered to the offices of president, athletic director, and football coach. Signed by Black as BSA chancellor, it demanded that Western Athletic Conference schools cancel and refuse to schedule games with the Mormon university, and that blacks and whites alike protest the "racist" policy of the Mormon church by wearing black armbands in any BYU contest. Similar problems had arisen previously at Arizona State, Texas-El Paso, and New Mexico, where students and athletes had protested the Mormon policy towards blacks. That afternoon, Eaton approached one of the black players and told him that "no way" could they wear the armbands during the Saturday game; he referred to his firm rule that no football players be involved in any demonstrations. As Eaton explained later,

We do not want our players taking part in demonstrations because to do so distracts them from their purpose in being here — to get an education through football. Because the majority of our players are C-average students, they cannot afford the time from their studies to participate in demonstrations. This rule is in effect during the entire school year, as long as a player is a member of the football team.

Fourteen black football players met that evening, and (in the words of one of them) "felt strongly about some form of protest." They resolved to talk to Eaton the next day.

Where "the Black 14" may have made their mistake was in wearing black armbands to the coach's office when they appeared there for discussion. Clearly, Eaton saw discipline being broken, and he was a disciplinarian above all. He marched the athletes into the fieldhouse stands and in less than ten minutes told them off. His language was not pretty, but his meaning was clear. He gave them little chance to respond. Angrily, he found them in "open defiance" and kicked them off the team.

Carlson was notified, and a series of frantic meetings began at once. Although Eaton refused to meet with the black players as a group, Jacoby agreed to do so; the meeting was fruitless. Jacoby had to support the coach. Trustees assembled, including the governor, and absent trustees were contacted by phone. They met with the players, with the coaches, and found only that positions had solidified; by evening, the blacks refused to play without armbands in the next day's game. Confronting a stone wall and a rock, trustees wondered frantically who might be found to coach the team through the Saturday game should they countermand Eaton's orders and should he refuse to coach. In the wee hours of the morning, in the face of intransigence on both sides, trustees opted to support their winning coach — or at least, not to reverse his decision. On the afternoon of the BYU game, the blacks entered the stands together in street clothes and — wearing their armbands — watched their teammates achieve a lack-luster victory.

Reaction to what became a season-long suspension of the black athletes was immediate and intense. In an emergency session on the Saturday of the game, the ASUW senate passed a resolution expressing "shock at the callous, insensitive treatment afforded fourteen black athletes who acted on a matter of conscience with restraint, with moderation, and with responsibility" and condemning both Eaton and the trustees as "not only uncompromising but unjust and totally wrong." The next day the Faculty Senate met to request that the administration change the athletes' penalty to temporary suspension pending investigation by a faculty-student committee, which was appointed the following day. On October 23, 1969, Carlson presented a summary of events to the Faculty Senate, but the ad hoc committee was not ready to report. When the committee did respond, it was only to recommend the passage of a statement on "rights and freedom of students" — a statement geared to prevent future crises rather than to express opinion on past ones.

During the next few weeks, it became clear that the campus was divided. The arts and sciences faculty condemned the action of Eaton as "unjust, unconstitutional and unwise," and the commerce and industry college followed suit; however, faculty in the College of Agriculture supported Eaton by a strong margin. So did students (in spite of the ASUW senate resolutions) — at least according to a journalism department poll. Meetings and demonstrations, primarily favoring "the Black 14," sparked campus life for several weeks, while two underground publications — *Revelations* and *Free Lunch* — circulated the latest gossip and news of gatherings: It is noteworthy that they consistently warned against violence. The local branch of the American Association of University Professors solicited funds for legal aid and got a promise of support from the American Civil Liberties Union. At least one English professor resigned his job to go "somewhere where students are valued as human beings," but it is doubtful that he took advantage of the Casper Quarterback Club's sarcastically proffered fund to relocate radical professors elsewhere. When the *Branding Iron* printed an editorial urging unity, caution, and a "cease fire" on the issue, its editor resigned in protest against the staff's conservatism.

Coe Library by night, c. 1958

Off-campus reaction seemed to favor the coach. The Alumni Association vigorously supported Eaton, and its president went a step further in suggesting that the resignations of faculty rebels should be "gratefully accepted." Letters to the governor ran almost unanimously in favor of Eaton's stance. The National Collegiate Athletic Association suggested in its official publication that Willie Black had acted on behalf of the Black Panther party, and years later both Carlson and Governor Hathaway were certain that the athletes' protest was inspired by outside agitators. Black himself always firmly stated that he had not even advised the athletes nor been in contact with them at all until after they had made their decision and their move.

Meanwhile, the fourteen blacks took their "civil rights" case to court, and eventually the courts decided against their plea. Almost immediately Eaton changed his rule about demonstrations; student athletes could demonstrate like everyone else, he said, although not during "team activities." Quietly, Carlson received permission from the board to invite the suspended athletes to return to campus to continue their studies under non-athletic scholarships — nine of them applied for financial aid during spring semester 1970, and seven actually enrolled in classes. A few of the players made professional football teams.

The situation remained tense, on and off-campus. Rumors reached the president that busloads of student radicals were preparing to arrive from Denver to support the Black Student Alliance in a massive protest. In February 1970, eighty people (mostly white) attended a rally sponsored by the Black Student Alliance before the Brigham Young basketball game. Although the leaders had agreed not to demonstrate during the game and black players never threatened to withdraw, highway patrolmen were brought to supplement the police force in the fieldhouse that evening. Sitting together, protestors ended by turning their backs during the singing of the national anthem and clenching their fists when BYU players were introduced. That spring, three black track athletes withdrew from the team.

In 1970, the football game with BYU was played at Provo, but angers flared in February 1971 during the basketball game between the two teams on the Wyoming campus. Again the Black Student Alliance sponsored a pre-game rally, and at the game police stopped marchers moving toward a "head-on collision" while spectators booed both sides. The confrontation came close to violence. Meanwhile, the besieged Western Athletic Conference devised all kinds of plans to cope with similar protests on many campuses. The addition of several blacks to the BYU team did not materially improve the situation.

In spite of Eaton's recruiting efforts and sometime assistance from black players, the spirit went out of the team, and the 1970 football season (one victory and nine losses) crumbled under the coach's feet. The team was depressed, and the whites and blacks felt alienated from each other.

It has hurt our ball team definitely. There were some excellent football players in the group. Our problems of depth right now are relegated [sic] back to that incident,

a frustrated coach reported. At the end of the 1970 season, Eaton was kicked upstairs into athletic administration, a position he left a year later.

Locally, as well as nationally, minority mistreatment continued to be a sore point and a source of discontent. In the growing consciousness of discrimination, equal education for minority groups seemed to provide a solution to what had been a national pattern of abuse. Anxious to avoid trouble and to play fair, the Carlson administration proposed a series of remedies to campus complaints. Recruitment of minorities to the University continued through a broad-based "special services" committee on educational programs and student life, although reports from the committee indicated that it was not always successful. The group tended to speak in terms of cultural activism, a concept that met with blank faces among high school students and hostility among high school administrators, who believed that the recruiters' remarks were "of a nature as to create dissatisfaction, discontent, and resentment on the part of our Mexican students." Pressed to denounce Eaton's treatment of "the Black 14," one important member of the committee — the president of Eastern Wyoming College — resigned because he believed his

continued presence on the committee could result in nothing beneficial, and indeed would most likely present a barrier to the establishment of the kind of climate which is going to be necessary if the committee is to function.

In addition to minority recruitment, efforts were made to assure that Chicanos, native Americans, and blacks might be assimilated more happily into campus life. W. Harry Sharp, guidance counselor and later dean of students, watched carefully over minority problems on campus, and the files contain his many sensitive and provocative reports. In 1971, Sharp conducted a series of interviews with minority students, probing their relationships with whites as well as with each other — for Chicanos, blacks, and native Americans resented being lumped together without distinction. On one occasion, Sharp encouraged and participated actively in a Chicano conference, sponsored by the Mexican-American student organization. His conclusions from the discussions were that everyone believed good intentions emanated from the administration but that most Chicano students wanted "more."

More seems to be in the academic area, particularly ethnic studies. I think what they are saying is more courses on the Mexican American culture taught by Mexican Americans.

When in the fall of the same year Sharp brought a number of native American students and their parents to campus, he reported that they felt like "a kind of museum piece — being put on public display" and that other minority groups regarded the special occasion as an example of favoritism.

To one complaint, faculty had a response, and during these years ethnic courses and programs were established on several levels. The English department began offering a course on Chicanos in the American Southwest. The arts and sciences college set up a minor option in minority studies. A program of special classes for blacks, native Americans, and Chicanos was established with the aid of Professors David Edmunds (history) and Anne Slater (anthropology).

Meanwhile, the Wyoming Union dedicated a special room to an Ethnic Culture Media Center. After considerable pressure from all sides, including an appearance before the board of James Tyler from the Black Student Alliance, the administration (through an advisory committee on minority concerns) hired a half-time coordinator for minority studies. Great difficulties in staffing plagued this office, as those of Upward Bound and Student Educational Opportunity, and a good many bitter words were exchanged. One particular problem centered around employment of whites in positions concerning minority problems, and in 1973 considerable complaint arose when a white was sent as director of the teacher corps to the Shoshone and Arapahoe area without what minority students regarded as proper consultation — although both tribal councils had approved the appointment.

Administrative efforts could not control all conflicts, and problems continued on many levels. In the fall of 1969, a group of native Americans formed the organization Keepers of the Fire with the purpose (its founders told trustees) of helping Indians make the difficult transition through "culture-shock" to campus life. The following spring a long-term Hispanic students' organization changed its name and began to take a more active role in student concerns. The Chicano drop-out rate at Wyoming was second only to that of native Americans, and a leader of the new organization, in a guest editorial in the student newspaper, contended his people were the "niggers of Wyoming." The Black Student Alliance continued to function vigorously. In 1970, Willie Black resigned his position as chancellor to become an instructor in mathematics. He continued to speak out on both racial problems and the Vietnam war; the *Branding Iron* quoted him as contending in a student meeting that

> *historically every time America has involved herself in conflict abroad, she has seen fit to make black Americans full Americans on the battle front.*

Black's position in the BSA was inherited by Mel Hamilton, one of the fourteen athletes who had returned to the University to complete his studies. Hamilton was understandably bitter about many administrative policies.

> *We're now in a stage where they tolerate and pacify us, so there will be no more black 14 incidents. They'll do anything to keep us pacified.*

When in 1971 the BSA voted to recommend the wearing of armbands during the BYU game, Hamilton bitterly protested the measure as not strong enough.

> *These times call for more radical action. . . . If it is up to me after all avenues have been exhausted as they have been, I will go to the battleground: meaning violence if necessary, and in particular violence. I feel this is the only way we are going to get some positive commitments. . . . I have always been a peaceful activist, but the time has come when radical action is necessary.*

Blacks and Chicanos in particular were concerned about discrimination in housing. Hamilton's suit against a Laramie landlord went to court, and when Judge Ewing T. Kerr decided in favor of the landowner, the *Branding Iron,* BSA, and the Chicano Student Coalition joined in criticism. "Wyoming is presently harder to live in than Mississippi or Alabama," Hamilton told the student newspaper in 1972. Fraternities and sororities were subject to specific criticism, and Hamilton was certain that although they had obediently stricken discrimination clauses from their charters, the Greeks "still make it almost impossible for a black man to join." In a special series of articles, the *Branding Iron* interviewed two Chicano students who found Wyoming and Laramie discriminating especially against Mexican-Americans.

> *I have traveled through several states, but in this state I have encountered a subtle kind of discrimination that's hard to deal with,*

said one, and another added,

> *This is the first place I've seen where there is a real "other side of the tracks" where the minorities live. I couldn't believe such a separated minority still exists.*

In 1971, one dormitory was reported split into racial groups and power struggles. Harry Sharp stood his grounds, however: When several sets of white Wyoming parents were upset because their daughters drew black roommates, Sharp refused to make a change on racial grounds, and indeed, one of the women involved refused to move. In 1970, a Chicano Laramie resident apparently filed a complaint against the University for its employment practices. In response to controversies over housing, employment, and educational philosophies, a sociology professor organized a campus branch of the American Civil Liberties Union in 1972.

In the 1973-74 files, categorized under minority concerns, is a compelling list of student angers and complaints, perhaps compiled by the advisory committee working on minority problems. Angers surface frighteningly in these brief statements, and complaints range from whites teaching black history to the small number of minority students enrolled on campus. Solutions, too, ran the gamut: from "input in discussions that concern us" to "less talk and more action" — throwing rocks, and even the suggestion that militant minorities "kill a few."

The closest the campus came to violence, however, lay not so much in the threats of minority activists as in the protest against the fighting of a long-enduring and unpopular Vietnam war. Here, too, Wyoming students were scarcely in the forefront of dissent, but the campus had seen its share of "peace" demonstrations, meetings, and organizations. Students who were "peacenik" on principle joined with those who were convinced the country was fighting without hope or justification in a situation where victory seemed ever more remote. Near-violence came to campus in May 1970, shortly after President Richard Nixon committed the United States to fight in Cambodia and less than seven months after the episode of the fourteen black athletes.

CHAPTER ELEVEN

The particular occasion for student protest was the slaying of four Kent State students by national guardsmen during confrontations on that university's campus. Early in the morning of May 5, a group of Wyoming students presented petitions with approximately 600 signatures to the University administration. The petition read:

We, the undersigned, hereby request that the University of Wyoming lower the flag to half-mast in a gesture of sorrow and sympathy for those who recently lost their lives in the Kent State tragedy. This flag shall fly at half-mast until the funerals of all four victims. We also ask that classes be dismissed on Thursday [May 7] so that all may reflect on what has happened and on what can be done to prevent such a tragedy from occurring here.

In the absence of Carlson, who was in Denver with his seriously ailing son, the petition was received by Elliott Hays. Hays agreed to convey the administration's answer by noon (before which time another 660 signatures were presented), and sensing disaster, called together administrators, the deans of the colleges, the Faculty Senate's executive committee, and the president of the ASUW. Carlson was contacted and so, by telephone, were trustees, including the governor. Deans (not unanimously) and the Faculty Senate executive committee (strongly) urged acceptance of both requests. Trustees agreed only to one of them.

At noon, when a group of perhaps 500 students assembled at the flagpole and marched to the administration building, Geraud was ready with the administration's answer: willingness to cancel Thursday classes (for a "day of contemplation and reflection on the issues involved" at Kent State) but rejection of the petition to lower the flag in mourning. Geraud's statement read:

It is our responsibility to conform to the protocol of the American flag. A request to lower the flat to half-mast falls outside the jurisdiction of the Board of Trustees and the administration of the University of Wyoming.

Presuming the statement to mean that the governor had jurisdiction over flag protocol, demonstrators dispatched six students to Cheyenne to consult with Hathaway in person.

Meanwhile, Carlson had begun a rapid trip back from Denver. On his way, he checked with Hays and other administrators by telephone, and on hearing from them that they were uncertain the demonstration could be handled, the president called the governor and reported that the situation was serious. President and governor agreed that additional police should be called in, but decided on the highway patrol rather than the National Guard because of the militant reputation of the latter.

By noon Laramie police had joined those from campus around the flagpole. A student who attempted to climb it to lower the flag to half-mast was arrested and paid a fine for breach of the peace. Geraud's appearance was unhappy, for his insistence that only Nixon could order the flag lowered was inaccurate, and his statements about the police presence were regarded as a threat. The highway patrolmen arrived on a tense scene. In early afternoon, after much debate on flag protocol, demonstrators opted to adjourn to the administration building for further interviews with officials, but there they found the police in occupation and the building closed to faculty and students, except for a few who gained entrance for routine purposes, such as paying bills. Elliott Hays met the protestors at the door. By now placards attacking the "pigs" and the ROTC were in evidence; a black flag had been hoisted on an improvised pole; and several cars (including one from the campus police) had been damaged by the crowd. Although no injuries were inflicted, one witness watched from a nearby building as three students raced to lower a small flag flying outside the post office building; the students were pursued by uniformed police, armed with billy clubs, and they pulled off the scene.

When Carlson returned to Laramie, he found a crowd of belligerent protestors circling Old Main. Trustees and administrators had set up headquarters across the mall in the agriculture building, and the president joined them there. This general staff maintained close touch with Bob Archuleta, president of the student body, and with the governor. Whether at Carlson's request or at Hathaway's suggestion, 99 members of the National Guard were quietly mobilized for potential service; they were located at the armory, well away from the center of campus but within minutes should they be called upon. From time to time in the late afternoon, Geraud or Elliott Hays (whose position as chief financial officer caused him to be in charge of campus security) approached the crowd, speaking on bullhorns or informally face to face. Carlson remained indoors; he was later accused of cowardice and of "hiding out."

By late afternoon, word came from the governor's office that Hathaway was unwilling to order the flag lowered. As Carlson acknowledged later, the administration had trapped itself, caught, he said, between radical students and conservative public. The situation was actually saved when police lowered the flag at 5 p.m. The Laramie police chief told the crowd it could do what it wished until the flag was raised again the following morning. What demonstrators did was raise an American flag and a black flag of mourning to half-mast position and then illuminate both with a spotlight to maintain proper night-flying protocol. The troopers withdrew.

Later a mix-up in communications almost led to violence. By 10 p.m., demonstrators had settled in; they were milling around the flagpole or sitting on blankets on the grass. Administrators, including Carlson, had left their campus post and retired to Hays' home, where they planned for morning and prepared to wait out the night. However, the governor, having heard garbled reports from frightened spectators in the area, opted to order highway patrolmen back to campus, this time with several army trucks, a hook and ladder, and additional police. Whether on command or at his own initiative, the ranking officer of the guard used his bullhorn to demand that the black flag be lowered, under threat of immediate violence. The ultimatum was issued in terms of minutes and countdown began. Carlson heard in time; to Hathaway he argued for the troopers' immediate withdrawal. A crisis was barely averted as Hathaway agreed.

Thereafter, overnight, about 200 people sang songs, played frisbee, kept vigil, and slept until dawn. At 6 a.m. a janitor appeared, escorted by police and tense administrators. Hays informed the crowd that the black flag must now be lowered and the stars and stripes returned to full mast. Demonstrators made a path as the janitor lowered the students' flags and raised the ordinary banners — state and U.S. — to the top of the flagpole. Someone read a statement.

In accordance with this philosophy of non-violence we have cleared a corridor for the officials of Wyoming to raise the flag of our Country. However, we feel that in accordance with

the action of the Administration, and in due respect to and tribute for the lives and families of the students who died at Kent State, the flag of the United States of America, the flag of the State of Wyoming, and a black flag of mourning [should] be flown at half mast. . . . We sincerely wish that the people of Wyoming, the Administration, and the Governor of Wyoming will also reflect this conscience. But none of us gathered here wish to see any form of violence.

As it turned out the Wyoming flag hung upside down, but nobody cared. With the flag at full mast, the demonstrators sang the national anthem and then dispersed. "Neatest thing I ever saw in my whole life," Carlson said later. "That's the end of the incident. One of the most touching things I ever saw."

The incident was over, but repercussions echoed on. During the flagpole episode, the ASUW senate had met late into the night, and although senators voted their sympathy for the Kent State students, they refused to pass resolutions condemning the Vietnam war and the invasion of Cambodia. The student body as a whole — answering questions on a poll — followed suit.

The stance of the ASUW caused radical demonstrators to form an alternative "Government in Exile," which took over the newssheet *Free Lunch;* issued proclamations and reports; and planned various events, often in coordination with other existing peace groups. To Hathaway, the Government in Exile wrote to "express dismay" over the presence of armed highway patrolmen on campus during the flagpole episode.

We feel that the action on your part was completely unnecessary and unjustifiable. We realize that there were communication problems between your officials and the campus. Nevertheless, you should have shown more foresight in obtaining the correct information before issuing your orders. . . .The mere presence of the state police aggravated the situation and caused many hard feelings. Unarmed, nonviolent students should not be intimidated by the presence of shotgun carrying, billy club toting policemen.

In a sheet entitled *Flagpole,* the Government in Exile attacked the rival ASUW and insisted on its own legitimacy.

Militancy does not imply violence. It does imply committed and aggressive action. Militancy is the backbone of the Government in Exile. . . .

Although the group's newspaper had accused Carlson of "hiding out" and called for his resignation, they were quite taken by the president in a meeting that they reported was a "fantastic success," and they thanked Carlson profusely for talking with them. Nevertheless, at a rally outside the dormitories on May 12, radical students passed a resolution censuring the administration for its actions.

Most alarming was the possibility of violence on Governor's Day, when the governor conducted an annual review of ROTC units on campus. Governor's Day had been planned for May 14, a week after the flagpole incident, as an ordinary part of commencement exercises. The Government in Exile announced a "nonviolent, nondestructive demonstration and student strike" to "protest America's militaristic spirit," but its negotiations with police and officials left no doubt that violence remained a possibility, especially when a counter-demonstration was organized by more conservative student groups.

As it turned out, the demonstrations passed without incident. But that afternoon Hathaway agreed to a public meeting in a campus auditorium in order to answer questions and to hear the students out. About 1,000 individuals — primarily hostile — showed up to hear him and Carlson questioned (sometimes belligerently) by a panel of concerned faculty and students. Carlson and Hatahway comported themselves with dignity under fire, and a few of the sore points — including the return of highway patrolmen to the flagpole during the evening of the demonstration — were actually explained. Panelists disagreed as violently with each other as with administrators on points like the cause of violence and the necessity for militant behavior.

Student field expedition, c. 1970

After the fact, Carlson and the board settled down to evaluate what they had done. Clearly, everything had not gone as smoothly as might be desired. The gap in communication that had ended in the governor's sending highway patrolmen back to campus with a threat of violent action had ended with no harm done, but events almost took a more drastic turn. There was uncertainty about where final authority lay. The board believed that the governor had been too much involved in the entire situation, and indeed that was Hathaway's opinion too. Trustees believed that Carlson should have been more prominent on the scene to announce decisions; perhaps the ASUW senate might have been called on for support, although the president, Bob Archuleta, was constantly in touch.

Hathaway shortly addressed a letter to Carlson outlining procedures for calling on the state highway patrol and in dire emergency the National Guard to aid police should a situation demand their presence. Clearly, the governor wanted Carlson in the future to take full responsibility for making the decisions. In any case, Hathaway ruled that the highway patrol would carry "regular" accessories, such as riot sticks and loaded sidearms. The National Guard, he said, would carry unloaded rifles with bayonets but no live ammunition. After a discussion with the president of the board and three other trustees following the Governor's Day demonstration, Carlson was authorized to call on the governor for aid (either highway patrol or National Guard) as he saw fit. But in the face of what must have been Hathaway's irritation, all agreed

not to confront the Governor with problems that we, the Board, should be assuming. Please do not misconstrue this to mean that we must not be in constant contact with the Governor on anything that he so wishes.

The board further responded by appropriating $12,000 to recruit, train, and equip an "auxiliary" police force of sixteen persons from the physical plant and maintenance division, to be paid for any extra hours of service; the force, it decided, would be uniformed but not armed. New working papers on civil disturbance and riot plans ran to even more complicated pages than before. In spring of 1971, perhaps anticipating more trouble during the next ROTC review, trustees invited the state attorney general to meet with them regarding legal action that might be taken against rioters and demonstrators, should violence break out. Meanwhile the Faculty Senate adopted a special resolution on professionalism in and out of the classroom, exhorting faculty to make a clear distinction between their roles as professors and private citizens, to support codes of ethics, exercise proper decorum, proceed by the principles of due process, and take care to assign grades and limit course content according to recognized academic standards.

Outbreaks of political and social protest in the early 1970s were accompanied by many less dramatic but almost equally important student demands, complaints, and achievements in campus life. Although disagreements existed, the president made an effort to consider what the students wanted. Indeed in 1969, with trustees' support, the legislature voted ex-officio status on the board to the president of ASUW. By 1971, in accordance with faculty and administrative rulings, students were serving on many university and academic committees, including those for academic standards, athletics, campus planning, the library, and others. The fact that such channels were open was credited later with having saved the situation from total disintegration.

Still, radical students were not always totally victorious, and the administration often advanced compromise plans. It was often difficult for trustees to accept completely the idea that University students were free adults with the rights and responsibilities of individuals living in any community situation. Such a concept lay at the basis of the "Bill of Student Rights," first devised in 1968 as a statement of constitutional guarantees. The original document focused almost exclusively on freedom from constraints.

Free inquiry and free expression governed by responsible freedom are essential attributes of the community of scholars. As members of that community every student is guaranteed those rights and privileges guaranteed to every United States citizen by the Bill of Rights and related amendments of the Constitution of the United States of America. In his independent search for truth and learning, every student is guaranteed certain other rights and privileges unique to the academic community.

CHAPTER ELEVEN

In May 1969, Geraud, as counsel for the trustees and presidential assistant for student affairs, reviewed the bill critically for trustees, who interviewed the student initiators and set up a committee composed of students, trustees, faculty members, and administrators to iron things out. After a full year's work, Carlson brought to the board a long series of regulations about students as proposed by Geraud; the "Principles of Student Life: Rights and Responsibilities" incorporated some of the original bill in amended form. Other sections provided for the authority of University officers, principles of student conduct, the appointment of a special magistrate for hearings on discipline, and a board of student appeals — the latter an important addendum to regulations, in that it provided for student appeal of any grade which the student believed unfair.

Although the appeals board had the support of the ASUW (and the Faculty Senate), the "code of conduct" included in Geraud's regulations was not presented for student approval, much to the ASUW senate's annoyance. Geraud was no favorite of the students. They disliked his ruling that "married women shall be accorded the same residence status [for tuition purposes] as their husbands;" the University's policy on legal room searches; and his frequent unavailability because of many other assignments he was handling for administration and trustees. The results had not been what the radical students wanted, but the ASUW gained a clear statement of procedure in terms of disciplinary actions and unfair grades.

Another major campus gripe of the early 1970s centered around restrictive dormitory regulations, as imposed more severely on females than on males. As students became "women and men" rather than "girls and boys," the University's role in *loco parentis* was ever more irritating to them. Men who were regarded as able to serve in the armed forces resented being told where they must live and when they should come home. In 1966, coeds ardently disliked the dean of women's

nightly room checks designed to keep them from "staying out all night or sneaking out." That same spring, the administration announced — apparently in error — that rules required all unmarried undergraduates to live in the dormitories. Assemblies, loud speakers, and petitions signed by 2,000 students marked a protest until the regulation was officially withdrawn. A May 1967, editorial in the *Branding Iron* took a strong swipe at "UW's Babysitters."

Students don't feel that some of their tuition should go to pay babysitters in the administrative offices, someone who makes sure they are punished for being late, someone who sets down a list of prescribed rules of dress for every phase of campus living and someone who forces them to live in a dormitory. . . . Until recently, students have tended to accept all of the rules and regulations as inevitable and have simply learned to live with them. But when a student is not allowed to attend a cafeteria to eat the meal he has already paid for because he is "improperly attired," he is no longer willing to take the Old Main policies lightly.

Actually, "Old Main" was more sympathetic to the students than they realized, for Carlson frequently took their side. The protest years saw regulations gradually relaxed, more cautiously by the deans of men and women than the president himself might have desired. In the fall of 1968, the dean of women responded to an ASUW resolution by permitting most women to stay out later, but she nevertheless clamped down more severely on freshman girls. In spring semester 1969, one of the dormitories — "inching," as the *Branding Iron* put it, toward freedom — allowed men residents twelve hours per month for "open house" visiting, during which friends of either sex might be entertained anywhere in the dorm. By the end of that semester, on Carlson's insistence to trustees, all students above the freshman level were permitted to live off-campus if they so desired, and dormitory "visiting hours" were increased. Subsequent pressure from individual students; the Residence Hall Association Council; the ASUW; and above all the *Branding Iron* — always with Carlson's sympathy — led to a new design in housing by the early 1970s — including unlimited visiting hours, male and female floors or sections in given dormitories, and a list of options for dormitory living from which parents and students might choose.

227

Liberalization of campus living regulations frequently evoked protest from students' parents, and Carlson found himself defending the policy on many occasions. In a sense, the president was caught again (as in the flagpole incident) between conservative Wyoming parents and liberated Wyoming students. One young woman's parents wrote the president that they would hold him "personally responsible" if anything bad happened to her. On one occasion state Senator L. W. "Dick" Jones referred to the University's housing arrangements as a "free love policy" comparable with condoning prostitution. The UW president stood his ground. He and Mrs. Carlson even made a hit with students by spending a night in the dorms in November 1973.

Of less immediate concern to students, but uppermost in the minds of trustees, was the fact that after 1966 dormitory space was remaining empty. In constructing student housing during the early 1960s, the administration had anticipated neither the leveling off of enrollment — the University was not much larger in 1973 than it was in 1968 — nor the growing desire of students to live in off-campus accommodations. The trend was national, and on many campuses dormitories were converted to other uses. But Wyoming had a particular problem because the income from living and eating facilities had been pledged to the retirement of construction bonds and payment of interest thereon. Empty dorms set the carefully-calculated financial arrangements in jeopardy. As early as 1966, trustees were forced to close Wyo hall because of nearly 600 vacancies in the men's dormitories. In 1970, Knight hall cafeteria was shut down, and plans were made to vacate both Knight and Ross dormitories in favor of newer buildings farther from the center of campus. In fall semester 1973, Crane-Hill cafeteria was closed, leaving only Washakie Center functioning as a dormitory food service. In 1971, the *Branding Iron* reported 800 dormitory rooms empty, and only through reestablishing many of them as singles did the University pull through at eighty percent occupancy in 1971-72. Even married student housing — generally oversubscribed — became a problem by 1973. With financial obligations uppermost in their minds, trustees could only hope to find money for bond payments from other sources (legislative appropriations, refunding of bonds) and at the same time, try to make dormitory life as attractive as possible.

Other acknowledgements of adulthood took time, energy, and patience. After 1976, beer was served at certain specified hours in the Union, but the issue had demanded a decision from students, trustees, legislature, and Laramie city council in turn; students had actually begun their agitation for beer at least ten years before. Issues of censorship of the student newspaper were even more difficult to resolve, since students, who were touchy about "administrative control," were at natural odds with trustees and administrators, who were not only the perennial brunt of *Branding Iron* editorials but also fearful of libel suits. In 1971, a crisis arose over the publication in the *Branding Iron* of an abortion referral notice. Threatened with legal action by a leader of the county Right to Life committee, the off-campus printer of the student newspaper refused to set the material. Geraud's citation of the state's anti-abortion statute called forth rallies, meetings, and debates, but eventually the issue faded. At about the same time, the decision by the Public Exercises Committee not to bring the musical *Hair* to campus (on the grounds that it had "undesirable features" and was too "provocative") raised a mild controversy.

More publicity, and indeed a threatened law suit, resulted from Carlson's cancellation of an "erotic film festival" to be presented in the Union in January 1974. Approved by the University Activities Council by a 4-1 vote, the showing was opposed by the Union's director as "stag and porno." Carlson's cancellation was based on Wyoming obscenity laws. The *Branding Iron* — always more radical than the student government — cried "Coitus Interruptus." As so frequently happened, the president's action was supported by at least 37 letters from parents and concerned citizens, some of which were actually in the form of petitions signed by a number of individuals. The ASUW called in a lawyer from the American Civil Liberties Union to defend the students' position, but the matter was settled out of court. The compromise policy on entertainment that was eventually reached defined obscenity; forbade students to book any entertainment that was blatantly obscene; and forbade the administration to cancel any potentially obscene showing except through court order. At just about this time, students petitioned for, and the trustees reluctantly agreed to, hiring a special half-time attorney for individual student counseling. The agreement made it clear that the attorney could not represent student organizations nor individuals if the University and its administration were interested parties.

Athletics came in for its share of criticism and problems. Here, too, the administration faced the gulf between state and Alumni Association — always pressing for a strong program — and campus radicals, who sought "de-emphasis" of athletics in favor of academic programs. Athletics for a quarter of a century profited from the leadership of "Red" Jacoby, who built a strong, smoothly-functioning, and frequently independent division that gained great respect from trustees and alumni. True, Fey as president returned the department of physical education to the education college on the grounds that all academic departments should have an academic base. Thereafter, Jacoby's influence over that department was lessened — at one time, he had urged and achieved the dismissal of a department head on grounds of conflict in academic philosophy. Conflicts occasionally arose, such as that in 1966, when the physical education department head vigorously protested the grading system of two of his instructors (the basketball coach, who taught the "Theory and Practice of Basketball," and the trainer, who taught "Prevention and Care of Athletic Injuries") on the grounds that awarding 210 "A's" compared to only three other grades seemed academically unjustifiable. Fey also put an end to a system of running athletic concessions whereby a number of faculty and staff members made money on the side. Other problems, such as the awarding of contracts to broadcast and televise University games, were a constant source of agony for Jacoby and board alike. In 1969, Carlson was pressured (against Jacoby's advice, for Jacoby was an old hand and a wise one) into permitting the formation of a Cowboy Joe Club, which aided in raising money for athletic facilities and programs but also represented an ultra-athletic and sometimes pugnacious faction.

"Jocks" and "cowboys" were equal targets for the new campus radicals. As early as December 1965, a group of students and faculty took to trustees a petition with almost 150 signatures requesting that the University resign its membership in the Western Athletic Conference, perhaps joining the smaller Big Sky Conference instead —

thereby permitting the channeling of current athletic funds into faculty salaries, library resources, and other academic needs. The "undue emphasis on athletics," the petition read, "upsets the desirable balance between the athletic and the academic purposes of a university." In 1970, the North Central Association of Colleges and Secondary Schools suggested in its accreditation report that trustees consider the probable overemphasis of athletics in campus budget and functions. In 1970-71, the year after "the Black 14" incident, when Jacoby found his budget cut by the legislature and sought to reduce minor sports without harming the football or basketball programs, the ASUW senate vigorously resented the elimination of soccer and tennis. That same year the senate refused to continue funding women's athletics, on the grounds that the University as a whole, and the athletic division in particular, should bear the costs of the program, just as they paid the price for men's sports.

An English graduate assistant had some angry suggestions about Wyoming's football program.

I suggest that the people of Wyoming, and the University administration, openly acknowledge what we all know to be true — that most college football is a thinly veiled professional enterprise. I suggest that football (and perhaps all major intercollegiate athletic programs) be taken out of the University program and put under a specifically designated (independent of the University) board of managers. I suggest that, if such a new program uses University facilities, it should pay rent to the University to the full amount of the cost of upkeep and capital expansion. . . . I suggest that a strong program of intermural (and/or intramural) sports would provide an adequate training ground for the coaches and Physical Education majors in the educational field as well as for those young people who play for the enjoyment of the sport and not as a profession. . . .

Although his ideas were rejected by an ASUW committee, protests about the supremacy of athletics over academics were printed in the *Branding Iron* throughout Carlson's administration and later.

By the mid-1970s, everything was winding down. For one thing, football and basketball programs had slowed to a crawl. Although Wyoming had been the first Western Athletic Conference team to win both basketball and football crowns in the same academic year (1966-67), the following seasons (perhaps because of "the Black 14" episode) were lacklustre indeed. The football coach was released in 1974-75 and the basketball coach in 1976. Over considerable protest by his supporters, Jacoby (aged 65) was retired by trustees in 1973. Frantic "cowboys" were elated with Coach Fred Akers, whose teams backed into the WAC championship in 1976 with an 8-4 record, but that proved a momentary flash in the pan. The conviction of alumni that the athletic program would be enhanced by better facilities — a large, domed stadium or a bigger basketball pavilion — led to major construction in the late 1970s, but that is another story.

Meanwhile, a few outbreaks of discontent haunted the early 1970s like echoes of the troubles of 1969. In 1972, the student newspaper still reported on boycotts, rallies, parades, and demonstrations. Once, in its words, tensions ran high. On one occasion, minority students charged campus police with using racially insulting epithets in a verbal confrontation at a student meeting.

But on the whole, the militant movement had passed its peak. The familiar names of the young rebels gradually disappeared from the *Branding Iron's* articles. The spate of underground newspapers and ad hoc student organizations of the early 1970s gave way to a willingness on the part of most students to operate through regular channels, like ASUW and its representatives on the board of trustees or various campus committees. Indeed, in 1975, Carlson made a special effort to increase routine contact with the student body president, who responded positively to the suggestion.

That fall, sororities reported a new interest in membership, and one reporter called the fraternity enrollment a "bumper crop for Greeks." In March 1974, campus was diverted by seven nude sprinters who "streaked" sorority row, and the following day a considerable crowd of men in the same condition made a similar dash. With few victories evoking little interest, the campaign to de-emphasize major athletics slowed and languished. The *Branding Iron* remained a campus gadfly, but by the mid-1970s it was characterizing students as "content" and "passive." Students still voiced complaints, but they were primarily focused on strictly local concerns. The "frustrated" students who sought to found a "pro-student league" in 1979 listed among their complaints the parking problem, the lack of enough day care for their children, and an irritating fence that had been constructed around the football practice field.

In the 1970-71 president's file labeled for Patrick Quealy, longtime trustee, is a sensitive report in the form of notes and comments on student concerns. Most students, the report reads, "have never been more aware and more sincerely dedicated to making this country and each individual life better."

> *Students feel a personal commitment and want a piece of the action. They are convinced that they can contribute immensely to the solutions to society's many problems. They are willing to take on many things and explore many areas that in the past have been so called "sacred cows" not open to review. I think this is great although they will make mistakes, will be overly impatient, but in the final analysis I strongly feel that things in general because of this generation of the probing, uncompromising student, will be far superior than today.*

The problems the students tackled — those of war, waste of resources, racial, economic and social injustices — were not confined to one state or one country but were major social issues in all societies. Change in education comes slowly, and patience is hard to find in youth, but a balance must somehow be struck peacefully. The memo suggests that University of Wyoming students were reacting like students all over the country. But certain special elements — the nature of student government, access to president, faculty, and trustees, the emphasis on undergraduate teaching, and in general the state's and the University's small size and physical isolation — came to Wyoming's aid, according to this document. The writer — like Carlson — saw the University as lucky and lauded both students and administration for their ability to avoid violent, disastrous confrontation.

Students of the 1960s across the country had protested both peacefully and violently for causes that they found vital and just. That these same causes were important to Wyoming students serves to demonstrate thoughtfulness, maturity, and involvement. That violence and destruction were avoided is to the University's credit. To her credit, too, stands the fact that at a time of distress, she did not remain isolated from the rest of the world.

COMMENCEMENT

omecoming may belong to the alumni, but that special weekend in spring is set aside strictly for celebration of commencement and its rituals. During the 95 years between 1887 and 1984, 52,773 students have marched across the stage to accept their diplomas (or replicas thereof).

The University's first commencement, according to Wilson O. Clough, took place in 1891. Two men received diplomas, but the ceremonies themselves lasted for three or four days. They included contests in oratory and declamation; baccalaureate exercises with a

Graduating class, 1889

sermon on "Essentials of Character," delivered by the new University president; the president's inauguration which followed; addresses by both graduates; and a speech by Senator Clarence D. Clark. Ceremonies then, and through 1924, were held in the Old Main auditorium.

University presidents gave the first ten baccalaureate addresses. Governors and senators were frequently invited to present the main commencement speeches. In 1912, Aven Nelson and Justice Soule both spoke to the graduates. In later years, commencement addresses were given by several University presidents who had moved elsewhere to make national reputations for themselves.

Until 1898, seniors (all of whom were required to present orations) carried flowers, but thereafter caps and gowns became regulation commencement wear, with the exception of a few years after

231

1911. Flowers, reported the Laramie *Republican* of May 5, 1897, were "not becoming the dignity of University graduates." Dignity, however, was not always uppermost in the seniors' minds. In 1911, the alumni play contained a flower dance, in which "five little tots . . . led by a dainty baby," all wearing pink and green dresses and large hats, ended their presentation with the shouting of a college cheer: "Rah! Rah! Rah! Zip! Boom! Zee! Let 'er go! Let 'er go! Varsity!," thus (as the *Boomerang* reported) "bringing down the house." That year (before football homecoming became a tradition) the five-day program included music recitals; baccalaureate ceremonies; the Cadet Ball; the alumni play; an alumni banquet with a riotous program to follow (one young lady sang a solo and a "mischievous little encore"); the commencement program itself; and any number of private celebrations, parties, and teas.

Faculty, Elmer Smiley administration, c. 1902

Later, commencements were held in the little theater, the half-acre gym, the arts and sciences auditorium, the fieldhouse, and (currently) the arena-auditorium. Until 1912, all diplomas were signed by the entire faculty, and even thereafter all the faculty signed pages that were attached. After 1928, faculty delegated the signing to president and the appropriate dean.

One special feature was initiated in 1921, when the University first granted an honorary degree. At a routine faculty meeting that spring in what R. E. McWhinnie has termed an "academic coup d'etat," Grace Raymond Hebard with the aid of June Downey proposed that the LL.D. degree be bestowed on Carrie Chapman Catt, a leading advocate of women's suffrage. "The Downey charm and expertise" persuaded the faculty to vote positively although not unanimously for the "Hebard brainchild," and Catt not only duly received her honor but made the baccalaureate address as well.

After 1932, the granting of honorary degrees became an accepted procedure, although the number awarded was irregular and in some years (1980-83) no honorary degrees were given. Thirteen Wyoming governors or acting governors have been honored, including Nellie Tayloe Ross, the nation's first woman governor. By 1984, 33 recipients (in addition to some of the governors) were University graduates; several were one-time presidents; and a number were faculty members, including Hebard, Aven Nelson, Justus Soule, Frank Trelease, Wilson Clough, J. David Love, William T. Mulloy, William G. Solheim, T. A. "Al" Larson, and Donald L. Blackstone.

Perhaps the most widely known of the luminaries received his degree in 1964; he was well-known entertainer Bob Hope, LL.D.

Chapter Twelve

The Search for Excellence
1964-1978

hese years at the University of Wyoming were years in which the institution focused on a new drive for research achievements and scholarly reputation. Academically, they were good years. Although enrollment increased only slowly, faculty was enhanced by the addition of vigorous young scholars. Programs in many areas received national recognition for research. The state of Wyoming was prospering with the energy crises, and the University budget prospered with it, permitting the hiring of faculty already famous in their fields, the acquisition of expensive research and classroom equipment, and the building of facilities that attracted graduate students and scholars. Publication and performance brought new prominence to faculty; this recognition was rewarding in spite of hard work and tough competition. In this rapid expansion, many problems developed, but the sum of academic achievements nevertheless rose to new heights.

"As an educational institution," said John T. Fey in his inaugural address as president in December 1964,

a university must devote its primary efforts toward the search for truth and knowledge. . . . Without a dedication to learning as well as to knowledge, to quality as well as to quantity, to understanding as well as to skill, and to creativity as well as to imitation there can be no true education.

Although Fey's definition of academic excellence laid classical emphasis on the breadth of the educational process, the president in his brief tenure did not fail to call for original research, both in its local aspect of service to the state and in its universal cast as discloser of new and essential knowledge. Even though Carlson's ideas were differently stated, he, too, sought to achieve excellence and to enhance the University's national reputation. Looking back on his first year on campus, Carlson wrote that he felt a mandate to generate University research where other presidents had been more committed to buildings or athletics.

When I first came here in September of 1967 as president-elect, I had the opportunity to look over the university for four months before I actually took over as the president on January 1st. I spent two or three days a week both in the university and around the state trying to assess what the people wanted. It was fairly evident that people wanted to develop what we had into a great university.

Carlson wanted, he said more than once, to "put Wyoming on the map academically." This president was sure that a university's greatness depended on the national reputation of its faculty for scholarship, performance, and research. Leaving office in 1978, he said he believed that the University had achieved in large measure the aims he set.

The reputation of the university or of a degree is really reflecting the reputation of the faculty. One of the greatest emphases we placed during this time was to bring in top people. I think if you go through those people who joined the university since 1967, we have in fact done that in an almost unbelievable way. We can go through department after department that have developed into truly outstanding programs, many of them national and some international. That's what makes a university.

Whether Carlson was right or wrong, the years from 1964 to 1978 were not easy years on campus. In a pattern set at institutions across the country, academic goals were changing, standards of achievement were shifting, and excellence in academe was being more rigidly defined. For faculty, administrators, and serious students, the constant striving for excellence was tense, tough, competitive, and sometimes hectic. The process was challenging and exciting too, but many believed it left some classic academic values — reading, reflection, self-enrichment, speculation — behind.

Academic reputation did not come cheap. Whatever its definition, it involved at a minimum bright and dedicated faculty, whose distinction in their fields became nationally recognized and for whom Wyoming had to be made attractive through competitive salaries, benefits, and rights. It involved research equipment of cost parallel to its complexity; a great library central to campus programs; an efficient support staff, from technicians to stenographers; and facilities of every kind that encouraged scholarship, research, and teaching.

Luckily, times were prosperous. In 1969, the legislature adopted a severance tax on the state's mineral resources — at a time when prices were high and energy supplies at a premium. Inflation presented problems but brought benefits as well. National grants were available to supplement the core of the University's state funding. For most of the years between 1964 and 1978, the legislature could afford to be generous.

The consistent upswing in legislative appropriations presents a clear pattern in these years. Through the presidencies of Fey, King, Person, and Carlson, budget requests always had to be justified. Sometimes projects were presented to several legislatures in a row before they made the grade, and restrictions on use of funds plagued UW administrators. Still, it was increased legislative funding which made new programs possible.

During Fey's single legislative session (1965) and in spite of a $1 million cut by the ways and means committee from the University's request, the state appropriation was increased by $3.5 million more than the previous biennium. This created 100 new faculty and staff positions (full and half-time) and permitted salary increases ranging from five to seven percent per year for academic and staff personnel. The next legislative year, 1967, has been generally considered a disaster, but such is not the case. King's original request for a $10 million

increase (including 140 new positions) was drastically cut by legislators, but the appropriation still totalled more than $20 million and represented a $5 million increase from the previous biennium. The University's allocation came close to representing one-third of the total outlay from the general fund.

The years of Governor Stanley K. Hathaway were good years. New President Carlson frequently consulted the governor, whose support (probably because of their mutual friendship with Colorado Senator Gordon Allott) he gained early on. In 1969, the University's appropriation was increased by $6 million, or more than 25 percent, and from the entire request the legislature cut only $300,000. F. Richard Brown, one of the president's closest assistants during the legislative session, wrote that the "overall attitude was one of genuine friendliness toward the University."

In 1971, seeking no new major programs, Carlson requested an increase of $4.8 million from the general fund for the 1971-73 biennium. For the first time, the UW president presented a total University budget to the legislature, including therein estimated income from all sources as balanced against essential needs, with the request that the general fund provide the difference. In his report, the president emphasized the "disturbing" extent of the reductions he had made following the first round of departmental requests for personnel, graduate assistantships, and equipment in particular. Hathaway reduced the request by $500,000 — a cut that Carlson probably anticipated — and the appropriations committee by an additional $200,000. The result was a final state operating appropriation of $30 million. Before the session of 1973, the University's appropriations request was cut by $2 million by the governor, but the increase still amounted to more than $6 million. Much of the governor's cut was voted back into the appropriation in the first short "budget" session of 1974.

Carlson appreciated Hathaway's policies, but when the governorship changed to the Democratic party in 1974, the president was less certain of support. In spite of the fact that Carlson did not feel the same camaraderie for Governor Ed Herschler, it was in 1975 that the operating budget made a quantum leap. In this year, the University pressed for a $19 million "inflationary" increase in what was now called the "standard budget," plus an additional $7.6 million for "expanded services," most of which was to be invested in studies of Wyoming energy and conservation problems. Herschler at once cut $12.7 million from the general fund request (eliminating moneys for the energy program and, among other items, the $600,000 trustees' discretionary reserve fund). To the joint appropriations committee, Carlson and the board argued heatedly for total restitution of the request, and the legislature ended by restoring a little more than half of the governor's cut. The result was a budget increase of almost $16 million from the general fund. In 1976, the president went back to the legislature with a similar restoration request: He asked funds for an energy research program, off-campus degrees, faculty and staff salary increases, the library, and computer development. The governor approved top priorities only, but the increases to the operating budget totalled almost $8 million for the biennium July 1, 1976 to June 30, 1978.

The session of 1977 raised the appropriation to $63,736,547 — an increase of only $700,000 compared to the $3.3 million that Carlson had requested. In 1978, the appropriation increased to nearly $70 million, with a total budget (from all kinds of funding) of $94 million. These increases took place during a time when student enrollments were fairly steady and actually in some years decreasing. They represented the general inflationary trend of the economy, the relative health of the state's treasury, plus the enrichment and enlargement of University programs.

The campus building program, too, continued apace, with only occasional brief setbacks. Almost every session the legislature approved appropriations or the issuance of additional construction bonds: for the classroom building; the science center (enhanced by $3.5 million in federal funds); three new dormitories with food service (1965); the fine arts center (towards which federal funds in the amount of $500,000 contributed); and a pharmacy building (financed primarily with federal money) called for by the accreditation team in 1965. In 1967, King casually volunteered to raise $1 million for an addition to the Wyoming Union if the legislature would appropriate $2.9 million; in 1969, the law was repealed and the legislature authorized bonds to cover the unavailable donations.

Still, 1967 saw an important King victory: The legislature gave trustees a blanket approval to refund bond issues by resolution rather than legislative mandate, when they deemed such action necessary. Thereafter bonds were periodically refunded (1967, 1970, 1974), and the resultant savings applied to construction projects. Because of refunding action in 1967, nearly $5 million was available for investment in a physical education facility and the new law college building that had been deemed desirable by accreditors. The legislature later authorized bonds for the completion of the projects. In 1973, trustees proposed a $7 million bond issue, including funds to complete the law college building, finance a $2.5 million library addition, and match federal support for the new infrared observatory at Jelm Mountain. The legislature balked, and the bill died on the recommendation of the joint appropriations committee. The legislature of 1975 reversed judgment on the law building and observatory, but failed to authorize funding for the library addition; that project had to await the $5.9 million appropriation of 1976. In 1978, trustees were authorized to issue bonds in the amount of $7.36 million to purchase new computer equipment.

Nor were athletics forgotten. In addition to the physical education facilities, the state, University, and football fans pooled enough resources to expand football stadium seating and facilities on one side of the stadium. In the mid-1970s, a flurry over the possibility of putting a dome on the stadium came and went, dying in spite of the insistence of the new football coach (Fred Akers) that winning teams were built on strong facilities. Carlson, on the other hand, argued that people who wanted to watch football indoors should pay for that luxury without draining funds from other University programs. In 1976, after considerable controversy had arisen across the state, the legislature insisted that the state's Department of Administrative and Fiscal Control investigate the need for a basketball pavilion (then called the "all-events center") before the house considered it. Subsequently, the legislature of 1977 authorized for University construction nearly $7.5 million (to be handled through the Capital Building Commission), two-thirds of which was designated for athletic facilities. Still, basketball funding was limited to plans for remodeling the fieldhouse. Not until the next year did an amendment allow that a separate new structure might be planned, and when Carlson left office in 1978, arena-auditorium designing was underway.

The University School derived its special role from the elementary teacher training program first established in 1906, but it took its nickname and part of its tradition from the earliest days of University history.

The concept of a school which might serve as a "laboratory" for Normal School students on their way to becoming teachers grew up under the tutelage of Ruth Adsit, who first came to Wyoming as a summer school teacher. In 1906, Adsit, who had graduated from a normal school in Iowa, brought together fifteen or twenty children in the first three primary grades and set up a model training school during the summer months. The success of the "laboratory" idea and Adsit's personal competence persuaded Tisdel and the board to establish the school as a permanent elementary entity. Adsit was retained as a year-round faculty member, and eventually she organized three other grades for the Normal School.

Few facilities were at first available, and children were assembled in various disconnected rooms and corners of Old Main. By 1908, four classroom teachers were associated with the venture, all UW Normal School graduates. In 1910, another teacher was added to the staff, with a music supervisor as well. Special training for rural school teachers was added in 1917, but the fate of this program fluctuated from year to year, suffering from rotating staff and the demands that other programs in the College of Education (officially founded in 1914) placed on the erstwhile model rural school building. For the elementary school, the space problem was greatly alleviated with the construction of a Normal School building in 1910.

Meanwhile, the high school level training inaugurated on campus in 1887 ran into trouble. This "State Preparatory School," from which "Prep" drew its name, together with similar high school curricula in agriculture, education, engineering, and other areas, ordinarily enrolled more than half the students on campus during the University's first twenty years. A state-supported high school designed especially to prepare students for college entrance might have been justified in 1887, but twenty years later district-financed high schools (including that in Laramie) were ready and able to take over the function. Complaints surfaced in the investigations of 1907, and as late as 1921, Aven Nelson told the board that the "Prep" problem had developed more "criticism and misunderstanding" than any other thing connected with the Normal School education program.

Such uncertainty of purpose was reflected in many bulletins which listed "Prep" as useful to offer high school training to boarding students who lived in areas remote from other schools; to serve as a model high school for other such institutions; and to "grow into a training school for the State Normal School" (1911).

Proposals to reevaluate the mission of "Prep" surfaced continually after that time, but it was Nelson (as University president) who took the bull by the horns. Clearly recognizing that the legislature would support a University School only to the extent that it was essential to teacher training, Nelson persuaded the board to

"Prep" School students, c. 1920

"PREP"

Indian exhibit, Preparatory School, c. 1948

restrict enrollment to pupils from areas where no high school was available and to adopt the official name "The State Training Preparatory School." The high school students thus joined elementary pupils as forming a "testing laboratory for pedagogical theory . . . as important . . . as the chemistry laboratory is in the department of natural science," as one *Bulletin* put it.

Plans to focus "Prep" around rural needs never made much progress, although the basic policy remained in effect. As high schools developed systems of transportation around the state, few rural youngsters volunteered. Boys' and girls' boarding facilities were closed in the 1940s and 1950s. By 1969, according to one survey, sixty percent of the "Prep" students were related to University employees, while almost all were from the immediate Laramie area.

By the late 1960s, "Prep's" role again was questioned. In 1948, the school had moved into the new education building, but twenty years later facilities were evaluated as out-of-date by national teacher education accreditation teams. In 1969 and 1971, surveys published in two doctoral dissertations indicated that faculty, administrators, and teachers throughout the state believed that the school remained traditional in outlook and had developed little reputation for educational leadership. In 1973, as a result of a new accreditation evaluation, grades ten through twelve were permanently closed. Parents, students, and faculty mourned the vanishing of part of a tradition. The last high school annual, wrote its staff, was "born of a union of fun, confusion, hard work, disappointment, dedication — a fitting chronicle to the last year of U.H.S." On the back cover was simply printed "30."

Old Main, entry to education, c. 1950

In spite of the increasing operating budgets and the rising volume of bond issues authorized for construction, there is every reason to believe that the University administration and a good many of the legislators were at odds. Mutual trust and respect often seemed lacking. Like Duke Humphrey before him, Carlson found that several powerful legislators remained suspicious of University operations. Some undoubtedly were responding adversely to the new president's program of building research and graduate studies; undergraduate education was always of prime legislative concern. Others resented the fact that trustees and their counsel considered themselves constitutionally exempt from fiscal and administrative rulings that were imposed by the legislature on other state offices.

Certain procedures utilized by the administration were subject to frequent legislative criticism. In 1968, the joint appropriations committee complained that the University had not sought legislative permission before beginning to buy up property surrounding campus with surplus funds. Similarly, the beginning of programs with "soft" or temporary grant money, uncontrolled by the legislature, frequently ended in pressures upon Cheyenne to continue financing once the soft money dried up — as in the case of salaries for certain faculty added to the science and engineering departments on the basis of federal and outside funding. For example, a development grant awarded to the geology department by the National Science Foundation included salaries for four professors and others

with the assumption by the NSF that the University of Wyoming would at the end of the three years assume responsibility for the salaries for people employed, together with the upkeep on any equipment secured.

The geology department had outside connections and its head, R. S. Houston, was able to solicit aid from various mineral companies. The department of social work was not so lucky. Formed in 1970 from its sociology core, it was financed almost completely by federal money; when federal funds dried up and the state was unwilling to replace them, much of the statewide instructional and internship program had to be phased out.

Similarly, the use of "reversions" — moneys not completely expended during the annual or biennial budget period, and particularly funds freed when a salaried individual quit — seemed suspicious to the legislature. Humphrey had quietly used reversions to help make bond interest payments. Later these reversions were freely and openly budgeted (although it was almost impossible to estimate the amount in advance), particularly for personnel and for funding sabbatical leaves. Carlson explained that

To avoid the hazards and waste of last-minute spending, the University purposely budgets one half million dollars in reversions annually. This amount . . . is occasioned primarily by position vacancies accompanying normal personnel turnover. If reversions were not budgeted, there would be a temptation for units to spend all funds allocated just to clear the books at the end of each fiscal period. Knowing that the total budget of the University depends on departments' reverting funds, units exercise greater responsibility and we avoid the hazards of unnecessary spending.

Through combinations of reversions, combined appointments, half-time funding, and salary adjustments, the administration gained considerable flexibility in making faculty appointments. Such funding was not deliberately concealed, but legislators were obviously concerned about its extent. In 1977, the legislature authorized the addition of fourteen part-time faculty and one full-time instructor for the Casper program without providing any additional funding. The oversight was probably a deliberate attempt to force personnel out of "reversion" research into teaching. Budget reversions met the expense.

To combat what it regarded as unauthorized spending, the legislature tightened its grip on fiscal procedures. A major step was bringing the University into compliance with rules established by the Department of Administrative and Fiscal Control, set up in 1971. DAFC began by setting the form of budget request (namely, funds for continuing programs as compared to expanded programs, and eventually a special section in which the University pled for exceptions to the common rule) and ended by establishing the principle of a line-item budget with no flexibility in transfer. In vain University officials protested that the inability to change funds from one category to another left them with inability to operate economically. "We want to be more flexible," board President Paul Hines told the joint appropriations committee in 1978,

more responsive to the changing needs of Wyoming. Therefore we ask you for greater internal budget flexibility. We ask you for leeway so we may better manage the affairs of the University. We ask you to give us the opportunity to do our jobs better.

Alfred Pence, board chairman at another time, also wrote that

the major financial problem facing the University is the inability of the Trustees to actually manage the University because of fund transfer restrictions. Effective management of any institution demands that management have the flexibility to make decisions regarding internal allocation of funds. If funds appropriated to an institution as large and complex as the University of Wyoming are rigidly restricted as to categories of spending, then the Trustees have effectively been denied major management options.

Years later, President Edward Jennings echoed the view that tight budget restrictions were the University's greatest problem. Jennings asked his legal assistant to check the law, but the answer was that trustees were clearly subject to DAFC budget control.

When a 1973 law required that funds from all Wyoming institutions be deposited with the state, the University began slowly and obviously reluctantly to transfer registration fees, income from agricultural sales, and income from athletic events; it stood firm on its retention of federal funds, gifts, and income from other sources. In 1975, the legislature began issuing special instructions about money, particularly about its reversion if not utilized by the end of the biennium, and specifying such matters as return of state funds to the treasury should other funds become available for a given program. As early as 1973, the total number of employees to be maintained on the payroll was specified in each legislative appropriation. In 1977, the mammoth construction appropriation was handled through the Capital Building Commission rather than directly by trustees.

In addition to various constraints on spending, the legislature also demanded special audits and investigations of University affairs. One of the most important of these occurred in 1973, when the biennial legislature let die in committee the University's capital projects request until such time as a subcommittee of the joint education, health, and welfare interim committee could conduct a thorough investigation of University affairs. The subcommittee, with Senator Roy Peck as chairman, designed an intricate questionnaire to be answered by the UW administration. The huge document contained questions ranging from the role of deans, the plans for extension, the "publish or perish" policy, the occupancy rate of dormitories to the women's athletic program, salaries

239

of the highest-paid administrators, the necessity for executive sessions of the board of trustees, and such questions as "Who does . . . actually run the University?" Final answers were forwarded to Cheyenne in December 1973, but in the meantime the University had received its share of criticism in public committee hearings in Rock Springs, Sheridan, Riverton and other communities. Particularly under attack were the emphasis on graduate programs and research; the "free love policy" induced by coeducational dorms; the dearth of statewide "outreach;" and the lack of orientation of both research and teaching toward problems of Wyoming.

In 1975, just two years later, the Wyoming Commission for Higher Education (established by the legislature in 1969) proposed to send a "management consultation team" to inspect and advise all higher educational institutions. The trustees' first reaction was negative, but thereafter (after a futile attempt to consult and agree on policy with the community colleges) the board decided to hire an external management review group of its own choosing and proceed with the audit as rapidly as possible. Indications that trustees wished to "keep the matter under close control" appear in — but were expunged from — the minutes. Eventually a team was agreed on, but it was a year and a half before the report was concluded; meanwhile Elliott Hays took a six-month leave from the finance office to study and analyze UW's administrative structures, procedures, personnel systems, and other pertinent areas. The final report set forth a number of specific suggestions for streamlined administration and more careful definition of policies and practices. It was forwarded to the Commission for Higher Education in 1978 just before Governor Herschler phased the latter out. Meanwhile another fiscal audit was requested by the appropriations committee in 1977; trustees agreed, although they pointed out that standard University procedures called for constant financial auditing by several experts.

In addition, the higher education commission completed its own survey of all higher educational facilities in Wyoming. It held public hearings; hired several consultants; and worked out a report on the status, needs, and finances for all two-year colleges and the University. The commission advised the University administration to expand its research programs, support academic activities especially needed by the state, and carefully evaluate Wyoming's need for University "outreach."

The final report suggested that no other Wyoming institution offer a full bachelor's degree program until the University achieved an optimum size of 12,000 full-time students.

The problem of educational outreach around the state worried the administration. By the early 1970s, seven two-year colleges, now totally independent from the University, offered freshman-sophomore (or "lower-division") classes in all corners of Wyoming. Of them, Casper College — with an enrollment of about 3,000 students in 1970 — was the strongest and largest. Legislative studies indicated a growing demand for four-year degree-bearing curricula, particularly among older, working individuals in areas remote from campus. In 1968, when Carlson came to office, the University offered a few upper-division courses around the state — extension classes in Cheyenne, field summer schools in various communities, correspondence courses, and occasional "short courses" that carried credit — but no off-campus degree opportunities, except for a troubled master's program in business administration at Warren Air Force Base. Rumors flew that Casper College, under the vigorous direction of President Tilghman Aley and with the aid of the Natrona County legislative delegation, was ready to fill the gap.

In principle, neither Fey nor Carlson objected to the community college system; both believed it would be to the University's advantage to focus on upper division programs, graduate work, and professional training. But a four-year college was different in terms of quantity of funding and quality of education. In the first year of his administration, a concerned Carlson brought in an expert from Fort Collins to evaluate Wyoming's program of educational outreach. Based on this report as well as statewide reaction during hearings at legislative sessions, a special office was created to expand and coordinate extension offerings, including those of the long-established Agricultural Extension Service. As vice president for extension, H. B. McFadden (psychology department) moved rapidly to take the situation in hand.

Under McFadden's leadership, educational activities were extended to many areas of the state while requirements were adapted permitting qualified individuals from off-campus to receive degrees. McFadden encouraged the College of Education to offer upper-division courses in Laramie County, where students were able to complete requirements for a bachelor's degree in close cooperation with two community colleges. The MBA program at Warren Air Force Base was opened to permit civilians to participate. Eventually, extension courses were expanded into other communities by University faculty members (who were flown to such sites for weekly evening classes) and on-site local teachers (who were always subject to approval by the corresponding University department).

An elaborate system of credit equivalents was set up with community colleges, and degree programs were altered so as to lower campus residency requirements. Since extension courses were always limited in number and scope, the College of Arts and Sciences designed a "distributive major," permitting a student to graduate with a major in science-mathematics, social science, or humanities and fine arts and thus avoid the previous necessity of accumulating numbers of credits in one narrower field. In the College of Education, James Zancanella devised curricula in vocational studies, carefully coordinated with community college offerings: Such "applied" studies had been in great demand at community colleges, and the University's program permitted students to continue to a full bachelor's degree, either on campus or off, as circumstances dictated. Less successful were efforts to integrate agricultural extension into the system; agricultural extension personnel in the field were concerned primarily with youth groups and advising services, and did not easily mesh with those field coordinators whose mission involved college-level and adult education courses.

Casper remained the sore point and the University's bête noire. Here, with increasing enrollment, the need for bachelor's degree programs was particularly acute. No one was particularly surprised when — in answer to the "clamor for baccalaureate opportunity" — Tilghman Aley proposed a four-year degree-offering program at Casper College. In spite of the previous negative recommendation from the higher education commission, such a bill was introduced into the legislature in 1971. It made no progress. In 1973, another proposal passed the senate but was defeated in the house.

Aley called attention to the special needs for bachelor's degrees in "general studies" and vocational or technical fields. In quick response, Carlson set up a special "Committee for the Expansion of Off-Campus Instructional Programs." Here faculty and administrators worked out a series of extension degree programs that might successfully be initiated in Casper. When in 1975, the four-year Casper College proposal was again introduced into the legislature, the University was ready with a sixteen-page counter brief. The University and the community colleges, it argued, should not duplicate roles: The latter should offer terminal vocational-technical curricula and two-year academic transfer programs, while the former provided baccalaureate, professional, and graduate work. No Casper degree program in "applied sciences" would be firmly-based without many junior-senior level support courses in all areas of study — courses which Casper was not prepared to offer. The University, on the other hand, already offered many such programs that were carefully "meshed" with community college curricula.

It cannot be emphasized too strongly that each of these [120] major areas prepares students either to directly enter the work force or to continue on to graduate school, if that is their wish.

Most importantly, the statement volunteered rotating University faculty to teach upper-level classes wherever demand existed. It proposed an immediate MBA program for the Casper area, an off-campus master's program for teachers, and sought increased travel funds for the offering of more extension courses.

In 1975, the four-year Casper College proposal was again defeated in the senate. Over the following year, McFadden met frequently with Aley and persuaded him to endorse a joint program for advanced degrees. Using Casper College facilities and employing faculty from that two-year college as well as the University, the agreement established a "general studies" curriculum, specifically conceived under the arts and sciences "distributive major" plan. In addition, UW was to offer the MBA degree at Casper, and plans were made to

241

introduce "applied studies" on the bachelor's level in the future. In 1976, legislators from Natrona and Albany counties caucused in circumstances that caused the press to complain of "secret meetings." On the floor, they voted together to approve the new "educational outreach" program. As one senator coyly put it, Casper College and the University became united in matrimony, if only through a "shotgun wedding."

Headaches predominated in the introduction of the program, especially since all parties — including the higher educational commission, which approved the cooperative program for two experimental years — were eager to get classes underway by fall semester. High-level committees of trustees and administrators were set up; Peter K. Simpson, Aley's special assistant, was named coordinator of the program; negotiations began in earnest. "I must emphasize," McFadden wrote in some frustration to Carlson,

> that Dr. Simpson and I cannot work together on day to day operations until there is a major policy agreement at the presidential and trustee levels. Unless he and I know what degree program is to be pursued, what governs the selection of courses and course content, whose faculty is to be used, and that the instructions from our respective institutions agree, we will be unable to proceed from this point in time.

By summer, planning began to smooth out, although many sore points remained. The selection of faculty from Casper provided special difficulties, as did the location of classes; eventually the MBA program was moved away from the Casper College campus to an old school building. Although the higher education commission was eager to see career-oriented programs, such curricula were put off for at least a year. Residence requirements and credit equivalents remained problems unsolved. McFadden, Simpson, and Joyce A. Scott from the University worked closely with Casper administrators on registration plans. In autumn 1976, 130 students enrolled, 35 of them simultaneously registered in lower division classes regularly offered at Casper College.

Simpson's several long reports make interesting reading. He was aware of many difficulties. Among them were faculty problems: Casper College faculty were irritated at having to apply for formal approval by the University, and most of them had taken on upper-division classes as a drastic overload in their schedules. Casper College administrators were sometimes slighted in the planning process. Courses were unbalanced the first semester, leaning heavily towards the social sciences and humanities; for that matter Simpson could not equate the hoped-for "general studies" with the distributive major plan as put into operation. Enrollees were primarily housewives, and Simpson was concerned about their commitment to completing their programs. In spite of everything, Simpson maintained an optimistic view of a liberal education that simultaneously prepared students for "life."

> If the program in Casper has any uniqueness whatsoever, it lies in its effort to imbue the upper division with a community college approach without sacrificing "standards" on the one hand or emphasizing graduate entry on the other.

In June 1977 — the very month of Simpson's resignation to accept the position of dean of instruction at Sheridan College — Aley appeared before the higher education commission to announce Casper's withdrawal from the joint enterprise. Although the legislature meant well, he said, too many problems had arisen.

> The present structure is simply not tenable with differing institutional missions, educational philosophies, two sets of work loads, pay scales of marked spread, and two controls — one being 150 miles removed. Growing resentment, insecurity and confusion as a result of two sets of standards and two administrative controls are growing [sic] to the point that the [Casper College] board feels it should no longer continue in the present configuration past the two-year trial period.

And he added:

> The presence of a second entity has sapped energies and has taken an inordinate amount of time of personnel, often to the detriment of our basic responsibility, the community college.

It was Aley's suggestion that the program be turned over to Casper College for management. He resented what he considered the overpowerful role UW had played.

> . . . the [Casper College] board wishes to express alarm about the state system that appears to be headed toward expansion of entrenchment of a single unit system. No monopoly is either as productive or as economical as those that must compete for service.

But the University's board of trustees had different ideas. At their next meeting, trustees accepted Aley's decision "with regret" and passed a resolution of appreciation for Casper College's help in "the successful launching of these educational opportunities for Casper citizens." Trustees reaffirmed their commitment to offer degree programs where demand existed and where students could not easily enroll on campus. The board made clear its intention to continue and develop distributive majors and the MBA program in Casper, even without two-year college participation.

The joint effort, although temporary, had indeed permitted the University to establish its Casper extension programs on a permanent basis. Although costs per student were inordinately high — more than twice those on campus — the legislature appropriated funds for two additional faculty,

Folk dances, Elizabethan Fair, c. 1976

and in 1978, a cheered administration embarked on the career-oriented curricula that the higher education commission had recommended. The first to be activated was a degree in social work; shortly after, when faculty became available, a political science program in the administration of justice was inaugurated. Meanwhile the School of Nursing, with federal support, planned an extended degree program in Casper and four other communities, and the College of Education was working to offer a full-fledged bachelor's degree in elementary education.

Although Casper College had withdrawn from the program, considerable cooperation continued in evidence. Because of space limitations, all UW classes were transferred to the Wilson school, which was duly remodeled through Herschler's contingency funds. But for many years UW students utilized Casper College library facilities, and the two-year college faculty occasionally participated in the program. Continued efforts of Natrona County legislators to expand Casper College were defeated, in part because of gubernatorial opposition.

In early 1978, with the program established and his mission accomplished, McFadden resigned his vice presidency for extension and the position was abolished. That same year, Herschler, with legislative approval, terminated the existence of the higher education commission.

The nature of the community college system seemed to underline one of Carlson's convictions: that University curricula should focus primarily on advanced work. Throughout the president's tenure, teaching and research programs burgeoned in many fields, but particularly in terms of upper-division, graduate, and post-graduate studies. Advised by James Ranz, his vice president for academic affairs, and with close collaborator E. Gerald Meyer, dean of arts and sciences, the president at first placed heavy emphasis on the centrality of the College of Arts and Sciences. Here the so-called hard sciences were already well-established, but Carlson's administration saw further progress and expansion.

In particular, the decade of Carlson's administration saw the employment of many new faculty whose reputations in their fields were already established. Thus, Carlson believed, the institution's reputation might be built. The president took delight in such faculty acquisitions. Writing to Morrill, the University's president from 1941-45, Carlson said:

Throughout the last . . . years we have worked very quietly but very hard to build the quality of the faculty at the University of Wyoming. I am sure this goal is the same one set by other institutions, but, perhaps through a combination of circumstances including the location of this institution, we have been able to attract competent people far beyond my fondest dreams.

With the president's blessing, both physics and chemistry benefited from Meyer's policy of importing widely-recognized research scholars to build graduate departments. Geoffrey Coates came as head of chemistry; known for his intensive research and many publications, he nevertheless insisted on personal involvement in undergraduate teaching over the years. Under the leadership of Derek Prowse, the physics department made what Meyer called a "quantum leap," increasing its undergraduate majors from eight to 62, its graduates from five to 65, and its outside grant support money from $8,000-$800,000 in a period of five years. With the help of Walter T. Grandy, who became department head after Prowse's sudden and tragic death, the astronomy program got a great boost with the construction of the largest infrared telescope in the continental United States, a project made possible by a National Science Foundation grant of $625,000 and a legislatively authorized bond issue of $975,000.

Other science departments, too, made remarkable progress. Historically united with philosophy, psychology broke off to become a department unto itself and soon established a clinical Ph.D. program that worked closely with state agencies. Both this department and the geology department acquired extra personnel, equipment, and funding through NSF development grants. The new chemical technology program was built on federal support in the amount of $400,000. Zoology continued its long-term research programs at Jackson Hole and its popular campus curriculum in wildlife management. In 1970, the small but strong botany department was the last of the science areas to begin a Ph.D. program; its research backing lay in the magnificent Rocky Mountain Herbarium, initiated and tended for many years by Aven Nelson.

In 1968, health sciences were brought together into a new college, combining programs in pharmacy, nursing, medical technology, pre-medical, pre-dental studies, and (later) the special program in speech pathology and audiology. Assisting Jack N. Bone, who continued to direct the pharmacy program and became dean of the college as well, were a special dean for nursing and an assistant dean to coordinate the paramedical and undergraduate curricula. Nursing soon began offering a master's degree, and a bachelor's degree in dental hygiene was added to college programs. In engineering, sciences did equally well. With an established research program dominated by two institutes, the college developed considerable outside funding and was able to increase its Ph.D. program to include such areas as atmospheric sciences, bioengineering, and mineral engineering. Chemical engineering became a bachelor's program in its own right. Commerce and industry expanded its master's degree offerings into the fields of finance and marketing. Its business administration programs attracted off-campus students at Warren Air Force Base and in Casper.

Arts, humanities, and the social sciences also expanded faculty and offerings during the 1960s and 1970s. As a new department, philosophy found an energetic head in Professor Benjamin Tilghman, but Tilghman resigned in 1967. Over the objections of its faculty, who regarded their small number and low support budget as inadequate to build a quality degree program, the history department became the first social science department to offer the Ph.D. (1965). Respected scholars Roger Williams and Walter Langlois came to build the departments of history and languages after the retirement of long-term department heads. American anthropologist George Frison brought new interest to the field research program in his department, already widely reputed through the work of William T. Mulloy on Easter Island. The English department embarked enthusiastically on an annual Elizabethan Fair, with original plays performed on the green, lectures on Elizabethan life, and concerts of appropriate vintage. In 1965, Professor Tom Francis founded a journal called *Sage*, but the administration's abortive efforts to bring in a new editor ended with the resignation of Francis, the summary dismissal of the overly experimental editor, and the end of the journal. Administrative disagreements, too, caused the premature demise of an experimental "humanities semester" — a system whereby students could fulfill all humanities

244

requirements in one hard-working semester through a visitor-taught core and locally-instructed complementary courses. The semester went down the drain, its grant actually refunded, primarily because of conflicts over educational approaches and personalities.

With its completion in 1972, the fine arts center lent new excitement and impetus to theater, music, and art departments. These programs all received special presidential attention. Perhaps because of his scientific background and his acquaintance with the limits of the Fort Collins curricula, Carlson set high value on the "impractical" but essential fine arts departments. With the aid of a growing number of scholarships that the president saw funded and under the leadership of its dynamic department head (David Tomatz), the music program flourished. Through the Western Arts trio the department attained national recognition; the collegiate chorale toured Europe and other areas; and the summer Western Arts Music Festival attracted artists from all parts of the world. With its new quarters, the art department gained a museum, which benefited from the vigorous development and collection policies of James T. Forrest. Separated in 1975 from the curriculum in "communications," the new theater department added a dance option in 1977 by absorbing the dance classes from physical education; the merger was marred by the dismissal (in spite of 2,000 objecting petition signatories) of one of the dance's most talented teachers.

Emphasis was laid as well on career-oriented programs. With its considerable backing in federal aid, the department of social work launched a curriculum that included internships all over the state, although, as noted, much of the program collapsed with withdrawal of its funding. Broadcasting became a subject in its own right, attached to the department of communications and bolstered by the greatly improved student radio station KUWR. Educational television, for which funding was rejected by the legislature in 1969, was gradually built into the curriculum. In 1971, the Faculty

Senate authorized and the board approved a special department of computer science, thus building into a degree-granting program courses that had been offered since 1965. "Internship training" was advanced through the public defender program in the law school. Such areas as wildlife management and recreation and park administration (a curriculum transferred entirely to arts and sciences after long joint association with physical education) appealed to students caught up in problems of ecology and environment. Although secretarial training was removed from the College of Commerce and Industry, it was rapidly integrated as a teacher training curriculum in the College of Education. Departments throughout the College of Arts and Sciences did their share by offering summer institutes for teachers under the auspices of the National Defense Education Act and other federal legislation; such institutes ranged from the sciences (mathematics, physics, chemistry, radiation biology) to the humanities (rhetoric, English). A year-round science-math teaching center constantly worked with teachers throughout the state. A humanities teaching center, also using the "portal school" approach, lost its National Endowment for the Humanities funding after several experimental years, however.

Research at the University kept pace with expanded academic programs. In his many addresses to alumni and friends before the legislative session of 1965, Fey stressed the "current emphasis on science and technology" that was causing universities across the country to develop research projects in areas previously monopolized by fewer than fifteen large institutions. Perhaps even more than Fey, Carlson believed research to be central to campus prosperity. Without it, he wrote,

the college atmosphere would be sterile. There would be few new discoveries, little new knowledge on which to build a better tomorrow. . . . We look to our teachers to engage in research to advance knowledge and to further their professional competency as teachers.

One of his concerns when he left the University — as expressed in a final meeting with leading faculty members in his home — was that students, parents, and legislators would abandon his vision of excellence and deliberately shift the University's emphasis from nationally-recognized research to locally-oriented teaching. In research Carlson saw the key to excellence in instruction and state service, the University's other functions. "We have encouraged the growth of research on our campus," he told the legislators in 1971,

> with two thoughts constantly in mind: the relation of the research programs to our own instructional programs; and the relation of those same research programs to the needs and the development of the State. We feel very strongly that an active research program, funded largely from outside sources, is one of the prime responsibilities of the University and that kept within the bounds described above will enhance our instructional programs and work to the benefit of the economy of the State.

With his background as a radiation biologist in veterinary science, Carlson was interested in Wyoming's research program from the start. Even before he was installed as president, he made the acquaintance of R. H. Denniston, zoologist, who had been appointed by Fey as director of research development in an effort, Fey wrote, "to coordinate research activities and to provide the President's office with more information on the development of our programs." In a special trip to Fort Collins in October 1967, Denniston reported on current projects at the University and noted his hopes for better coordination; more research support for certain areas (social science, humanities, arts); and some unique programs that might be developed in conservation, ecology, and population studies of the state. Denniston was obviously enthusiastic.

> Ever since I initiated and organized our first all-university office for research administration, ideas have been accumulating that I have been eager to try out in a favorable environment. The level of our research effort could be increased several-fold. But, there has not been a sufficient understanding of the importance of research in the whole educational and service structure. Until now, innovation in research administration of the University has not been feasible. There is adequate representation of the teaching and service functions of the University at top administrative levels; there is no corresponding position representing research activity.

Apatosarus skeleton, geology museum

Following his interview, Denniston again wrote Carlson on research development possibilities in such fields as bioengineering and speech pathology.

Although Denniston and Carlson shared much the same goals, they seem never to have worked well together. Denniston slipped out of his position in 1972, first to spend a year in Afghanistan with the University's AID project, then on a leave of absence for 1973-74. Carlson apparently was closer to Ranz, who shared and strongly influenced his opinions, and to Meyer, whom he later appointed vice president for research in Denniston's stead.

Research on campus was organized (and disorganized) in many ways. First of all, there were officially designated institutes and research coordination offices in several of the colleges. The Agricultural Experiment Station and its substations throughout the state provided the oldest formal network. The Natural Resources Research Institute, established just after World War II, was intended to attract state contracts for locally important engineering research, primarily the uses of coal, other minerals, water, and similar resources. Later the Water Resources Research Institute was set up as a separate operation because federal funding demanded that it be an "all-University" effort. It remained, however, primarily confined to engineering with the exception of its ties to Dean Frank Trelease's land and water center in the law school. The Division of Business and Economic Research was a similar formal structure set up in the College of Commerce and Industry. These institutes regularly accepted commissions (usually from state and federal agencies) for research projects, which were then directed by full-time staff or associated college faculty. After 1976, efforts were made to set up a similar regional institute for energy research based on an initial donation of $350,000, but although numerous projects of Wyoming interest were presented to the legislature, the necessary additional funding was not forthcoming.

Philosophical and administrative uncertainties often caused difficulties for these separate research establishments. Should they focus strictly on locally-oriented research problems, or should more theoretical and basic research, keyed to universal problems, take precedence? How could permanent personnel best be funded, and what should be the institutes' relationships to academic departments and teaching? The Division of Business and Economic Research suffered a series of short-term directors, partly because irregular financing made problems of staffing acute, partly because college faculty seemed generally uninterested in research, with the exception of William C. Guenther, who was a publishing scholar. Eventually, the division broadened its scope to include governmental and political projects, and came to be jointly administered by commerce and industry with the arts and sciences college. For years the NRRI was regarded by the engineering dean strictly as a source for funding: for students, graduates, faculty, and equipment as needed. In 1971, the institute's relationship to the college was called into question, particularly as concerned teaching assignments given to researchers without proper procedural authorization. To clarify functions, several NRRI staff members were relocated and Donald L. Veal became head of a new department of atmospheric sciences with the result that NRRI (to the irritation of several of its staff) became strictly a mining and mineral resources research institute.

In most fields, faculty conducted individual or team research on a more ad hoc basis. The astonishing scope of topics for research can hardly be covered in any single document. They ranged from the geology of Antarctica to Afghanistan's crops, from gasification of coal to Mexican immigration, from nutrition to Shakespeare to weightlessness in space. For faculty on regular appointments, release time from teaching encouraged consistent research efforts; through this policy, state-paid salaries were in part sponsoring faculty scholarship. Outside grant money awarded to individuals or teams financed many projects of statewide and national import. The University set aside funds for matching when such were necessary (particularly for the purchase of special equipment) and charged a regular fee against the grant for overhead costs. A division of basic research in arts and sciences was funded out of general University appropriations to award "seed money" for equipment purchase and travel in connection with faculty research. Summer fellowships for faculty research were made available on a limited and highly competitive basis through University budgeted funds.

Funding for research makes a fascinating study. In 1968-69, for example, an administrative study indicated that grant and contract awards still active at the end of the calendar year totalled more than $6.4 million, not including federal funds for agriculture, construction, the overseas AID programs, the special air force degree programs in Cheyenne, or National Defense Education Act fellowship allotments. The grants received this year included a vast array of project topics, from purchase of physics equipment to archeology, from mosquito control to studies of boating accidents. Awards came from the National Science Foundation, the National Endowment for the Humanities, the U.S. Office of Education, the army, the departments of interior and public health, private foundations, corporations, and research-oriented associations, to name only a few. Ten years later the trustees regularly accepted outside research funding and grants in the amount of nearly $1 million a month; more than $1 million was not unusual.

Such increased funding for research made temporary employment of personnel on so-called "soft money" almost irresistible. During the 1970s, a number of appointments funded by research grants were made. If clearly understood by all concerned, such appointments provided little cause for trouble, for when the grant was terminated, the faculty member simply went his way. Complications arose through misunderstandings and unclear hiring practices. Derek Prowse, physics department head, brought several faculty members to campus to be paid by grant money, but failed to make it explicitly clear that the appointments were temporary and could not become tenured because of limited funds. A large physics department turned out to be based in great measure on temporary funding. Upon termination of their grants and appointments, several individuals involved contended that they had understood their appointments to carry the possibility of tenure. One such case — that of a Japanese physicist, Professor Shinzo Nakai — went to a faculty committee for adjudication; the committee found that Nakai had reason to believe his appointment might lead to a permanent position and recommended that he should be transferred to a tenure-track appointment. A similar situation concerned Professor J. P. Biscar, who ended by taking trustees, president, department head, and dean to court. In this instance, a district court judge eventually decided in favor of the University, and Biscar's dismissal — upon the termination of the grant under which he was funded — was confirmed.

Meanwhile faculty, like administrators, were involved in the pursuit of greatness and prestige. The 1970s saw a great deal of talk of academic excellence — about how to focus limited resources so as to attain and retain it; about how to expand programs without watering them down. A series of self-analyses were dedicated to the search for improvement. Such minute — and time-consuming — self-evaluations formed the basis of the University's long reports to the North Central Association's accreditation teams in 1970 and particularly in 1980. In 1971-72, a series of "priority review" committees analyzed programs on both administrative and academic levels. In 1965, and again ten years later, the administration with faculty participation devised a ten-year plan. Every legislative meeting saw the involvement of personnel from instructor on up in the formulating of budget proposals with hard figures, programmatic decisions, and justifications. For professional and technological programs, reports for accreditation kept faculty and administrators alike constantly on their toes.

Everyone was agreed that academic excellence was important, but not all faculty and administrators developed similar criteria for defining excellence or similar academic philosophies in general. Humanists could not help deploring the scientific emphasis in programs, to which most federal funding was awarded. Building the new department of philosophy, Professor Ben Tilghman found President King pessimistic; such programs were expensive, could anticipate little outside support, and were not related to immediate Wyoming concerns. In the face of 1967 gubernatorial budget cuts, Tilghman, Larson, and other humanists drafted a special statement for King, who duly adopted it in his budget campaign. But Larson was soon irritated at the college and University administration. Having insisted on a doctoral program for history and aware of the department's needs listed in the ten-year academic plan, the administration had cut his request for three new positions — even though physics was rumored to be receiving five. Physics, Larson reported, had half the students but double the faculty of the history department. Similarly, the botany department — in response to remarks in a "priority review" — protested that new programs could not be expected to attract large numbers of students except through gradual building. Efforts to establish a native American studies program never got off the ground, partly because of cost and the difficulties of staffing the suggested courses: in Arapaho and Shoshoni languages and native American dance.

Most degree programs retained rigid requirements both in breadth and in specialty courses. Many universities and colleges had proclaimed great flexibility of requirements in the 1960s — either to cope with an influx of minority students, guaranteed their places in school by federal legislation, or to accommodate young rebels who demanded the right to make their own decisions about courses and curricula. At Wyoming, several all-University requirements had been dropped without fanfare, but neither represented an incursion against the academic core. One was ROTC, an activity demanded of able male students since the University was founded, voted out as a requirement by faculty during Fey's administration. With even less fanfare, the physical education activity requirement was lowered from four semesters to two in 1970.

A few other walls crumbled a little at the edges, making life somewhat easier for students. By vote of the faculty, a system of satisfactory- unsatisfactory grading was established, primarily to encourage students to take courses that they might otherwise regard as too rigorous or too remote from their own majors. The period during which classes might be dropped was extended, and rules for academic suspension and dismissal gave marginal students a second chance. Although the dictum of admission open to any Wyoming high school graduate was never in effect for graduate degrees, Wyoming residents were in some instances given an edge over out-of-state students. A faculty adviser's signature was no longer required for enrollment, and an appellate system was set up for students who believed they had been unfairly graded. The new academic policies caused a concerned faculty member to write to his dean in ironic vein.

We may view the operation of a University class as follows. It is a happy group in which no student works too hard because an S/U situation is easily manipulated, and to which no student feels a responsible commitment because he may withdraw from it without penalty, and which he entered without background knowledge of the material and without advisory consultation, and concerning which (if the above measures fail to make his life easy and happy) he may appeal to a faculty/student committee which will hold his hand and gently comfort him, thereby soothing the psychic wounds inflicted by any faculty member who tries to maintain academic standards.

A harsh judgment — for standards were not abandoned. Arts and sciences, the University's largest college, never gave up its insistence that students enroll in a balanced program of science, social science, humanities, and fine arts, although it compromised when it eliminated a foreign language from requirements and substituted instead additional humanities courses.

If anything, scientific, professional, and skills-oriented programs became ever more rigorous, building class upon class until students had few options for electives. At one point, the objection of some faculty to such a specialized (as compared with general) education was embodied in a committee report proposing a core program of common courses for all University freshmen. Although the idea provoked discussion and evoked enthusiasm (from, among others, the vice president for academic affairs), it was never activated. Posing problems by adding courses for those in professional colleges, it might also have been difficult for less capable students, in the judgment of the head of the counseling center.

I feel that in theory the idea is excellent. However, because of the nature of our admission requirements, I feel it may do a disservice to certain kinds of students such as those who come from culturally deprived backgrounds, those who have certain physical and or emotional problems, and those who have marginal ability.

Instead, arts and sciences developed a broadly-based honors program for exceptional students, as directed by Professor Glyn Thomas (English) and supported for its first few years by a federal grant. The argument between specialists and generalists only proved that excellence was not always attained by the same road or even defined in the same terms.

Along the rocky path, two colleges in particular seemed to need assistance. In 1964, the College of Education had been accredited only provisionally because of excessive faculty teaching loads, inadequate laboratory experience for students, the limited curriculum for elementary teachers, and its student screening procedure. In 1969, following another accreditation visit, Carlson called on a member of the team to "consult with him and his colleagues relative to the most effective means of moving the College of Education within the University setting to a position of greater excellence." The consultant — H. K. Newburn, dean of education at Arizona State, — suggested more aggressive leadership, a more clearly defined mission, more selective graduate programs, stronger and more independent departments heads, a research program, and either great improvement or the end to the University School.

The response of the education dean was a long report on which Carlson's notations clearly indicate that the two did not see eye to eye. True, the report spoke of attaining lofty heights and of an "insatiable desire to perform these tasks better than they have ever been done before and to place the college among the elite in the nation." But it also contained specifics: a call for a center for research, full-time professional advisers for students, more public relations, a new building, and extra positions in almost all areas. Carlson was unimpressed and even irritated, as his notes indicate (for example: "Faculty develop [research] in each area — the need for a center comes way later to coordinate active programs"). Even more clear is his memo to a vice president: "They really don't understand the needs, priorities & methods to accomplish goals. I am about to give up on their leadership." The attempt of the dean to appoint an all-education committee to name a replacement for a resigning department head seemed the last straw.

In early 1970, Dean Ivan Willey was pressured to resign; the board granted him a sabbatical until July 1, when he would return as an education professor. Reaction around the state was angry, and the files contain letters attacking the decision: "Could it be that there again is an attempt to make the College of Education a department under Arts & Sciences?" one protestor wrote. Carlson stood firm. He appointed Lawrence Walker, a longtime friend from the Boy Scout Council, as acting dean. A year later the committee to search for a replacement recommended that Walker remain permanently.

Meanwhile a special statewide advisory council was appointed to make suggestions and watch over the college's programs. Several department heads resigned their administrative duties to become full-time teachers instead. An overextended graduate program in guidance and counseling — which had in one year admitted 97 graduate students and which had burgeoned with now-withdrawn federal aid — was cut back, much to the dismay of many of its numerous Ph.D.s, who wrote to protest. The upper grades of University School were phased out

in 1973; the school's small program and inadequate facilities had been a subject of criticism by evaluators for many years. In 1971, Carlson went to the legislature and gained seventeen new education positions, several of which were anchored half-time in traditional academic departments outside the college. In 1973, the college was accredited by the National Council for Accreditation of Teacher Education for a six-year period.

In agriculture, too, the administration insisted on a series of program reviews. Carlson's familiarity with the agriculture school at Fort Collins undoubtedly enhanced his expectations and his knowledge of what a college of agriculture might contribute, through federally financed teaching, research, and affiliated extension services. In 1973, a statewide review committee was set up to consider problems. Two years later in 1975, an outside reviewer (Professor C. P. Wilson) suggested a more careful definition of mission and goals for all agricultural programs and, specifically, the establishment of a permanent statewide advisory council similar to that recommended for the College of Education. In May 1976, Dean Neal "Dutch" Hilston sent in a progress report: The advisory council had been set up, departments were working on academic plans for the future, and other recommendations were being considered. Hilston was most concerned, he told trustees, with

> the image of the college, especially with regard to public relations in the state; policy questions; organization, supervision and operations; program determination, management and delivery; subject matter deficiencies; and physical plant requirements.

The next year, shortly before Hilston retired, Carlson brought in an outside evaluator again. This time J. C. Hillier, professor emeritus from Oklahoma State University, was asked to concentrate on the agricultural research program and extension service. Although his report was generally positive, the observer found that a "lack of direction" within the various divisions had "led to an indifferent attitude on the part of some faculty." His tour of the various state experimental farms, he wrote, made him aware of their inadequate equipment, minimal research programs, and the lack of definite research goals. "A hard line," wrote Hillier, should be taken relative to unproductive or outdated projects," and someone (perhaps Carlson) has written in the margin "AMEN!"

Verdi "Requiem," University and high school musicians, December 1976

In 1976, Harold J. Tuma was named dean designate, in anticipation of the retirement of Hilston, who had held the deanship for nineteen years. After months touring Wyoming, Tuma returned keen on relevant research and communication. "We need to listen to the people and to tell the people in the state about the University's agricultural programs," he told the board in a long, first interview. He turned his energies at once to the experiment substations and brought about considerable improvement, particularly in physical facilities. With Tuma at the helm, Carlson seemed less troubled by the operation of the agriculture college.

As before, for many programs excellence was defined in terms of national accreditation standards. Accreditation was particularly important in areas like the health sciences, where the critical nature of exact knowledge was a matter of public concern because of the careers undertaken by graduates. Accreditation trouble was at the heart of the incorporation of the College of Nursing into a College of Health Sciences (together with pharmacy and several paramedical and pre-professional programs). In 1966 and 1968, the administration received "warnings" from the National League for Nursing that "continuation of accreditation . . . will depend upon the presentation of evidence that substantial progress has been made." Trustees and Carlson were alarmed. With the establishment of the health science college, ailing Dean Amelia Leino took a sabbatical and then a sick leave and later retired. With hard work and keen analysis, Dorothy Tupper managed to bring nursing back into the good graces of the NLN in 1971. Meanwhile, the program for medical technicians, which had been operating under contracts with Laramie

251

County Memorial Hospital in Cheyenne since 1954, was challenged by the American Society of Clinical Pathologists because of the dearth of trained teaching personnel in hospital service. Carlson had to go to the legislature to request additional staffing. The speech pathology and audiology clinical curriculum, which had come under considerable criticism from the State Department of Education, was accredited in 1974 by the American Board of Examiners in Speech Pathology and Audiology.

A critical problem again arose for the College of Law when a joint inspection team from the American Bar Association and the American Association of Law Schools threatened the college's accreditation in 1972 on the grounds of inadequate library facilities and physical plant. Research productivity, high turnover in instructors, and certain curricular policies also came in for criticism, as did the uncertain support accorded the public defender program ("with the result that one can only say that, at the moment, there is either an uneasy truce or a watered-down clinical program that is of inadequate value to the student body"). The law school was accredited, but additional reports to the committee were required. With great support from the Wyoming Bar Association and individual legislators, Dean E. George Rudolph shortly received a considerable increase in book budget — plus funding guaranteed to replace a projected building addition with a brand new building, construction beginning in 1975.

Evaluators frequently commented upon the inadequacy of the University's support systems. Carlson, Ranz, and Meyer needed no accreditation team to tell them that University facilities and particularly equipment had fallen behind. If the science center brought new laboratory space to arts and sciences faculty, engineering was consistently reported as lagging when accreditation teams called. McFadden remembers taking Edward Jakubauskus (then academic vice president) on an unannounced tour of agriculture laboratories, where beginning students and graduate researchers battled for facilities. Both of them emerged disturbed, depressed, and determined. Only with the building additions completed did laboratory space become adequate.

Meanwhile, scientific research equipment was increasing constantly in complexity and cost. The atomic reactor so gladly received by Humphrey turned out not to be appropriate to much of the engineering research. Geologists sought the latest in microscopes; the education college needed a media center fully equipped. If astronomers delighted in their infrared telescope, broadcasters sought equipment for televising and taping. In 1969, the University received $300,000 from the NSF to upgrade the Sigma 5 computer then in operation; but within a few years the system was outdated and lacking in storage capacity for research and other data. In many areas, essential assistance was at a premium. Caretakers and technicians were lacking for the sciences; historians and sociologists typed their own manuscripts; and the new theater department operated for a time without a carpenter to aid in constructing sets. In these regards, part-time help was always at a premium. Improvements came slowly over the years.

At the core of the support program for humanities and social sciences stood the University library. Between 1964 and 1978, expenditures for library books, staff, and facilities steadily increased, with the exception of some backsliding during King's legislative year (1967). In 1970, the North Central Association accrediting team was critical of the "inadequacy" of the library holdings and Carlson, in 1971, gained support from the legislature for a library budget of more than $2 million, an increase of sixteen percent from the previous biennium. Similar inflationary increases came steadily until 1976, when the library was designated by trustees as a "top priority" item and when Carlson, according to one of his colleagues, "worked his heart out" to persuade the legislature of the importance of budget increases. In this he was highly successful. The operating budget in 1976 increased by 46 percent, and in the same year the legislature authorized more than $5 million for an addition to the library building.

As part of an on-going campaign, library director Robert Patterson sought an evaluation of operations and collections. As a result the Association of College and Research Libraries denied the University membership in the organization and pronounced the system to be "seriously substandard in both collection and staff size." Strongly seconded by Jakubauskus, vice president for academic affairs, and supported by Carlson, Patterson campaigned for continuing help. Since the small number of periodical subscriptions had come in for special notice, trustees requested $45,000 of the governor for special emergency funds, and although Herschler came through with only $24,000, he supported the University's efforts to achieve increased funding in the next legislature. In 1978, the library's budget was increased by another 25 percent.

CHAPTER TWELVE

Probably through the influence of Ranz, his first academic vice president, Carlson became an even stronger supporter of the University archival program. In his previous role as librarian, Ranz had brought Gene M. Gressley to campus in 1956. Thereafter the manuscripts, papers, rare books, and Western art that formed part of the archival collections dramatically increased in volume (6,000 archival collections by 1977). It seems likely that Ranz brought Carlson and Gressley together and that the president was impressed from the start, especially since archival holdings meshed well with the research orientation that Carlson appreciated. Gressley frequently expressed to Carlson his wish that Wyoming faculty members and students would orient their work around the archival collection; he shared the president's interest in stimulating research and advanced graduate programs.

> *. . . the main problem is the lack of research by the resident faculty. . . . I am . . . strongly of the opinion that when we have a sizeable graduate program with highly oriented research faculty in the humanities and social sciences the matter of archival use will solve itself. . . .*

Among other plans, Gressley (with assistance from Humphrey, then retired) hoped to develop a business history center that would encourage research in archives relating to cattle, petroleum, mining, railroads, lumber, and other business areas.

It seems clear also that, recognizing the possibilities for future expansion, Gressley took pains to involve Carlson in his collection activities. Having contacted the president-elect before his assumption of office, Gressley reported to him frequently on individual donors and their responses (sending 69 letters to the president in academic year 1969-70); wrote in 1968 a particularly long and interesting report on his needs and plans; and involved the new president in many of his travels (in the first six months of 1972, Carlson traveled with Gressley to New York, Chicago, and California in search of donors and collections). At a time when little effort was being made to attract donations to University projects, Gressley was surely the University's prime development officer.

It was Carlson who supplemented Gressley's previous functions (as assistant director of the library for the division of rare books and special collections, research professor in American studies, and professor of library science) with the new title of American studies director. It seems likely that the president and his immediate staff were not particularly pleased with the activities of the former program nor its directorship. A search for an eminent outside professor to occupy the Coe chair in American studies following the retirement of Wilson O. Clough led to several refusals. The administration gladly turned to T. A. Larson who accepted the chair as of 1969; Larson's resignations left vacant the headship of the department of history and the directorship of the School of American Studies. Undoubtedly, the history department was in Carlson's view needful of change. Its new Ph.D. program had been refused a spot on the "acceptable" list of the American Historical Association. Larson had found it increasingly difficult to work with E. Gerald Meyer, dean of arts and sciences since 1963. After a national search, the headship of the department was assigned to an eminent research scholar, Roger L. Williams.

As for the directorship of American studies, Ranz and Carlson vetoed the suggestions of Larson and others; and in August 1969, Carlson recommended to the trustees that Gressley be given the position in addition to his other assignments. "These two programs," he told the board,

> *— American studies and archives — have much in common, can be meshed together to the mutual benefit of both, and Dr. Gressley is uniquely qualified to guide both.*

Trustees agreed, but the entire tenured faculty of the English and history departments wrote to protest an appointment made without consultation during a summer month when school was out of session and faculty were gone.

Under Gressley's supervision and with Carlson's approval, the Coe program was drastically changed in direction. It seems fair to say that neither president nor archivist particularly appreciated its focus on teaching rather than research. Transferred at once to the College of Education, the summer institute for teachers devoted a few sessions to the less-than-popular topic of semantics and then was quietly phased out. By 1972, the winter scholarship and fellowship program was allowed to lapse, in accordance with a recommendation that came from Ranz, who had brought Gressley to campus and remained a close friend.

> *Of late, there has been some difficulty in getting really qualified applicants for these awards. Discouraging too has been the fact that enrollments in the American studies program have*

consisted in large part of students receiving American studies scholarships. Although these awards are unquestionably of value to the students receiving them, the University as a whole profits little from them and Mr. Coe's intentions in setting up the program seem little furthered. Accordingly, it is recommended that these scholarships be suspended for a trial period, and the funds used for other purposes which it is hoped will more directly achieve Mr. Coe's purposes.

Faculty objected strenuously to the new arrangements — particularly Wilson O. Clough in a brilliant letter dated May 25, 1972. At least two deans protested — Meyer and (later) Dean Riley Schaeffer of arts and sciences. To Meyer, Gressley responded that the teaching program could continue without funding if courses were provided through regular department offerings. He wrote the dean that he would be

glad to go all out, even if I personally have reservations about the wisdom of such a course, in the development of an American studies graduate program (including a doctorate), but this will require a University commitment of staff, curriculum and budget; a commitment, which I sense will not be forthcoming now or in the immediate future. Therefore, I have suggested that if we desire an American studies program at Wyoming, we should run it the way most American studies programs in the country are supported.

In 1971, then, the "School of American Studies" was "re-directed," as Gressley put it later, "to encompass the fostering of research and teaching in the humanities through the allocation of a series of departmental project grants." Gressley wrote that as salary commitments were slowly decreased, he hoped to increase funding for lecturers, institutes, travel, and concerts, among other items. If graduate and undergraduate curricula were continued, it was basically with the primary aid of Professor H. R. Dieterich and, outside of several core offerings, through other departments' classes.

The conversion of American studies funds represented a potential problem with the Coe Foundation, for William Robertson Coe had provided that funds be withdrawn rather than suffer diversion from his expressed programmatic purposes. As early as 1972, Carlson wrote to Robert Coe (at his

residence in France) expressing a desire to talk with him about the necessity of an addition to the library and ideas

for the development of our American Heritage Center. This program already has a national significance and our hopes are that we can have a truly national center, in a beautiful building at the University of Wyoming dedicated to our past great heritage.

In the summer of 1973, however, Carlson and Coe missed connections when Coe was in Cody and New York.

Later that year the situation became alarming when members of the Coe Foundation board learned of the change in the program — whether through Arad Riggs or through some other source. President and archivist shared concern about what they considered "distortions" of their actions. Carlson managed to speak with Marguerite Pettet, Coe's one-time secretary who was then vice president of the foundation, and caused her (he reported) to change her mind on "the matter of fellowships." In December 1973, Gressley drafted letters to Pettet and Coe for Carlson's signatures, writing the president that

After considerable thought on this I really tried to avoid mentioning names. I am dubious of the wisdom of that approach, especially if [Pettet] shows that letter to Bob Coe. What we did want to get across was that we are well aware of the undermining that is going on, the outright lies and viciousness, and I hope I have relayed these points across.

At Ranz's suggestion, Carlson toned down Gressley's drafts, but the president wrote both Pettet and Coe in January 1974. To Pettet, he repeated that he was

extremely disturbed and distressed to learn of the erroneous reports that have been floating about regarding the development of our American Studies program at Wyoming; indeed, and of my administration of The University of Wyoming. In fact, I do not know how I could express myself anymore than to say that I am amazed and bewildered at these rumors. Not only are these reports misguided and misleading, they are patently untrue. There is no other university president in the United States who would hold beliefs that would come closer to William Robertson Coe's than I personally cherish. . . . After a considerable amount of reflection on this matter, the only conclusion that I can reach (and I must admit reluctantly) is that most of these rumors and reports have resulted from petty jealousies and a degree of malicious intent.

To Robert Coe, Carlson again expressed his desire for a personal meeting during which he hoped to explain and "clarify" several matters. He wrote:

After reading [Coe's] will and having discussions with various administrative officials involved, I decided to make several alterations which I firmly believed would be more in line with achieving the objectives of your father and would fulfill his wishes. In this connection, after discussing my ideas and concepts with Mr. Arad Riggs and many other colleagues and officials of the University, I first decided to make a change in the Director of the American Studies Program. Secondly, we altered the focus of the William Robertson Coe Summer Institute of American Studies toward a direction that we thought would more closely conform with the original objectives of your father's bequest.

Thereafter, Carlson explained that College of Education personnel had focused summer programs around "the development of semantics in the American Heritage" through always emphasizing "the contributions of the conservative philosophy to the development of our American ideals;" and that through the "winter program," although he did not specify the awarding of grants, the "Jeffersonian tradition" had been followed in funding various projects in music and fine arts as broad parts of American life and culture.

Any problems with the Coe Foundation were circumvented when later that year, the foundation formally terminated its existence, thereby paving the way for institutionalizing the new focus of the Coe endowment. In 1975, the legislature recognized the existence of a Western Heritage Research Center for which trustees were empowered to seek funds. In 1976, the WHRC was more clearly

defined in a regulation adopted by the board, and the new American studies program was explained.

The American Heritage Center shall be composed of special programs relating to the American heritage and shall specifically include the School of American Studies and the Western History Research Center, each having its own distinct and definite academic goals and functions. The Center shall be headed by the Assistant to the President for the American Heritage Center [Gressley] who shall be responsible to the President, and through him to the Trustees, for developing and administering all programs within the Center. With regard to the School of American Studies, the Assistant to the President shall consult with the appropriate academic officers of the University in formulating and initiating interdisciplinary programs in American Studies. The objective of the Western History Research Center shall be the acquisition, organization and management of all University archival collections relating to the history of American civilization, with particular emphasis on the American West.

The official formation of the American Heritage Center with its assistant to the president did not by any means end problems. As before, the status of such matters as the rare book collection; space in the University library; budgeting of certain items such as freight (although the final separation of budgets helped); and staff assistance caused constant friction between the AHC and the University library. In 1973, Librarian James H. Richards, Jr., resigned over the "archives situation" and the "mutual distrust and acrimony" among himself, Gressley, and Ranz; although Ranz persuaded him temporarily to retract his resignation, he affirmed it again the following year and left on June 30, 1974.

Others, too, complained. Especially after the construction of the fine arts building, the art museum director became irritated at Gressley's solicitation of paintings and sculpture in rivalry with his own, especially because he considered himself professionally more competent to restore and evaluate such acquired items. Faculty contended that AHC collections were not useable because collecting had outstripped inventories and storage facilities, and Gressley retorted that faculty were not properly orienting their research around archival holdings. When Meyer complained that the "collection policy needs a better focus" and suggested a faculty advisory committee, Gressley resisted the idea. To Carlson he wrote in 1974:

> *The name of the game is acquisition. Great libraries became great only by the catholicity of their collections. We, of course, view the development of archival resources in an identical light. Obviously, quantity alone does not make a distinguished library or archive, but the equation between quantity and eminence is remarkably high.*

Gressley's vigorous archival collecting was part, but only part, of increasing interest in development, or the accumulation of outside gifts and funding for University use. Without detailing all of the problems of mounting a major development campaign, one might note that the administration of the development program was excessively complex and subject to constant reassessment and change. The University of Wyoming Foundation, a tax-exempt corporation with a complicated set of Class A, Class B, and later Class C directors, was supplemented by a president's development officer, the Alumni Association, the Cowboy Joe Club, and a committee of trustees — not to mention Gressley in his special fields of collecting and individual departments in theirs. Periodic dissatisfactions with the complex arrangements only led to poorly-concealed mistrusts or, as the development committee once put it, a lack of rapport between the trustees and the foundation.

On occasion, potential donors were alienated too. In 1971, one of the trustees wrote to another that

> *I feel it only fair to indicate to you that the concern of the Directors of the Foundation arises from specific instances in which recent potential donors have felt thwarted in their efforts to make contributions to the University of Wyoming. It is not the intention of the Directors to indicate whether the donors were justified in their feeling; however, the very fact that they have indicated a problem would make it imperative that the Board establish definite policy decisions in this regard.*

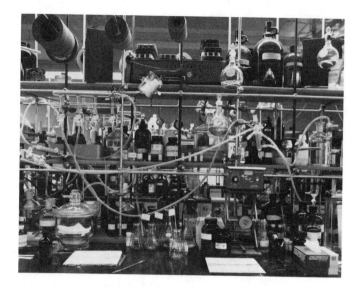

Research equipment

The problem of development administration was never truly solved during Carlson's administration. Still, the University profited from generous gifts apart from that of William Robertson Coe: Funds provided for an endowed chair and other purposes in economics by John S. Bugas; the Milward L. Simpson fund in political science was raised by a series of alumni and friends; and there were also the generous gifts of Chacey C. Kuehn of Dubois — to mention only a few.

Gifts alone could not enhance academic excellence, nor could the multiplicity of curricula and burgeoning research funds. As teachers, researchers, and those from whom the University derived its reputation, faculty lay at the core of campus operations. "In large measure," Carlson wrote as he left office in 1978

> *the faculty determines the quality of education we are able to offer at the University of Wyoming. One of the most satisfying aspects of my tenure as president has been to observe the great people who have joined us this past decade. They are putting us on the map academically and will do so even more in the future.*

Attracting faculty was a special problem. A competitive salary scale was essential, and increasing salaries was a project that Carlson personally took to heart. To this, he gave his all, as one administrator recently reported. To legislature after legislature, the president argued that good teachers and researchers would not come to Wyoming without financial inducement, nor would they stay if better-paying opportunities at prestigious universities called them away. National studies of faculty salaries were regularly compiled by the American Association of University Professors and other organizations, and from them administrators devised charts and texts to use in persuading legislators of the need for salary adjustments.

In this matter, the administration was rather spectacularly successful. Legislators responded; luckily, times were good. In 1968, Wyoming was ranked in the lowest tenth percentile among comparable state universities in salaries paid to faculty; ten years later, the University stood above median, near the sixtieth percentile point. Only full professors ranked somewhat lower. When Carlson left the University, he wrote that

Working together, we have provided faculty raises that have exceeded the national average nine out of the last ten years and tied the remaining year. We have provided a total of 72 percent increase during the last ten years while the rest of the country averaged 52 percent. . . . I doubt that that record was surpassed anywhere.

In addition, faculty profited from a greatly enhanced program of fringe benefits. In this regard, initiative came primarily from teachers themselves. The active group of faculty that founded the University Faculty Association in 1975 and affiliated with the National Education Association through its Wyoming branch was concerned primarily with matters of tenure and financial security. The notable effort mounted by Professor Burton Muller (physics) — an effort which included lobbying at the legislature — vastly improved retirement and insurance systems. Muller, together with Russ Hammond (education) and with the support of Elliott Hays, worked tirelessly, and provisions that permitted a better income for University retirees may be counted his personal achievement. By 1975, all University employees of more than half-time status were "benefited" in health insurance, life insurance, and later dental insurance. An increasing proportion of this was paid by the state. In addition to the greatly improved Wyoming retirement system, the legislature also agreed that employees might choose to place funds in a national teachers' retirement plan as a complement to, and substitute for, the state plan.

During the same period, regulations concerning the employment and pay of women and minorities were reconsidered and redrawn. In February 1965, Fey persuaded trustees that married women should be permitted the same tenure as married men. However, his proposal for a change in the nepotism rule was tabled by trustees, and not until 1971 — pressured by the federal Office of Economic Opportunity — did the board lift its prohibition of married persons' employment in the same "unit;" hereafter such employment was permitted unless one of the couple was in a supervisory position over the other. The question of women-faculty pay and sexual discrimination rose on several occasions in the early 1970s before an education professor finally demanded a formal hearing. Eventually, an authorized investigation revealed considerable differential in male-female salaries, and the rates for a number — not all — of the University's women professors were adjusted upward. Again the UFA was actively involved. In 1977, civil rights legislation required the University to devise a long and complicated regulation on equal employment opportunity and affirmative action. Grievance procedures were approved in 1978 for personnel problems of faculty and staff. This document was the result of long labors by an ad hoc committee: the vice president for academic affairs, the Faculty Senate, deans and department heads, the employment practices office, and many other individuals.

Whatever the policies, at least the procedures of faculty self-governance were carefully established during the decade ending in 1978. In accordance with a strong national trend, a Faculty Senate was established and held its first meeting in October 1968. Twenty years before, such an organization had been voted down as superfluous, but now the faculty was larger, and its regular semester meetings had become awkward — better vehicles for administrative announcements than for faculty decisions. Nor did the former president's advisory committee, with its representatives from the various colleges, seem adequate to mirror faculty concerns. The immediate occasion for the establishment of a senate and the composition of careful bylaws was probably the fact that at Fey's request, the trustees were re-formulating rules and bylaws into what would eventually be called UniRegs. Faculty leaders sensed this as a good time to move. After review by the faculty as a whole, the president recommended that trustees approve the constitution and regulations of the new organization.

257

On May 31, 1968, they did so, making it clear, however, that having a senate did not enhance the powers of the faculty as provided in the trustees' own regulations.

Thenceforward elected faculty representatives debated University policies and voted regulations. Careful procedures were established for changing the UniRegs that were constantly being amended. Although the president had a veto over all regulations, his negative vote could be overridden and the trustees called on for final judgment. Faculty committees — including those on courses, retirement, research, probation, scheduling, and many other matters — were transferred to senate jurisdiction. Unlike the president of the ASUW, the chairman of the Faculty Senate never became an ex-officio member of the board of trustees, although the suggestion was brought to the legislature time and time again. Instead, senate chairpersons were informally invited to attend trustee meetings. Relations between Carlson and the Faculty Senate chairman were generally calm, and the new organization operated smoothly. In 1976, after considerable criticism of personnel policies and continuing misunderstanding about personnel rules, a parallel Staff Council was established and approved by trustees. It replaced several review and advisory committees previously in operation.

Among the first concerns of the new senate was the adoption of procedures and rulings concerning promotion, tenure, reappointment, and similar matters of faculty status. The award of tenure, representing a statement of permanent employment except under extraordinary circumstances, was the most important step for a young faculty member and a demonstration of his quality performance. For ten years, senate committees worked and re-worked statements of procedures and criteria for the granting of advancement and tenure. All of the statements were laboriously complex. A minutely defined set of procedures included evaluation at many levels. Should a faculty member feel disgruntled, a careful grievance and appeal procedure was written into the regulations.

What made for faculty excellence was less easy to determine. Many elements were written into criteria for evaluating faculty performance, the most universal being research (or artistic endeavor), teaching, and service to the state. All of these matters — especially in *quality* of performance — represented judgment calls. However specific might be the "allocation of an individual's time," as a general memorandum for the 1971-72 "priority review" put it, the evaluation of the particular percentage devoted to research or teaching was still a matter of personal assessment, and such a mathematical scheme as devised by Meyer (as arts and sciences dean) could never truly solve the problem.

One particular area for concern was student evaluation of a faculty member's teaching effectiveness. Although it took different forms from time to time, such a procedure had long been campus policy; occasionally, ratings were compiled and published by the ASUW. When a new computer card form was devised so that results could be processed by machine, such a form was rated by the Faculty Senate as a "compromise" and regarded as having "numerous deficiencies." In 1974, when the faculty committee on scholarship standards reviewed the procedure, it received numerous complaints from faculty who found the questions inapplicable and ambiguous, deplored the "crude reduction of the learning process," and pointed out that card-checking systems were of almost no value for improvement, whereas written statements might be.

Constant questions arose as to whether students could measure teaching ability without reflecting the grades they had been awarded. Hours of work by the committee on scholarship standards and the faculty tenure and promotion committee produced little agreement. The system in use (wrote Clifford D. Ferris, at one time chairman of the academic standards committee)

tends to affect faculty morale adversely, and if misused could be disastrous in tenure and promotion recommendations as well as in recommendations for faculty teaching awards. . . . I would suggest the establishment of a questionnaire which elicits written comments from the students with, perhaps, some very general guidelines, but that the present "canned" question approach be abolished.

Ferris's view was eventually adopted and student evaluations came to be requested in writing on blank sheets of paper with only the most general guidelines. The validity even of this system remained under attack.

Although teaching abilities were probably the most difficult subject for objective evaluation, it was undoubtedly the research component that caused the greatest problem in matters of promotion and tenure. For one thing, the "publish or perish" idea was new; senior faculty and faculty in many of the teaching-service departments (like physical education or English) had been employed with little concern for research abilities and proclivities. For many of them, the new criteria were devastating. They called for professionalization of individuals heretofore devoted to institutional, or teaching, goals. The definition of scholarly excellence as national recognition, achieved primarily through research publication or performance, caused problems for those who had not anticipated that such criteria would become part of their job descriptions. Many departments came to be split between senior faculty and new.

Since personnel files were kept confidential, an examination of the reports on promotion and tenure cases does not generally indicate the reason for denials. It seems apparent, however, that under the new system, the University took a dramatically hard line. The key organization in the procedure came to be the University promotion and tenure committee, appointed by the Faculty Senate as advisory to the president. Its membership consisted of representatives (later elected) from all colleges, with the president (later the dean of academic affairs) sitting as an ex-officio member. The committee's function was to examine all (later only disputed) cases of tenure, promotion, appointment, and certain other recommendations filtering upward from department heads and college deans.

In 1968-69, the University committee overruled both dean and department head in fourteen instances, frequently denying tenure and promotion

rather than granting them. In all cases, Carlson approved the committee's decision; in the two cases of a tie vote, the president endorsed one and turned down the other. In 1969-70, sixteen of the individuals recommended for promotion and/or tenure by both dean and department head were not approved by the University committee. One department head claimed that the administration pressured the committee to deny promotion for "individuals who were (and are) regarded as outstandingly good teachers, on the grounds that their publication record was inadequate."

Carlson occasionally — though not frequently — vetoed some of the committee's negative decisions. In spring 1973, the president postponed tenure in spite of the committee's negative vote in at least four cases. In 1974-75, the committee was less vigorous in its denials and reversed only six decisions of the lower administration. The following year, Carlson vetoed the committee's *denial* of promotion for at least five individuals, although he went along with many others; there were seventy cases considered altogether. Although the board always seems to have approved the president's recommendations, it did request that he indicate those cases on which he disagreed with the University committee. In 1977, there was only one such on the tenure list; the committee split in a tie vote (and then requested a delay), but the president (and the board) approved.

Of course there were many complaints. Deans and department heads resented being overruled and contended, with considerable justification, that they knew their faculty better than any president or University committee. The whole procedure "smacks of autocracy," wrote a department head in 1973. Another deplored the system whereby a committee could overrule

recommendations strongly supported by the tenured colleagues of a department, department heads, and deans, made on the basis of at least four years of professional contact. In earlier times at this institution, what is now called the Tenure and Promotion Committee served largely in the capacity of screening the recommendations of department heads and deans as a means of protecting faculty from unjust or arbitrary actions by their superiors. As the committee now functions, it has assumed a role which, in my opinion, cannot be justified. . . .

Angrily attacking the system that had postponed tenure for several of his faculty, Dean E. George Rudolph of the law school drew powerful support from an American Bar Association committee on campus for an accreditation visit. He and the committee insisted that law schools operated differently from other academic departments, that low teaching loads were the norm, and that high productivity in publications should not be set as a standard. Not only did the committee deplore the "lack of control that the law faculty has over its own development," but it suggested that the administration was quantity-minded in terms of research publications.

There appears to be a rather singular focus on an article in a "scholarly journal" or in a book as the evidence that a teacher is doing meaningful research and is, in fact, a scholar in his field.

Rudolph won his point and the faculty in question were tenured the following year. Even more difficult to decide were tenure criteria for such faculty-equivalent staff as the library administration.

In the president's files are preserved many poignant letters from individuals protesting their own situations. A professor of geography who had received the highest ratings in the student course evaluation poll left before tenure became an issue. "Every school has its own philosophy," the student newspaper quoted him as saying, "and I just don't fit in. I'm interested in teaching." A professor of education, who had been rejected for promotion by the college committee, favored by the University committee, and then (apparently) negatively assessed by the academic vice president, was emotionally distressed.

I would like to appeal to you to do something to change the present procedure. This is a de-humanizing ordeal. . . . I think this ordeal is cruel and very upsetting to the ones involved. Therefore, I would like to spare others the hurt that I have received.

Others accepted the standards and wrote three and four page letters underscoring their accomplishments. Carlson usually replied soothingly — on occasion with a personal interview.

As in universities across the country, the "publish or perish" approach to faculty evaluation became a public issue. In response to student protest, Carlson, in 1972, told the ASUW that publication was not essential to tenure or reappointment, but justified the call for research on grounds that it made for better teaching and a reduction of otherwise heavy teaching loads — a matter of considerable concern in merit evaluation. Unconvinced, the *Branding Iron* published a tongue in cheek editorial on one of the students' favorite professors who was leaving for another campus.

And Bill sayeth unto them, "Publish or perish. Go forth and multiply and cover the earth with publications in order that we might come to be looked upon as a great seat of learning.". . . .

But it came to pass that not all heeded the wise council of Bill and forgot the ways of his wisdom, for in the Geography Department was one professor, a thoroughly wicked fellow who desired only to teach. . . .

And a decree went out that the wicked Professor should be exiled to the wilds of Montana, never to set foot in the state again. . . .

"Praise be to Bill," said the multitude. "May his name be honored forever."

A few months later, a prominent University trustee wrote to Ranz in more thoughtful vein.

As you know, I am in full support of the doctrine that there should be evidence of original research and thought on the part of a man who is designated a member of the faculty of a university. I am a little in doubt as to the strict definition of "research" and even more worried about the strict interpretation of the word "publish." One of the most valuable lessons which I have had drilled into me is the necessity for recognizing the grays in almost every situation. I can, for instance, imagine several situations in which research might take such unconventional guises as quiet and meditative thought without

CHAPTER TWELVE

the use of any sort of tools or aids such as previous publications or instrumentation. . . . I am also perturbed by a too literal definition of publish. . . .

More vital was opinion among legislators. In 1965, Fey told the legislature that research was essential to a faculty's professional growth and cited such research as an expanding element in a University's responsibilities. But the "publish or perish" dictum was rejected by many, including one leading member of the joint appropriations committee who wrote that he

like many other members of the Legislature, would be more inclined to grant larger salary increases if greater emphasis were placed on teaching and less on research. . . . [This] is an attitude acquired from personal observations and conversations with university students.

But demands for recognized faculty research efforts continued in Wyoming as across the nation.

This chapter would not be complete without consideration of an issue of curriculum that combined problems of quality, accreditation, funding, faculty, and service to the state. The problem of medical education had for many years concerned Wyomingites who sought to place sons and daughters in medical schools and provide physicians — but also dentists and veterinarians — to practice in the state's small, isolated communities. In the mid-1970s legislature and governor got together and sponsored a plan for in-state medical education, with which the University necessarily became closely involved.

Such education had been a special problem for many decades. As early as 1948, the dean of the University of Colorado medical school entered into an agreement with Humphrey whereby Colorado reserved some medical school slots for qualified Wyoming students. This agreement shortly became the basis for a Western Interstate Commission for Higher Education, of which Humphrey was one of the founders. WICHE assessed fees against state governments and arranged in exchange for the training of local students in out-of-state medical, dental, veterinarian and other professional health care schools. WICHE was never popular with legislators because it charged high prices (actually subsidizing medical schools with its fee payments); it did not attempt to reserve slots for students from any one of its thirteen member states; and it made no guarantees that medical school graduates

Monitoring Wyoming range and livestock, c. 1980

would return home after their residency programs. Indeed, statistics showed that residents usually practiced wherever they finished their training.

Various measures were proposed to circumvent the problems. As early as 1950, a legislator sought to establish a medical school in Wyoming, but his suggestion gained little support. In 1962, a committee appointed by Humphrey suggested the possibility of a two-year medical curriculum. Two years later, a study indicated that it would be a decade or more before the less populated Western states could afford to build large hospital facilities necessary for quality medical training. Accordingly, Fey proposed that a contract program be established — with or without WICHE support — whereby students could enter agreeing medical schools at specified costs to be borne by the state — at least on a loan basis. Other proposals included the erasure of indebtedness if students would agree to return to Wyoming for a certain period of practice. A few years later, it was suggested that the four states with smallest population build a common medical school jointly financed. Included in the proposal was the notion of family practice: "combining the concentrated knowledge and skills of the specialist with the broad understanding, wisdom, and continuing care of the generalist."

Aroused to interest, the Wyoming State Medical Society determined on a professional consultant and survey. Enthusiastically, Governor Hathaway matched the society's funding, and with the aid of a grant from a health planning council, the society employed a Palo Alto, California, firm to conduct an in-depth study. The consultants' report, published in December 1972, recommended several possible programs. The legislature balked at the recommended appropriation of $750,000 for the nucleus of a faculty, but it did (in 1973) appropriate $100,000 to pay a "director of medical education," whose task it would be to work with the society and University in detailing a medical school plan. Selected was Dr. Stephen C. Joseph.

Dr. Joseph's plan closely paralleled that of the original California consultants. In 1974, he presented to the hesitating trustees, the medical society, and finally the Wyoming legislature a scheme for a four-year medical school centered around family practice. The core school would be located on the University campus and coordinated with health education and science facilities at both the University and the community colleges. Clinical training would occur at Wyoming community hospitals or special family practice centers, while physicians in the state would be called on to provide "internships" for medical students at their own practice sites. Out-of-state facilities might also be used for hospital training, but a Wyoming faculty member in residence would make sure that family medicine remained the "integrative theme." Joseph envisioned fifteen faculty at the campus "Medical Education Resources Center," ten at clinics, and a good many medical doctors who would give part-time service. At full operation, up to thirty under-graduate students would be working on campus and 24 others would be in the residency stage. As start-up costs, he anticipated $500,000 the first year, $1 million the second, and an annual budget of $3.5-$4 million, not counting immediate building construction costs.

Opposition to a full-fledged medical school — on the grounds of financial drain and maintenance of quality — began almost at once. In the files is some friendly and sympathetic correspondence between Carlson and Tilghman H. Aley, head of Casper College. In early 1974, Aley had analyzed the program and emerged with several doubts: The cost, he thought, might be prohibitive; the clinical facilities would never equate with those of larger hospitals in more populous areas; and there was little guarantee that the resulting family doctors would settle in hamlets, where they were needed, instead of towns, where they were not. "While reluctant to do so," Aley reported to Carlson early in 1974,

> *several of my physician acquaintances have serious doubts of the efficacy of the experimental construct now under study.*

Instead, he suggested that Wyoming might make one-on-one deals with area medical schools for fees and admissions (to be fully paid by the state).

Carlson responded with conditional approval.

> *I think Wyoming may be forced into this type of arrangement on a broad scale, but I am sure you realize that the implications on the direct subsidization of medical education are very far reaching as far as our exchange programs with WICHE are concerned. I suspect that the moment we would adopt a direct cost reimbursement basis for medical education, we would be forced to follow the same procedure for both veterinary and dental education. This of course, does not absolutely rule out this possibility, but it does require some rather serious soul searching before we move in that direction.*

At the same time, a Faculty Senate ad hoc committee began investigating the medical education planning. Having met with doctors, administrators, and Joseph, the committee made a careful report. It included "pros" (the increased activity and moneys for health science personnel, the greater likelihood that Wyoming residents would be admitted to a program, the possibility of more health care personnel in the state) and "cons" (cost, competence, accredibility and quality, effect on higher education budgets). Most of all it asked, will the plan work? Will physicians really stay in small communities? Will the residency program at small hospitals provide enough variety and intensity of training? The report was submitted to trustees but went no further.

CHAPTER TWELVE

The 1974 legislature refused to appropriate funding for a medical school complex although it did appropriate $60,000 for continuing investigation. A few months later, Joseph presented a supplemental plan that recommended a phase-in approach to the system: To begin with, several family practice residency centers in Wyoming, where students were sent out-of-state for their primary training, would be required to assume internships. Shortly thereafter Joseph resigned. He accepted another position, but in truth he was worried about administrative problems. Would the governor's office be coordinating medical education, or would the chore fall to the University, an alternative that he preferred? Was there enough commitment and funding to continue planning even on a minimum scale? Joseph was unsure.

In 1975, Joseph's replacement, Dr. Thomas A. Nicholas, saw his predecessor's recommendations become a reality. The legislature authorized the establishment of special agreements between Wyoming and out-of-state institutions for the payment of tuition costs (provided students agreed to practice in Wyoming or to repay the amounts involved); the establishment (with an initial budget of $1.87 million) of a family practice residency program in state; and the continued planning for a medical school. Specifically, legislators budgeted for medical school contracts at approximately $1 million, construction of buildings at $250,000 for planning, and a staff not to exceed 28 individuals. That year, special contracts were negotiated with Utah, Creighton, Nebraska, and Kansas State for medical, dental, and veterinary students, but the administration took care that WICHE handled the negotiations and that relationships with that organization were therefore not jeopardized.

In 1976, the legislature appropriated $4.5 million for the biennium to recruit faculty and staff at Laramie, to develop Casper and Cheyenne family practice residency programs, and for student contracts at Creighton and Utah. In 1977, it appropriated an extra $1.9 million for additional fiscal-year expenses, and the medical education program seemed a reality.

That spring, Dr. Robert M. Daugherty, Jr. was appointed dean of the College of Human Medicine (referred to as the medical school), and administrative faculty was actively recruited. Assistant deans for special programs were designated and hired, as were directors for the family practice residency centers in Cheyenne and Casper (the sites of the state's largest hospitals). UW campus faculty members were assigned teaching chores. Daugherty was a strong and fast mover; his report on development, addressed to Carlson in autumn 1976 and distributed to the trustees at that time, contained considerable planning for curriculum development on campus; a chart of administrative responsibilities; as well as Casper and Cheyenne construction details. The program, wrote Daugherty, had after all been initiated by "the physicians of the state and the people through the legislature" as a means of helping to "solve their severe health care problems." The envisioned curriculum reflected

a balance between traditional structured didactic presentations, small group interaction, and individualized learning. The curricular goal is to produce physicians strong in the basic natural sciences who also have broad training in the social and behavioral sciences and who understand and are sympathetic to the special needs of medical practice in rural America in general and Wyoming in particular.

In the spring of 1978, a good many plans fell apart. Medical school funding had been included in the standard appropriation request. Trustees now announced their "full support" and urged legislators to approve the budget proposed by the governor. Although the house passed the package by a vote of 35-27 on one occasion and 37-25 on another, the senate deadlocked 15-15 and apparently was not to be moved. The legislature adjourned in anger without passing any appropriations bill, in spite of the fact that Daugherty had taken 22 pre-medical students to Cheyenne to lobby and the governor (Democrat Ed Herschler) had clearly indicated support.

263

Many queries had arisen, and University officials wondered if their policies had been politically astute. Were legislators objecting to the expenditure of $14 million for another campus building? Had the medical school better be located at Casper, as Senator Roy Peck had suggested? Was a four-year school really essential to support those residency programs which were designed to keep physicians in the state? Were salaries too high? Should personnel have been phased in gradually? Was there any problem of University control when the program had been originally stimulated by the governor?

Following the legislative debacle, in a memo addressed to Daugherty by Carlson but drafted by Joe Geraud (March 23, 1978), the president asked the dean to tell his staff that positions were subject to termination according to legislative decision.

While the Governor has announced that he will call a special session within the near future, it is uncertain that availability of funds for the support of personnel positions will be known at a time that will permit utilization of the normal notice periods to personnel with regard to employment by the University.

In April, a not-yet-daunted Daugherty made a long and enthusiastic report to the board on the medical school plan. Trustees brought up many problems. Clearly their "full support" was tempered.

As it turned out, meetings were in vain, plans went for nothing, and dour predictions proved correct. At the special legislative session called by the governor early in May, the bill funding the medical school was defeated in the house by a vote of 31-30. Although the house later voted a compromise proposal that would have authorized funding of staff already hired, the senate developed objections and turned the compromise down. Some legislators may actually have been turned off by Daugherty's intensive lobbying, but on the whole

finances seemed the major consideration. T. A. Larson, now a state legislator, was one of the leading opponents to the scheme; his objections were founded not only on the expense of medical education but on the difficulties of maintaining quality without larger and more intricate facilities.

To add to difficulties, the school's application for a "faculty development training grant" in family medicine was turned down by a federal agency. The department of biochemistry, only recently switched to "College of Human Medicine," had to be relocated, and plans to integrate the student health service had to be dropped. Faculty administrators, funded only through the end of 1978, sought other positions and began to drift away. Daugherty shortly resigned; replacements were difficult to find.

In the long run, however, the purged program continued to function. In 1978 and thereafter, the legislature regularly funded students who attended out-of-state medical schools, either on one-on-one agreements or through the WICHE program. Residency centers were duly established, first in Casper and then in Cheyenne, although administrative difficulties so plagued the former that many early students resigned rather than follow programs to fruition. A staff of coordinating administrators in Laramie oversaw operations, advised pre-medical students about courses and careers, and taught occasionally in the pre-professional curriculum on campus.

The defeat of the medical school probably did not greatly distress trustees; after all, the plan was not of their making. It had been promoted basically by the governor. In the long list of programs developed, researches accomplished, faculty hired, and facilities improved, the medical school defeat ranked as relatively unimportant. Other achievements were more important. Ten years after he became president, Carlson estimated "subjectively" that nineteen departments had made outstanding improvement, 25 had done well, and seven were unchanged. "Many of the departments showing most improvement are in the College of Arts and Sciences," he said. In these ten years, the president counted eleven new bachelor's degree programs,

Student art exhibit preparation, c. 1982

fifteen on the master's level, and four new doctorates. He spoke of individual and departmental research achievements; in a decade, faculty had increased outside research funding by about 500 percent. Not only had the legislature raised the operating budget appropriation, but private funds solicited had increased by nearly 1,000 percent. Faculty salaries were up, as were fringe benefits; a viable system of self-governance was in operation. Not only was campus life (in Carlson's view) richer than before, but cultural outreach was bringing performances and exhibits to Wyoming citizens wherever in the state they lived. New computer programs, increased library funding, and the American Heritage Center provided more support. New buildings and additions enhanced facilities.

"This is probably the greatest decade that the University has had and will ever have," said the former president in August 1978.

RESEARCH

hree University of Wyoming off-campus research facilities testify to the interest of faculty and students in the unique conditions offered by the state.

Chronologically the oldest, the Jackson Hole Biological Research Center was founded after World War II, when this research facility for the new Jackson Hole Wildlife Park came into being through efforts of the New York Zoological Society and the Wyoming Game and Fish Commission. The station soon became an outpost for research by UW faculty and professors from many other institutes and universities on the special environment and life of the Jackson Hole area. After 1947, the station not only welcomed but housed researchers and provided limited laboratory facilities. Through the years, heat, water, electricity, and more appropriate quarters (a group of cabins) were added. From the establishment of the center, UW professor of zoology L. Floyd Clarke served on its executive board. In 1953, Clarke became director of the station; he was followed in 1976 by Professor Kenneth L. Diem. A year later, the research center moved its operations to a new facility and the New York Zoological Society discontinued its affiliation. The University of Wyoming-National Park Service Research Center is now officially located in Moran. High atop Jelm Mountain, thirty miles southwest of Laramie, the University's infrared telescope reaches for the stars. Formally dedicated in July 1978, the observatory was financed in part by the Wyoming legislature and primarily by the National Science Foundation, to a total cost of more than $1.6 million. High altitudes, clear skies, and cold winter weather make for extraordinary vision, impossible in areas where the atmosphere is polluted by smog, ground light, and vapor. At the time of its construction, the 92-inch telescope was one of the largest of its type in the world. The design of the instrument was the work of University Professors Robert Gehrz, John Hackwell, and W. T. Grandy. The observatory, used by faculty, students, and scientists from all over the world, permits the study of the spectral area between visible light and radio waves. It is not too much to believe, astronomers say, that it will assist in unraveling the secrets of the origin and evolution of the universe.

Located where a state fish hatchery once stood and less than ten miles from campus, the Red Buttes Biological Research Station is the youngest of these three special facilities. In 1957, the state turned the old hatchery barn over to the University, and for fifteen years it served as a site for research on fish, badgers, beavers, and coyotes. In recognition of the growing array of Wyoming-oriented research projects dealing with zoology and the environment, the legislature, in 1981 and 1982, appropriated funds for construction of a more useful and up-to-date building. Today, Red Buttes contains pens for small mammals, large mammals and birds, holding tanks for fish and aquatic animals, and laboratories for experimental work. Laboratories are used for both research and teaching. The list of student and faculty projects at the facility ranges from fish

L. Floyd Clarke and Kenneth L. Diem, directors of the Jackson Hole Biological Research Center

Assaying class, 1897

culture to animal behavior and from endocrinology to environmental physiology. Researchers are working on antelope, deer, and elk; on bear and beaver; and on badgers, coyotes, ground squirrels, ducks, mice, frogs, fish, toads, and salamanders. As Professor Harold Bergman (zoology, physiology) has pointed out, the research comes "at a crucial time in Wyoming, when the state government and citizens are attempting to place resource conservation and resource development in proper balance."

Chapter Thirteen

Focus on the Presidency
1970-1982

A university president — especially in a public institution — constantly walks a tightrope to maintain support and approval among the constituencies he must impress. Alumni, students, trustees, faculty members, voters, and legislators comprise the list, and frequently the aims and outlooks of these groups are diametrically opposed. A president can hardly satisfy everybody, but strong presidents cut an image of "leadership" — whatever the term may mean — that garners respect from those most important to a university and its purposes.

Leadership implies the quality of strength, but for a university president, strong decisions must be tempered with consultation on all levels, particularly with trustees, faculty, and administrators. Too much consultation, of course, signifies weakness and lack of leadership; too little causes a president to seem withdrawn, secretive, and even dictatorial. Many established systems — faculty governance, open meeting laws, complex legislative rulings — call for a different type of leadership from the old brand of assertiveness and dictation. Still, in some ways, leadership can become a matter of personality and public presence.

During Carlson's administration, a range of complaints — some often contradictory in themselves — surfaced on the score of administrative methods. Eventually, an erosion of confidence in the president, particularly among faculty, played its role in his resignation. Subsequent presidents worked to reestablish the image of leadership and the balance of consultation with decisiveness. This chapter will attempt to tell the story.

The administrative team through which Carlson operated during his presidency stood at the center of a complicated system. When he arrived at Wyoming, the new president found a great many officers already in place, with responsibilities and chains of command that resembled, when charted, a number of great spider webs. Most of the positions had been established by Humphrey during his

many years as president. Although Fey had called for a review and any necessary revision of University regulations, he had not remained on the scene long enough to see it to its conclusion.

In 1967, there were six major administrative divisions whose chiefs reported directly to the president: finance, student affairs, research, academic affairs, athletics, and "University relations" (the latter consolidated and retitled the division of information). Several of these divisions headed complex structures — such as that for academic affairs, which included fourteen different subdivisions (including all the colleges) as well as several areas of joint responsibility (computer services and American studies). Student affairs and finance were almost equally complicated organizations. The situation bothered even the trustees, who in 1971, concerned about (in Carlson's words) "proliferation of staff, proliferation of programs, sharply rising costs, and reorganizations effected and contemplated," requested and received a report on the exact functions of divisions in "student affairs."

Carlson had indeed made some changes, but it is hard to say that administration was simplified. Shortly after his arrival, he eliminated the research office (although he later revived it) and added one for University extension (which was later abolished, having apparently fulfilled its purpose). In an effort to straighten out chains of command, he designated four vice presidents (extension, student affairs, finance, and academic affairs) plus two assistants (for development and for information, the latter which came to include alumni relations), plus a director of intercollegiate athletics.

From among these administrative leaders Carlson chose his close advisers. Through them he communicated with deans of the colleges. His other contacts with campus affairs came through officially

 268

recognized organizations, like the Faculty Senate or the ASUW. Carlson's advisers were important, for the new president leaned heavily upon them. He tended to refer matters of import to vice presidents for decision, and the files are filled with memos that demonstrate this practice. Even when he himself had strong opinions, the new president seemed to gain confidence by conferring with his administrative colleagues. Most policy documents in the files are marked for their attention and advice.

Of necessity, the president leaned most heavily on those he trusted and with whom he felt at ease. It is difficult to tell what he felt for Elliott Hays, vice president for finance; but he expressed considerable admiration when he recognized how implicitly Hays was trusted and respected by the legislators. With Geraud in student affairs — and also for some time legal counsel to the trustees — Carlson seemed to feel an affinity that grew out of like-thinking collegiality. In later years, he came to respect H. B. McFadden, vice president for extension, and indeed might almost have been thinking of him as a successor. But when he first came to Wyoming, Carlson's right-hand man was clearly the important vice president for academic affairs, James Ranz.

Ranz was in a central position. More than other vice presidents, he had contact with campus academics, and he shared Carlson's view of building academic excellence. An old hand, Ranz had begun his Wyoming career as a librarian. After a hiatus elsewhere, he had been summoned back by Humphrey in 1963 to take over the office of academic affairs. Among Ranz's early close friends was E. Gerald Meyer, who held the key position of dean of arts and sciences after 1963. At first quiet, pleasant, and glad to be of help, Ranz was a natural aid to a new president acclimating to a new campus, and an easy man to work with besides. Carlson undoubtedly welcomed his knowledge of the faculty and appreciated his criteria for academic excellence. It is impossible to tell exactly what decisions were made by whom, but it is apparent that Ranz soon assumed great importance in administrative policy making. By 1972, he was surely *the* man in Carlson's administration, and

indications are that he was beginning to assert his authority over even such a long-term administrator as Elliott Hays.

Exactly how far Ranz's authority ranged was a matter between himself and the president and may never be determined. Rumors of the vice president's power spread across campus — and even farther — and did not fail to evoke adverse comment. Among the many anonymous letters preserved in the files of all presidents, there is one (1973) directed to Carlson which complains that Ranz was "running the University" and suggests that "very few people can handle power wisely." By 1973, Ranz was evoking irritation among his administrative colleagues, all of whom had admired his intelligence and his dedication to academic standards. He was frequently away and left much of the running of his office to his knowledgeable and efficient secretary, and rumors circulated that he was manipulating secretly behind Carlson's back. Ranz's motives were obscure to his colleagues, but to several of them he seemed to have changed.

Confronted with overt criticism and covert gossip, Carlson finally — and it seems reluctantly — set about remedying matters. Trustees may well have suggested that he do so. Sometime in 1972, he began a series of regular meetings with staff and deans, with whom his dealings had previously existed through Ranz's office. "I feel that I am not in as close touch with each college as necessary," the president wrote later to Ranz. "It has been particularly so lately as compared to the early part of my administration." Ranz may have been hurt. In early 1974, he and Carlson disagreed strongly on a matter of budget, a problem that probably involved Hays as well. Thereafter Ranz and the president, to the distress of the latter, were scarcely communicating.

That spring, Ranz's position and policies became the subject of discussion at a board meeting, probably at the insistence of the trustees themselves. There are no records of a subsequent meeting between president and his now-alienated assistant, but one probably occurred. Carlson was disturbed. In a letter to Ranz, he blamed himself for his

poor description of the situation in face of your obvious and understandably emotional strain and your suspicion that this was a personal attack on you.

He added that

> *In discussing this matter with the Trustees, I never once mentioned a derogatory thing about you. I spent most of my time in praise of your work. I stated unequivocally that the progress that has been achieved in the past years just would not have been possible without you. I clearly stated that you were acting under my directions at all times, and that I accepted total responsibility for any unpopular reactions resulting; that you were in my opinion completely loyal to me and the University. I stressed at least six times that this cannot be considered a disciplinary matter, only a difference in philosophy and a changing situation being instituted by the president.*

The truth is that with growing criticism, undoubtedly shared by the board, Carlson had to cut bait. His statements to trustees and later to others indicated that he realized that he had to take more administrative authority into his own hands. He wrote that

> *After being appointed as President of the University of Wyoming, I did delegate much authority in the academic area to the Vice President for Academic Affairs. Over the past two years I have concluded that the President should* personally *exercise general administrative direction over the deans of the academic colleges. I am now of the opinion that a basic difference in philosophy exists between Dr. Ranz and myself as to whether the President of the University and the Vice President for Academic Affairs can both effectively function if I pursue my intentions as to the manner in which I should meet my responsibilities.*

In April 1974, with the approval of trustees, Carlson informed Ranz that he would soon be assigned to a different position in University administration. The long letter was obviously written under stress. It expressed concern, characterized by a combination of remorse and frustration, and indicated that the president was greatly disturbed by the lack of communication between himself and his vice president. When shortly thereafter he was assigned to become acting director of the library (for Richards had just resigned), Ranz apparently assumed the shift was temporary; once before, in 1967, he had so served while a search was conducted for a new permanent librarian. Professor Conrad Kercher from animal science was appointed acting vice president to conduct daily

business in the office of academic affairs, but Ranz clearly counted on returning to the post when a new librarian was appointed. Rumors circulated that Ranz would be dismissed, but he was not.

Men's rugby game, c. 1981

Meanwhile, Carlson made efforts to balance the administrative seesaw. In September, he recommended to trustees the re-creation of a vice presidency for research. Several members of the board objected on the grounds of the proliferation of administrative offices and three voted negatively, but the recommendation won a majority vote. The position was offered to Meyer, but only on an "acting" basis. A search committee was established to make recommendations for a permanent research vice president, and in November, acting (again with some reluctance) on the committee's recommendation, trustees appointed Meyer to the permanent position. Ranz was clearly upset. The beleaguered vice president accused his colleagues of manipulating against him. Although he had worked closely with Hays and Meyer, their relationships rapidly disintegrated.

Carlson must have discussed plans with the trustees, because at this same November meeting, the board felt compelled in a resolution to "declare their continuing support and confidence in President William D. Carlson to execute and carry forth his responsibilities as President of the University." Now the president officially informed Ranz that his rank as vice president would be terminated. Even before the dismissal was formally approved by the board, Ranz bitterly released the story to the press. President and vice president found themselves locked in public controversy.

In December, trustees formally accepted Carlson's recommendation, and Ranz was officially relieved of the academic affairs position, although as a tenured official he retained the title of acting director of the library. To the board, the president suggested a reorientation of his upper administration.

The President of the University is responsible for the total operation of the University, the majority activity being academic programs. It appears that the president must clearly be in the position of exercising personal direction over the academic deans and programs. The current trustee Regulations provide that the Vice President for Academic Affairs exercise general administrative functions over the academic units of the University, under the direction of the President. The functions of this position should be described in a manner that clearly places the President in immediate supervision of the academic deans.

Meanwhile, the Ranz demotion generated fireworks, both on campus and off. In a special meeting, the Faculty Senate failed to pass a bill "deploring" the action of the president, but did pass a resolution calling on Carlson to "seek input from college deans, appropriate campus and Faculty Senate committees" before making decisions that "affect the academic community," and affirmed the need for a "continuing and uninterrupted office of academic affairs." An "ad hoc committee on academic decision making," appointed to report on the duties, functions, and responsibilities of vice presidents, eventually fulfilled its charge with a long and sensitive report on liaison, communications, and responsibilities. At the same time Carlson inaugurated an all-University study of the mission, goals, and responsibilities of the institution. In response to all the investigations, trustees approved several revisions for the UniRegs in early 1976. The vice president for academic affairs, the revised rules states,

shall have overall responsibility for the University's instructional program under the general direction of the President, in consultation with the cognate administrative and academic officers and with the advice of faculty and staff.

By mid-1976, Ranz had resigned his "acting" position and left campus. Former Dean Ed Jakubauskus of the College of Commerce and Industry was installed as new permanent vice president for academic affairs.

The situation and dismissal of Ranz was only one of the administrative and personnel problems that dominated the Carlson administration. Deanships, too, were subject to considerable change, if not rotation. True, a certain shifting of the old guard was inevitable, not only because of differences in personality or educational philosophy, but also because of retirement of many administrators who had been in office since the early days of Humphrey's administration. Retirement removed Hilston from agriculture and Clare Mundell from commerce and industry — not unhappily replaced by Carlson (after considerable consultation) with Harold Tuma and Jakubauskus respectively. Following considerable conflict with the administration, E. George Rudolph stepped down from the law deanship with what was probably relief in 1979, but Peter Maxfield who replaced him had no reputation for complacency. The merger of nursing into a new College of Health Sciences effectively demoted a dean, who subsequently resigned, but it was accomplished only after considerable consultation and probably to the benefit of dean and college alike. On the other hand, Jack N. Bone, who became dean of the new college as well as of the pharmacy program, seems to have served with little trauma through Carlson's administration and beyond.

In the round of reorientations, several appointments at dean levels caused the administration more difficulties than it would have liked. The resignation of Ivan Willey from the deanship of education (on presidential request) was part and parcel of Carlson's plan to revamp and reinvigorate the college; it evoked dozens of letters of protest from fans and friends throughout the state. In 1972, A. J. McGaw of engineering was promoted upstairs to become presidential assistant for development. His replacement, J. F. Sutton, was named by the board with some uncertainty, for the president's recommendation in this case ran counter to the governor's inclination and general salary guidelines.

As dean, Sutton's interests lay in solving statewide technological-industrial problems, and from the start he suggested that students and faculty apply research to "real problems" instead of

271

theories. As it turned out, engineering shared a dilemma with agriculture, and Sutton ran almost at once into trouble with what came to be called the "academic" research orientation — a conflict that had also plagued the NRRI. To Ranz, one trustee wrote facetiously in 1972:

It may be true that real academic research in economics and engineering must always be so theoretical that it is of absolutely no benefit to the Governor when he calls for research statistics or aid on industrial problems. To get such practical help perhaps we should organize a new department and call it the Natural Resources Research Institute and shortly after it was formulated the people in the academy could insist that it was not true academic research and, therefore, should be reorganized into the Academy.

Ranz insisted that engineering had funding enough for both practical and theoretical research; in particular, faculty members were benefiting from comparatively low teaching loads so that research might be emphasized. "I think," he wrote,

we must guard against overlooking the substantive considerations here and simply concluding that industry and the academy are not meshing. This would be easy to do for there are many predispositions in both quarters.

Although Ranz urged patience, Sutton was not so sure that he fit into either the academic or administrative pattern. He left the University after two years, accused by at least one of his faculty of permitting a "vacuum of administrative leadership." Samuel D. Hakes, who was promoted to the deanship in 1975, caused less argument and apparently adjusted more easily to campus and college life.

By far the most controversial situation in regard to deanships occurred in the College of Arts and Sciences with the appointment of Riley Schaeffer, a chemistry Ph.D., as dean in 1975. Schaeffer insisted on immediate tenure, and after a careful review by the tenure and promotion committee, tenure in the chemistry department was granted on the basis of his scholarship, teaching experience, and administrative background. Almost from the start, Schaeffer and the administration were at odds. The new dean knew what he wanted and did not mince words in asking for it. Files contain his protests about the budget (which he viewed as "grossly deficient of current needs of the College") and his plans — or threats, however one reads the documents — for cutting back on college

services unless funding was improved. He criticized the distribution of and salaries for graduate assistants; and he protested the diversion of Coe funds, on the basis of his research into the original provisions of the bequest. On at least one major tenure controversy — the Villemez case, to be discussed at length — he took a view highly unpopular with the administration. Documents may not reflect all of the suggestions, requests, and demands that he made in an effort to build the college. However, they clearly indicate that on Carlson's recommendation, but with little faculty consultation, Schaeffer was relieved of the deanship and reassigned to the department of chemistry in the summer of 1977. He received no more than a few days' notice.

The demotion evoked immediate protest when the faculty returned to campus. The senate questioned the "due process" of Schaeffer's dismissal, and in December 1977 asked its executive committee to conduct a thorough investigation. In response to the committee's request for "a complete written account of the procedures and reasons employed in the Schaeffer reassignment," Carlson only wrote that "The Trustees of the University and I regard this matter as a closed issue." In a letter to the president, nineteen department heads, including the acting dean, deplored the lack of proper procedure. In October, the *Branding Iron* printed a long article based on the former dean's complaints, in particular that he had been dismissed with 24 hours' notice and that he had never been specifically informed as to cause. Schaeffer speculated that he had continually complained that the college had not been properly treated, that he was not given "sufficient authority to deal with even minor problems" in the college, and that

Carlson was unwilling to have someone as an administrator who was going to both push for what is necessary for the college and who was not afraid to speak and in fact use publicly available data to support that position.

He denied "rumors" suggested by the student reporter that he was too often out of town, that he was not on good terms with other deans, and that his budget presentation was inadequate. Cornered, Carlson responded only "Let me assure you, he knows why he was dismissed." In spite of all pressures, the administration kept mum.

The Schaeffer affair attracted most notoriety, but during Carlson's administration scarcely a year passed without a deanship vacant. Frequently committees were seeking deans for several positions at once. The situation was troubling, because administrative turnaround made for instability and uncertainty. Often the resignation of a dean was accompanied by withdrawal of those department heads who had worked most closely with him. Sometimes the turnover was embarrassing, especially when highly-paid deans or department heads withdrew to ordinary teaching positions, taking their salaries with them — a situation about which the board complained but could not rectify. Most discouraging to faculty was that although officers were usually hired on the basis of committee recommendations, the same procedure was not used in dismissals. Schaeffer was removed following no known faculty recommendation. Other deans were called on to resign and agreed to do so without formal protest or consultation.

A Faculty Senate which deemed consultation essential found a partial solution in 1973 when it passed legislation requiring periodic review of all administrative officers by faculty committee. As one respected department head wrote to the president,

Authoritative government, such as any university must have, depends for its effectiveness upon the intellectual and personal integrity of those who wield the authority; and in a democratic society, they should not fear to place their authority on the line. The alternative usually is authoritarian government, where rank conveys privileges and powers without any checks or balances.

At the time, Carlson told senate Chairman Glenn Mullens (engineering) that he disliked ratings not conducted by peers; accordingly the system was instituted (at least partially) for department heads, but not for higher administrators. It was a measure of the administration's distress at many complaints that Carlson asked Kendall L. Baker (political science), senate chairman in 1975, to institute the full administrative review procedure. In that year, perhaps informally, Lawrence Walker, dean of cation, was reviewed highly favorably by his department heads. Thereafter, such reviews became mandatory, although the system occasionally broke down.

Still, the numbers of review committees appointed in the wake of the firing of Ranz and of Schaeffer could not solve the problem. There remained too many questions of leadership versus consultation, decisiveness versus dependence, and secrecy versus communication. Carlson's personal inclinations and administrative philosophy called for him to lean for support and advice upon close associates, while his dislike of adversarial challenge and confrontation caused him to draw them around him as a barricade against unpleasant and even nasty situations. The result was a kind of inner circle to which (as the Ranz situation indicated) even the deans did not necessarily belong. From this circle, faculty members came to feel more excluded, until it seemed to them that regular communication was totally lacking and that important problems were subject to more or less furtive decisions. Some faculty members — particularly those associated with the University Faculty Association — believed that the president held himself out of reach and referred them to other administrators.

Keeping the channels of communication and consultation open had bothered many University presidents before, but with the strong movement towards faculty self-governance, the matter became crucial. Humphrey may seldom have bothered to consult with his faculty, but Fey did. When King was dismissed in 1967, trustees were probably startled to realize how wrong things had gone. At that time Harry Roberts, ex-officio trustee through his position as superintendent of public instruction, sent a long memorandum to the board about what he called "philosophy and goals."

I have been very concerned about a lack of communication in relation to objectives and goals that apparently was present during the administration of President King at the University. As one visits with University people it becomes more and more apparent that there was virtually a complete breakdown in communications, a tremendous divergence between the aims and objectives of President King and the aims and objectives of the University Deans.

Roberts suggested that trustees might help by devising a common statement of educational philosophy with the deans and "academic people." Apparently, nothing was done.

focal point for campus as never before, the fine arts building (1973) has united art, music and, theater and dance in facilities already outgrown but always throbbing with the vitality of performance and programs. In the past few years, these departments have generated excitement for students, faculty, and visitors from across the nation. Let these pictures serve as examples of the creativity that shapes these essential elements of campus life.

"The Garroters," drama department, c. 1900

CHAPTER THIRTEEN

But when the Carlsons arrived — and notably before their son become critically ill and the family deeply concerned — the president made a concerted effort to be friendly and communicative, particularly with students. A year or so after Carlson's arrival, one of the trustees commended his relations with a group of students, who had reported that

> *Dr. Carlson was doing a tremendous job in getting the confidence and further the aims and purposes of the students [whose only fear was that] the Board of Trustees was going to fire you in the very near future because no Board of Trustees would allow such a liberal person to give away the University to students.*

Commending student contact, trustees recommended even more, and subsequently, the president attempted regular meetings with student living groups.

Nevertheless, high spirits did not last. The slippage in communication and confidence was gradual, but it was real. By late 1969, the board made note of the administration's "lack of contact" with faculty and students, and scheduled for itself some one-day meetings and campus tours. During the flagpole demonstration, at least in the opinion of some trustees, Carlson lost credibility by not being more visible to the student crowd. Meanwhile, faculty were beginning to realize that appointments (Gressley's, for example) and dismissals (Deans Willey and Schaeffer) were determined without consultations; occurred often over the summer vacation months when campus was deserted; and were never fully explained to those concerned. In many cases rumors exaggerated circumstances, and sometimes administrative silence was maintained to protect the individual involved, but, of course, nobody could tell. In the autumn of 1974, Carlson was accused at a faculty meeting of being a "phantom president."

When the University Faculty Association was formed in 1975, it was in part to push for a stronger system of salaries and benefits, but also to support the faculty claim to participate in decision making. One professor writing in the UFA's journal decried a particular suggestion that

> *a university, like a factory, should be "run from the top" and the judgments of mere employees ignored as valueless. This is not an uncommon view of the relative responsibilities of university administrations and faculties. Indeed it is held by some faculty members and by some administrators. Such views do not, however, prevail in the high quality universities which we so often profess to emulate. Nor should they be allowed to prevail here. It is an important part of the responsibilities of faculties and especially of administrators and board members to understand, explain, and protect the unique institutional character of the university, which is centered more than anywhere else in the integrity and freedom of the critical intellect of its faculty.*

It was probably unfortunate that Carlson refused to deal at all with the UFA, for a little recognition might have gone a long way. By no means did he disagree with all of its aims, and the record shows he worked for faculty salary increases as hard as any president before or after. Because the senate was officially the faculty representative body and because the UFA frequently maintained the kind of adversary position that Carlson disliked, the president, as much as possible, avoided contact with the latter organization. Petty conflicts and misunderstandings (Had the UFA threatened to oppose publicly the University budget? Was Carlson hiding material of vital importance in refusing to release details of a biochemistry department review?) only made matters worse. In these situations, Carlson was not always politic, nor did he seek to be. He often spoke out sharply and stuck to his guns — qualities that could easily alienate those who opposed him.

By 1972 students, too, felt left out. The *Branding Iron* proposed to send the president a map of campus "so he can discover what exists outside Old Main," and a student editorial urged "Communicate, Mr. Carlson," while contending that the president operated "behind the scenes" and used Geraud as his spokesman. The president's seemingly good-humored acceptance of a pie in the face at a festive student gathering did not help his image at all. In 1977, Vern E. Shelton (assistant to the president for information) designed an interesting and sensitive memorandum regarding channels of communication, and ended by recommending more regular staff meetings, newsletters, and particularly the confrontation of gossip arising through "the grapevine."

Gossip and rumors should be countered quickly with fact. When questions arise or when rumors are being circulated, every effort should be made to answer the questions and to circulate the correct information. This can be done verbally in the coffee rooms or back through the grapevine, but it should be reinforced with a written statement such as a memo, a news release, or an information circular.

By then Shelton had already been excluded from participation in staff meetings because of (he believed) his efforts to seek an end to secretive decision making and establishment of a policy of openness, particularly with the press. Although the president made a few efforts — he held monthly press conferences for a year or so — such policies were not his style. And once communication faded, it was difficult to reverse the image.

Communication problems were inadvertently compounded by the situation on the board of trustees. Trustees during Carlson's administration were twelve in number, appointed by law by the governor and confirmed by the state legislature. Ex-officio members of the board included the state superintendent of public instruction, who was often absent from meetings; the governor, who was seldom there; the president himself; and, after 1969, the president of the ASUW. The role of trustees during Carlson's years was particularly strong. In 1970, the North Central Association in its accreditation report observed that the board retained too many powers that should be delegated to the president. The "management audit" report of 1978 put it more succinctly.

The board and administration should examine their present practices as they might relate to the blurring of the separate roles of policy-making by the board and policy-execution, administration, explication, and presentation of policy issues to the board, etc., by the administration. Changes calculated to clarify the separate roles and establish appropriate "distance" should be made where feasible. The role of, and rationale for, a non-voting student trustee should also be reviewed in this connection.

Bagpipe player, Elizabethan Fair, c. 1979

With the board, the problem of secrecy was even more acute than with Carlson. Board meetings had always been private, and although minutes had been made public, they represented the bare essence rather than the stenographic record of what had occurred. Although in the late 1960s the board officially opened its meetings to those interested, little publicity was accorded to the change, and apparently few observers ever attended. However, in 1973, the legislature passed a law requiring open meetings of all boards set up by the Wyoming constitution and defining what kinds of questions might be considered in executive, or closed, sessions. The measure received considerable publicity, and representatives of the press began to show up for meetings on a regular basis.

With the press present, the nature of board meetings changed. Personnel decisions were regarded as confidential and important. These were determined in executive sessions which frequently absorbed hours of trustees' time, and it was not unusual for visitors to be excused at once and refused admittance for the entire day. Media representatives were frustrated at being asked to wait outside for hours on end. As Shelton reported after the first open meeting, "Although those in attendance recognize the need for executive sessions, suspicions were created by the timing and duration." Rumors of secret transactions abounded. "Many things are done secretly here at the university," one professor told the *Branding Iron*. Called on to define the new law in regard to the University budget, which had always been kept confidential until figures were finalized, Geraud wrote Carlson that there was no way to hide, and suggested even that a summary of the budget be made available for public distribution. With the open meetings law in effect, trustees decided that the minutes must more clearly reflect decisions and agreed that negative votes should be recorded by name. Still, what had been intended as a measure to let the public know rebounded because of the length of executive sessions that served only to emphasize the confidential nature of many board deliberations. The situation further alienated the Casper press representatives, with which Carlson had already been at odds.

Complaints might have continued or been buried eventually in the sand had it not been for two episodes in 1977 that caused a crisis — and eventually sounded a knell — for Carlson's administration. One instance concerned a faculty grievance of broad repercussions, and the other had to do with the University's athletic program.

The case of Clarence L. Villemez, Jr., was the first to come up for special hearing before the trustees under the new grievance procedure and represented a traumatic crisis for faculty and administration alike. Villemez had joined the faculty of the biochemistry division (the College of Agriculture's term for department at that time) as an associate professor in 1972. He was promoted to full professor and several times reappointed on probationary status before, according to UniReg provisions, he arrived at the moment for tenure decision.

By then, this outspoken professor had become deeply embroiled in controversy within the biochemistry division. It seems likely that the argument was based on the essence of the division's mission and research, for Villemez, together with a number of young scholars, focused research efforts on human nutrition and health-oriented problems, while another faction of the division called for the primacy of animal and agriculturally-oriented service scholarship. In personal and abrasive conflict with his division head, Villemez with several other faculty chose to write Carlson with the suggestion that the head be replaced with "an outstanding biochemist from another university."

In early 1975, the Villemez tenure case came up for decision. Although supported by his department, Villemez received a negative vote from both division head and dean. Called in by Carlson for considerable discussion and negotiation, the young professor agreed to a postponement of the decision while Carlson made an effort to iron out some of the problems and antagonisms.

As one solution, the administration proposed to transfer some, if not all, of the biochemistry faculty to the chemistry department in the College of Arts and Sciences. Unfortunately for his plans, Carlson met the stubborn resistance of that department's head, who proclaimed a set of unnegotiable demands in terms of extra space, laboratory equipment, and funding that would be needed should biochemistry faculty be merged with their chemistry colleagues. In this extraordinary situation, the whole division of biochemistry was moved, becoming instead a department in the nascent College of Human Medicine, where its dean — Daugherty — agreed to act as temporary department head. One professor in biochemistry requested transfer instead to the home economics division (agriculture), where research might more easily be focussed on human nutrition. This transfer was denied by Carlson, in part because of funding problems.

Even as these negotiations were proceeding, Carlson brought in an outside review committee to evaluate the departmental situation. Tensions ran extremely high. The outside committee — the report of which was revealed to departmental faculty but otherwise kept confidential — hardly offered help. Instead it reported that

The animosity between the various factions is so great as to be scarcely credible; none of us has ever encountered anything remotely resembling this situation. The divisions are so deep that we can see no conceivable way of composing the differences.

The following year, Carlson suggested to Villemez that he agree to another postponement of his tenure decision. But this time the biochemistry professor — already in contact with available legal consultants in regard to his rights and procedures — refused to delay. Consequently, in 1976, the tenure case of Villemez again went through standard University procedure. After some debate, the biochemistry faculty voted in favor of tenure; indeed, Villemez had a record of research and publication that proved difficult to criticize. Nevertheless, the division head firmly recommended that tenure be denied and was backed by the dean of the agriculture college. (The change in colleges was effected too late to influence the Villemez tenure decision.) Accordingly, the case went to the faculty tenure and promotion committee for investigation. Here the vote favored granting tenure status. Carlson vetoed the decision and took the case to the trustees.

In the debacle that followed, Villemez contended that tenure had been denied because of his opposition to his division head's management and that therefore his right to freedom of speech under academic and constitutional canons had been violated. Many concerned agreed with him. As a supporter in the department put it to the tenure and promotion committee,

Certain comments made to me have clearly pointed out that disagreeing with college of agriculture administrators is in itself grounds enough for having a negative tenure recommendation sent to the tenure and promotion committee. . . . I sincerely believe it has been Dr. Villemez's attempts to improve the academic and research standards in our division that has placed his tenure in jeopardy.

The chairman of the subcommittee assigned by the tenure and promotion committee to investigate the Villemez case wrote in the same vein upon learning of Carlson's decision.

I was very shocked and even embarrassed to learn of your recommendation concerning the tenure of Dr. Villemez. . . . The only reasonable inference I can draw as to the reason for your decision is that he was quite impolitic in his views about the quality academically or rate of development academically of his department. It's a sorry day for the University when a faculty member cannot speak out freely on any subject, let alone the subject of academics on his own campus.

In a letter to Villemez, Carlson ordered the young professor to "refrain from saying anything against the division head that would cause further problems."

Before making their decision, trustees debated long on the merits of the case and ramifications of what they might say. One vice president strongly urged that they grant tenure and not make an example of the Villemez case; he was certain that while an employee could be fired for insubordination, a tenure decision had to be based on teaching, research, and general academic achievements. Another vice president argued equally firmly that the case could be won. Under the circumstances, trustees opted to support their administrators and denied tenure to Villemez. Threatening to take his case to court if necessary, Villemez promptly initiated a grievance claim.

With a fanfare of publicity that reached as far as the National Education Association, public hearings took place in December 1976. Three trustees sat in judgment: They were Joseph Sullivan, Gordon Brodrick, and Cameron McEwan. A series of witnesses, including the dean, division head (who had in the interim resigned), and Carlson, as well as faculty members, testified on both sides. Devastating controversies and dirty linen were exposed to the public eye. In the midst of the hearings, Villemez's division head refused to reveal certain of his notes and correspondence on the case, and Villemez threatened to take the administrator to district court with a demand for release of the documents. "If it gets to the national news that the acting head of the division did not give up papers when ordered to do so, the University of Wyoming will be the laughing stock of the university community," predicted one pro-Villemez biochemist. Apparently the trustees agreed. The hearing was adjourned — supposedly to permit time for Villemez's lawyers to take his case to court. It never was reconvened.

278

Cowboy offense, c. 1980

In February, trustees began quiet negotiations with Villemez. Eventually agreement was reached, and Villemez agreed to drop all charges and legal actions if the board would reverse itself and act favorably upon his tenure. To their April meeting, trustees summoned Daugherty, now Villemez's official department head, who rapidly recommended tenure for the controversial professor. Academic Vice President Jakubauskus as rapidly concurred. Trustees then voted to tenure Villemez as a professor of biochemistry, effective at once. The case was thus settled out of court. If it left a bitter taste for those to whom it represented public embarrassment, for others it was a milestone — a turning point in the understandings of faculty rights and governance.

On the surface the second event that caused increasing lack of confidence in the administration was less compelling, because it concerned the athletic rather than the academic program. Nevertheless, it turned more frustration and irritation against Carlson from throughout the state than did any situation of an intra-university nature.

The problem focused on football. Following the episode of the fourteen black athletes, the football program at UW had disintegrated and coaches seemed unable to post winning seasons. Carlson always believed that unique problems in black recruitment did not lie at the basis of the difficulty in building a winning team; he blamed instead changes in the rules of the Western Athletic Conference that raised the standards for admission and eligibility and forced Wyoming to compete for players on an equal basis with the strong midwestern teams. Whatever the cause, many alumni tempers ran high. Carlson later remembered a group of irate citizens with whom he and George McCarty, athletic director, met in the board room: "They sat across the table . . . they were screaming at me. . . . By God, if we have to cheat to win, you're going to cheat." Nor did members of the Cowboy Joe Club mince words; created in an effort to compensate for "the Black 14" disaster, the club's ardent supporters frequently proffered as much advice and complaint as funding and support.

By the mid-1970s, coaches and football fans adopted the line that facilities were at fault and insisted that a winning program could be built only if the stadium were enlarged and domed. Although trustees agreed about enlargement, which was eventually accomplished, Carlson's investigation indicated that construction problems would make doming the stadium impossible without vast expense. A further crisis evolved with the withdrawal of the Arizona schools from the WAC, an event which caused considerable discussion about the conference's future. There naturally surfaced the possibility of de-emphasizing football (in accordance with the 1970 accreditation report, among other suggestions) and settling the University in a minor less-competitive league where victory might more easily be accomplished. To this the board responded firmly that

> the trustees of the University of Wyoming reaffirm their commitment to sustaining a major intercollegiate sports program and to pursuing that commitment as vigorously as the dictates of the people and the resources of the State permit.

Meanwhile, alumni demands probably played their role in the resignation of Coach Fritz Shurmer after the 1974 losing season.

In the midst of all the controversy about how to build a winning team or whether even to try, the board hired Fred Akers as new football coach. In two years, Akers turned the situation around. Although his 1975 record was an unprepossessing two wins to nine losses, in 1976, he posted the first winning season since "the Black 14" year and with a score of eight games won, four lost, scooped up the WAC championship. When it was announced that Wyoming was to play in the Fiesta Bowl, football fans were elated, and Akers became the hero of the hour. Mindful, he said later, of the fact that coaches, athletic director, and trainers would have to put in extra hours and that Akers might anticipate offers from colleges all over the country, Carlson with the support of the athletic director persuaded trustees on December 10, 1976,

to vote bonuses to the staff in a total amount of $62,000. Money was distributed before the game so that recipients might have extra cash to spend in Arizona. It was anticipated that Fiesta Bowl revenues would cover the bonus payments. The entire episode was kept secret, against the emphatic advice of Vern Shelton, the president's assistant for information.

Almost immediately, everything began to go downhill. Wyoming lost to Oklahoma by a humiliating score of 41-7. Bowl receipts turned out to be nowhere near the $115,000 that the board had anticipated. To top it all, Akers accepted another position and, with a string of assistant coaches in tow, left for the University of Texas.

When the bonus story inevitably broke, flak in the state was immediate and resounding. Editorials called for an audit of University funds to determine the source of the bonus money. Two state senators announced they would sponsor a bill for a complete financial investigation to "dissipate the dark cloud" hanging over the University. In Casper, the trustees were sued by an irate citizen who demanded that they personally reimburse the University for the $62,000 total. To make things worse, the board had to go to the University Foundation for help, because of the shortfall in Fiesta Bowl income. In irritation, foundation directors at first refused, and trustees had to humble themselves further to persuade their colleagues that they had at least "made a decision in good faith" in an effort to retain Akers as coach. "We got taken," Carlson later said. "I never spent a more humiliating day in my life." Governor Ed Herschler added contritely, "We have egg on our faces for all to see."

A governor might ride out the criticism, but a university president was far more subject to pressures around him. As a direct result of the Villemez case and the bonuses paid to football coaches, one of Villemez's colleagues in the troubled department of biochemistry introduced into the Faculty Senate a bill seeking a faculty vote on Carlson's administration. On January 17, 1977, the Faculty Senate adopted the resolution by a vote of 24-16, and the faculty was accordingly polled. The question was:

> Do you think President Carlson is administering the affairs of the University of Wyoming in a manner that best serves the interests of Wyoming, the University, the students, and the faculty?

Seven hundred and fifty-one faculty members received ballots, and 547 returned them. Of those returned, 48 ballots were not counted for they contained no vote, indicating abstention. Of the rest, 35 were undecided, but 319 (58.32 percent) voted no, and only 145 (26.51 percent) said yes.

Reaction was immediate. The "loss of confidence" vote was published in press across the state. Many newspapers — including the *Wyoming Eagle* and the Laramie *Boomerang* — defended Carlson from the attack. The *Eagle* editorialized:

> *Timed, as it was, during the regular session of the 44th Wyoming State Legislature, it could only hurt the University of Wyoming from which the faculty members get their paychecks. . . . It was a nasty, vindictive action on the part of a few faculty members. And we suggest that if those few are unhappy at Wyoming University they go to some other university and see whether they can get its president ousted. We have known many university professors, including deans and department heads. We have known very few, indeed, who would be capable of running a university. Some had considerable trouble running a class and teaching one subject.*

In a news conference, the governor, too, defended the president, but upheld the right of the faculty to conduct a poll — "I assume we live in a democracy" — and equivocated when asked what he thought of the University administration. Opposed faculty members, particularly from agriculture, engineering, and education, called for a special faculty meeting to review and reconsider the senate's action. Trustees, to whom Carlson reported on the entire episode, released a resolution deploring the poll on principle.

> *For some years there has generally been a harmonious relationship among those involved with University governance. . . . Recently, however, a series of disruptive events have damaged the internal harmony and the external image of the University. While certain decisions of the administration and of the Trustees can be questioned and may on occasion prove to have been wrong, no group has the right to take actions which plunge the campus into harmful disunity. The ill-timed and ill-conceived faculty vote concerning the President has been such a disruptive act. This action not only abrogated a year of work by a joint faculty-staff administration committee which was establishing procedures for review of administrators, but it used an evaluative technique which the faculty itself eschewed.*

The resolution went on to state that the trustees had sole responsibility for appointing and removing University presidents and would support the president while he remained in office. Carlson himself refrained from comment.

Pleas for silence and unity were to little avail. The University Faculty Association, representing activist faculty, resented the assumption that faculty objected to student ratings similar to the poll and devoted a column to refuting news releases and media that so claimed. The faculty vote, read the leading article in the UFA newsletter,

> *is only one indication of the deplorable state of morale and confidence at the University of Wyoming, a state for which no individual or group bears so much responsibility as does the present structure of power and prestige, of governing mechanisms, and of their attendant assumptions of responsibility.*

The senate itself resented the trustees' term "disruptive," and its chairman wrote Carlson that the trustees' resolution

> *has been perceived by many faculty as an inflammatory act which serves only to further polarize the relationships between the faculty as well as between the faculty and the administration.*

It submitted to Carlson a series of recommendations for improving faculty-administration relationships, which included the appointment of the Faculty Senate chairperson as *ex-officio* member of the board; a reconsideration of the Villemez case still in adjudication; and periodic review of principal administrators as recommended by a recent committee. In response, Carlson met with the senate executive committee and faced a full senate meeting late in March.

In the interim, arts and sciences department heads discussed the administration with Vice President Jakubauskus and later had to deny a news report that they had recommended the president's dismissal. Individual professors got into the act with strong and public opinions one way and the other. Students could not be left behind, and the ASUW authorized a poll too; about forty percent of the students were reported as critical of the administration.

A month later, the University Faculty Association (affiliated with the National Education Association) took a poll of its own. Of 511 respondees, 74 percent believed that the trustees spent "too much time" on athletics, 82 percent believed that faculty members were "kept in the dark" about many things that they should know, and 83 percent agreed that many misunderstandings had resulted from poor communications.

Having unwittingly fanned the fires with their resolution, trustees moved rapidly to attempt some kind of understanding and reconciliation. To the board in February, H. A. True reported that there was

confusion, dissension and misunderstanding in and around the University and the State. The Trustees have heard from the media and other sources that two occurrences more or less triggered the confidence vote by the faculty regarding the administration. The two issues were the Villemez situation and the granting of extra compensation to the football coaches and the athletic director.

On March 17, teams of trustees spent an entire day with faculty from the various colleges in open meetings and with the aim of mending the "credibility gap," as one faculty member put it. Promptly the senate passed a resolution commending the board for its efforts "to establish an open dialogue with the University faculty as a whole." But all was not well. In April, trustees shared their findings. Complaints came from biochemistry regarding its transfer to the College of Human Medicine; from the humanities about administrative merry-go-round and decisions without consultation; from everyone about funding needs and paperwork and trustee executive sessions. The administration, said one professor, was always on the defensive; it did not come up with constructive ideas. Carlson was attacked for too little leadership as well as too much.

There is too much of a dictatorship attitude in Old Main. A total lack of communication between the president and vice presidents, on one hand, and the department heads and faculty on the other. . . . The president refuses to discuss problems with faculty — refers them to vice presidents who are unable to make decisions. . . . This has resulted in extreme frustration.

As one trustee team reported:

. . . there has been a decided lack of communication between the administration in Old Main, the department heads and the faculty. The morale appears to be very low. . . . Taking all this into consideration, we recommend that the Board of Trustees take a strong look at the problems which exist and make immediate and effective plans to correct them.

In May 1977, the trustees firmly renewed Carlson's contract for another year. In June, they studied a thoughtful report from one of their members on "goals," and apparently resolved to do an administrative self-study; set forth a ten-year academic plan; evaluate graduate programs; and tackle some more specific programs: equipment, a new computer, library holdings. A formal resolution called for the establishment of priorities and a study of potential and advantageous degree programs.

The next academic year passed quietly, but those around him believed the president seemed more and more withdrawn. The files include some surveys of faculty about particular gripes, but nothing resembling the vote of no confidence; to some of them Carlson responded and attempted to help, such as the perennial complaint of too much administrative paperwork. H. B. McFadden, vice president for extension (until his retirement from the position in January 1978), found considerable administrative burden shifted to his shoulders, particularly in terms of following through on decisions made jointly by vice presidents and other officers. Carlson appreciated McFadden, although they were not close personal confidants; perhaps even through the winter, he was quietly grooming McFadden as a successor. Other friends found Carlson remote. Some of them quietly urged him to resign, but the president kept his own counsel and only further isolated those who were critical.

The legislative session of 1978 was a University success in spite of the special session that had to be called. Legislators ended by approving a $7 million computer system and increased the operating budget by $15 million besides. The storm over the medical college may not have bothered trustees as much as others; it had been the governor's program, not the University's. Although Carlson went to Cheyenne for some time during the special legislative session that decided the medical school's fate, he quietly disappeared and did not show up at the key hearings.

The real storm that broke the calm came later. Shortly after the special session in May, twelve legislators addressed the State Management Council demanding a review of "the leadership activities at the University of Wyoming of the Administration and the Board of Trustees." "What kind of institution do we have?" the group demanded. It included an Albany County legislator who was the wife of a faculty member. The request was for an investigation that did not focus on facilities or curricula, but rather on internal management. In connection with the request, the local legislator was quoted by news media as calling the University a "diploma mill." Later she enlarged without explaining.

> *All of us want the University to be a good academic institution doing the job it was designed to do, in the manner appropriate to the latter part of the 20th century. . . . Because of no clarity of thought or consensus as to philosophy, goals and purpose of the institution by the Legislature, the Board, and the Administration, the citizens of the state, the students, faculty and staff have become pawns in a gamesmanship that can destroy the institution we are supposedly trying to protect.*

Nothing could more effectively have united board and administrators. President, vice presidents, trustees all fought back in what the *Branding Iron* called a "media battle" — a situation, Carlson freely admitted, that he had always hoped to avoid. Legislators' complaints apparently arose in part from the defeat of the medical school, which they chose to interpret as another vote of non-confidence in the University administration. Tempers raged, compounded by press interviews granted by all sides.

When the affair died down, Carlson accepted another contract extension for the following year. Still, rumors circulated about the possibility of his resignation. In mid-July, governor, trustees, and the State Management Council apparently met together with certain legislative leaders but in the president's absence. Trustees continually refused comment about the president's plans, although Casper papers in particular hinted a move was underway.

To the board on July 28, Carlson finally tendered his resignation. He and his wife, he said, had been considering the change since January, and he hoped that trustees would at once begin on a search for his successor. Although there was little doubt of his distress and that of his family, the message he read to the board was upbeat. In subsequent interviews with student journalists, he maintained a cheerful and positive attitude. The summary of the accomplishments during his eleven years as president reflects his efforts to put the University "on the academic map." The things that had ultimately gone wrong reflected an administrative philosophy and personal attitudes that led to growing mistrust and disrespect. The board accepted Carlson's resignation with regret and accepted, too, his recommendation for an acting president. Their choice was H. B. McFadden, who (considerably astonished and with fifteen minutes' notice) agreed.

Known through the University community as a faculty member and administrator since 1939, McFadden picked up the reins calmly and professionally. In the aftermath of Carlson's resignation, the student newspaper called on the trustees to appoint a strong leader.

> *Dissention [sic] among UW faculty, staff, students, and Wyoming people about Carlson's management (or lack of it) has been prevalent in the last three or four years. . . . The UW Board of Trustees should learn from past experience as it considers people for the UW presidential position and insure that the next president is someone who will face issues and problems and solve them — with a minimum of evasiveness.*

The governor noted that "the president we had lost the confidence not only of faculty and students but of the people of Wyoming," and referred to a "lack of administrative leadership." As an immediate restorer of confidence, McFadden carried an aura of the elusive quality called leadership into the president's office. His demeanor and his bearing bespoke confidence. His administration opened doors that had been closed and began again to restore the consultation and even camaraderie that had vanished in Carlson's later years. Among other policies, McFadden regularly brought vice presidents into trustees' meetings.

Budget was first on the acting president's mind, and at once he set a policy of involving deans and department heads in the budget requests. Once proposals were made, McFadden consulted on priorities, and he remembers many hours in the "board room" hammering out policies with vice presidents, deans, faculty, and students before the final document was prepared. The "budget" legislature of 1979 increased the University's total operating budget for the ongoing biennium by $2,860,402, of which only $402,951 represented increased appropriations from the general fund. Among major items, the legislature agreed to a larger program in women's athletics, an engineering option in mining, and faculty salary increases. McFadden stated outright that reversions from salaries would be utilized to pay for faculty sabbatical leaves. In construction, the legislature authorized a coal fired steam plant as well as plans for additional agricultural facilities on campus and at the state farms (which the board had toured the previous autumn). On the basis of a careful analysis, McFadden opted not to lobby against the four-year college plan for Casper, and the bill as anticipated went down to defeat. When the board praised the acting president's performance, trustee Gordon Brodrick noted that the session was most cordial in terms of the University's relationship with the legislature in general, and Herschler himself gave much credit to the open and effective presentations made by McFadden in Cheyenne.

Not that McFadden's role lacked in challenge. In September 1978, the attorney general issued his report on Legislator Matilda Hansen's accusations of "serious midconduct" on the part of University employees. Most allegations were determined to be baseless, but one case of criminal misconduct, apparently being investigated by the University at the time of Hansen's public statement, was found by county and state attorneys to have insufficient evidence to merit legal prosecution. Scandals in collegiate athletics across the country caused McFadden to request, and the trustees to agree to, a thorough investigation of athletes and scholarship to become part of voluminous material being prepared for the North Central Association's accreditation visit in 1980. The state farm inspection convinced McFadden that facilities had fallen desperately behind, and in an effort to move ahead, he was able to raise agricultural salaries and upgrade the positions of agricultural extension agents. McFadden, too, reinstituted a one-time Carlson investigation into salaries of faculty women through a new committee with Patsy McGinley (Center for Counseling and Testing) chairperson, and set about integrating the medical school into University principles and practice, with the promise from Herschler that the entire project and its funding would be turned over fully to the University.

Meanwhile the search for a new permanent president began. As early as August 1978, the trustees set formal criteria, adopted a time framework, outlined a number of issues that needed further definitions, and listed some principles for the presidential search. Among the latter, it recognized that as governing board, the selection responsibility was its own, but it acknowledged the "crucial participative roles for constituencies." It urged its committees to be sensitive to political issues without politicizing the selection process, and to retain also sensitivity to strictly academic values and expectations. Among the criteria for judgment were scholarship, enthusiasm for the arts and sciences, and belief in academic excellence; appreciation of special problems of a state university; administrative ability; support for major intercollegiate athletics; ability to communicate with students; "a personality with a sense of humor; and the ability to make decisions and take action to implement them." Thereupon trustees authorized a search and screening advisory committee, to be elected and selected by faculty, students, deans, and staff, and a selection and evaluation committee, consisting of trustees Gordon Brodrick, Donald Chapin, and Leo McCue. Chairman of the former was Robert S. Houston, geology.

By October 1978, 84 candidates had applied or been nominated for the presidency. A month later, the number was 187. By December 15, there were 292 applications and nominations. In late January, the Houston committee presented the trustees' committee with seven names, and by February 29, 1979, the trustees named a new president: Edward H. Jennings, formerly vice president for finance at the University of Iowa.

In March, when the full board confirmed its commitees' decision, trustee Patrick Quealy had special words of thanks for the acting president.

I first became acquainted with the Univerity of Wyoming and the various presidents thereof more than fifty years ago. In the intervening half century, it has been my pleasure to know and work with in various capacities most of the presidents of this great school. Dr. McFadden has served in the capacity as Acting President during the last several months with great distinction. Never to my knowledge has any president of this University been more suited to the position by reason of character, training, or experience.

As an expression of what they called "exceptional leadership," trustees then appointed McFadden the University's eighteenth president, to serve as such from March 30 to July 1, 1979. As he worked ever more closely with Jennings, McFadden made himself useful to the point of becoming indispensible, and at Jennings' request, he remained on a half-time appointment as special assistant to the president for the 1979-80 academic year.

With his personal ease of manner, his own calm self-assurance, his sense of humor, and even his deep voice, Jennings exuded a confidence that was immediately contagious. Like McFadden before him, he seemed outgoing and friendly. He was "most open to student input and like a breath of fresh air," wrote the *Branding Iron*.

At his inaugural speech in October 1979, the new president told the University audience what it wanted to hear in the way it wanted to hear it. He would, he said, emphasize the quality of existing programs as a priority over expansion. Service to the state and region must be supplemented by use of the advantages that the state had to offer. Teaching and research, he said,

are not separate activities . . . excellence in either cannot be achieved without excellence in both.

The new president emphasized that he would maximize the "freedom for faculty, students, and staff to be innovative and creative," and that accountability demanded a system of evaluation at all University levels. He insisted that

undergraduate education is the heart and soul of our educational enterprise. We must not depreciate graduate education, but we must continuously keep in mind that excellence in undergraduate education cannot take a back seat to other activities.

He spoke to education across the state by way of new and experimental methods, and emphasized that the curriculum must be founded

on the premise that change is the nature of society and that our students must be prepared to adapt to those changes through a broad based general education whatever the specific course of study.

Jennings set to work almost at once to build an administrative team. As acting vice president for academic affairs, to replace Jakubauskas, who resigned in summer 1979, he appointed William R. Steckel, a longtime professor of history. A year later, after a national search, Allan Spitz, formerly dean of the liberal arts college at New Hampshire, assumed the permanent post. The academic vice president, Spitz said,

is the academic officer of a college or university and a primary spokesman for the academic program. Although he is responsible to all students and faculty, he should remember the primary missions of a university — research and teaching.

Spitz entered into his job with an enthusiasm based on the confidence he had in University faculty and administration and what he called "a vigor here not always present in major institutions."

With the resignation of Geraud, who went back to his position in the law school, the responsibilities of the vice president for student affairs were turned over to an assistant in the academic affairs office. Meyer withdrew from his post as research vice president, to be replaced after a search (in early 1981) by Donald L. Veal from the department of atmospheric science. In 1980, Jennings appointed a special assistant for athletics and legal advice in the person of William G. Solomon from Athens, Georgia. The new president retained assistants for information and development and — after some consideration — for the American Heritage Center (Gressley).

Changes in deanships saw Edward A. Dyl become first acting and then permanent dean of commerce and industry; Joan K. Wadlow appointed as the first woman dean of arts and sciences; and John Dolly eventually becoming dean of education to replace Laurence Walker. Susan B. Leddy was appointed in 1981 to replace resigning Marion Shrumm in the School of Nursing; and, in 1979, Peter Maxfield became dean of the law school following George Rudolph, who had announced his intended resignation the previous year.

Enthusiasm for reform was shared by the trustees. Early in Jennings' administration — whether at his instigation or through their own decision — trustees moved to set up a personnel committee to consider and make recommendations on all appointments, tenure, and promotion cases; this wise move at least mitigated the problem of the long secretive-seeming executive sessions. At the same time, Shelton was given considerable leave to publicize board actions as he saw fit. In the spring semester of 1980, Jennings brought to board meetings a series of faculty members and administrators to speak to the University's mission. Meyer and Professor Robert Jenkins (zoology) talked on research efforts; Steckel on the history and rationale of the tenure system; Wadlow on the centrality of arts and sciences; and Professor Tom Preston on a "general education" curriculum shortly to be adopted by the arts and sciences college. David Tomatz was called in to speak about music, particularly about the band program. Letters in the files indicate that trustees appreciated Jennings' openness and friendship. Happily, the new president also enjoyed a good game of golf.

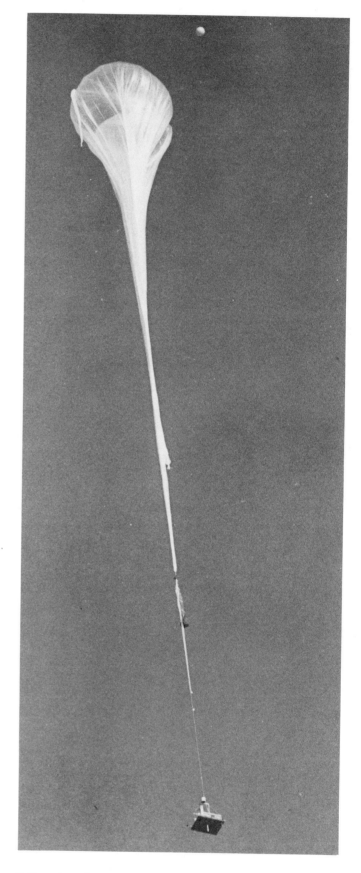

Balloon launch equipment

Legislators, too, had confidence in the Jennings administration. In 1980, as usual, the appropriations committee raised many questions. Legislators sought information on administrative salaries, the Casper program, the extent of the law library, the status of athletes and the athletic program, and the high salaries in the College of Human Medicine. Still, Jennings' presentations helped to increase the University's total biennial budget (July 1, 1980-June 30, 1982) to $146,680,153, of which nearly $100 million was appropriated from the general fund. Most capital expenses came from the general fund too: That included primarily the completion of projects begun and renovation of animal science and biochemistry facilities.

The following year, one member of the legislative education committee wrote Jennings in no uncertain terms.

I have been reading the budget requests for 1982 for the University of Wyoming. To say that I am disturbed at the scope of these requests is expressing it mildly. . . . I know the State of Wyoming has plenty of money, but I do not like to see what we are experiencing by a number of state institutions and state departments, requests for money which just amount to a big "rip off" of State funds.

Jennings responded like a veteran enjoying the fight. There seems to be a misunderstanding, he wrote, and went on to explain that in this "budget" year the University was seeking an "emergency" increase in its appropriation of less than one percent. Jennings won. The legislature upped the budget by approximately $3.1 million, including a considerable appropriation for the new computer network, and the president got just what he wanted in terms of capital outlay. In an unusual measure of respect, Herschler requested Jennings' advice about a number of bills concerning education, such as the ban on Iranian students, limit on athletic scholarships, and a statewide purchasing system to include the University. After the session, one senator wrote to the president in great good humor.

How awkward and embarrassing this must be for you! All the kudos and all the compliments are very flattering — I want you to know that I agree with everything they say. . . . I have reservations only about the way you stroke sidehill, downhill, three-foot putts!

In one area, however, Jennings was unsuccessful, and he later cited this as a great weakness in the Wyoming system. He was unable to achieve one of his most sought-after goals: flexibility in budget that would permit the University administration to reassign moneys where it believed them most needed. Consistently and concisely, Jennings insisted that the University could be trusted and that its annual financial statement "reinforces accountability to the Legislature by showing precisely where each dollar appropriated is spent." Nevertheless, when Jennings left office, the University still operated on a tight and unchangeable line-item budget, and the appropriations committee regularly commanded information as to numbers of part-time employees or the replacement rate of individual typewriters and office machines.

In his relation to faculty, Jennings maintained his open and easy stance. In his attitude towards faculty rights and self-government, he seemed like one of the crowd. One of his first actions was to write the chairman of the Faculty Senate to seek inauguration of a review system that would encompass all academic administrators. From the beginning, he endorsed specific terms in office for department chairpersons, with a mechanism of regular peer review. Although Jennings did not believe that limited terms were appropriate for deans, he sought periodic reviews of performances and guaranteed that appointments and dismissals would always be made with faculty consultation. To the chairman of the senate, the president wrote that any review system must be constructed to avoid rigidity in criteria.

I firmly believe that judgments regarding these matters cannot be made without the advice and consultation of the faculty and that any procedure established must be designed to prevent insofar as possible the crisis atmosphere that can develop when the abilities of a given administrator come into question. I also believe that policies and procedures developed to address such problems must reflect the diversity of departments and colleges within our university.

The new president liked the way the tenure system operated at Wyoming. He reviewed it and approved, although he was bothered by the amount of paperwork, the complexity of the review system, and the decisive power of the all-University committee. He understood faculty concerns about the emphasis on research as well as teaching.

With regard to the amount of research required for promotion this, of course, is a function of the activity in which the individual is involved. It seems appropriate that at least some evidence of research be available prior to the tenure or promotion decision. I do not believe that effective teaching can be accomplished without some activity in research; nor do I believe that research can be accomplished without the stimulus of the classroom.

He followed carefully the investigations into student teaching evaluations conducted by a faculty committee, which was looking into more effective forms. In 1980, he persuaded the legislature to permit a range of eleven to twelve percent increase in campus salaries, with an emphasis on merit. With the aid of a Faculty Senate committee, he followed through on McFadden's investigations of women's pay scales and authorized an adjustment in cases of potential discrimination. Unlike Carlson, he met without rancor with the University Faculty Association and told a colleague afterwards that he found its members sharp and well-informed, that he shared and understood their concerns.

In terms of academic programs, Jennings kept his word and made little effort to add to the University's offerings. True, Casper added several degree programs — a bachelor of science in business administration, a joint master's in the same field to be accomplished along with a bachelor of arts degree — but on the whole, faculty focused on enhancing what was in place. In 1981, a major program was cut back by withdrawal of federal funding; it was the Wyoming Energy Extension Service, attached to the College of Agriculture. In spite of staff anger and disappointment, Jennings was unable to retain the service or its employees. In 1978-79, a number of professional programs were accredited, including speech pathology, several fields of engineering, and social work (a program that had been on probationary status); but the following year the National Council for Accreditation of Teacher Education refused status to the master's program in education, primarily on the grounds of course content, low residence requirements, and the need for more advanced classes — criticisms centered around curriculum and were not excessively difficult to correct.

By far the most trying curricular problem involved the integration of the College of Human Medicine into the University structure. McFadden had recognized the difficulty; he frequently spoke to Dean Joel Lanphear about matters such as out-of-scale salary payments and expenses. The legislature also requested reports since Herschler and legislators had actually inaugurated the program. When Jennings arrived, however, Herschler turned both administration and funding over to the University. Jennings set up a review committee to look into high salaries and high ranks. Dr. Virgil Thorpe, Newcastle physician on the board of trustees, requested special reports.

The truth is that the deans of the medical college, practicing physicians all, knew little about the operation of a university. It is possible that Jennings was not sold on the system, for a high-paid staff in Laramie had minimal supervisory duties. Obviously, Lanphear's initial report to Jennings was not well-received by the new president. After Lanphear's resignation in summer 1979, Jennings dealt with Dr. John J. Corbett as acting dean; but almost at once frictions arose about salary levels, the high ranks the dean recommended for his faculty, travel allowances (in which the medical staff sought exception to state regulation), and above all promotion and tenure criteria. The latter, the subject of a long report written by Corbett in December 1980 and an even longer meeting called by Jennings early the following year. Although little could be done to accommodate salaries to general University levels, the president insisted (over much of the staff's objection) that standards of tenure and promotion include research as a component. Meanwhile, the problems of administration that caused all but a few of the student-residents to abandon the Casper program after its first year were only slowly overcome. The Cheyenne center opened with six resident positions in 1980, and an additional six scheduled the following year.

Nor was the reassociation of the division of biochemistry with the College of Agriculture entirely happy. Delwood C. Collins, recruited as department head by Daugherty during the division's brief affiliation with the medical college, had foreseen difficulty when he resigned in July 1978; the bifurcation of research interests between agriculture and nutrition would again cause conflict, he predicted. New head, Ivan I. Kaiser, managed the division for several years before turning to Jennings for assistance. His letter concerned facilities above all, but he believed strongly that

CHAPTER THIRTEEN

Sculptured entryway, College of Agriculture

biochemistry remained a stepchild in the agriculture college. In spite of the journal articles written, the research grants earned, and the general productivity of the biochemistry staff, Kaiser wrote, division members still received far less support and commitment than was their share, and the dean of agriculture seemed remote and uncommunicative. Jennings had to step in and agree to relieve the laboratory and equipment situation with special legislative help.

Two staff problems of magnitude caused considerable grief during the Jennings years. One concerned the head of the State Veterinary Laboratory, whose opinions were outspoken, whose professional practices and policies were constantly criticised, and whose connections throughout the state permitted him considerable independence of operation from the College of Agriculture, through which the Veterinary Laboratory was supposedly supervised. In December 1980, he was relieved of his duties by the dean and returned to his position as professor of animal science. More painful was the situation of Donald L. Stinson, longtime head of the department of mineral engineering. Apparently without anticipating rancor, Dean Samuel Hakes in November 1980 asked Stinson to step down as department head. His letter was filled

with appreciation and praise for Stinson's accomplishments and gave no reason for the request except for his belief that all departments needed periodic changes in leadership — as did, he said, colleges — for purposes of "invigoration." In asking Stinson to resign the headship, Hakes admitted that he had someone else in mind for the job; he actually violated procedure by making an offer that subsequently had to be withdrawn. Shortly, too, the department was split into petroleum and chemical engineering areas.

Stinson's angry reaction to Hakes' request that he step down was no more vigorous than that of his students and professional colleagues throughout the West. Letters of protest poured into the president's office in such numbers that a form letter had to be designed to respond to them. Faculty protested Hakes' action, which had been taken against their advice. Students wrote letters in the *Branding Iron* hinting that Stinson was removed because the administration sought to "gain some of his power." On appeal, Spitz and Jennings both refused to reverse Hakes' decision. In a long letter to Stinson dated January 23, 1981, Jennings defended the principle of rotating department chairmanships. His effort to convince the former administrator that the reassignment to teaching should not be regarded as down-grading, necessarily, failed. When trustees upheld Hakes' decision, Stinson resigned from the faculty with a bitter letter to the board.

During the past months I have been subjected to arbitrary and capricious decisions without explanation. By ignoring the input from faculty, alumni, and students and by confirming the actions of underlings without conducting a hearing on the subject, you have abrogated your constitutional and statutory obligation to manage this University. Quite frankly, I have no desire to be associated with an organization governed by such principles or lack thereof. Your actions have imperiled the program and the hopes and aspirations of the over 250 students presently enrolled in the program. I challenge you to rebuild what you and your administration have severely damaged.

The Stinson affair left a black mark never quite erased from the Jennings administration.

In only one other regard was the ship threatened during the Jennings captaincy, and in this instance the president leaned heavily on McFadden, Solomon, and others for support. In 1978, in connection with the anticipated North Central Association review, but inspired also by a series of national problems, McFadden had called for a complete review of athletics at Wyoming. A committee was assigned to follow through, although it was urged by trustees to keep its work as confidential as possible. When Jennings came to the presidency, he supported the investigation and turned it over to McFadden, Joyce Scott (assistant to the vice president for academic affairs), and to some extent Solomon (who was to coordinate the athletic program).

Revelation followed revelation. Some football players, whose eligibility might have been in jeopardy, had raised their grade point averages by enrolling in fraudulent summer classes in another state — classes from which they transferred "A" credit without ever having attended at all. One former football player charged the University athletic staff with padding averages by giving "A" grades with impunity to leading athletes. In the end, athletes' scholastic records were investigated individually and reevaluated. Only one individual was found to be actually ineligible. To the physical education department, through which coaches gave instruction, a number of measures for quality control were detailed and at least one class was permanently canceled. Plans were made for careful monitoring of athletes' scholarship ratings, and a special adviser was appointed to watch over programs, making sure that each was directed to progress toward a degree. When McFadden reported to the Western Athletic Conference, he was able to present his own long analysis of February 1980 and to indicate measures taken to remedy the situation. Under the circumstances, the WAC commissioner opted not to penalize either the University or the athletes beyond measures already undertaken by the administration itself.

Stronger complaints were lodged with the WAC regarding crowd behavior at a basketball game with Brigham Young in early 1981. Here responsible students, the athletic director, and the president joined together in urging restraint; and a series of positive steps seemed to help. Enthusiasm for basketball dominated the student newspaper, although the formation of a gay group called GLOW (Gays and Lesbians of Wyoming) took a close second in 1980-81.

Jennings' success as an administrator did not escape the notice of higher education officials throughout the country. In 1980, the president declined to be a candidate for positions as vice president of the University of Wisconsin system and as chancellor at the University of Kansas. In April 1981, nominated as a candidate for the presidency of Iowa, Jennings said he was not interested in leaving Wyoming. But with the offer of the presidency of Ohio State — one of the largest universities in the country — the situation changed. In June 1981, in spite of efforts to hold him with a salary that raised the eyebrows of certain legislators, Edward Jennings resigned to accept the Ohio State position.

"He leaves us," said the president of the board of trustees,

with an outstanding legacy of organization, leaders, and intentions that will strengthen us in the future. We have lost him for the future, but we have benefited enormously from his presence.

Jennings responded with praise for "the policies the faculty, the board, and the administration have established." Privately, one trustee wrote a touching letter.

The way I feel today is confusing; I am extremely sad that you are leaving the University of Wyoming and [we] will certainly miss you and Mary Eleanor, as we consider you among our dearest friends. I feel about you as I did about my [son], when he decided he no longer wished to be associated with us in our family business, it really hurts.

But when you get over the shock, you become extremely proud. [My son's] father after he got over the shock is nothing but proud. I am extremely proud of you too. It is a compliment to our search committee that two years ago they found a man . . . that turned out to be the best prospect in the United States that Ohio State could find today.

With Jennings' resignation, the trustees appointed Donald L. Veal, vice president for research, as acting president. Veal promised a vigorous administration even during the search for a presidential successor. "I want to emphasize," he told the student newspaper,

that the university must continue to progress throughout the presidential search process. I intend to carry out the programs that started under the leadership of President Jennings.

The acting president was pledged to a policy of openness. Before the faculty senate in 1980 he had insisted that

Institutions of higher education must pursue their purposes openly and always in full view of society and must be willing to participate in making the educational experience available to a broad cross-section of society.

Even in his research position and as a researcher himself, he strongly advocated excellence in teaching as a faculty requirement.

Excellence in the classroom is the minimum expected from a university faculty member. Without excellence in the classroom, it is hard to see how any of the subsequent goals can be realized for the benefit of our central purpose of providing a quality educational experience for our students. . . . Teaching and research are inseparable. Excellence in the classroom and excellence in the advancement of knowledge are equally important at a major institution of higher education.

In the selection process for a new president, the board opted to follow the procedure used when Jennings was hired. Members of the faculty-staff-student search and screening advisory committee eventually accumulated 322 names, although 89 of the original nominees declined to be considered. For its own use and that of the committee — again Robert S. Houston was chairman — trustees evolved a set of criteria that might have been designed to fit Jennings himself. Among them was commitment to academic freedom; to the principle of accountability, meaning the "implementation of well-defined processes for review and evaluation of all University programs;" and

evidence of physical and intellectual stamina, energy, and enthusiasm which permit the several and various responsibilities of the University presidency to be carried as exciting opportunities.

Six finalists were eventually selected, and the three-member trustee committee arranged for interviews on campus. Among the candidates was Veal, who underwent the interviewing process with the rest. In April 1982, Donald L. Veal was appointed twentieth president of the University of Wyoming.

ROMANCE OF THE DANCE

et it not be said that University of Wyoming students ever overlooked an opportunity to trip the light fantastic — at least until chaperones and ballroom dancing became passe.

The Cadet Ball was probably the first annual dance to be established on campus; it became one of the most elegant of the formal dances, a spring event that often lasted until daybreak. After a hiatus during the years of World War I, the ball was revived in 1921. Meanwhile, the junior prom became an annual event after 1911 — one of the most beautiful formals ever given, reported the *Wyo* in 1918, commenting in particular that "coral pink was the color" and the supper was "served at dainty candle-lighted tables on the [gymnasium] track." The first annual Engineers' Ball came in 1916 and the gym was "decorated electrically in a manner symbolical of Engineers." Fraternities and sororities sponsored dances following their appearance on campus near the years of World War I. From time to time, special dances crowned the whirling calendar. A series of "hard-time" dances graced the years of World War I, one of which saw as decorations not only tin cans and rusty stoves, but the remains of the Old Main tower, pulled down to much local distress. The *Wyo* in 1918 described an "Ag and Home Ec Barn Dance," held in the loft of the stock farm's dairy barn, at which "sturdy farmers with their bonnie lassies" glided on hay-strewn floors, and "luxurious bales of hay about the room provided comfortable tête-a-tête places between dances." Beauty queens graced pages of the *Wyo* and reigned at balls. In later years, faculty dances provided their own memories — of such as the strains of Les Elgar's "big band."

Otto Gramm, board president, 1897-1911

One particular event towers in the memories of those who were there. One November evening in 1933, a group of intrepid law students, several of whom have since made national reputations, set their budding talents to kidnapping the queen of the Engineers' Ball. By dint of intricate plotting, abetted by the secret assistance of a traitorous engineer, and served by a getaway car in the form of an ancient Ford, the conspirators performed their deed by dousing the lights and firing a gunshot to frighten the crowd just as the lovely queen took her formal position on stage. In the pandemonium that followed, the engineers were forced to name the runner-up as reigning ruler, and when the real monarch was finally permitted to return, she was dubbed only honorary queen instead. "Villians," cried the displaced queen's sorority — and her irate father too. "Childish," wrote the *Branding Iron* of the episode.

It may be hoped that the days of the dance are not gone forever. On the other hand, some think they are.

SOCIAL DANCES

Gym decorated for fraternity dance, 1910

Chapter Fourteen

Past to Present

With the selection of President Donald L. Veal, this history comes to a close.

The University of the 1980s is a far cry indeed from the institution that opened its doors 100 years before. In every conceivable way, it has expanded. Campus itself would be unrecognizable to John Hoyt, who once (according to legend) watched Aven Nelson shoot rabbits on Prexy's Pasture, the central campus mall. More than 10,000 students from all over Wyoming and the world can count themselves heirs to the few dozen Laramieites who enrolled in those first classes. The handful of dedicated faculty assembled by president and trustees in 1887 has burgeoned into more than 750 teachers and scholars who called the University of Wyoming their workplace in 1985. The massive investments in research equipment — laboratories and archives, telescopes and microscopes — were unknown in previous ages. About all that a Rip van Winkle might recognize on awakening are the peaks of the Snowy Range to the west and the Laramie mountains to the east.

Anyone looking back on the University's first 100 years realizes that the first quarter of a century was the hardest. Although those involved would have been reluctant to admit it, the University was probably born before its time. Cries for an institution of higher learning in the frontier territory came not from hard-working, isolated citizens still battling stern climate and unyielding soil, but from a handful of far-sighted idealists who recognized the value of education and a clique of officials intent on dividing the spoils of statehood before the state was even established. Those problems have been summarized in the first chapters of this

Boys' boarding club, fall 1897

history. They include the nature of the student body — primarily Laramieites under the age of 18; the sources of funding, the great majority of which came from the federal government; and the numerous administrative missteps and misconceptions. In its struggle to stand firmly on its feet, the University had the aid of a devoted faculty, who taught, researched, wrote, traveled, argued, and groped their way upward, and of dedicated students who grew with their institution.

In the long run, the crisis of 1907 was a positive step, whatever miseries it brought to those immediately involved. The governor's investigation revealed to the public a good many petty malfunctions on campus and in Cheyenne. Slowly, state officials and University administrators took steps to remedy many of them. A handful of Democrats began to show up on the previously solidly Republican board. A series of stronger administrators took courageous — if sometimes futile — stands. An effort was made to restructure the student body into statewide and college-age dimensions. True, the administrations of Presidents Merica, Duniway, and Nelson (particularly the latter) were not without strains, and the State Board of Land Commissioners continued for some time to manipulate land deals with University property, but a good many of the 1907 ailments gradually began to heal. By the time of Arthur G. Crane's long administration (1922-1941), the University had pulled itself into the twentieth century.

Crane added his share. Little concerned with curricular development, he set the patterns for University financing for decades to come. Following an example set previously by the trustees, he ensured that oil royalties from University or public lands would be treated as endowment and used only for permanent construction. He established the precedent for issuing revenue bonds and set the policy whereby such bonds were frequently redeemed (in the case of income-providing facilities like dormitories or the stadium) through revenue from the buildings themselves. It was Crane who first persuaded the state treasurer to invest special Wyoming funds in University securities, and he who first tapped federal sources for aid in campus construction. It was Crane's fate to stand at the helm through the years of the Great Depression, but he weathered the storm and saw calmer waters ahead. He was less lucky in his relationships with faculty and board. Never an expansive or easy-going individual, he found himself at odds with politicians and alumni, and in 1941 he was relieved of his job.

The war years were difficult for the University. Depletion in faculty and students was only part of the picture. To keep its doors open from 1941-45, and to aid in the nation's war effort, the University participated in the War Department's numerous plans for college-level draft-eligible young men. It paid a price, for the variety and transciency of federal policies prohibited any kind of planning or certainty about the future. Faculty members arrived at class with graded papers to return, only to discover that class had disappeared and new students were on their way. Still, the University survived, in great measure owing to strong leadership and healthy dedication.

The past forty years have seen slow but continual progress, with only a few stumbling

moments along the way. Increasing enrollment has provided the impetus for campus construction, faculty employment, and rising state and federal appropriations. Little of the expansion occurred overnight and less of it without effort and exertion, sometimes on heroic scale. Changes were perhaps less dramatic than those of the early days, when the addition of one building changed the entire physiognomy of campus. Nevertheless they occurred, against a background of frequent ups and downs.

"The Freezer Section," UW basketball game, c. 1981

"Welcoming" Cowboy opponents, c. 1981

The administration of George Duke Humphrey — the longest in the University's history — brought to Wyoming more campus buildings, more imaginative financing, and a series of winning athletic teams. Humphrey was a politician above all, and his relationships with legislators and political figures frequently (but not always) gave the University boosts forward. During the second longest presidential tenure in post-war years, William D. Carlson (president 1968-1978) complemented Humphrey's efforts by solidifying existing programs (often proposed by faculty) and by establishing patterns of faculty scholarship and productivity.

Neither of these presidents was particularly popular on campus, but the University's ability to survive and prosper marked a certain maturity, through which presidents might come and go (for all of their differences and diversities) without uprooting the structure that had grown sturdy over the years. Presidents indeed came and went — seven of them in twenty years — some sorely missed, others aided on their way. Faculty, too, moved in and out during prosperous years of upward mobility. The University was not made of rocks, for it heaved and groaned with complaints, angers, and frustrations, but at least it had long since learned to survive.

Certain persistent problems confronted campus in the postwar years. One administration after another opposed the expansion of a rival college system, but eventually accommodation and even cooperation were achieved. In the multiplicity of new programs, the maintenance of quality was a constant struggle, especially since small-scale efforts and funding often failed to meet national standards set for larger operations. Competition for faculty with larger or more prestigious institutions called for increasing scales not just of salaries but fringe benefits and special research support facilities. The admission of all Wyoming high school graduates as students (by legislative mandate) called forth questions of maintaining quality standards both on campus and (by periodic crusade) in the state's secondary schools, while administrators devoted increasing efforts to attracting superior students to campus. Funding was frequently a problem for Wyoming, for even the friendliest legislatures were bound by rising and falling tides of inflation and income.

In its last twenty years, Wyoming has become an integrated segment of the national higher educational picture, with all its turbulence, troubles, and rewards. Although the echoes came late and somewhat faintly, campus participated in the student unrest of the 1960s. At first remote from the protests of the McCarthy era, a stronger faculty (by the early 1970s) came to demand a voice in campus governance such as its Berkeley colleagues had earlier fought to achieve. The dictum of "publish or perish" hit Wyoming too, just as completely as inflation and recession governed legislative appropriations and the budget's expansion and contraction. In the post-war years, a student body which had generally been steered around the jazz age and the Charleston grew up with love-ins, sit-ins, and membership on the board of trustees.

Donald L. Veal came to the presidency of an institution which had survived many crises during its first 100 years and emerged stronger than it had begun. Still, problems remained and others lurked on the horizon. The idealistic hopes of the men of 1887 —that the University of Wyoming would some day become great — may never be permanently realized, for greatness demands constant reassessment and continual struggle. Much has been accomplished, but all is not necessarily well. The next 100 years will be crucial.

A Note on Sources

WILSON O. CLOUGH

Clough's *A History of the University of Wyoming, 1887-1964* (1965)* stands in a category all its own in terms of its contribution to the present work. Combining his previous *History of the University, 1887-1937; The University in War, 1939-1946;* and *The Third Quarter, 1937-1962;* the 75th-year chronicle is a gold mine of information and delight. Clough's work has been consulted at every step, as he himself — a good friend and esteemed colleague — has been consulted on procedures and sources. Without the Clough *History,* the present author would have been sunk for a lifetime in an unmanageable sea. The assistance to a safer shore is hereby acknowledged.

BIBLIOGRAPHICAL AIDS

The author wishes to acknowledge with gratitude the assistance of Registrar Emeritus Ralph E. McWhinnie, who has supplied me with several check lists of sources published and unpublished. His bibliographical acumen has steered me frequently in the correct direction. Beyond the statistics prepared by McWhinnie and the short bibliography in Clough's *History,* there is no full published bibliography of sources and archives relating to the University of Wyoming. I have, however, made use of the following:

Ridings, Reta W. *Checklist of University of Wyoming Publications.* University of Wyoming Publications, V. III, l937.

This is a thoughtful and careful compilation of all University publications, from reports of the board of trustees to the pamphlets of the Agricultural Experiment Station to occasional departmental and committee publications. It does not include mimeographed materials.

Edwards, Zona M. *Scholarship on the Wyoming Plains: Seventy-five Years of University of Wyoming Publishing, 1887-1960.* University of Wyoming Publications, V. XXVI, 1937.

A helpful update.

*The place of publication is Laramie unless otherwise indicated.

TRUSTEE DOCUMENTS

Minutes of the Meetings of the Board of Trustees of the University of Wyoming, 1887-present. At first irregular; by 1905, quarterly; after 1922, monthly.

These documents are essential not only because they set forth trustee policies and resolutions but because they often serve as a guide to whatever is happening on campus and whatever difficulties might be present. Kept in the president's vault, Old Main. Copies of these minutes for the period of Crane's administration may also be found in the papers of E. O. Fuller and of Fay Smith, University archive in the American Heritage Center. During Crane's years, the executive committee of the trustees held interim meetings between the trustees' quarterly sessions; these minutes are available in the Fuller and Smith papers.

Report of the President of the Board of Trustees to the Governor of the State of Wyoming, 1891-present.

The official annual published report of the University. These reports from earlier years make interesting reading; today they are detailed financial and statistical statements. Available in early years as one of the issues of the *Melange* (1904-1913; thereafter called the *University of Wyoming Bulletin)* these documents have also been published separately in pamphlet form.

President's Reports to the Board of Trustees, 1891-present. Annual to 1907; thereafter semi-annual, quarterly, and finally monthly (for every meeting of the trustees).

These documents are far more interesting than the minutes themselves, for the presidents reported at length on campus matters of importance. At first, these reports were regarded as highly confidential; those of presidents Johnson, Graves, and Smiley are in a special box in the University archives, American Heritage Center. Merica began the publication of these reports, a practice continued by Duniway and Nelson. They become confidential again with the Crane administration; Crane's reports can be found in the Fuller and Smith papers, while those of Merica and Humphrey (to 1950) are contained in a special file in the president's office storage room, attic of Old Main. Since 1950, the presidents' reports have been filed with the trustees' minutes in the president's vault.

Fiscal Agent, Secretary: *Reports to the Trustees.* 1922-1940.

Like the presidents' reports, these are available in the Fuller and Smith papers. Smith reported on most financial and budgetary matters, while Fuller (whose primary initial task had been the management and inspection of University lands) reported on land income, royalties, and many special projects. During the Humphrey administration, these reports were merged into the president's reports; after 1949, the two offices (as they had existed) were abolished.

Special trustees' publications:

A Statement Concerning University Lands. [1911].

A Ten-Year Post-War Building Plan for the University of Wyoming. 1944.

PRESIDENTIAL DOCUMENTS

For reports to the trustees, see above. During the Merica, Duniway, and Nelson administrations, the published reports to the trustees were listed as issues of the *University of Wyoming Bulletin;* they are bound therewith in the William Robertson Coe Library, but many seem to remain in separate pamphlet form in the Grace Raymond Hebard room.

In addition the following are very useful:

President's Ten-Year Report to the Board of Trustees, published as the December 1932 issue of the *University of Wyoming Bulletin.*

A report by Arthur G. Crane.

Crane, Arthur G. *A Pioneer Comes of Age.* 1940. Published in pamphlet form, but also labeled *Bulletin*, and called internally the President's *Eighteen-Year Report.*

Report of the President, University of Wyoming. Issued annually 1945-64 by G. D. Humphrey.

Especially useful in that it contains summaries of the various divisions and colleges with their activities for the academic year. The initial publications were simply designed, but they became more elaborate (color photographs, larger format, quality production) as the Humphrey years progressed.

Several special publications should be mentioned here:

Lewis, Charles W. *Wyoming's Contribution to Higher Education.* 1904.

Duniway, Clyde A. *An Open Letter . . .* 1915.

The University of Wyoming Developmental Study. 1948-49. 4 vols.

This is also called the Klein report, named after Arthur F. Klein, who was commissioned by President Humphrey to examine and make recommendations for the administrative structure and existing regulations of the University. The report far exceeded Humphrey's intentions, for it became a mammoth self-study, compiled by all departments and units. Available in the G. R. Hebard Room.

Institutional Profile Documents . . . For the North Central Association of Colleges and Secondary Schools. 1969 and 1979.

The former is available in the G. R. Hebard room; the latter in a notebook binder in the president's office storage area, attic, Old Main. Reports on all units of campus for the accreditation procedure.

University Priority Review, 1971-72.

A report, written by W. D. Carlson, on this university-wide study of needs and priorities; available in the G. R. Hebard room. Materials for this report can be found in the president's office storage area, attic, Old Main.

FACULTY DOCUMENTS

Minutes of the faculty of the University of Wyoming, 1887-present.

Much routine business was transacted in faculty meetings. I am grateful to Professor Richard L. Hillier for his topical summary of matters of importance covered by faculty minutes since 1931.

Minutes, Faculty Senate, University of Wyoming. Since 1968.

These and minutes of many meetings of faculty committees are kept with the president's files in the attic of Old Main. Senate chairpersons regularly communicated important legislative actions to the president, and I have found these reports and presidential reactions most useful.

University Faculty Association. *The Sounding Board.*

A journal focusing on faculty concerns and complaints during the Carlson administration.

OTHER USEFUL DOCUMENTS, PUBLISHED AND UNPUBLISHED

University of Wyoming Bulletins, 1887-present.

The official catalogue of regulations, courses, fees, programs, etc., which gave its name to a very different set of documents, the bulletins published irregularly but several times a year, which include the catalogue as one issue, but also trustees' reports, presidents' reports, summer course listings, various college brochures, etc.

The earliest catalogue for 1887-88 was called a *Circular for General Information*; thereafter the term catalogue was used, and after 1904 the bulletin was included first in the *Melange*, after 1913 in the *Bulletin*.

These documents are essential for following new programs and old, determining fees and tuition, course requirements, and many other important items.

Reports of the various colleges.

Such reports were periodically published as part of the *Melange* or the *University of Wyoming Bulletin*. However, many annual or biennial unpublished reports were required by the presidents. Such may be found with the legislative materials preserved by President Crane; in the files of presidential correspondence, attic of Old Main; and for some years, in special drawers or boxes in the attic storage room. Very useful material, especially in its unpublished form. Deans of colleges are likely to be arguing the need for new faculty facilities, equipment, support services, etc., and their statistics make interesting reading.

The annual reports of the Agricultural Experiment Station are useful especially for early years.

Faculty and University committee minutes and reports.

Filed for the most part in the attic of Old Main, but there are some committee reports with the materials on legislative requests in the University archives, American Heritage Center. Early minutes of the executive committee for the Agricultural Experiment Station are in a special box in that archive and labeled "agriculture."

Much material here is routine. I have generally checked committee minutes only when something special was indicated. Many reports of committees are located in the president's office files.

Miscellaneous publications and reports.

There are too many such items to be listed individually here.

Among the most important are the reports of the many special accreditors and review teams that came to campus, as, for instance, the Carnegie Foundation for the Advancement of Teaching, the Klein report, the various self-studies compiled for accreditors, and the "priority review" of 1972-73. Reports on individual colleges are usually kept in the president's files.

In addition, many brochures, pamphlets, and books exist, most of them available in the Coe Library or the G. R. Hebard Collection. Such documents were published whenever a building was dedicated, a new program begun, a president inaugurated, special facilities opened, and on anniversaries, homecomings, and many other special occasions. At Coe Library, programs for concerts through the years have been bound together. Athletic programs have likewise been very useful.

WYOMING STATE SOURCES

Reports of the Territorial Governors of Wyoming to the Secretary of the Interior. Annual, 1878-1890.

Governors of Wyoming Territory, *Messages to the Legislatures.* 1869-1890.

Council Journal, Territory of Wyoming. 1869-1890.

House Journal, Territory of Wyoming. 1869-1890.

Wyoming Territory, *Session Laws.* 1869-1890.

Journals and Debates of the Constitutional Convention of the State of Wyoming. Cheyenne, 1893.

Governors of Wyoming, *Messages to the Legislature.* 1890-1965.

Wyoming Legislature, House of Representatives. *Journal.* 1895-1955.

Wyoming Legislature, Senate. *Journal.* 1895-1955.

Digest of Senate and House Journals of the State Legislature of Wyoming. 1957-present. (published in separate series since 1975).

Session Laws of the State of Wyoming. 1890-present.

State Superintendent of Public Instruction. *Biennial Reports.* 1890-present.

A NOTE ON SOURCES

Collections housed in the Wyoming State Archives, Cheyenne:

I have used in particular the papers of several governors, especially John W. Hoyt, Francis E. Warren, and B. B. Brooks. Collections have been consulted in regard to particular University issues rather than systematically read.

IMPORTANT SERIAL PUBLICATIONS

The Wyoming Student, 1898-1923.

The Branding Iron, 1923-present.

The Summer Round-Up (and other titles).

All of these student newspapers are invaluable for their insights into issues, their reporting of programs and policies, and their portrait of what students were doing and thinking.

WYO, 1909-present (not issued 1934-39, 1944, 1978-81). Dating system varies.

Superior for pictures and for student activities. During its suspension in the depression years, it was to some extent replaced by the less ambitious publications *Swingout* and *The Wyo Magazine.*

Alumnews, 1943-present.

A fine source for feature stories about the University, particularly when it was edited by June Schrib.

Statistical Summary. Published by the Office of the Registrar and allied services. Annual, 1934-35-present.

All you ever want to know about students and more; a useful compilation.

PERSONAL PAPERS AND CORRESPONDENCE

For the Presidents:

Hoyt: Few papers remain beyond his briefs and letters regarding his dismissal from the presidency. These are contained in the files of the secretary to the trustees; see below.

Johnson, Graves, Smiley, Lewis, and Tisdale: What remains of their files has been collected and labeled, perhaps by Grace Raymond Hebard or an assistant. These materials (presently in boxes labeled "President's Office," but frequently misnumbered and misdated) are in the University archives, American Heritage Center, University of Wyoming. One bound volume of Tisdale's letters to students and potential students remains in

the same archive; the label seems to indicate that it was one of several, but no others can be located.

Merica, Duniway, and Nelson: According to Wilson O. Clough, *History of the University of Wyoming,* p. 85, Merica destroyed his papers when he left office. Duniway's correspondence seems in great measure preserved; it is in files located in the president's office storage room, attic of Old Main, and labeled "Pre-1927." Few of Aven Nelson's letters are available, but Roger L. Williams was able to use the collection for his recent biography.

Crane: Some but not much correspondence remains for the period 1922-27 in the attic file labeled "Pre-1927;" from 1927 on, the collection is far more complete. Crane's working papers on legislative matters contain pertinent correspondence. They are in the University archives, American Heritage Center, in boxes (often mislabeled) containing all legislative campaigns and arranged by year.

All presidents since 1941: Files of correspondence seem complete and are located in the storage area, attic, Old Main.

For other important figures:

When Grace Raymond Hebard was secretary to the board of trustees, she kept a file of her own correspondence and of important letters signed by the chairman of the trustees; these are now in a carton in the University archives, American Heritage Center, marked "Hebard correspondence." A similar box labeled "Agriculture" contains Hebard and other correspondence relating to the College of Agriculture and the Agricultural Experiment Station.

Correspondence of trustees, if such relates to the University, can often be found in copies directed to the president; this material is filed in all presidential correspondence files under "Trustees" with the name of the individual.

In the papers of E. O. Fuller and Fay Smith, both of whom left files in the University archive, American Heritage Center, there is little correspondence but many working papers and documents regarding financial matters, lands, etc.

NEWSPAPERS

The Laramie *Boomerang* (1887-1924 and 1933-present) and *Republican-Boomerang* (1924-1933) have been used as a primary newspaper source, although no effort has been made to examine these newspapers day by day.

Other Wyoming newspapers have been consulted as necessary.

The "Clipping File" in the Reference room, Coe Library, has been used in limited manner to collect biographical details.

REMINISCENCES, AUTOBIOGRAPHIES, AND INTERVIEWS

In this category, there are almost too many items to count. The following, but not exclusively the following, have been used:

McWhinnie, Ralph E. *Those Good Years at Wyoming U.* 1965.

A collection of charming tales, mostly reminiscences, by students at the University through the years.

Hoyt, John W. "Autobiography." Mss.

This typewritten reminiscence was completed after his death by his son Kepler Hoyt. Copy in the John W. Hoyt Collection, Wyoming State Archives, Cheyenne.

Smiley, Edith. "Pioneering with Wyoming University." Mss., 1936.

A reminiscence contributed by the president's wife to Wilson O. Clough on the occasion of his 50th-year history. In the files of the American Heritage Center.

Miscellaneous written reminiscences or talks contributed by Associate Director (Admissions) Charles C. Chase, and Professors Emeritus Gertrude Gould Lindsay, Ralph E. McWhinnie, and Allan A. Willman.

The following kindly consented to interviews, which were taped and then transcribed:

Associate Director Charles C. Chase (May 1983)
Registrar Emeritus R. E. McWhinnie (October 1983)
Professor Emeritus Richard L. Hillier (October 1982)
Former President Edward Jennings (March 1983)
Former President William D. Carlson (June 1984)
Former Governor Stanley K. Hathaway (February 1983)
Former Governor Clifford P. Hansen (June 1984)
Former Trustee Willard Wilson (June 1984)

A NOTE ON SOURCES

Many others were interviewed or questioned less formally. Notes on these interviews have been preserved in the files. Among the most important were President H. B. McFadden (August 1984), Dean E. Gerald Meyer (June 1984), Vice President Elliott Hays (March 1985), and Assistant to the President Vern E. Shelton (several occasions). Thanks are owed to many individuals for their willingness to answer questions and provide information.

BOOKS AND MONOGRAPHS

In regard to Wyoming, I have leaned heavily on T. A. Larson, *History of Wyoming*, second edition (Lincoln: University of Nebraska Press, 1978). Occasional reference is made to other works, particularly Frances Beard, *Wyoming from Territorial Days to the Present* (Chicago and New York: American Historical Association, l933). Special mention should be made of a volume that appeared during preparation of this history: the delightful *Aven Nelson of Wyoming* (Boulder: Colorado Associated University Press, 1984) by Roger L. Williams.

The following short histories or histories of specific departments were useful:

Bruce, Robert H. "The Graduate School at Mid-Century." *University of Wyoming Publications,* XXIII, No. 1 (July 15, 1959).

Daly, Major B. C. "Historical Sketch of the Military Department." Mss., 1936. American Heritage Center archives.

Diggs, D. Teddy, "Ideology of the Land-Grant Movement: The Cases of Utah and Wyoming," M.A. thesis in history, Utah State University, 1984.

Hewitt, William L., and Welch, Deborah S. "Gossard vs. Crane: National Issues Brought to the University of Wyoming in the 1920s." Mss., yet unpublished, supplied by the authors.

Hewitt, William L. "The University of Wyoming Textbook Investigation Controversy, 1947 to 1948, and its Aftermath." *Annals of Wyoming,* v. 56, No. 1 (spring 1984), pp. 22-34.

Hill, Richard H. "A Study of Institutional Vitality at the University of Wyoming: Perceptions of Faculty, Administrators, Students, and Trustees." Ed.D. dissertation, Educational Administration, 1979.

"A History of the Registrar's Office of the University of Wyoming." Materials compiled by Debbie Phillips Smith, 1975-77.

Hudson, Ruth. *Here Is Wyoming: The University and its State Background.* 1948.

Jackson, W. Turrentine. "The Administration of Thomas Moonlight, 1887-1889." *Annals of Wyoming,* XVIII, No. 2 (July 1946).

Miller, Lyle L. *A Half Century of Guidance in Wyoming: From Vocational Guidance to Counselor Education.* 1981.

Orr, Harriet Knight. The University of Wyoming: A History of the State Normal School, the College of Education. Compiled in 1937. Coe Library, Grace Raymond Hebard collection.

Rasmussen, Richard E. "The Laboratory School in Teacher Education as Related to the University of Wyoming." Ed.D. dissertation, Department of Curriculum and Instruction, 1969.

Ringert, Alice B. "The Territorial University." Typewritten mss. preserved with the Hoyt correspondence, President's Office, University archives, American Heritage Center.

Watson, Eddie D. "History of the Organization and Growth of the University of Wyoming with Constitutional Provisions and Legal Enactments." M.A. thesis, 1935.

Woodward, George R., "History of the College of Education, University of Wyoming, 1887-1947." Ed.D. dissertation, Department of Educational Foundations, 1971.

Yount, John R. "Priorities and Functions of the University of Wyoming Laboratory School." Ed.D. dissertation, College of Education, 1971.

SPECIAL COLLECTIONS

I wish to acknowledge with gratitude the access to particular personal files granted me by Professors Richard L. Hillier, T. A. Larson, and William R. Steckel, and, in addition, the material on Grace Raymond Hebard collected and proffered by Virginia Scharff, M.A. in history from the University of Wyoming.

Credits

Photographs in this history are provided courtesy of the following sources (Identifications, when available, are given as complete as possible.):

p. 3 . . . . . *Hartwell and Sons, Laramie*

p. 5 . . . . . *Pratt and Ferris Cattle Company Collection*

p. 8 . . . . . *W. G. Richardson Collection #22*

p. 12 . . . . *Studio portrait*

p. 14 . . . . *University Archives Collection*

p. 17 . . . . *University Archives Collection (Top row: Henry Merz, W. I. Smith. Middle row: A. M. Swain, Irene Morse. Bottom row: President A. A. Johnson, Justus F. Soule, John D. Conley and Aven Nelson.)*

p. 22 . . . . *University Archives Collection*

p. 23 . . . . *Early collodian print*

p. 24 . . . . *Book 3, S. H. Knight Collection #140*

p. 27 . . . . *Baillie Collection*

p. 29A . . . *Fills' Studio, Manila, Escolta 105*

p. 29B . . . *University Archives Collection*

p. 32 . . . . *B. C. Buffum Collection #230*

p. 37 . . . . *Collection #142*

p. 40 . . . . *Book 3, S. H. Knight Collection #140*

p. 43 . . . . *Book 2, S. H. Knight Collection #140*

p. 44 . . . . *Collection #142*

p. 46 . . . . *Book 2, S. H. Knight Collection #140*

p. 48 . . . . *W. S. Ingham Collection #113*

p. 50A . . . *University Archives Collection*

p. 50B . . . *Weyle Barber Studio, Laramie*

p. 51 . . . . *Formal studio "carbon type" portrait, Endean Commercial Photographers Studio, Chicago*

p. 53 . . . . *University Archives Collection*

p. 56 . . . . *S. H. Knight Collection*

p. 62 . . . . *University Archives Collection (Above: Ada Wilkinson, Evangeline Downey, Wilburta Knight, Lottie Crawford, Miss Stoner, unidentified, Elsie Rodgers, Susan Brown, Lillian Paln, Esther Johnson, Myrtle Ware, Georgia Cook, Helen Cordiner and Loretta Butler.)*

p. 64 . . . . *University Archives Collection*

p. 65 . . . . *Collection #142 (Back row: Herbert Brees, Sam Wilson, Wallie Pease, Ross Mordy, Robert Smith, Paul Paulson, Charles Rigdon and Van Winkle. Middle row: H. Robb, John Rigdon, Neil Suddoth. Bottom row: George Trabing, Emory Land, Harry Houston, George Sheldon and Fred Brees.)*

p. 66 . . . . *University Archives Collection*

p. 71 . . . . *Aven Nelson Collection #164*

p. 74 . . . . *G. R. Hebard Collection #8*

p. 75 . . . . *Aven Nelson Collection #164*

p. 76 . . . . *Book 2, S. H. Knight Collection #140*

p. 81 . . . . *University Archives Collection*

p. 84 . . . . *S. H. Knight Collection #140*

p. 91 . . . . *Roland Brown Collection #4459*

p. 92 . . . . *University Archives Collection*

p. 93 . . . . *Clarice Whittenburg Collection #364*

p. 95 . . . . *Clarice Whittenburg Collection #364*

p. 99 . . . . *University Archives Collection (Standing: Fay Smith, Fred Geddes, J. M. Schwoob, President A. G. Crane, Frank A. Holliday, J. A. Elliott, DPB Marshall, Will Lynn. Seated: Patrick Quealy, Katharine Morton, Governor Emerson, Harriet Grieve, Anna Haggard.)*

p. 100 . . . *University Photo Service*

p. 101 . . . *University Archives Collection*

p. 104 . . . *University Archives Collection*

p. 109 . . . *University Archives Collection*

p. 112 . . . *University Archives Collection (Left to Right: Buchner, Beckwith, Ferren, Kenkel, Olinger, Isberg, Shoemaker, Peterson, Sam Knight.)*

p. 114 . . . *University Archives Collection*

p. 118 . . . *Collection #H-249*

p. 119 . . . *University Archives Collection*

p. 121 . . . *University Archives Collection (Left to Right: Tracy McCraken, Harold Johnson, Governor Leslie Hunt, Fay Smith, P. M. Cunningham, President George Duke Humphrey, Milward Simpson, A. L. Keeney, Mary Edelmen Cope, A. P. Wattenpaugh, Joseph Sullivan.)*

p. 124 . . . *Major Beverly C. Daly Collection #3474*

p. 127 . . . *University Archives Collection*

p. 128 . . . *University Archives Collection*

p. 133 . . . *University Archives Collection #19089*

p. 136 . . . *University Archives Collection*

p. 137 . . . *University Archives Collection*

p. 142 . . . *Collection #249*

p. 143 . . . *University Archives Collection*

p. 145 . . . *University Archives Collection*

p. 149 . . . *University Archives Collection*

p. 153 . . . *University Archives Collection*

p. 156 . . . *Herb Pownall, Laramie*

p. 159 . . . *University Archives Collection*

p. 163 . . . *University Archives Collection*

p. 165 . . . *University Archives Collection*

p. 168 . . . *Svenson, Ludwig Studio, Laramie*

p. 172 . . . *Mark O. North*

p. 177 . . . *University Photo Service*

p. 179 . . . *University Archives Collection*

p. 182 . . . *University Photo Service*

CREDITS

p. 183 . . . *University Archives Collection*

p. 186 . . . *University Archives Collection*

p. 191 . . . *Herb Pownall, Laramie*

p. 197 . . . *Dean Conger, Bethesda, MD*

p. 200 . . . *Frederick Hutchinson Porter, Architect, Cheyenne, Wyoming, Porter Collection*

p. 205 . . . *University Photo Service*

p. 208 . . . *Ted Edeen, Laramie*

p. 215 . . . *University Photo Service*

p. 216A . . *University Archives Collection*

p. 216B . . *Book 2, S. H. Knight Collection #140*

p. 217 . . . *Book 2, S. H. Knight Collection #140*

p. 220 . . . *Robert C. Warner, Laramie*

p. 225 . . . *University Archives Collection*

p. 231 . . . *Collection #142*

p. 232 . . . *University Archives Collection*

p. 236 . . . *University Archives Collection*

p. 237 . . . *Chuck Rue, Clarice Whittenburg Collection #364*

p. 238 . . . *University Photo Service*

p. 243 . . . *University Photo Service*

p. 246 . . . *University Photo Service*

p. 251 . . . *University Photo Service*

p. 256 . . . *University Photo Service*

p. 261 . . . *University Photo Service*

p. 265 . . . *University Photo Service*

p. 266 . . . *Ken Diem, Laramie*

p. 267 . . . *S. H. Knight, S. H. Knight Collection #140*

p. 270 . . . *University Photo Service*

p. 274 . . . *Collection #113*

p. 276 . . . *University Photo Service*

p. 279 . . . *University Photo Service*

p. 286 . . . *University Photo Service*

p. 289 . . . *University Photo Service*

p. 292 . . . *Mrs. Neil Roach Collection #902*

p. 293 . . . *Book 3, S. H. Knight Collection #140*

p. 294 . . . *University Archives Collection*

p. 295A . . *Leslie Blythe, Laramie*

p. 295B . . *Leslie Blythe, Laramie*

Index

INDEX

INDEX

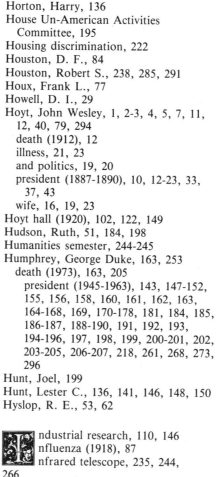

INDEX

INDEX

INDEX